Robert Harley

Portrait of Robert Harley reproduced by kind permission of Christopher Harley.

ROBERT HARLEY

*Speaker, Secretary of State
and Premier Minister*

Brian W. Hill

1988
Yale University Press
New Haven and London

In memory of
William Richard Hill and
Hannah Frances Charlotte Hill

9 2
H285h

Set in Goudy Old Style by Best-set Typesetter Ltd., Hong Kong.
Printed and bound in Great Britain at the University Printing House, Oxford by
David Stanford, printer to the University of Oxford.

Library of Congress Cataloging-in-Publication Data

Hill, Brian W.
    Robert Harley, speaker, secretary of state, and premier minister/
by Brian Hill.
        p.   cm.
    Bibliography: p.
    Includes index.
    ISBN 0-300-04284-1
    1. Harley, Robert, Earl of Oxford, 1681–1724.   2. Statesmen – Great
Britain – Biography.   3. Great Britain – Politics and
government – 1702–1714.   4. Great Britain – Politics and
government – 1689–1702.   I. Title.
DA497.08H5   1988
941.06'9'0924-dc19
(8)

CONTENTS

PREFACE

'A WHOLE ANTHOLOGY of abuse', writes a historian of Augustan pamphleteering, 'could be compiled on the character of Robert Harley.'[1] Hundreds of lampoons and tracts attack Harley with a virulence which is unusual even for the time. Yet he did not lack defenders who felt, like the anonymous reviewer of one critical memoir, that 'the picture of Harley is at least partially drawn, all the deformities are heightened, and the beauties, for beauties of mind he certainly had, are entirely omitted'.[2] Alexander Cunningham, a political opponent, maintained that personal motives played no part in Harley's character – a high claim on behalf of any man – and called him 'a man of great soul and firm in his resolutions'. Harley's colleague the Earl of Dartmouth testified to his probity in an age when ministerial venality was almost acceptable, calling his ministry of 1710–14 'four years cessation from plunder'.[3] Few British politicians have aroused more speculation as to their aims, either in their own lifetime or later. His frequent incoherence, his tergiversation, and the secrecy with which he loved to surround his slightest actions, all became legendary early in his career; it should be noted, however, that the soubriquet Robin the Trickster, often taken to be a description of his character, was not so much that (the contemporary historian John Oldmixon tells us) as a reference to Harley's fertility in parliamentary expedients and in exploiting procedures. 'No man', recorded another observer, 'knows better all the Tricks of the House.'[4] Nevertheless Harley's quirks, particularly his love of secrecy, make interpretation of many of his actions subject to dispute after nearly three centuries. Nor are

1. M.R. Foot, The Pen and the Sword (1957), p. 62.
2. The Gentleman's Magazine, xii (1742), p. 131.
3. Cunningham, n. 417 18; Burner, vi, 50. For other evidence of Harley's incorruptability, see, Holmes, British Politics, p. 267 and note.
4. Oldmixon, p. 459; John Macky's 'character' of Harley: Memoirs of the Secret Services of John Macky (Roxburgh Club, 1895), p. 84.

matters helped by his ungrammatical prose and difficult handwriting, exacerbated in later years by arthritis. In Sir Winston Churchill's exasperated words 'no greater disservice can be done to his memory than to read his letters', and even allowing for Churchillian hyperbole there is some truth in this assessment of Harley's correspondence.[5]

Problems surrounding Harley's complex character, and the extremes of reaction which he provoked among his contemporaries – from love and loyalty to distaste and violent censure – may be partially responsible for the dearth of biography, either in his own day or since. Jonathan Swift's projected study of his old patron would have been invaluable but was never written. Daniel Defoe, who acted as Harley's personal agent for many years, could have given fascinating sidelights on his more obscure activities but left little more than a formal statement, in *The Secret History of the White Staff*, of his non-party policy and support for the Protestant royal succession.[6] Harley's claim to respect was probably his moderation and middle-of-the-road political stance, but as one who stood somewhat aside from both political parties he achieved little prominence in the pantheons of Tory or Whig historical writing in the eighteenth and nineteenth centuries. His purpose was appreciated best in the first generation after his death by David Mallet, an early biographer of Henry St John, Viscount Bolingbroke, Harley's colleague and would-be supplanter during the ministry of 1710–14. Mallet wrote of Harley 'it is rather wonderful that he sustained himself so long than that he sunk at last. In a Nation agitated by Faction, he who will not be of a Faction must be crushed between them.' Mallet was, curiously enough, one of Harley's stoutest defenders in print, even pointing out that in later years Bolingbroke was obliged to recommend Harley's 'old scheme, under the new title of a coalition of Parties'.[7]

In the early Victorian era Lord Macaulay recognized Harley's importance in the immediate post-1688 period, but viewed him with prejudiced eyes as one who had stood against his own hero, King William III.[8] In any case Macaulay did not take his story as far as Queen Anne's reign, when Harley's ministerial career took place. Much of the later nineteenth-century historiography followed Macaulay's deprecatory line and considered Harley, when it considered him at all, as one of the quarrelling team of 'Harley and St John' in Queen Anne's last ministry. His entry in that great late-Victorian repository of historical knowledge,

---

5. Churchill, ii, 79.
6. Defoe maintained that Harley's overthrow in 1714 was engineered by Jacobites, who were 'planet struck' when the Duke of Shrewsbury, not Viscount Bolingbroke, was appointed in his place (p. 14).
7. David Mallet, *Memoirs of the Life and Ministerial Conduct of the late Lord Bolingbroke*, in *Works* (1754), pp. 277–8, 337.
8. Thomas Babington Macaulay, *The History of England from the Accession of James II* (1848–55).

the *Dictionary of National Biography*, was full and reasonably accurate but uniformly hostile in the prevailing tradition, conceding only that Harley was incorruptible in financial matters. The first book-length biography, by E.S. Roscoe, appeared in 1902 but was little more than an expanded version of the *Dictionary* article, if more sympathetic.[9]

A real appreciation of Harley's role in politics from 1689 to 1714 had to await the publication of the best of his political correspondence by the Historical Manuscripts Commission in the late nineteenth and early twentieth centuries.[10] It was Sir Keith Feiling and G.M. Trevelyan in the 1920s and 1930s who gave him his rightful place in the roll of major British statesmen and placed him accurately as a leading influence in the development of post-Revolution parliament and government.[11] After the Second World War, the situation was again transformed by the Duke of Portland's generous loan to the British Library of the Harley manuscripts in his possession, an enormous collection containing much of interest and importance in addition to the originals of the letters already published by the Historical Manuscripts Commission. Since these papers became available to scholars there has been a serious 'attempt to elucidate Harley's political personality' by Dr Angus McInnes, in *Robert Harley, Puritan Politician* which, despite its author's disclaimer of full political biography, is an important guide to the religious springs of Harley's political conduct. The Portland papers now available have also been used by many other scholars to throw light on various aspects of the period, and in the process many further facets of Harley's career have emerged.[12] On the whole, post-war studies have continued to be beneficial to Harley's reputation. One exception is Professor Edward Gregg's biography of Queen Anne which, while exonerating the Queen from a desire to further a Jacobite restoration after her death, maintains that such a Machiavellian purpose was the keynote of Harley's policy.[13] The view has not been much supported, and even Gregg admits that Harley's correspondence with James Edward, the Old Pretender, 'repeatedly stressed that the Pretender's conversion to Protestantism was essential if a Stuart restoration was to be secured'. More recently Dr D. Szechi has given convincing evidence re-affirming that Harley's approaches to the Pretender were inspired by motives other than a desire for the latter's

9. E.S. Roscoe, *Robert Harley, Earl of Oxford* (1902).
10. H.M.C. *Portland*, i–x and H.M.C. *Bath*, i and iii.
11. Feiling, *A History of the Tory Party, 1640 to 1714* (Oxford 1924); G.M. Trevelyan, *England Under Queen Anne*, 3 vols (1930–4).
12. In addition to the many other books published since the 1950s on Harley's period (for which see the Select Bibliography below), authors dealing specifically with aspects of his career include Downie and Biddle.
13. Gregg, p. 376 and *passim*.

succession to the throne.[14] The present work gives reasons for supposing that the more conventional view of Harley in 1714 as a preserver of the Hanoverian succession, which he had helped to establish in the Act of Settlement of 1701, is the correct one.

More important than problems of personality in explaining the complexities of Harley's behaviour were the unusual problems of his day. His main political career coincides with the quarter of a century which lies between the Revolution of 1688 and the accession of the House of Hanover. It was a period of uncommonly tense issues. Although the senior line of the House of Stuart was rejected in 1688, the possibility of its return did not cease to be a matter of everyday importance until 1715. And, while the succession remained unsettled, there remained also the closely related question of religion. These two problems of Church and State, inseparably intertwined, were the combustible material of every major political decision throughout Harley's career. At the same time, conditions of unnatural stress produced, in an effort to meet them, a situation unusually favourable to institutional change. In retrospect the period has often appeared to historians as the one in which modern parliamentary government of the British pattern took its distinctive shape: annual meetings of Parliament with a two-party alignment, the national funded debt and the Bank of England – all were on probation in these years. To Harley's contemporaries, it is true, the situation appeared differently; they were well aware of the importance of the new developments, but doubtful as to their permanence. Where later historians saw the emergence of a constitution fit for centuries of bloodless government, contemporaries wondered only whether there would be a repetition of the events of 1642 and 1688 which had ended the efforts of two successive generations to settle their differences in a parliamentary way; where the historian thought of the settlement of a comfortable, unredeemable National Debt, they constantly feared the return of the national bankruptcy usual under the Stuarts.

Yet the fact remains that Harley's political lifetime probably witnessed more advances towards constitutional and financial security than any which has followed. So great, indeed, were the changes in the pattern of government at this period that the remainder of the eighteenth century and the early part of the nineteenth were to pass before they were fully assimilated. For many of the new developments were premature. In the hothouse temperature of politics after the Revolution of 1688, the

14. *Ibid.*, p. 364, *Cf.* Downie, p. 185, who writes 'In many ways it would have been true to say that of living Englishmen, [Harley...] had done most to secure the peaceful succession of the Hanoverians. He regarded it as his life's work.' Another recent author sees Harley's procrastination with the Jacobite court as simply a means of obtaining the votes of Jacobite Members of Parliament: D. Szechi, chp. 9.

common process by which the radicalism of one age becomes the conservatism of the next was accelerated. Even before 1714, many of the
period's achievements were seen to be precarious; religious toleration
had been granted but barely survived; the new fiscal system was almost
stifled in its cradle. Soon after 1714 the Whig and Tory parties, which
were well defined to the subjects of Queen Anne, underwent change in a
situation where the Whigs had the monopoly of office for half a century.

Both the changes in the pattern of government and the immaturity
of these advances need to be borne in mind in order to explain much
of Harley's career. He worked in an adolescent body politic in the post-
Revolution era. The now regular meeting of Parliament from 1689 on-
ward made possible a new kind of politician, the permanent 'parliament
man', of whom he was one of the first to reach the highest offices. Born
a generation or even a decade earlier, he would have had to satisfy his
political aspirations by introducing himself at court or by remaining content with the smaller world of local politics. Before his day, the only men
to put an opposition policy into effect had to wade through a rebellion to
do it, and their achievement did not endure. Harley, for his part, did
not slough off all the old ways of thinking, any more than the nature
of politics changed overnight after 1688. He was a pre-party man in an
age of parties, a moderate in an epoch of extremism, a religious man
in an age when religion was in decline. If his thinking was sometimes
obscure and his actions tangled, the acrimony and complexity of events
in the post-Revolution era must bear some of the blame. He reached
the highest office, made a European peace which lasted half a century,
helped to settle and preserve the Protestant Succession, and established
a compromise on the government fiscal system which still exists today:
but his achievements cost him and his reputation dear.

I would not like to omit the usual acknowledgements, however inadequate. Among the many who have helped me my first thanks are
due to Professor John Kenyon, for guiding my early Ph.D. research on
Harley. To my colleague Professor Robert Ashton and to Dr Robert
Baldock of Yale University Press I own the encouragement to take up
this study again after a lapse of years. For allowing me access to private
collections of documents I am especially indebted to Mr Christopher
Harley, to their Graces the Dukes of Portland, Buccleuch and Marlborough, and to the Warden and Fellows of All Souls, Oxford. Some
of the collections are no longer where I consulted them, or are now
more easily available in very good printed versions; particular mention
might be made of the Blenheim MSS., since deposited in the British
Library, and the parliamentary diaries of Narcissus Luttrell and an anonymous writer, now published by Henry Horwitz and W.A. Speck
respectively.

I also record my warm thanks to Madge Robinson, Hazel Bye and Vera Durell, who shared the typing of this book in difficult circumstances, often fitting in my complicated drafts between my, and other colleagues', administrative typing.

As always my closest supporters, and the chief sufferers, were my wife and children.

Brian Hill
School of English and American Studies,
University of East Anglia,
Norwich.

ABBREVIATIONS

Unless otherwise stated, dates are given in the old style, but with the year beginning on 1 January, and the place of publication of printed works cited in the footnotes and Select Bibliography is London.

Add. MS(S)	Additional Manuscripts in the British Library
AHR	*American Historical Review*
BIHR	*Bulletin of the Institute of Historical Research*
CB	Court Book of Bank of England directors
CHJ	*Cambridge Historical Journal* (see also *HJ*)
CJ	*Journals of the House of Commons*
CSP Dom	*Calendar of State Papers: Domestic Series*
CTB	*Calendar of Treasury Books*
Econ. HR	*Economic History Review*
EHR	*English Historical Review*
HJ	*Historical Journal* (continuation of the *CHJ*)
H.M.C.	Historical Manuscripts Commission
HLB	*Huntington Library Bulletin* (see also *HLQ*)
HLQ	*Huntington Library Quarterly* (continues the *HLB*)
JBS	*Journal of British Studies*
JMH	*Journal of Modern History*
LJ	*Journals of the House of Lords*
NS	New Style
PRO	Public Record Office
TRHS	*Transactions of the Royal Historical Society*
WMQ	*William and Mary Quarterly*

CHAPTER 1

The Harleys and their Background: Civil War, Restoration and Revolution

THE FAMILY OF Harley were gentry with an estate at Brampton Bryan in the north-west corner of Herefordshire on the Welsh border. The property was large enough to make its owner a substantial local magnate without placing him in the class of great landowners. Thus he was neither rich enough to be a member of the traditional ruling group, the wealthy aristocracy, nor sufficiently poor to have to depend upon court favour or office if he wished to sit in Parliament. Like hundreds of his kind, Robert Harley was a country gentlemen whose main income came from his landed property. In 1656 when his father inherited the estate it was valued at £1,500 per annum.[1] From its locality the property differed from most other British estates in that a major crop was timber, which grows to magnificent size in the area. In the hurricane which swept over England and Wales in November 1703, Harley was noted by John Evelyn, diarist and arboriculturist, to have lost 1,300 trees, blown down on the low slopes which are the beginning of the hills of Wales.[2] On the English side of the border tenanted farms on the rich soil of lower ground supplemented the estate's income.

From the fourteenth century Harleys were settled at Brampton Castle, playing a leading part in the life of Herefordshire and neighbouring Radnorshire. The first of them to have a place in national affairs, other than by occasionally serving as a Member of Parliament, was Robert Harley's grandfather, Sir Robert, who rose to be Master of the Mint under Charles I. Few men better illustrate the hazards of life in the period than Sir Robert Harley. The prevalence of disease and high mortality, especially among children, is seen in his early loss of his first two wives

---

1. Henning, *sub.* Harley, Edward; The size of Harley's estate was discussed at the time of his elevation to the peerage in May 1711, and was held by many to be insufficient to support a title. Jonathan Swift wrote: '[Harley] makes only one difficulty which is hard to answer: he must be made a lord, and his estate is not large enough, and he is too generous to make it larger', *Journal to Stella*, 22 April 1711.
2. John Evelyn, *Sylva*, (1706), p. 341.

and all nine offspring of these marriages. His third marriage, concluded in 1623 with Brilliana, daughter of Sir Edward Conway, was more fortunate: six of their seven children survived. A highly religious man, Sir Robert was a Presbyterian. His knighthood had been conferred as early as James I's accession to be English throne in 1603, as a part of that monarch's initial attempt to conciliate the Presbyterians of his new kingdom. In the Long Parliament of Charles I, Sir Robert Harley was Member for Herefordshire and took the parliamentary side against the King, as did most men of his religious convictions. During his absence under arms in the Civil War which followed, Lady Harley had to defend the castle against local royalist troops, for theirs was not a Puritan locality, and after withstanding a siege successfully she died in October 1643, worn out by her exertions and complaining in one of her last letters to her husband that there was still 'scarce time to write' while a new assault was threatened. After her death the siege was renewed, Brampton Castle was dismantled by the victorious royalists, and three of Sir Robert's younger children were taken prisoner, though later released.[3]

In London Sir Robert was appointed Master of the Mint for a second term in 1643, this time by Parliament, and also served on a committee to investigate idolatrous monuments in churches. Many such valuable works were destroyed under his supervision in London and elsewhere. But though a zealot, he became increasingly opposed to Fairfax, Cromwell and the new extremism in political and social thought exhibited among many members of the New Model Army. On 6 December 1648 Sir Robert was imprisoned briefly for voting to negotiate with Charles I, and six months later he was discharged from the Mint on declining 'to stamp any coin with any other stamp than formerly'. Regicide pushed him towards royalist sympathies, and he spent his remaining years during the Interregnum ill and increasingly isolated from public affairs, dying in 1656.[4]

Sir Robert Harley's eldest son Edward was a man of similar outlook and ability. Born in 1624, his studies at Oxford were cut short after two years by the crisis of the Long Parliament in 1640. Two years later he took arms under Sir William Waller and was wounded in several engagements. Elected for Herefordshire in 1646, Colonel Harley, as he now was, incurred impeachment by the army for his share in an ordinance attempting to disband it, and was imprisoned. Along with his father he attempted to prevent Charles I's execution, writing to Fairfax that the army was 'hastily digging a miserable supulchre for all the beauty and

---

3. *Dictionary of National Biography, sub* Harley, Sir Robert and Brilliana; H.M.C. *Portland,* iii, 117, 122, *passim;* John Webb, *Memorials of the Civil War as it affected Herefordshire* (1879), i, 20. Brilliana Lady Harley's letters, mainly to her son Edward, were published by T.L. Lewis, *Letters of Lady Brilliana Harley,* Camden Society (1854)
4. *Dict. Nat. Biog., sub.* Harley, Sir Robert; H.M.C. *Fifth Report,* appendix, p. 116.

strength of our native kingdom'. Edward Harley was not released until after the King was beheaded. For further intransigence he was expelled from Parliament and forbidden to remain in his native Herefordshire. Although he never swerved from his Puritan convictions his new discontent with military government, which he shared with so many Britons for the rest of his life, grew during the Protectorate of the Cromwells.

Colonel Harley took his seat in the revived Long Parliament in February 1660 and on Charles II's Restoration was knighted and appointed Governor of Dunkirk, which had been recently captured by Oliver Cromwell: Sir Edward's period of favour was brief, for having held the port against several attempts at recapture he had to be dismissed for refusing to give it up when the King ordered its return to the French in 1661. Sir Edward spoke out openly against what he considered to be the ignominious and harmful sale of the French privateering port by a corrupt restored court. He again represented Herefordshire in the short-lived Convention Parliament of 1660, but in the general election which followed its dissolution a year later he lost the seat when the court backed rival candidates. In the borough of New Radnor, however, he had more success against a courtier opponent and was returned in what was to become known as the Cavalier Parliament. In the following years he unsuccessfully opposed the anti-Puritan legislation of the 'Clarendon Code', which excluded Presbyterians and other more extremist religious groups from the right to public worship and from a wide range of office holding.[5]

Sir Edward himself was realist enough to accede to most of the new legislation from the start, while privately favouring dissenting preachers. Though a landowner and a Puritan who carried his austere outlook into the new reign and beyond, he was also a man whose circle of acquaintances extended beyond the dissenting Protestants and who had a wide range of interests beyond those of the landed class. He became an early member of the newly-formed Royal Society, which numbered most of the leading scientists and thinkers of the day among its members. Sir Edward was by all accounts a generous as well as a pious man. Soon after the Restoration he was allotted the sequestered estate of Sir Henry Lingen, who had led those who besieged Brampton Castle, but Sir Edward returned the estate to Lady Lingen. The Castle itself was a ruin and was replaced as a residence by a house, though its shell remained to remind the family of their chequered past. Having lost his first wife, Sir Edward married, in February 1661, Abigail Stephens, the daughter of a Gloucestershire neighbour. Her family may have leaned towards a milder form of worship than his, for though she was devoutly religious, her letters,

---

5. H.M.C. Portland, iii, 166–7; Dict. Nat. Biog., sub Harley, Sir Edward; Henning, sub Herefordshire and New Radnor.

unlike his, lack the distinctive phraseology of the Puritan. Their first
son, Robert, was born on 5 December 1661 and baptised on the following day at the church of St Paul, Covent Garden.[6]

Robert Harley's earliest years passed at Brampton with much the same
joys and crises as most children's, though his father's periodic absences at
Westminster left a correspondence which chronicled the events better
than usual. At ten months 'we have caus to bless God he toothes so well';
and on Robin's first birthday, 'The Lord grant many happy, that is, holy
days'. At seven 'Robin has a good memory and learns apace', while his
brother Ned will soon be able to read. Another brother, the infant Brian,
was 'ill again much as he was before', and died soon after, aged eleven
months. At nine their mother reported Robin to be associating with
the servants, 'getting a strange clownish speech and behaviour'; he also
caught an ague: Sir Edward wrote anxiously, 'I beseech the Lord to spare
his life'. In short, Robert Harley grew up in his first ten years in the midst
of a devoted family.[7] In his father's generation there were Sir Edward's
sisters and his brother Major Sir Robert, and in Robert's own generation there were his half-sisters Brilliana and Martha, by Sir Edward's first
marriage. Robert's younger brother Edward, later his inseparable follower
and defender in politics, was followed by another brother, Nathaniel,
and a sister, Abigail. During Robert Harley's early years the lives of this
extensive family remained centred for the most part on the new house
and rebuilt church at Brampton (it too had suffered in and after the
siege); though Sir Edward's brother roamed abroad, as Nathaniel was
later to do, they often returned to their place of origin.

Even in the earliest years Robert's circle of knowledge was not confined to the family and remote Herefordshire. Sir Edward brought home
many unemployed preachers, deprived of their livings and homes by
legislation of the Clarendon Code, whose wanderings brought them into
contact with a wider world. Sir Edward's parliamentary and intellectual friends ensured that the diet of visiting worthies would not be too
narrow. During Robert's childhood there were many exciting reports
of national and international affairs. The series of persecuting statutes,
accompanied by wars with the Calvinist United Provinces, modern Holland, brought about a growth of parliamentary disillusionment with the
royal court, followed by the fall of the King's minister the Earl of Clarendon and of the 'Cabal' ministers who succeeded him. The excesses of the
Restoration court, and the re-emergence of Roman Catholicism among
many of its members including even the King's brother the Duke of York,
disquieted the Cavalier Parliament. The Royal Society provided reports
of exciting discoveries in natural science but also led to a new question-

6. H.M.C. *Portland*, iii, 245, 248, *passim*; Daniel Hipwell, *Notes and Queries*, 7th series, 12 (1891),
    p. 363; extract from the parish register of St Paul, Convent Garden.
7. H.M.C. *Portland*, iii, 266, 270, 312–13, 319, 322.

ing of religious authority and an atmosphere of 'latitude' even among the clergy, which was to lead eventually to more tolerant attitudes about doctrinal and other religious differences. Much of this ferment must have been absorbed, consciously or unconsciously by a boy who was bright and of retentive memory.

Nevertheless, Robert was brought up in an atmosphere highly charged with a religious fervour which owed little to the newer influences, whether of 'latitude' or licence, emanating from Restoration society. When he was about nine years old, Lady Harley described to his father a mood of self-questioning into which he had fallen:

> I was asking him this evening what it was that troubled him for Nan told me he prayed that God would rebuke the tempter. He said it was sin. He had heard of the sin against the Holy Ghost which was unpardonable but did not know what sin it was and was afraid to ask lest he had committed it or the devil should tempt him to commit it. The poor child with tears told me he was afraid if he died he should go to hell. He asked whether he should think oftener of scripture at prayer, for he said then he was tempted to vain thought which he could not help.[8]

Many echoes of the young boy's piety were to sound in his later life, for though he became a successful politician well able to practise the compromises with truth needed for that occupation, he retained the habit of religious observance and also, if more arguably, a basic probity which he drew from it. As to the first there is no dispute. When he was Queen Anne's leading minister a Scottish divine heard that 'sometimes he takes a botle; but otherwise he is morall, and never fails to pray with his family at night; and be it never soe late ere he comes in on the post nights, yet still they must all wait till prayers.'[9]

Until his tenth year Robert was educated at home with his brother Edward. By that time, however, Lady Harley was writing to her husband that Robin was reported by his instructors to be 'sometimes extremely lazy' though perceptive and willing. His mother's apprehension of laziness may have contributed to the palpable myth sometimes put forward of Harley's sloth; he was, in fact, most industrious later in life. She advised sending him away to school. Sir Edward agreed, made enquiries, and selected an academy run by a former Puritan chaplain of the Parliamentary Army who had subsequently been ejected from a civil living. Accordingly Robert went, in the summer of 1671, to Samuel Birch's school at Shilton in Berkshire, where he remained, except for short holi-

8. H.M.C. *Portland*, iii, 317.
9. Wodrow, *Analecta*, i, 324.
10. H.M.C. *Portland*, iii, 319, 321.

days, for over eight years.[11] Concerning his schooldays little is known that is reliable, except that two of his fellow pupils were Simon Harcourt, later Lord Chancellor, and Thomas Trevor, whose modesty kept him Lord Chief Justice of the Common Pleas.[12] As to Robert's education we learn from later achievements that he was taught to speak Latin but not French.

During the years he remained at Shilton, Robert continued to hear periodically of many tense events in national affairs. The Cavalier Parliament continued in its seemingly interminable career, and from the point of view of an old parliamentarian like Sir Edward matters became worse the longer an election was postponed. The King undertook secret commitments to France in 1670 and was suspected by many of being a crypto Roman Catholic, while his brother's adherence to that religion was notorious. Anglican opinion in Parliament, in reaction against these tendencies, passed in 1673 a Test Act which excluded Roman Catholics as well as Protestant Dissenters from national office. Fortunately for Sir Edward his conscience did not prevent him from taking the Sacrament of the Eucharist in an Anglican church, the test required for his continuance as a Member of Parliament, and he thus became one of the earliest of those who were later to be censured as 'occasional conformists' to that Church while continuing to worship for preference at the Meeting House.[13]

Church of England opinion was right to suspect Charles II, who relied increasingly on support from the proselytizing Louis XIV and had undertaken to announce his own conversion to the Roman Catholic faith when the time seemed appropriate. By the time Robert left Birch's school in 1779 an attempt at Anglican government by the Earl of Danby was seen to be hollow, especially as the King's heir was his avowedly Catholic brother James, Duke of York. Sir Edward Harley was numbered among an opposition party led by the Earl of Shaftesbury, and not even Danby's masterstroke of an arranged marriage between James' Anglican daughter Mary and the Dutch leader of European Protestantism, Prince William of Orange, could allay their fears entirely. Such fears lay behind the opposition's unfounded accusation in 1679 of a 'Popish Plot' by members of James's entourage against the King. The accusers' real fears, which they could not state openly, were of a joint plot by King and Duke of York against the Protestant religion. The Cavalier Parliament was dissolved on the verge of further allegations, and the subsequent series of manipulated trials showed little mercy to James's Catholic associates. Meanwhile three successive short Parliaments saw desperate attempts by

11. For Samuel Birch, schoolmaster, see *Alumni Oxonienses* (ed. J. Foster).
12. T.P. Armstrong, *Notes and Queries*, 148 (1925), 31.
13. H.M.C. *Portland*, iii, 336. Sir Edward obtained a certificate from the incumbent stating that the sacrament had been administered to him according to law.

Shaftesbury's followers to pass legislation which would exclude James from the succession, attempts which were frustrated by Charles II's tactics and the use of his right to dissolve the legislature.

No doubt the troubled times had something to do with Sir Edward's decision not to send Robert on to Oxford, a royalist centre, as he had originally intended. Instead, he went from school to the academy of a Monsieur Foubert, a French Protestant who had taken refuge in England. Foubert's Academy was a fashionable London finishing school, in Sherwood Street, near the Haymarket, for 'riding, fencing, dancing, handling arms and mathematics'. After a year, however, Robert left this institution, apparently in disgust at the licentiousness of his companions.[14] In March 1682 he enrolled at the Middle Temple. There he retained rooms for many years, but was never called to the bar, for as eldest son he had no need to regard his law studies as a professional training. His brother Edward however, was 'bred to the law'.[15]

To those who met him as a young man appeared to be of a grave, steady nature, set apart from the fashionable debaucheries of the day. In 1683 the Scottish minister Gilbert Burnet, who later became a political enemy, wrote of Robert to Sir Edward: 'I never saw him but with a secret joy in my heart when I observed so many fair and excellent beginnings in him, which makes me hope he is born to be a blessing to the rising generation'.[16] Burnet did not find his hope fulfilled, and the later political estrangement had all the bitterness of disappointed friendship. But if Robert's personality early impressed the later Whig bishop, his ability too was not to be despised, for the learning he carried, though desultory, was considerable in fields which would be useful to a politician. His legal studies gave him a good basis for the wide and recondite knowledge of political and constitutional history for which he was afterwards famous. From Jonathan Swift comes a later account which throws light on the way Harley's studies brought historical analogies easily to mind. In 1711, soon after an atempt by the Marquis de Guiscard to assassinate him, he received an anonymous note which he discussed with Swift. It read:

Though G———d's knife did not succeed
A F———n's yet may do the Deed.

The first concealed word was clearly 'Guiscard', and for the second Swift put forward the suggestion of 'Frenchman', but Harley thought it should

14. *Ibid.*, iii, 366; Harley's disgust is inferred from a letter from Edmund Nicholas, 9 Jan., 1682–3, *ibid.* iii, 374; 'The academy stands were it did, but seems only like a sodome that you have left for fear of a punishment on yourselfe'.
15. 'Certificate of Admission' to the Middle Temple, 18 March 1681–2, Loan 29/162/7; H.M.C. *Portland*, ii, 230.
16. H.M.C. *Bath*, i, 44.

be Felton, referring to John Felton the assassin of James I's favourite, the Duke of Buckingham. To Harley's excellent memory Swift bears testimony, writing 'He is master of a very great and faithful memory, which is of mighty use in the management of public affairs.'[17]

Robert was in London for much of the time the Exclusion crisis raged, from 1679 to 1682. Sir Edward was returned for New Radnor or Herefordshire in each of the three 'Exclusion' Parliaments of those years. In the first and doubtless in others too he voted for the bills brought by Shaftesbury's followers, now called 'Whigs' by their opponents, to exclude the Duke of York from the succession.[18] Robert witnessed at first hand, from the galleries, the efforts of Charles II's parliamentary supporters, dubbed 'Tories', to prevent this outcome. The last of the three parliaments was called at Oxford to avoid the support London gave to the Lower House at Westminster; but the Oxford assembly too seemed bent upon the exclusion Bill, and was dissolved after only a week. Robert Harley's later determination to prevent the misuse of royal prerogative and to ensure the dominance of Parliament, particularly the House of Commons, was greatly strengthened by what he observed at this time.

From 1683 the court went over to the offensive. The Rye House plot against Charles II's life gave the same excuse for an orgy of trials as had the 'Popish' plot four years earlier, only this time it was the leading Whigs who were condemned, executed, or driven into exile abroad. Shaftesbury died in Holland. Corporation boroughs which had returned Whig members to vote for Exclusion, were given new Tory membership by a renewal of their corporate charters set in motion by the King. Sir Edward Harley was not involved in the plot and suffered little more than failure to obtain a seat in the new Parliament summoned by James II in 1685, when Charles died after receiving the last rites of the Roman Catholic Church. For a few weeks Sir Edward endured semi-impisonment on suspicion of wishing to join a rebellion headed by the Protestant Duke of Monmouth, eldest illegitimate son of the late King. The suspicion was unjustified, for the Harleys would not support an illegal cause; Robert wrote to his father announcing Monmouth's defeat: 'we are not a little rejoiced at it'.[19] But the rounding up of rebels and severe punishments meted out to suspects by Lord Chief Justice Jeffreys and other judges brought out the full force of Robert's indignation even years later when he called for justice upon the royal judges.

Meanwhile Robert had courted and, on 14 May 1685, married Elizabeth Foley. His bride was daughter of Thomas Foley of Witley Court, Gloucestershire, who stood alongside Sir Edward Harley in all

17. Swift, *Journal to Stella*, 14 and 16 Nov., 1711; H.M.C. *Bath*, i, 228.
18. Andrew Browning and Doreen J. Milne, 'An Exclusion Bill division list', *BIHR*, xxiii (1950), 25.
19. H.M.C. *Portland*, iii, 386.

three Exclusion Parliaments and like him had been defeated in the elections for the Tory Parliament of 1685. Her grandfather, the greatest ironmaster of the day, had been a friend of the great Puritan divine Richard Baxter, who was also on close terms with Sir Edward. The match was suitable in other ways too, for the Foleys resembled the Harleys in being a large, clannish family equivalent or better off then the Harleys in ownership of landed property. The marriage laid the foundation of a long-lasting political alliance; for after 1688 the Harleys and Foleys acted as one group in Parliament. The alliance was cemented by the subsequent marriage of Robert's brother Edward to Elizabeth's sister. Through an earlier marriage, that of a third sister to John Hampden the Younger, Robert also now became connected to one of the greatest of old Puritan families. Most important of all for Robert's future career was Thomas Foley's brother Paul, who was to lead the Foleys and Harleys in a decade of post-Revolution Parliament and precede Robert as Speaker of the House of Commons.

Robert's marriage was a happy one, a match of love as well as a momentous family alliance. For a few months the newly married pair lived in the Harley lodgings in London, in King Street, but as it became clear that James II had no intention of continuing his Parliament, they moved to Brampton Bryan to bring up their children. There were born two daughters, Elizabeth and Abigail, and there in 1687 died Lady Harley, 'your dear and precious mother' as Sir Edward still called her to Robert's sister Abigail many years later.[20] The presence of this unmarried sister, and sometimes of other members of the widely-flung family, made the children's early life at Brampton closely similar to Robert's own.

He was now actively seeking a parliamentary seat. James's Parliament of 1685, loyal though it was as the result of Charles II's activity in manipulating the borough franchises, had proved to be not loyal enough for the new monarch's aspirations; even the Tories baulked at James's programme of toleration for Catholics in a year when neighbouring France was taking the final steps to rid itself of its Protestant citizens. This Parliament was prorogued after a few weeks and never met again though there were increasing signs that James hoped to replace it eventually by another when he could be sure of obtaining a less obstinately Anglican majority. James commenced a policy of conciliation towards the Protestant Dissenters and even Whigs, hoping to make them his allies in obtaining concessions for both Roman Catholics and Protestant Dissenters. Robert's father-in-law Thomas Foley appears to have been one of the relatively few Whigs who responded to the monarch's blandishments, but the Harleys held back. Robert, acting on his father's behalf in July 1688, refused a Privy Council place when the King, after the

20. *Ibid.*, iii, 548.

birth of a male heir the previous month by his Catholic second wife, was redoubling his efforts in the hope of obtaining support for his infant son against any claim to the succession by his daughter Mary, Princess of Orange.[21] The birth followed a series of incidents in which James aroused the fears and wrath of the Church and Tory party, culminating in the trial of seven bishops who refused to promulgate his policy of 'indulgence' to religious dissidents. By this time Robert Harley was acting as his father's agent in canvassing support for the Orange and Protestant cause in the general election which was expected to be James' next expedient. He reported to Sir Edward Harley on 4 August 1688, some months before the Prince of Orange set sail with his army for England, that he had seen 'Lord Ch[andos]' who 'will adhere to the Prince's interest and steer as Sir E. will desire'. A careful reading of the letter by a government official would not have carried conviction that it referred solely, as it purported, to electoral matters.[22]

James II's realization that he was in danger of losing his throne came too late. His ejection of Tory corporations by a new onslaught on the borough charters had the result of replacing some of the ejected voters by Whigs, but the gamble did not pay off. Like the Harleys most Whigs and dissenting sympathisers refused to be seduced, while others who accepted royal favour soon showed that they felt no obligation to the monarch and his Roman Catholic advisers. When the Prince of Orange landed in Torbay in November there were few to oppose him. At the first reports of the invasion Sir Edward and Robert Harley put themselves at the head of their friends and tenants and marched in support of the Prince, taking possession of the key city of Worcester in his name. Robert was sent on to report to the Prince, whom he duly met at Henley. By this time William was virtually in control of the country, James having fled after his commander-in-chief the Earl of Marlborough led his army into the Prince's service. Writs for new elections, prepared by James but not yet sent, were supplemented by missives from the victor and a Convention Parliament was summoned. Sir Edward Harley became Governor of Worcester, while Robert was commissioned as a major of militia foot in Herefordshire, a function in which he continued for several years.[23]

In the Convention which assembled in January 1689 Sir Edward Harley recaptured a seat for Herefordshire but Robert, despite great anxiety to take a part in the assembly which would determine the settle-

21. Henning, *sub* Foley, Thomas II; H.M.C. *Portland*, iii, 415.
22. Loan 29/184, f. 102.
23. Jones, *Revolution of 1688; Hatton Corr.* ii, 113. 'Memoirs of the Harley family, especially of Robert Harley, first Earl of Oxford', by Edward Harley, H.M.C. *Portland*, v, 644. Substantially the same as this document, but containing many additional passages, is the 'Account of the Earl of Oxford by his brother', in Landsdowne MS. 885, which on this event contains the words, not in the printed version, 'A message was sent to the Prince by R.H. etc.', (f. 11).

ment of Church and State, did not at first manage to obtain a seat. As the eldest son of a local landowner he could aspire to a borough seat in either New Radnor on the Welsh side of the border or Leominster in Herefordshire, but the election was an unusual one. The tide of public opinion was again running in favour of Whig candidates in constituencies where they had enjoyed support in 1679; but in both boroughs experienced Exclusionists appeared, and Robert did not have the prestige of men who could boast that they had already fought in the front line.[24] So while Sir Edward made for London in his sixty-fourth year to serve in the busiest Parliament of his busy life, Robert was left to keep Herefordshire secure for the Prince and to retrieve the Harley electoral fortunes for himself.

At first there was some hope that the successful outsider Richard Williams might be unseated at New Radnor. Williams unexpectedly obtained the seat, largely on the strength of his being one of the twenty-five members of the Radnor corporation and winning his fellows to his cause. Other towns and villages, the 'out-boroughs' also included in the Radnor constituency, were largely loyal to the Harley interest. But the confusion in which many constituencies returned members in the hurried elections of 1689 was reflected at Radnor, where Williams had found himself unopposed by the Harleys who were attending to the Prince's business elsewhere. The Rhayader burgesses boycotted the election out of a preference for the Harleys, and those of Knighton, Painscastle, Huntley, Knucklas and other boroughs appear to have been confused by the failure of the usually dominant family to make a poll. Williams' election on a show of hands was, however, protested by another candidate, William Probert.[25]

While a petition alleging wrongful election was pending in the House of Commons, Robert set about securing support for himself in the event of a successful outcome and of Probert's expected withdrawal to permit a re-election thereafter. On 29 January he was able to write to Sir Edward 'I have secured most of the burgesses of Radnor. Not twenty besides the twenty-five are against me.' Soon afterwards he reported that he thought he had promises from some of the twenty-five also, though he added uneasily that he wished the support of the powerful Radnorshire landowner Sir Rowland Gwynne could be obtained.[26] In the event the Commons proved to be in no mood to upset loyal Whig supporters, and Williams' election was confirmed. But Robert's brisk efforts to re-establish the Harley interest were to prove useful later when he had to face another formidable challenge, this time from Gwynne.

24. Henning, *sub*. Williams, Richard, *and* Colt, John Dutton.
25. *Ibid.*, *sub* New Radnor.
26. H.M.C. *Portland*, iii, 425–6.

For the rest he waited anxiously for the news from Westminster, where the Whigs were united by a determination to resist the reinstatement of James II, under any circumstances, and to adopt his nephew the Prince of Orange as successor. Less single-minded were the Tories; having forced James to take refuge in France they now either toyed with the idea of his return, duly chastened, or supported the candidacy of Mary, as closer to the throne than her husband and more sympathetic to the established Church. If James's action in placing himself under the protection of the Roman Catholic King of France seemed to make his restoration, upon any terms, daily more unlikely, those of William were not well calculated to soothe the fears of a Church party. Sir Edward Seymour, leader of the West Country Tories and one of the first to join the Prince at Exeter, remarked that the countenance William was giving to the Dissenters 'gave too much cause of jealousy to the Church of England; who...if they were not supported, we should run into a Commonwealth, and all would be ruined'. To such a cry the Earl of Clarendon, influential as the son of the great Clarendon and uncle to the Princesses Mary and Anne, gave strong support. Mary was still absent in Holland, beyond the reach of Clarendon's influence, but Anne was available and listened willingly when he mentioned a rumour that William and Mary were to be proposed as joint King and Queen with William to continue as King if he outlived his wife. Anne replied that 'she knew very well the commonwealth party was very busy; but she hoped, the honest party would be most prevalent in the Convention, and would not suffer wrong to be done her'. Her husband, Prince George of Denmark, went so far as to issue a denial that she would consent to a change in the succession. As uncertainty and rumour grew, the convention had to face some of the greatest decisions ever met by the legislative body.[27]

On 28 January the House of Commons expressed its mood by choosing as its chairman Richard Hampden, mover of the Exclusion Bill of 1679, son of John Hampden the opponent of Ship Money in Charles I's reign and father of Robert Harley's brother-in-law John ('Jack') Hampden. The debate soon centred upon a motion by Gilbert Dolben stating that, James II having 'voluntarily forsaken' government, it was thereby in demise. In the course of a long parliamentary career Dolben never made any other contribution comparable with this. His intervention gains signficance from his standing, for he was a Tory lawyer and son of a former Archbishop of York. Though other Tories opposed the motion as too extreme they were not averse from considering an alternative to James II. Some suggested a Regency of Prince William, in James's name, and others favoured Mary. But against the divided Tories their opponents were able to obtain a resolution that James had broken the

---

27. Diary of Henry, Earl of Clarendon, *Clarendon Corr.*, ii, 238, and 255; Schwoerer deals with these decisions in detail.

'original contract' between king and people, withdrawn himself from the kingdom and thereby left the throne vacant.[28] When the House of Lords proved less than willing to adopt this root and branch approach a constitutional crisis was at hand, but the Whigs in the Lower House remained firm. On 5 February Sir Edward Harley rallied the Herefordshire members to vote against Lords' amendments to the abdication vote.[29] Finally, however, a compromise was reached whereby William and Mary would reign jointly. Sir Edward Harley was also active in adding to the decision to change the line of succession a series of limitations on the power of the new monarchs; as he wrote to Robert, it was only prudent to secure existing rights from royal interference by drawing up a Declaration of Rights.[30] This document duly prefaced the declaration of William's and Mary's sovereignty by a long list of statements condemning James II's prerogative Courts of Ecclesiastical Causes and High Commission, the claimed royal right to suspend or dispense with legislation, the levy of taxes without parliamentary consent, the raising of a standing army in peacetime, royal interference in elections and other practices complained of under previous monarchs. On 13 February Sir Edward heard the Declaration being read before both Houses of Parliament assembled in the Banqueting House of Whitehall Palace, where Charles I had stepped on to the scaffold, and witnessed the Prince and Princess being declared King and Queen.

At home Robert Harley busied himself with the proclamation of the new order. With 'thirty-six horse and two trumpets' he rode to Leominster, and thence to Hereford in greater style with three trumpets and fifty horses, to attend the proclamation. Afterwards there were fireworks; he reported that they were 'well designed but did pretty much fail in the execution'.[31] The hunt for a parliamentary seat continued. From Hereford, for which Paul Foley had again been returned, came the news that his fellow member was retiring on being given a judicial post. Robert gave the matter much thought but in the end informed his father that 'probably I might, with great expense have come in for Hereford, but it was not a place in which I could expect a continuing interest'. In March he became High Sheriff of Herefordshire, but more as a duty than by inclination; the post was an unpopular one among country gentlemen on account of the considerable expense and likelihood of causing enemies, especially at election time when the incumbent might have to add the duty of returning officer to his other responsibilities.[32]

From Westminster news of continued problems of government con-

28. Grey, *Debates*, ix, 7–25; *CJ*, x, 14; H.M.C. *Portland*, iii, 424; Luttrell, i, 499; Schwoerer, chapter 9.
29. Henning, *sub*. Harley, Sir Edward.
30. 29 Jan. 1689, Add. MSS. 40, 621, f. 7.
31. H.M.C. *Portland*, iii, 429.
32. *Ibid.*, iii, 432 and 435.

tinued to trickle in. The new monarchs appointed the experienced
Danby as Lord President of the Council, with the title of Marquis of
Carmarthen, but they also made many Whig appointments, much to
the jealousy of Tories who considered themselves the natural men of
government. Edward Harley, accompanying his father in London, wrote:
'The clergy and many Tories do with all malice imaginable express their
dislike of the Present Government.'[33] The omission from office of most
of their best-known leaders was a blow to those whose expectation of
King William was, despite their belated and reluctant assistance for his
cause, scarcely less than that of the Whigs. Henceforth, Clarendon and
his brother the Earl of Rochester, who had been dismissed as Lord High
Treasurer for opposing James but was now ignored, placed their chief
hope of future favour in Princess Anne. The Tories' mood was important
for the Harleys and their like, for the next important matter to be dealt
with in Parliament's settlement of the nation was the position of the
Protestant Dissenters. The issue of religion was one of great complexity
involving, as well as the dissenters' disabilities, the future safeguarding
of the Church of England and the doubtful loyalty to the new monarchy
of clergy long imbued with the doctrine of Divine Right. Because the
Protestant Dissenters had given little encouragement to James II, despite
considerable incentives, responsible Tories like the Earl of Nottingham,
one of the new Secretaries of State, were pledged to alleviate some aspects of the harsh legislation against dissenting worship. Many Whigs,
however, were by no means satisfied by the prospect of merely religious
toleration, and they pressed also for alleviation of the political disabilities
imposed by the Corporation and Test Acts which kept Dissenters out of
Parliament and local and national offices.

On 25 February, the Whig politician and dramatist Sir Robert Howard
brought this matter to the fore in the Commons by proposing the removal of the sacramental test imposed in the Corporation Act, by which
the stricter dissenters were excluded from corporations and municipal
offices. To give strength to the demand, the Whigs devised a bill enforcing the new oaths of allegiance and supremacy upon clergy and officeholders; such a requirement would act as a counter-test, for the scruples
of the lower clergy about taking the oaths were widely known. Despite
this threat, however, no further softening in the Tory position became
visible. In the Upper House the Tory Nottingham introduced two bills,
one for the toleration of the Dissenters' public worship and the other for
the comprehension within the Church of their least radical element,
the Presbyterians; but no offer was made to raise the political tests. The
Whigs' bill accordingly went forward, and although the churchmen
struggled long to obtain a concession that the oaths should be tendered

33. Edward to Robert Harley, 23 Feb. 1689, Add. MSS. 40, 621, f. 26.

to the clergy only in selected cases where loyalty was suspected, the Commons were induced to stand firm upon this point. While the Whig bill was under consideration the King personally intervened by means of a speech on 16 March calling for the way to office to be opened to all Protestants. Speculation ran rife that he was willing to exempt the lower clergy from compulsory oath-taking if the sacramental tests were lifted for dissenters. If this was the case William greatly misjudged the temper of Parliament. Both Carmarthen and Nottingham deserted him and voted against the raising of the tests, and an Anglican demonstration of strength was joined even by eminent Church Whigs such as the Earl of Shrewsbury, the other Secretary of State, and the Earl of Devonshire, one of the principal pillars of early whhiggery.[34] In the Commons the Tory rally took the form of a vote on 26 March, by 188 votes to 149, to add a proviso to the coronation oath binding William and Mary and their successors to uphold the Church of England as by law established.[35] All these events, following closely upon one another, were followed avidly by Robert Harley from his relations' letters and from newsletters by more professional news vendors. Probably it was only the need to 'make his interest' in local constituencies which kept him from joining his father and brother in London, upon which was centred the nation's close attention.

The parliamentary arrangements for the settlement of religion represented a *modus vivendi*. Though the Comprehension Bill was finally dropped, the Toleration Act was passed, giving freedom of worship to all Protestants. The Dissenters remained politically disadvantaged under the Corporation and Test Acts, but this did not affect such as the Harleys, who had always been willing to conform, and was seen by some Church Whigs as useful, ensuring the Dissenters' continued support for Whig parliamentary candidates.[36] Less calculating Whigs were disappointed at many aspects of the settlement. Edward Harley wrote to Robert concerning the debate on the coronation oath 'you may guess the whole design by the fact that...a debate began whether the King should swear to maintain the Church of England established by law'.[37] But the nation was strong in defence of the Anglican Church, and its triumph had to be accepted. Over the next few years old Whig families such as the Harleys and Foleys, Harcourts and St Johns, were to move further towards conformity with the Church, as an alternative to sinking in the social scale by refusing the established form of worship and incurring resultant exclusion from office.

As the later stage of these debates continued, there came at last a turn

---

34. Grey, *Debates*, ix, 111, 218–26; Burnet, iv, 13 16; Foxcroft, *Supplement*, pp. 315–16; Foxcroft, *Halifax*, ii, 213 and n. 5; Lacey, p. 233; Browning, *Danby*, i, *Life*, 447–48.
35. Grey, *Debates*, ix, 190–200.
36. Lacey, p. 236; Burnet, iv, 20–1.
37. H.M.C. *Portland*, iii, 435.

in Robert Harley's personal fortunes; in March arrived news of the death
of one of the representatives for the borough of Tregony in Cornwall,
Charles Boscawen. His brother Hugh Boscawen had influence in the
borough and was looking for a candidate of suitable views. Among those
consulted was Jack Hampden and the result, as Sir Edward wrote on the
30th, was that both Robert Harley and Paul Foley's son Thomas were
considered and Robert was chosen.[38] The electors being compliant, he
was elected on 6 April in his absence, on Boscawen's recommendation.
Pausing only to appoint an under-sheriff to carry out his duties, Robert
made haste for London. His family did not accompany him; Elizabeth
was six months pregnant with the child who was to be their eldest son
Edward, young Elizabeth was not much out of the toddling stage and
'Little Aby' was still on mare's milk. In his eagerness to get to Westminster while great matters were still being discussed he probably had
little prevision that his chosen career would make him, for the next three
decades, virtually a Londoner who took annual vacations in the country.

38. *Ibid*, iii, 435–7.

CHAPTER 2

Coming into Notice

THE CONVENTION PARLIAMENT in which Robert Harley took his seat in the spring of 1689 was to be a very different institution from its predecessors. Continuing in session several months after Harley's arrival, it contrasted sharply with the recent pattern of short-lived assemblies in Charles II's last years and James II's reign. After playing a key role in changing the line of the royal succession, Parliament was to assume a new importance with regular meetings of many months' duration every year rather than the short sessions, often measured in weeks or even days, with intervals sometimes lasting years, which had marked the rule of the Stuarts. Parliament's transformation from an intermittent to a permanent institution during Harley's career reflected the determination of almost all members to prevent any recurrence of royal attempts to dispense with the nation's representatives. Though the full effect of this change was not yet visible when he took his seat it was to transform him and his fellow members into a new breed of full-time parliamentary politicians rather than, as he probably envisaged in 1689, gentlemen of substance meeting occasionally in Parliament.

To some extent Harley's family connections ensured him a reputation which preceded his entry into Parliament. Sir Edward already had a secure and well-defined niche, from his long service and puritanical outlook. Even before Robert took his seat he had heard, as he wrote wryly, of his father's reputation as 'very worthy but not for the church'.[1] Equally well-known were the proclivities of Harley's sponsor at Tregony. Jack Hampden was a Whig who habitually spoke with the fervour of an extremist and a religious terminology more suited to his grandfather's period than to an era of growing religious latitude. Harley's first actions in the Commons placed him firmly alongside his relatives in furthering the Toleration Bill's progress even though his early hope of 'an equal

1. H.M.C. *Portland*, iii, 428

settlement of religion', by comprehension of the Presbyterians within the Church, had already been shown to be misplaced. He also joined enthusiastically in helping to beat off a Tory attempt to amend the en-acting bill of the recently-adopted Declaration of Rights by leaving a loophole for the restoration of James II's infant son in the event of his becoming a Protestant. This attempt, as Robert excitedly wrote to Eliza-beth, had 'been long in contriving' and was 'designed to overthrow all former proceedings'. His suspicion of a resurgence of Tory aspirations was to be greatly inflamed in the coming months. But for his own parlia-mentary début he chose a subject close to his heart for several years. On 14 May, in his maiden speech, he reminded the Commons of recent Tory persecution, calling for justice particularly over the draconic punishment of Monmouth's humble and ignorant followers after the rising of 1685.[2] Former Lord Chancellor Jeffreys, of the 'bloody assize', died in the Tower to the regret of few.

Robert's early letters home describing the state of the House reflect the confusion felt by the Harleys and their like when the Calvinist king failed to resolve the situation according to their expectations. William had to share the throne with his wife, who as an Anglican was the Tories' choice, even though Mary placed unrestricted executive authority in his hands. He had also to please both parties which had supported his invasion and to make compromises in the interest of practical adminis-trative needs. The Harleys were inclined at first to attribute the King's less acceptable activities to evil councillors or ignorance of the English system. He was about to take his new country to war with Louis XIV, who in March had backed a landing in Ireland by James II at the head of a substantial force. To raise an army for war on the Continent and in Ireland funds urgently needed to be raised in the Commons, caus-ing William to have recourse to the traditional court 'managers' of the House, a proceeding far from pleasing to the Whigs. Robert recorded for his wife his bafflement and frustration, writing gloomily 'there is a party setting up to play the old game', though he added hopefully 'I am sure the King is of our side'.[3] In the following weeks however, his hope of William's co-operation disappeared when faced with the realities of war and taxation, while his discontent with new policies gained ground. His disillusionment was a reflection of the views of many Whigs and other country gentlemen at Westminster. Their mood was expressed increas-ingly in their refusal to make a permanent settlement of royal revenue, such as the last two monarchs had enjoyed, and in the adoption of votes of war supplies for only limited periods of a year or less.

A matter which especially interested Harley during his first weeks

2. Robert to Elizabeth Harley 11 May 1689, Loan 29/164/2; *Henning, History of Parliament, 1660–1690, sub.* Harley, Robert II.
3. 1 June 1690, Loan 29/164/2.

in the Commons was King William's proposal for an indemnity for all political activities in the last two reigns, a measure intended to prevent the continuance of old feuds but one seen as mainly favouring the Tory transgressors. On this subject Harley made a major early speech, welcoming the proposed indemnity with the ominous qualification that 'God said He would not pardon the shedding of innocent blood'.[4] The blood of Whig martyrs cried for vengeance, and like many survivors the Harleys were convinced that exceptions should be made from this general indemnity, especially where offenders were still in office. Some Whigs were already arguing that exception should be carried much further by the introduction of a measure to penalize old enemies at constituency level, preventing them from sitting on the corporations which in many boroughs constituted the whole body of parliamentary electors. The king himself conceded the principle of exceptions in some cases. But Church and Tory members responded by advocating that only a very limited number of named individuals, whose crimes were too serious to be overlooked, should be excepted from the indemnity.

This proposal was by no means acceptable to the Whigs. Their reaction was to attack Carmarthen, the most obvious author of evil counsels and one who was vulnerable by reason of his many enemies among Tories as well as Whigs. Threatening to renew the impeachment from which he had narrowly been saved by Charles II they succeeded on 4 June in obtaining a resolution stating that a royal pardon was not pleadable by the accused in the case of a parliamentary impeachment. A former Speaker of two Exclusion Parliaments, Sir William Williams, expressed a sentiment which appealed to more than his own party when he claimed 'if a pardon from a Prince be a bar to impeachment, farewell to redressing grievances'. Appeal to country sentiment was sufficient to get the Indemnity Bill shelved for the moment.

Another measure which met the same fate was a bill intended to give statutory force to the Declaration of Rights. In this case both Whigs and Tories were, for different reasons, responsible for the obstruction, which centred upon a clause added in the Lords at William's behest to entail the throne, after the King, Queen and Princess Anne and their descendants, upon the Princess Sophia and her descendants of the Protestant House of Hanover. Opposition from Tories, who were reluctant to preclude the eventual restoration of the Stuarts, was predictable: the objections of the Whigs smacked of studied intransigence, when they claimed that the clause prevented the future choice of a monarch by Parliament. But, intransigent or not, Whig obstruction turned the balance, and William reluctantly abandoned the bill until a more auspicious occasion.[5]

4. Grey, *Debates*, ix, 247.
5. CJ x, 165; Grey, *Debates*, ix, 244–52, 345–6; 'Spencer House Journals', Foxcroft, *Halifax* ii, 223; Burnet, iv, 28; Oldmixon, p. 11.

To allow time for tempers to cool, William and Mary prorogued the Convention Parliament late in August 1689 after seven months' almost continuous sitting. Harley was able to pay a brief visit to Herefordshire, though even at home the prospect of unfinished parliamentary business occupied a good deal of his thought. The Whigs' determination to punish their former persecutors and to frustrate William's intended indemnity was undiminished, and the Declaration of Rights still awaited its final passage into law embodied in a bill. To remove Whig objections to a new Bill of Rights when the Convention asembled for its second session in October, William agreed to give up the clause specifying ultimate succession to the throne by the House of Hanover. The bill was passed easily, but in other matters the House proved truculent. In a series of debates on military misfortunes in Ireland and heavy losses to merchant shipping during the summer, country members often combined to press for enquiries. Thus, the subject of naval mismanagement found the Whig Admiral Edward Russell defending himself against not only the powerful Tory Sir Edward Seymour but also Paul Foley, who was followed in his stand by Harley and other relations and neighbours. The same significant combination of country Tories and Whigs was visible in criticism of the provisioning of forces in Ireland; Commissary-General Henry Shales was selected for special censure, and both Foley and the Tory Sir Christopher Musgrave were prominent in calling for punishment to be carried to a higher level still. Despite a warning from the cautious Whig lawyer Sir John Somers that such probing would give 'great advantage to those about the King to tell him that the Commons go beyond the bounds of his dignity' the Whig office holders did little towards defending the government, and on 29 November the House resolved to address the King for information as to who advised the appointment of Shales.[6]

As a result of these attacks William drew closer to the Tories, and particularly to Secretary Nottingham, whose energy and ability had more than justified his appointment and whose loyalty, together with that of his brother Heneage Finch in the Commons, had been proved except over the repeal of the religious tests. Nottingham was now able to point to the fact that in the summer the great majority of the clergy had, contrary to Whig forecasts, taken the oaths of loyalty, thanks to a new wording inserted at Nottingham's own suggestion to prevent the embarrassment of having to taken the same form of oath to William and Mary as formerly to James. The lead thus given by the clergy was crucial, for if the Tories were willing to accept the new monarchy *de facto*, (if not *de jure*) their capacity for loyalty was well demonstrated. By the beginning of December Nottingham was telling his friends that the King 'was now convinced that he had taken wrong measures in relying so much

6. C.J., x, 286, 298; Grey, *Debates*, ix, 411–21, 450–1, 456.

upon the dissenters, and that he would hereafter put himself into the hands of the Church of England'.[7]

A fortnight before Christmas the Whig attacks on the ministers were renewed with a fury and desperation which suggest that Nottingham's claims were now generally known. Howard asked whether 'any man is for the Government who was for the regency', and Jack Hampden attacked the ministerialists Nottingham, Godolphin and the Marquis of Halifax as former adherents of James II. In a sharp party tussle the Tories rallied strongly. Even Seymour, whose animosity was limited to Whigs and to his personal enemy, Carmarthen, defended the beleaguered ministers. Led by Paul Foley, however, the Whigs succeeded in carrying an Address to William 'to appoint affairs to be managed by persons unsuspected, and more to the safety of His Majesty and satisfaction of his subjects'. This victory boded well for the prospects of a bill, of which Harley had high hopes, to restore former corporation charters and hence the Whig majorities in many borough constituencies. After successfully cutting the Christmas recess to a brief week, during which they remained in London, the determined Whigs renewed their attack when the House of Commons reassembled, denuded by the season's continuing festivities. Harley voted in a majority of 133 votes against a mere 68 for the most farreaching proposal offered, a clause drawn up by the extremist William Sacheverell to exclude from office for seven years all who had connived in the surrender of the borough charters in the late reigns. This triumph was short-lived, however, for in succeeding days returning Tory members, aided by moderates alarmed by the extent of the proposed proscription, succeeded in reversing this vote. A point of decision had at last been reached: the country was tired of extremism and was now almost ready to rally to the King in ridding him of opponents as intransigent as Sacheverell.[8]

King William was contemplating a dissolution of the Convention Parliament which had done so much to establish the new monarchy but now threatened to destabilize its own achievements and delay urgent government business by prolonged partisan struggles. The last few days of the session in January 1690 saw the Whigs again locked in conflict with their opponents over the king's proposal for a general indemnity. A fierce struggle ensued in which, as the author of one tract put it, 'when an article is moved that toucheth the friends of one party, the others for

7. Looking back after William's death, one Whig was to concede ruefully that 'The Tories... prevailed by the assurances of their peculiar regards to regal power', Sloane MS. 4224, f. 83 ('K.W. Character', transcript, attributed to Thomas Wharton); For Nottingham's assurances see Diary of Clarendon, *Clarendon Corr.*, ii, 296. *Cf.* his conversation with Sir John Knatchbull, Add. MS. 33,923, f. 465, printed by Sir Hughe Knatchbull-Hugesson, *Kentish Family*, pp. 88–9, where the speaker Nottingham is mistaken referred to as Halifax.

8. *CJ*, x, 309–23: Grey, *Debates*, ix, 480–8, 490–3 510–20; Robert to Elizabeth Harley, 14 Dec., Loan, 29/164/4; Browning, iii, *Appendices*, pp. 164–72.

want of better weapons to oppose with, move for other articles which shall reach the friends of their adversaries'. The main quarrel turned upon whether those to be excepted from indemnity should be selected as individuals or by the wide categories of offences as favoured by the Whigs in order to incriminate the largest possible number of offenders. Harley found occasion to speak strongly in favour of categories, observing that if the Commons adopted the method of excepting named persons, a process already begun at random in the House, the innocent might suffer and the guilty escape among the exigencies and chance of debate. This was a sensible and persuasive appeal to moderate opinion, in view of the heat with which cases were being discussed, and the Whigs were enabled to obtain the narrow majority of seventeen votes. But William had seen enough, and late in January he prorogued the Convention for the last time. A few days later he finally dissolved the assembly which had passed the Bill of Rights and the Toleration Act but signally failed to avoid contention or provide him with more than short-term supplies for war. He was tired of the Whig desire for protection or revenge, and in a message to the electors he urged them now to 'choose Church of England man'.[9]

In preparation for the general election both Tories and Whigs circulated lists of their more extreme opponents in the Convention, with Sir Edward's and Robert Harley's names appearing among those of members who had supported the Sacheverell clause. 'I hear a list of the Commonwealth's men, as they call Whigs now, is printed' wrote the younger Edward Harley. Such lists were useful electoral material for informing the voters of the past record of candidates. The Harleys, Foleys and their like had gone too far in disrupting Parliament by pursuing vendetta, and were among those who now found themselves penalized in the national reaction which responded to the King's election appeal. Sir Edward Harley was unseated by the forty-shilling freeholders of Herefordshire, whom he had first represented as early as 1646, and Robert felt the force of local opinion the Tregony. Here, however, a more personal element of motivation also played a part in his rejection. He had not yet found time to cultivate his constituents by a personal visit, and they now rejected the pressure and advice of the magnate who backed him; the voters were reported as saying 'they will have no stranger for their burgess'.[10]

In his home border country too there were formidable problems, with Gwynne taking the field against him at New Radnor boroughs while another powerful landowner, Thomas Coningsby, opposed the Harleys

9. CJ, x, 332–3, 338; Grey, *Debates*, ix, 520–2, 538–47; *A Letter in Answer to an Enquiry touching an Act of Pains and Penalties. . . January 1689*, MS tract, Add. MS 32, 524, f. 2; *Clarendon Corr.*, ii, 304.

10. H.M.C. *Portland*, iii, 444–5.

for Leominster and Herefordshire. At Radnor Sir Edward generously waived his own claim and supported his elder son, though himself ousted for the county seat. The election, however, was fiercely disputed and it was Gwynne's name, not Robert Harley's, which was forwarded to Westminster by the returning officer. Harley immediately instituted a formal protest based upon an interpretation that the burgesses of several out-boroughs who had pitched for Gwynne were not in fact entitled to vote. The issue would be decided by the Commons' committee of elections when the House assembled. Everywhere elections were equally hotly contested, one observer reporting 'hardly any county or town but they stand double'. Contested elections were far from inevitable, in an age when less expensive 'accommodations' could be reached between rival interests willing to share the seats for two-member constituencies, but the proportion of bitterly fought polls was to remain relatively high during the whole of Harley's career in an age of keenly-felt issues. The King wrote with satisfaction to his friend Willem Bentinck 'it seems to me that the Tory party will be larger'.[11]

So it proved when the new House of Commons assembled, with Sir Edward Harley, Sacheverell, Williams, Jack Hampden and many other prominent Whigs conspicuously absent. On court recommendation a Tory lawyer, Sir John Trevor, was elected Speaker to replace his Whig legal counterpart, former Speaker Henry Powle. And when the monarchs caused an Act of Grace to be introduced, extending indemnity for past offences to all but a few offenders, the measure now passed in both Houses with little attempt at opposition. Because of the disputed result of the Radnor election, Harley had to spend the first few months of the new Parliament as an observer rather than a participant. Meanwhile, there was a tragedy at home. His infant second son, Robert, was struck down unexpectedly in the summer of 1690 by 'strangling fits', a description sufficiently wide to avoid classification, and never recovered.[12] With the impact of this loss scarcely behind him, and taking a worse toll upon Elizabeth, Robert Harley arrived in London in October having arranged for a coachload of witnesses from Radnor to arrive in time to support him in his petition against unwarranted exclusion from the electoral return. Their testimony turned the balance in his favour. On 13 November the representation for Radnor was amended in Harley's favour, and he took the oaths enabling him to take his place in the House of Commons.[13]

With the delays and frustration of the election dispute now behind him, Harley took care to cultivate the patrons and electors of the Radnor boroughs for the future, building up his 'interest' whenever possible, and

11. Luttrell, ii, 16; Japikse, i, 140.
12. H.M.C. Portland, iii, 449.
13. Ibid., iii, 450-2

his assiduity ensured his continued return for the borough during the remainder of his career in the Commons.[14] In London he settled comfortably in rooms in the Middle Temple, where he was within easy reach of Westminster Palace by riding or walking. He was determined to make his mark by regular attendance, unlike many of his less dedicated fellow members. Perhaps as a result of chastising experiences during and after the election he was now also in a more moderate mood than at the time of the Sacheverell clause. On 5 December, his twenty-ninth birthday, he had the opportunity to display this moderation in a vote on a bill providing for the forfeiture of the estates of Irish rebels defeated by William in the campaign culminating the previous June in King James's defeat on the River Boyne. Harley found the measure 'not relishing' for, as he explained in a letter to Sir Edward back at Brampton: 'Too many are in hopes of grants out of it. I therefore strove for a vote that would have rendered the bill useless.'[15] A few days later he continued in his more responsible line by refusing to join in a new attempt to impeach Carmarthen. 'My little experience', he told his father, 'shews me when these things vent in noise, little is the execution'.[16] Such studied avoidance of the sort of attempt at persecution which had already resulted in the exclusion of so many Whigs from Parliament was the right course for a young man with his way to make.

Before December was out, Harley's growing reputation assured him of an appointment which placed him at the centre of a more generally acceptable type of opposition than he had displayed in the Convention. He was elected by his fellow members as one of the parliamentary commissioners paid £500 a year to 'examine, take and state' the accounts of the kingdom since the coming of the Prince of Orange. The Commons were increasingly alarmed at burgeoning war expenditure in Ireland as well as on the Continent. From the start Harley demonstrated a remarkable devotion to the commission's as well as to other business, as was later described by Lord Raby:

> In King William's time . . . I heard it then said that, though he had but £500 a year he spent half of it on clerks to copy out what papers were given to the House of Commons concerning treaties etc., so that Mr. Blathwaite and others of the King's people were almost afraid to speak before him.[17]

---

14. In the following year Harley succeeded in obtaining the royal stewardship of Cantref Moelynaidd, to which was later added control of other manors in Radnor county, strengthening the Harleyite electoral interest: W.R. Williams, *Parliamentary History of the Principality of Wales* (1895), pp. 180–1
15. H.M.C. *Portland*, iii, 454.
16. *Ibid.*, iii, 456.
17. *Wentworth Papers*, p. 132.

Harley continued for several years to be placed on such commissions, which were to become one of the Commons' most powerful constitutional weapons against the royal executive after the Revolution.[18]

This early tribute to his abilities was due to his hard work in the House of Commons. He spoke as often as possible. Some of the reasons for his success as an orator are evident from the few recorded fragments of his speeches. His style was frothily rhetorical, but it had a basis of solid fact culled from a wide reading of parliamentary precedents and lawbooks; he divided his remarks into numbered headings an sub-headings, and rammed his points home by frequent repetition. The effect, though not artistic, was of closely reasoned argument rather than verbal dexterity. Furthermore, his encyclopaedic knowledge was shown at its best in the conditions of debate, where many a dubious precedent could be contradicted by factual accuracy, and many a timely hare could be set off by a piece of abstruse and interesting information. During his first years in Parliament, Harley's time was much taken up by the committee for accounts and similar bodies set up for financial estimates of war supplies. His chief concern, in the words of his brother, was 'endeavouring to be frugal by good management' on behalf of the public.[19]

This endeavour was to remain a major pre-occupation of his career even after he took government office in the next reign. In summer, while his fellow commissioners went into the country, Harley remained in London on this business; for he reflected 'how many mouths would be open in the winter if any umbrage were given for an accusation of neglect'. It is not surprising to find that by June 1691 he was reporting to Sir Edward he had taken the chair, not for the first time, while the chairman was incapacitated.[20] Harley plunged eagerly into the minutiae of accounting and financial administration; he willingly undertook the toilsome duty of preparing statistics for use in the House. The knowledge of government finance he thus gained, at a time when new and complicated techniques were rapidly developing, was to be of service when he was at the head of the Treasury. Before long his extraordinary vigour brought him a personal ascendancy not only among his closest associates but in an increasingly widening circle.

Harley's range of friends in the Commons had its nucleus in the family group and was always more remarkable for debating power than for numbers. Sir Edward being out of the House, the most powerful members

18. From the beginning the Commission of Accounts remained a jealously-guarded perquisite of the Commons, who felt so strongly about their sole right to control expenditure that when, on renewal of the commission in 1692, the House of Lords claimed a share in the Commission's composition, and rejected the enacting bill, the Commons tacked it as a clause to a money bill, in which form it passed owing to the Lords' customary inability to reject such financial measures: Bonet, in Ranke, vi, 178–81.
19. H.M.C. *Portland*, iii, 481.
20. *Ibid.*, iii, 494 and 467.

were Paul Foley, Harley's close relative, Harley himself and Sir Thomas Clarges, a leading back bench Tory. Much of the new Parliament's business concerned the voting of financial supplies for the King's ambitious war plans, which involved placing England in the forefront of a Protestant crusade against the France of Louis XIV. This expense, the immediate reason for the establishment of the Commission of Accounts, was the price the country paid for the new monarchy which replaced James II. William, as ruler of Holland, had been engaged for two decades in placing limits to Louis's overweening ambitions, and England was on the whole not averse from taking a fair share of the burden which the Stuarts' pro-French sympathies had placed upon the smaller protestant nation. But at the same time the country – through its representatives the 'country' element in Parliament – was determined to keep war expenses within limits and also to use the grant of taxes as a lever with which to enhance the legislature's power to avoid any possible recurrence of activities found reprehensible in Charles II and James II. A number of measures were placed on the statute book during the first and second sessions; but some major matters, including a bill to prevent the use of treason trials to suppress political opposition, and others to reduce the number of officeholders in Parliament and to ensure more frequent elections, were held up by the reluctance of government to countenance measures detrimental to its power.

At the time of the election, William had altered his ministry considerably by bringing in a stronger element of known Tories, some of whom had served under the last two monarchs.[21] But in spite of the now predominantly Tory complexion of the administration, party differences were soon seen to be relaxed considerably in the 'Officers' Parliament', as the body elected in 1690 was later called in view of its large element of officeholders. This change from partisan strife resulted not least from the actions of Harley and his friends, who now showed themselves willing to play down old differences and work alongside any country Tories who appeared to share their desire for good and frugal government. Thus, the chief development of the 1690–1 session was the beginning of a more permanent alliance of Whig and Tory back bench members. This combination, in which ideology counted for little and country patriotism was paramount, had been visible on several occasions since 1689, with Whigs such as the Harleys and Foleys finding themselves voting alongside country Tories like Clarges and Musgrave in criticism of both Whig and Tory ministers. The incipient alliance was sealed by the appointment of the Commission of Accounts and its successors in succeeding years.[22]

21. Hill, p. 48.
22. A convenient summary of the successive commissions of accounts is the 'Abstract of several acts enabling commissioners to examine, take and state the Public Accounts', Add. MSS. 38,329, ff. 102–9.

The indispensible member of this body was soon seen to be Harley. Although in many ways a personification of the landed gentlemen in the Commons, he differed from the type by his understanding of such intricate subjects as finance and constitutional procedure. His occasional verbal incoherence served only to endear him to his fellows, who often suffered from similar difficulties, and his knowledge frequently confounded his more articulate opponents. Even what later became his most famous characteristic, the obscurity with which he loved to surround his intentions, worked in his favour in the role of investigator of accounts. On the wider parliamentary scene his role was that of younger spokesman in a new age for both Whig and Tory gentlemen who were finding common cause against the court. From 1691 the strident tones of militant Puritanism were softened by the mellower notes of former Cavaliers, and there developed the momentous alliance of country Tories with the Harley and Foley families which, nearly seventy years later, was to cause the great Duke of Newcastle to regard the appointment of Edward Harley, fourth Earl of Oxford, to a post in George III's bedchamber as the symbol of a revived Toryism.[23]

At first in the early months of 1691, the new commissioners of accounts were content to amass information. The main theme of their research was national expense. 'I hope', wrote Musgrave to Harley in October, 'all animosities will be buried and all heartily join in preserving the public'. Battle was joined with government supporters in a committee of supply on 6 November, when Paul Foley called for a statement of England's treaties and quota commitments to the Allies – a suggestion containing too radical a challenge to the King's right of conducting foreign policy to find general acceptance at that moment. The following day Clarges criticized Admiral Russell, who had been unable to bring the French fleet to action in the summer to revenge the disgrace of the navy at Beachy Head under Admiral Lord Torrington in 1690.[24] The scope of the attack quickly broadened. On the 9th Foley successfully united with Clarges and Musgrave in obtaining a special committee to examine naval estimates for the next year, Musgrave piously claiming that 'the poverty of the nation calls upon us to be as good husbands as we can'; and five days later Harley reported from this committee in favour of cutting the estimates, on the grounds that overlarge sams had been provided for the Navy in the previous session. In the meantime the commissioners of accounts presented their first report, laying stress upon excessive salaries, fees and perquisites. From this it was but a short step to demanding a scrutiny of current ministerial requests for supplies, and on 14 November Harley reported to the House a select committee's recommendation

23. Sir Lewis Namier, *England in the Age of the American Revolution* (2nd ed., 1961), p. 135.
24. Musgrave to Harley, 1 Oct. 1691, Loan 29/312; Parliamentary diary of Narcissus Luttrell, 6 Nov., All Souls MSS. 158a, pp. 1–2; Grey, *Debates*, x, 162–7: Bonet, in Ranke, vi, 164; H.M.C. *7th Report* (Denbigh MSS), p. 206.

that naval estimates should be reduced by £279,000 from £1,855,000.[25] Army supplies were similarly subjected to parliamentary scrutiny under the leadership of Foley, Harley, Clarges and Musgrave, so that much of the session's work became a close-fought tussle between ministerialists and commissioners for control of supplies.[26]

Co-operation with the Tories on the Commission of Accounts was the first step towards misunderstanding with some of the Harley-Foley group's Whig associates. A lack of communication became apparent with the introduction of a new Treason Bill. Country Whigs, who had suffered under the last two monarchs, and Tories who feared that treason trials might be used against them in the new reign, combined to pass the bill through the Commons; but government objections received strong backing from many other Whigs who took their lead from some of their number who had survived as officeholders the purge of 1690, notably Sir John Somers and Sir George Treby. Their stand signalled a change of direction by leading Whigs in anticipation of their party's eventual return to favour with William. It was a notable step towards regaining the King's confidence when the patrician Charles Montagu boldly asserted that the law of treason should not be weakened in time of war and national emergency. From this court-oriented Whig tactic, however, the Harley-Foley element stood conspicuously apart, sharing with the country Tories a vociferous disappointment at successful ministerial obstruction of the bill in the House of Lords.[27]

Early in December 1691, in the midst of the parliamentary campaign, Robert Harley was stunned by the news from home that Elizabeth had died a few days earlier from the scourge of smallpox, her constitution weakened by grief over the death of their son. The new loss was to strengthen, if anything, the ties which bound Robert to his fellow-mourners, the Foleys. The strong love demonstrated in his letters to his wife leaves no doubt as to the extent of his grief. He redoubled his activities at Westminster but, though his career continued to wax, a return of his old poor health after Elizabeth's death was accompanied by fainting fits which brought his spirits to a low point. In sombre vein he wrote to his father: 'Tho rest is the thing we al pretend to seek after, we will search for it everywhere, but the only place where it is to be found. Vanity and vexation was the quintessence the greatest chymist could ever extract out of the largest and most unbounded enjoyment of the creature.'[28]

25. Horwitz, p. 71 sqq.
26. Luttrell Diary, 9 Nov., All Souls MSS 158a, pp. 10–14; CJ, x, 552; H.M.C. _Portland_, iii, 482 and 485; Bonet, in Ranke, vi, 166–7.
27. Hill, p. 53.
28. H.M.C. _Portland_, iii, 488.

In 1692 King William was not yet ready to change his ministry and turn to the new-model Whig courtiers who had opposed the Treason Bill and other country measures. He continued to rely mainly on his Tory ministers, especially Secretary Nottingham, to raise supplies for the summer campaign in the Low Countries. But the situation was complicated by a new portent in post-Revolution politics, the rise to royal favour of the second Earl of Sunderland, sometime Secretary of State to James II, now returned to England and duty penitent for the policies which had made him the best-hated of James's ministers. The knowledge that William was receiving advice from so unexpected and powerful a source induced in Nottingham a fear that Sunderland was being considered for a ministerial post, a development which could only do harm to the modest reputation of the Tories for loyalty to the new monarchs. In fact the returned exile's general unpopularity was sufficient protection for Nottingham, who was assured by the King that Sunderland was not to be appointed, though he remained a potent background figure. Meanwhile the campaigning season in the summer of 1692 drove a wedge between the King and the Tories. At sea Russell's victory over the French fleet at La Hogue established British and Dutch naval supremacy and made the Whig admiral, a close associate of Somers and Montagu, a national idol. In Flanders William's failure to hold the key fortress of Namur occasioned the Tory ministers much heartsearching about the cost of the land war, causing them to advise him that British forces in the Low Countries should be reduced. This advice, couched in such a way as to be effectively a demand, was one which the King, mindful of his homeland's defence, could only reject.[29]

The meeting of Parliament which began in the autumn of 1692 was thus a crucial one for the ministry, and it also confirmed the emergence of Harley as a major parliamentary figure. Despite personal afflictions and recurrent poor health he threw himself with vigour into a renewed endeavour to control the executive, which was itself deeply divided between the major Tory element and Whig challengers for power. Paul Foley wrote, while Harley was still in Herefordshire in September, that 'an endeavour will, its said, be used when the King returns to change hands'. If such an attempt was made behind the scenes it was unsuccessful, for William made no further major appointments for the moment. From the opening of Parliament on 4 November, a well-organized campaign was devised by Somers, Montagu, Russell and another vociferous Whig Thomas Wharton to demonstrate to the King their ability to control the House either in favour of his wishes or, if necessary, against them. This 'Junto' of politicians was now increasingly differentiated from the Harleys and Foleys by its naked ambition for office. A major

29. Hill, pp. 54–5.

rift was exposed in debates over severe losses in Flanders resulting, Harley believed, from the subordination of the English contingent to Dutch general officers. After stormy debates the House resolved on 23 November, on Harley's motion, that future appointments in English foot regiments should be filled by English nationals. But ministerial Whigs were not slow to point out, with some justices, that such opposition arose from the country members' fundamental mistrust of the army which was dear to William's heart.[30]

The Junto's main efforts were reserved, however, for the naval debates in which they could denigrate their Tory colleagues. From early in the session a quarrel developed between Russell and Nottingham concerning the responsibility for the former's lack of activity after La Hogue. On 11 November Montagu seized the initiative, deflecting an attack on naval mismanagement away from Russell by obtaining a vote of thanks which was unquestionably due to the Admiral for the victory itself. In the succeeding debates Russell's friends made much of the fact that the fleet had received many of its orders not from the Admiralty but from Nottingham. Foley and Harley made ineffectual efforts to defend Nottingham because of, as Harley put it, 'the selfishness of those that attack him as much, and for other ends than public good'. Although the House of Lords took Nottingham's part, a committee set up in the Commons to investigate all aspects of naval miscarriages decided in favour of Russell, and feelings ran high against the Secretary.[31] The Whigs were quick to exploit this advantage, transforming their case against Nottingham into a matter of party principle by dragging in his well-known *de facto* acceptance of William and Mary. John Smith told the House, 'There is a coolness in peoples' minds to this Government which arises I think because they believe you have not a rightful King but only *de facto*.' Tory speakers argued weakly, from the evidence of Privy Council records, that the ministers were better attenders at Council that their traducers. 'The mischiefs', Thomas Wharton retorted angrily, 'do not proceed from some gentlemen's not attending but from some men who ought not to be there at all.'[32]

Even more distasteful to Harley than the Junto's attack on Nottingham was their treatment of a new Treason Bill. This met, as before, the full weight of the court Whigs' obstruction. In reply to their argument that the cure proposed in the bill was not suited to the disease Harley

---

30. Foley to Robert Harley, 17 Sept., Loan 29/135/7; Luttrell Diary, 23 Nov., All Souls MS. 158b, pp. 270–81; H.M.C. *Portland*, iii, 508; Bonet, in Ranke, vi, 195.
31. Bonet, in Ranke, vi, 183–5; Nottingham to Hatton, 13 Dec., Add. MS. 29,594, f. 265; CJ, x, 698; Luttrell Diary, 11 Nov., All Souls MS. 158b., pp. 11–13; H.M.C. *Finch*, iv, 512–13; Harley to Sir Edward, 6 Dec., Loan 29/186/224.
32. Luttrell Diary, 30 Nov., All Souls MS. 158b, pp. 110–16; *cf.* Bonet, in Ranke, vi, 191.

answered succinctly 'then let it be made so', and he called for it to be passed as soon as possible. In this proposal he was supported by Musgrave and other country Tories. But although the measure had too much support to permit its outright rejection, its opponents were able to wreck it on 1 December by gathering a majority of 145 to 125 for postponing its operation until after the end of the war, despite a vigorous attempt by the leaders of the Tory-Herefordshire Whig country coalition to fix the date not later than 1695.[33]

Harley's associates were further disillusioned by Somers' Abjuration Bill, which was intended to cause maximum embarassment to the Tories, and to prevent their officeholders from siding openly with them. This bill would have imposed upon 'placemen' an oath abjuring King James, with dismissal and imprisonment for refusal and the penalties of high treason for a second refusal. Denial of the sovereignty of William and Mary, either in writing or by word of mouth, would also have been made treasonous. While placing many Tory officeholders of the *de facto* school in a cruel dilemma, the bill would hardly have trapped many dedicated Jacobites, and a rising Tory, William Bromley of Baginton, later to be one of Harley's closest associates, remarked with justice that it was 'a snare to catch good conscientious men and will not hold the bad'. Though most ministerial Whigs and their followers supported the bill its opponents included, as well as the great body of the Tories, the Whigs of the country coalition, led by Foley, Harley and Sir Francis Winnington, committed as before to damping down rather than reviving party animosities. In general the moderation of the majority of the Commons prevailed in refusing to commit the bill by 200 votes to 175.[34]

Harley gave his full support to two measures; one a bill to diminish court patronage by excluding placemen, holders of government office or emolument, from the Commons; and another intended to limit the life of any one Parliament to three years. Both these bills were extremely popular, appealing as they did to a longstanding country resentment against court management and the appetites of placeholders. The Place Bill required that members elected after 1 February 1693 who accepted an office of profit under the Crown should be expelled from the Commons. Harley described one sitting as 'the largest debate on one question that I ever knew', and added 'I hope we have shown the parts of honest men and lovers of our country'. Carried through all its stages in the Commons, the bill was rejected in the upper chamber by the strong contingent of ministerialists. In later years Harley, as minister, was to

---

33. *CJ*, x, 730; Luttrell Diary, 28 Nov. and 1 Dec., All Souls MS. 158b, pp. 94–6, 122–3; Grey, *Debates*, x, 249–52, 285–91.
34. Luttrell Diary, 14 Dec., All Souls MS, 158b, p. 181–90; Bonet in Ranke, vi, 197–8.

change his views, and fend off place bills which would have diminished his governmental majorities; for the moment, however, he lamented court influence which struck down his favoured project.[35]

The Triennial Bill passed both Houses without much difficulty. Its long-term object was to cut down the court's control of the House of Commons by providing the electorate with frequent opportunities to refuse re-election to ministers and other placemen. This end appealed to the country Whigs, whose sentiment was declaimed by Foley: 'if this House would not punish ill ministers, 'twas fit the people should send those that would'. The Earl of Shrewsbury, who introduced the bill in the Lords, was committed to its main objects, but some of his fellow Whig ministers were not, in view of the King's known opposition. In the Commons the bill was given its first reading on 28 January 1693, and its second speedily on 2 February. Somers and Montagu sat silent, not caring to raise too open an opposition while even some of their fellow Whig ministerialists supported the popular measure. In the course of the bill's passage, Harley brought himself to notice by drawing from his pocket and reading out a copy of the Prince of Orange's Declaration of 1688 promising frequent parliaments; and he went on to expatiate on the corruption of long-lived assemblies which were no longer representative of the people who elected them: 'A standing parliament can never be a true representative; men are much altered after being some time here, and are not the same men as sent up.' As usual, he had ready precedents back to the reign of Henry VIII, to support his arguments.[36]

The court's objections to the Triennial Bill took the form of outright rejection of it, expressing William's extreme dissatisfaction not only with this measure but with the session which had seen the voting of addresses against the management of the war, in particular the campaign in Flanders, and the passage of popular bills in the Commons. The Tory ministry had often been powerless, and without the responsible attitude taken by Foley, Harley and their associates the voting of war supplies might have been seriously impaired. Paul Foley, indeed, was responsible for rescuing the Treasury by suggesting a highly successful 'million loan', which was carried into effect by Montagu, as a newly appointed member of the Treasury commission. Harley pointed out to Sir Edward that it had been the Commons' own commissioners of accounts who 'found all the money'.[37] Nevertheless, the principal gainers from William's dissatisfaction were the Junto group and their associates. Somers became Lord

---

35. H.M.C. *7th Report*, (Denbigh MSS) p. 212; Bonet, in Ranke, vi, 198–200; H.M.C. *Portland*, iii, 509.
36. Bonet, in Ranke, vi, 206 and 212–13; Foxcroft, *Supplement*, p. 181, and Burnet, iv, 192; Luttrell Diary, 28 Jan. and 2 Feb., All Souls MS 158b., pp. 307–13 and 318–20; *Grey Debates* x, 299–39; H.M.C. *Portland*, iii, 512.
37. 9 Feb. 1963, Loan 29/187/28.

Keeper of the Great Seal while an extreme Whig, Sir John Trenchard, was appointed as Nottingham's fellow Secretary and Montagu's star began to rise at the Treasury. Ministries were not customarily changed altogether, but the new arrangements signalled a shifted balance in favour of the new Court Whigs whom Harley was beginning to despise.

The spring and summer of 1693 marked a climacteric in Harley's political career. The session which ended in March had shown him to be at the forefront of country pressure on the court. A few weeks before the end of the session Sir Edward Harley had slipped quietly back into Parliament, on a bye-election for Herefordshire. But if he wished (and there is no reason to suppose that he did) to resume leadership of the group of border MPs and their associates he returned too late. Robert Harley, now strengthened by his father's presence, was second only to the much older and more experienced Paul Foley in the leadership of a dozen or so Old Whigs who had acquired a distinct group personality even more strongly because of their alliance with Tories of similar social standing and ideas, centred upon their leaders' shared membership of the Commission of Accounts. Their achievements, in terms of legislation, were not yet great, but their restraining effect upon governmental decision-making and upon those responsible for endemic corruption was already considerable. The conjunction of country Whigs and Tories was a situation little envisaged by Harley and his friends even three years earlier, at the election of the Officers' Parliament, but new circumstances had brought new methods and new liaisons. Harley's personal sorrows were still raw, but now he was ready to submerge them by working harder than ever to make his mark in Parliament.

CHAPTER 3

Country Spokesman

DURING HARLEY'S FIRST years in Parliament he and his friends often, as
we have seen, found themselves at odds with those ministerial Whigs
who relied on the support of the court. Differences were accentuated by
the country Whigs' working alliance with Tories of their own type whose
activities in criticising King William since 1689 had brought about a
similarity of outlook. The Harley-Foley group, still clinging to traditional
Whig opposition, thereby distinguished themselves from those of their
fellows who looked increasingly to such men as Somers and Montagu
to lead them into royal favour and the chance of lucrative officehold-
ing. Country members opposed all aspects of what they considered to be
the arbitrary use of government power or taxation. Their characteristic
stance was xenophobic, they disliked the newly-developed land tax, and
they advocated reliance on the navy as a necessary permanent expense,
rather than on land forces. Harley denounced venal ministers, placemen, and all who profited too much by giving financial credit or other
services to the government; his beliefs were sometimes muddled and
even self-contradictory, and to his opponents, the harassed ministers,
he often seemed the very acme of obstructionism; but to the 'gentlemen
of England', whose judgment he so often invoked, he appeared the stern
and impartial guardian of national honour.

The group of ministerial Whigs which was to be the Harley-Foley
group's principal target in coming years was still amorphous. In 1693
the group was taken to include the Earl of Shrewsbury, but by the mid–
1690s his sponsorship of the Triennial Bill sufficed to cut him off from
his fellows. Somers and Montagu, together with the inspired political
improviser 'Tom' Wharton and the hero of La Hogue, Edward Russell,
formed the leadership of the court Whigs whom Harley's friends denounced as the 'New Whigs'. Harley's personal vendetta with them
became an important constituent in the changing politics of their time
after 1695. The Whig Junto acted almost as one man in all matters of
importance. Their growing alliance with the mainly dissenting financiers

of the City of London strengthened them immeasurably in view of the government's pressing need for wartime loans. The Junto stressed the need for administrative improvements, particularly in the fiscal system, rather than the constitutional safeguards favoured by the country opposition: the executive rather than the legislative tradition. Their approach naturally had more appeal for the rich men of the City, mainly Dissenters eager to lend to government at high rates of interest, than did the financial frugality and low taxation advocated by the country gentlemen. Harley later dated his own breach with the Dissenters from about 1694, writing of them seventeen years later, to the minister Daniel Williams:

'. . . there has not been a good bill during that term of years which they have not opposed in the House of Commons contrary to the practice of the very few dissenters which were in Parliament in Charles the Second's time, who thereby united themselves to the country gentlemen, the advantage of which they found for many years after: but now they have listed themselves with those who had first denied our Saviour and now have sold them.[1]

Harley's objections to the Junto characteristically concentrated most often on a single aspect of their outlook, the avowed atheism or deism of most of them. In 1701 he wrote in an anonymous letter to the unrepentantly Whig Archbishop Tenison 'you are entirely under the influence of those who have not only discharged themselves from all obligations of religion, but also have for many years been promoting, first Socinianism then Arianism and now Deism in the state'.[2] And eight years later he was lamenting that 'what used to skulk in corners and shelter itself under the names of latitude and freethinking, they publicly own; and Deism is the bond of their Society'.[3]

But in 1693 the worst of this antagonism was still in the future. During the summer recess Harley paid only a brief visit to his family at Brampton. The Commission of Accounts continued its difficult, but for him interesting and rewarding, enquiries into government mismanagement and malversation. London buzzed with rumours as the new Whig ministers had clandestine meetings with Sunderland, currently their strongest advocate among William's advisers, and as Somers in his new Chancery office energetically rooted out Tory magistrates and replaced them by Whigs. At sea this summer heavy mercantile losses, particularly in the Mediterranean convoy, brought further discredit for the remaining Tory ministers; no one was surprized when, on the eve of Parliament's meeting in November, the King deprived Nottingham of his seals of office as

1. Dec. 1711, Loan 29/160/8
2. H.M.C. *Bath*, i, 52
3. Carstares, *State Papers*, p. 775.

Secretary of State. The extremist Trenchard was left for the time being as sole Secretary; Shrewsbury was offered the seals again but refused them and thus emphasized his growing differences with the new Whig ministers. He remained free to support a new Triennial Bill and drew closer in sympathy with the country members. His alliance with Harley, so crucial for the latter's ministry in the last years of the next reign, was rooted in the common cause which the two men found at this time.

Thus while the King drew closer to the ministerial Whigs of the emergent Junto, many Whigs who preferred Shrewsbury now found themselves in alliance with the Herefordshire-centred group based on the Foleys and Harleys. These were again much in evidence at the opening of the session, together with their country Tory friends. New military failures, including William's costly defeat in a pitched battle at Landen as well as the loss of the 'Smyrna' Convoy, aroused further discontent among the country coalition. Fortunately for the King country alarm at the conduct of the land war was overshadowed by indignation at the convoy disaster, and the admirals concerned were acquitted of gross negligence by only nine votes in a very full house.[4]

After this the Commons turned to the perennial problem of ensuring more frequent elections. At the outset Harley attempted to settle the problem by a characteristic expedient. In the course of his researches into the history of Parliament he had discovered a statute of Edward III's reign which seemed suitable for his purpose. He called upon his fellow members to declare the legality of annual elections under this unrepealed measure and uphold the old adage that 'there was an act already and it should be observed'. He struck a sympathetic note in the House when he maintained that while the crown's prerogative always increased the liberties of the people were at a stand. But, though his sentiment was appreciated, his antiquarian approach proved too recondite for the majority of his listeners: the motion he offered was lost, though only by 40 votes. Succeeding days found Harley speaking for a new Place Bill, which passed in the Commons, and supporting Paul Foley and Clarges by strongly criticizing the King in a jealously guarded area of the royal authority, foreign policy. Harley urged boldly that England should not pay twice as much as the Dutch in subsidizing German allies. For good measure he spoke on 5 December in favour of caution in granting a new excise for military expenses, urging the Commons to be careful 'that what we give this year we may be able to give the next, without filling the nation with publicans and the House with Excise men'.[5]

A Triennial Bill initiated in the Lower House having been narrowly

4. Add. MS. 17,677 NN, f. 364; H.M.C. *7th Report* (Denbigh MSS) pp. 216–17; Grey, *Debates*, x, 333–8, and 344–8.
5. Grey, *Debates*, x, 329–30, 338–44, 358.

defeated, a similar one was brought toward in the House of Lords, was passed and duly sent to the Commons. Here it met the some fate as the first, and was rejected after attempts had failed to extend its scope to annual parliaments. Harley as usual, was in the forefront of debate, inspiring Sir Edward to write to Abigail Harley on one occasion, 'The Lord was pleased to enable your brother to speak so that some in the House called upon me to bless God that vouchsafed to give me a son so to speak'.[6] The bill's supporters could do little, however, for they provoked a reaction against themselves by confusing the triennial parliaments issue with the more extreme one of annual elections. Soon after Christmas the country leaders were roused to the highest fury when, after a Place Bill had passed all its stages in both houses, the King refused to accept it. A debate on 26 January 1694 on the State of the Nation culminated in a resolution, on Clarges' motion, to inform William that those who had advised him to reject the latest bill were 'enemies to Your Majesty and your Government'. Harley told the House ominously, that if the King could veto bills, they could withhold supplies. He urged the country gentlemen that 'the King indeed hath a negative voice: so have you in money'. Wharton, Montagu and Russell combined in attempting to turn the onslaught, but failed to counter Harley's motion for an address to the King representing how rare it was for bills to be rejected by the crown. At the end of the session a groundswell of discontent remained, promising ill for William if he continued to resist every attempt at reform.[7]

In the end the King recognized the strength of the forces he had roused against himself and he was wise enough to yield gracefully. In March Shrewsbury at last agreed to resume the vacant secretaryship on William's undertaking that in the next session the Triennial Bill, at least, would be accepted. But at the same time changes were made in the Treasury after Montagu launched a vicious attack in the Commons on his colleague Seymour 'showing', as the Prussian Resident in London reported to his court, 'his inconsistency in changing party' and 'his attachment to his own interest rather than that of the public'. Obliged by this action to choose between the two men the King promoted Montagu to Chancellor of the Exchequer and brought in another vociferous Whig, John Smith, to replace Seymour. At the Admiralty Russell was reinstated as First Lord in place of the undistinguished Falkland. The latter's fate was expected but the dismissal of Seymour, despite mainly loyal service to William in the Commons for two years, was a portent of a new situation in which service to the crown was insufficient without acceptability to the dominant party. Finally, dukedoms were conferred upon leading

6. H.M.C. *Portland*, iii, 548–9.
7. Grey, *Debates*, x, 375–81, 381–6.

Whig aristocrats who had assisted in bringing William and Mary to the throne, the Earls of Shrewsbury, Bedford, Devonshire and Clare. The last-named, as Duke of Newcastle, was later to be linked to Harley both politically and by marriage between their children.[8]

Montagu had been able to please the King by carrying a bill to fund a loan of £1,200,00 and incorporate the subscribers in a Bank of England. The Bank raised the required amount easily, in a City market which now had confidence in the reconstituted ministry, and was to be a generous conduit for many further loans to an embattled government. The ministerial Whigs celebrated their advance by continuing throughout the summer to manoeuvre their supporters into national and local office, especially in view of the elections which an expected Triennial Act might soon bring about. Harley's friends witnessed with frustration the accelerated exclusion of all but ministerial supporters from lord lieutenancies, magistracies, the customs, excise and other tax services, carried out ruthlessly by the triumphant Junto.[9] Reinforcing their political advance, William's military campaign in Flanders went better than for several years, aided by the more generous financial provisions made in the last winter. Thus it was in vain that Godolphin, still nominally head of the Treasury commission, protested to the King at 'removing some men that are of one party, and gratifying some that are of another'.[10] As the time drew near for Parliament's autumn sitting Godolphin, like Shrewsbury, was engaged in discussion with Paul Foley about 'the excises' and other anticipated business, including a new Triennial Bill.[11]

The same season saw a new and important development in Harley's life. On 18 September (not, as sometimes stated, 4 October) he was married quietly to Sarah Middleton, aged 22, the daughter of a London merchant Simon Middleton of Hurst Hill, Edmonton. The new marriage was to be a contented one, for Sarah shared the religious outlook and vocabulary of the Harleys, and Robert's references to her are tender, but there were no children of their union. That his second marriage was as much a love match as that with Elizabeth may be doubted, but Sarah brought stability back into her husband's life. She was not destined to be a fashionable hostess, and her somewhat strait-laced virtue caused malicious amusement among some acqaintances, but such things mattered not in the Harley household. Years later Jonathan Swift, after enjoying the Harleys' hospitality for an evening, was to pen the sentence

8. Bonet, in Ranke, vi, 240, 245; H.M.C., *Kenyon*, p. 286.
9. Musgrave to Harley, 24 Sept. 1694, Loan 29/312; H.M.C. *Kenyon*, 273–4, 285–6, 290–1; H.M.C. *Downshire*, i, 512, 582.
10. Godolphin to William III, 5/15 June and 3 Aug. 1694, Portland (Nottingham) MSS, PwA 471 and 472a.
11. Horwitz, p. 135; H.M.C. *Bath*, i, 51–2; H.M.C. *Portland*, iii, 560.

'Lady Oxford is a silly mere old woman', often quoted to her detriment, but he did so at the end of an account which testified to the united warmth of the family over which Sarah came to preside in lieu of Elizabeth. Of her loyalty to her husband and concern for her stepchildren there is no question, and she brought up the children during his frequent absences. Happily the marriage appears to have been acceptable from the start to the Foleys too; at least, if so much may be assumed from one jocular comment by Harley's father-in-law, Thomas Foley, who wrote that 'you have been so taken up with the public accounts and your amours, that I durst not trouble you'.[12]

Perhaps as a result of his recent discussions with Shrewsbury, Harley was designated by the Commons to bring in the new Triennial Bill. This time there was no opposition from the government side, although the court spokesmen succeeded in obtaining an extension of one year, to 1 November 1696, to the permitted life of the existing Parliament. Among the leading Whigs only Tom Wharton stepped out of line, and his intervention caused some passing confusion among those members who were accustomed to considering his interventions as coming from the King. But by arguing for a return to the last permissible date specified in the original bill, 1 November 1695, Wharton was apparently acting upon his own initiative, with the object of ensuring an early dissolution. His attempt was unsuccessful, for Montagu made the King's true intentions clear, and William was thus permitted a choice between 1695 and 1696 for ending the sitting Parliament. Thereafter, it was enacted, Parliament must be held at least once in three years and could continue for not more than three years. In practice the Act, until superseded twenty-two years later by the Septennial Act, resulted in even more frequent elections than Harley or Shrewsbury envisaged, for on average there was to be a general election every two years during this period. In return for the ease with which the bill was allowed to pass, the country gentlemen voted more financial supplies with greater grace than they had ever done: opening the debate on army estimates Paul Foley pronounced these to be reasonable and engaged his friends to consent.[13]

During the Christmas recess a new turn was given to political life by the death of Queen Mary from smallpox, at the age of thirty-two. She had been a self-effacing but indispensable partner in the early years of post-Revolution monarchy, standing as the symbol of Tory yearning for legitimacy. Her loss, coming so soon after William's unmistakable swing towards the New Whigs, greatly aroused Tory fears of persecution. Even before Mary's death Nottingham had privately expressed his support for a new Treason Bill to afford greater protection against triumphant Whig-

---

12. H.M.C. *Portland*, iii, 557–8. *London Marriage Licenses, 1521–1869* (1887), ed. Joseph Foster; Swift, *Journal to Stella*, 31 Dec. 1712.
13. Bonet, in Ranke, vi, 252.

gery. He now declared himself of the opinion that a new approach was needed in a new situation.[14] In January 1695 he joined with Rochester in leading an attack in the House of Lords on war policy and government finance. On the same day, the 25th, Harley, representing the Commissioners of Accounts presented the Lower House with their latest observations on corrupt officials and agents.

This concerted move, if such it was, provoked some dramatic reactions in following weeks. The ministerial Whigs moved swiftly to use the commission's and other revelations to incriminate their rivals. The first major figure to suffer was Sunderland's friend Henry Guy, Secretary of the Treasury, sent to the Tower after a debate on 15 February for accepting a bribe of 200 guineas. Guy's true offence, as a survivor of the former administration, was that of holding a key post in the disbursement of Treasury patronage. Following this success country and court Whigs together turned their attention to Speaker Trevor, a Tory whose blatant distribution of bribes in the Commons was resented by the country gentlemen as corrupt and by Montagu as rivalling his own management of the House. On 7 March Harley, again as spokesman for the Commission, induced his fellow parliamentarians to commit James Craggs, a contractor for army clothing, for refusing to produce account books. In the midst of these heady scenes Harley also found time to deliver a petition to the Commons on behalf of the homeless Protestant refugees from Europe who dragged out their existence in thousands in London and elsewhere. As a result of passions aroused over official malpractices a new Commons committee including Paul Foley and Tom Wharton was appointed to inspect the books of the East India Company and the Chamberlain of London, and Foley reported from this committee on the 12th with the staggering information that the Speaker had received a gratuity of 1,000 guineas from the City. Trevor was immediately resolved guilty of high crimes and misdemeanours, and two days later the House decided to elect a new Speaker.[15]

Up to this point the court and country Whigs had found more in common than had been possible of late. They now parted company abruptly. Wharton, for the court, nominated Sir Thomas Littleton as Speaker, but the country preferred Foley and carried his election. His campaign in search of government corruption had been zealous but fair and popular. His reward, while imposing a stern warning against any repetition of official misconduct, brought the group he led to their highest point. And with Foley's assumption of onerous new duties, Harley's responsibility for leadership within the group became still greater.

The search for high-placed culprits did not end with Trevor's disgrace.

14. To Hatton, 22 and 29 Dec. 1694, and 3 Jan. 1694/5, Add. MSS. 29,595, ff. 69 and 72.
15. Torbuck, *Debates*, iii, 3–4, 9–16; Hill, pp. 62–3: Horwitz, pp. 145–51; H.M.C. *Downshire*, i, part i, 462.

The next attack, however, smacked more of ministerial Whig ambition than of genuine indignation; and when Wharton rose on 27 April to move the impeachment of Carmarthen, now Duke of Leeds, for alleged-ly receiving bribes from the East India Company, the King had seen enough. On 3 May he prorogued Parliament rather than permit further divisive activity in his government. Leeds, however, was effectively neu-tralized and henceforth had to be forbidden to take an active part in administration or even to attend Council meetings. Some months of anxious thought followed for the monarch while he decided whether to call an early general election and, if so, whether to give further support to the Junto in their election campaign. They had presumed too far, using Parliament's justifiable anger at malefactors in office for their own ends, as in the attacks on Leeds and Sunderland's associate Guy. The country gentlemen, on the other hand, had recently given strong sup-port to demands for war supplies, and the Triennial Act which they had demanded as the price of their support was directed more against the ministry than against the King himself. William went overseas for the year's compaign without taking a final decision, leaving the increas-ingly trusted Sunderland to put out feelers to both court and country Whigs with a view to obtaining some kind of juncture in support of his government.[16]

The court's protracted negotiations kept Harley in London during most of the summer but produced little result. Any hope which Sunder-land may have entertained that the country leadership would find minis-terial Whig patronage more acceptable than their present ill-defined status was soon disabused. In a negotiation through the mediacy of Guy, now released from custody, Foley and Harley proved unco-operative. They firmly refused to work with Montagu or Wharton, professing to believe, as Guy reported to the King's Dutch confidant the Earl of Port-land, that the ministerial Whigs were superfluous to any future arrange-ment. But Foley's claim that 'by a little pains the Whig party will totally leave Mr Wharton and Mr Montagu', did not convince government negotiators that the King could safely dispense with the present ministers altogether. When William on his return to England began preparations for a general election he did so without changing his ministers. On the other hand he had no intention of declaring, as in 1690, against any particular party. As a result the nation went to the polls with little royal guidance other than the knowledge that William, though unwilling to drop the ministerial Whigs, was not sufficiently pleased with them to penalize their opponents. His only discernible personal approbation was shown to irresponsible favourites such as Portland and Sunderland.[17]

16. Browning, *Danby*, i, 517–24; Burnet, iv, 238.
17. Guy to Portland, 18/28 June, 5/15 and 12/22 July, Portland (Nottingham) MSS. PwA 503, 504 and 508; Kenyon, *Sunderland*, pp. 275–6.

The general election in the autumn of 1695 reversed the Tory gains of 1690 but was less satisfactory for government Whigs than for what their supporter Bishop Gilbert Burnet coldly called 'the sourer sort of Whigs'. Harley again secured his own election for New Radnor without much difficulty, and his brother Edward was returned for Droitwich with the backing of the strong Foley interest in that borough. Henceforth, Edward Harley was increasingly to become Robert's right arm in Parliament, an effective politician and a loyal follower. The newly elected members swelled the ranks of those who were now on the point of cutting their final ties with the ministerial Whigs and taking a regular stand with the Tories. And if the Junto could take little comfort from the strengthened position of their country brethren, they were hardly more assured of the co-operation of those court nominees who took their cue from Sunderland. In such circumstances the elections, though a *prima facie* loss for the Tories were no clear gain for the Whig ministers.[18]

The key developments of both this Parliament and the next were to be closely associated with the behaviour of those Whigs centred on the Harleys and Foleys, and it is necessary at this point to consider the group's growing relationship with the Tories. One old ally was gone: Sir Thomas Clarges died in October. Sir Christopher Musgrave remained but was forced to relinquish his prestigious county seat at Westmorland for one at the borough of Appleby. With the loss of Clarges and the undisputed re-election of Paul Foley as Speaker, the country Tories, as well as their Old Whig counterparts, looked increasingly to Harley as their spokesman. The Harley-Foley group already had in common with the Tories the outlook of landed gentry and, by closer consideration for the Church, were continuing to absorb the mores of their new associates. Sir Edward, it is true, continued until his death to speak and write in the distinctive language of Puritanism, and even his sons Robert and Edward were liable throughout their lives to drop into the same idiom upon occasion; but their adherence to the Church was more than a formality. Nor was the commerce between the Tories and Old Whigs all one way, for the latter brought to their Tory colleagues a willingness to indulge in open opposition quite foreign to many who until recently had supported the court and who still thought of themselves as natural government men. One shrewd if hostile observer, the third Earl of Shaftesbury and grandson of the founding father of Whiggery the first Earl, was to write years later that Robert Harley played the leading role in converting the main body of Tories to opposition: ''Tis he has taught 'em their popular game', he claimed, 'and made them able in a way they never understood, and were so averse to as never to have complied with, had they not found it at last the only way to distress the government.'[19]

18. Burnet, iv, 288; Hill, p. 65.
19. *Locke Letters*, p. 146.

In 1695 however, the working alliance which the Harleys and Foleys had already achieved with some Tories did not yet have a general approval from all of that disposition. The Old Whigs were long regarded with suspicion by those who had been able, in the early years under William and Mary, to continue proclaiming vestigial aspects of the original Tory credo. The difficulty was particularly marked in the case of men who took a strongly High Church stance, it being hard for those who spoke of Charles I as 'the Blessed Martyr' to accept the alliance and leadership of former Roundheads. And Robert Harley's habit of keeping up old ties with some Whigs – for, like other men conscious of the mutability of political fortunes, he liked to keep more than one string to his bow – could cause an infuriated Tory to exclaim that 'he would never trust a Presbyterian rogue more'.[20] But, as already noted, some Tory leaders such as Nottingham and Rochester had wasted no time after Mary's death before they stood alongside the country alliance to signal their discontent. Their way was made easier by the circumstances of King William's accession to what was in their eyes a de facto (rather than a de jure) monarchy to which opposition was not ruled out by theoretical considerations of passive obedience. A leading Tory in the Commons, Sir Edward Seymour, had allied himself with the country coalition by the time of the elections and concerted with Harley to throw his weight, and that of the West Country Tories he led, behind Foley's candidature for the Chair of the House.[21] Where these influential men pointed the way, most other Tories were to follow as a result of misfortunes which befell them during the next two years.

When the new Parliament assembled, Harley honoured an undertaking to Guy the previous summer to assist the passage of the year's supplies.[22] In other respects, however, the country party proved less amenable, and the next few months witnessed a number of important bills or attempted measures further to restrict the royal powers. The Treason Bill was at last passed, for so anxious were its sponsors to secure its passage that they made no further difficulty about accepting a Lords' clause for the trial of accused peers, and William was not willing to challenge his new Parliament so early in its existence by the use of the veto. Henceforth, trials for treason were to be conducted in a manner which gave the accused a fairer means of defence, with a copy of the indictment prior to the trail; further, condemnation could not be secured without the evidence of at least two witnesses to an overt act of treason. But other causes which the country members furthered were less acceptable. William's gifts of crown property in Wales to Portland had occasioned deep resentment among the Welsh squires for the loss of estates of

20. Hatton Corr., ii, 232; Vernon Corr., ii, 444.
21. Seymour to Harley, 13 Nov. 1695, Loan 29/156/6.
22. Lexington Papers, p. 148; Guy to Portland, 5/15 July, Portland (Nottingham) MSS., PwA 504.

which they had long enjoyed the lease or stewardship. Although Harley had undertaken to Guy to prevent further attacks he proved unable, or unwilling, to restrain his friends and neighbours from voicing their grievance. The Commons resolved on 14 January 1696 to request the King to resume ownership of the properties in question, and he did so with considerable anger.[23] The new year saw also a struggle over Harley's own proposal to set up a Board of Trade, with its members to be nominated by Parliament, in place of the existing Lords of Trade. The measure arose out of a general discontent over heavy losses which had been suffered by British commerce at sea. In a close contest the ministry succeeded on the 20th in inflicting a setback to the bill by grafting on provisions for tendering an abjuration oath to members of the proposed board and for excluding Members of Parliament from it. But in a renewed debate on 31 January both these provisions were deleted with Harley speaking against abjuration alongside Seymour and William Bromley, the last of whom was now taking the prominent place among Tory orators he was to occupy for the next generation. The Tories had need of their allies, for the crucial question of the oath was decided by a narrow margin of seven votes in a packed House, the voting being 195–188.[24]

It was probably at about this time that Harley refused a government offer of the lucrative Auditorship of the Exchequer, when the current holder was thought to be dying, in return for giving up his place on the Commission of Accounts. He had no intention of losing his independence, and in the annual ballot for a new commission, which took place on 1 February, he achieved the highest support, five votes ahead of Foley.[25] Two days later both men were ready to broach their main business for the session. This was no less ambitious a project than the foundation of a Land Bank to serve the agricultural interest as the Bank of England served the 'monied' interest. Harley and his brother, in conjunction with the Tories, had laboured for months to produce a scheme, and it was adopted over the next few days in the Commons in spite of strong opposition from Montagu. Even before the foundation of the Bank of England had given offence to the 'landed interest' there had been a general idea that some way might be found to urilize the value of land as a backing for paper credit. In 1696 no fewer than four schemes were afoot to this purpose. The object of the one which was adopted was of relatively limited scope, namely to raise capital in order to make advances upon mortagages. The Harley's plan was a Joint Stock Bank, for which

23. Japikse, I, ii, 59–61; Feiling, pp. 317–18.
24. H.M.C. *Hastings*, ii, 253; R.M. Lees, 'Parliament and the Proposal for a Council of Trade, 1695–6', *E.H.R.*, liv (1939), 49–52; Burton, Riley and Rowlands, *Political Parties in the Reigns of William III and Anne*, pp. 6–7.
25. Horwitz, pp. 165–6; H.M.C. *Portland*, iv, 451. Sir Robert Howard, the incumbent, did not in fact die until 1698.

the prior approval of the King was obtained through Sunderland.[26] The Land Bank agreed to raise a subscription of over two and a half millions to lend to the government in return for a parliamentary annuity of 7 per cent. It was hoped that land-owners would benefit by borrowing from the Land Bank at the low rate of 3½ per cent per annum, and subscribers of the loan would receive an additional security from the fact that the estates mortgaged would be subject to half of any losses incurred. The scheme was technically sound but it assumed, mistakenly as it proved, that the City of London would be able, and if able then willing, to give support to an institution intended to help the gentry and the country opposition.

Strengthened greatly by close co-operation over the Land Bank, Treason Bill and Board of Trade proposals, a growing understanding between the Old Whigs and a wide range of Tories was now tested by an unanticipated hazard. This was the discovery of a conspiracy to assassinate the King, to be followed if successful by a French invasion in support of James II. Harley was recovering from one of his recurrent bouts of ill-health when both he and Foley were given the details by Guy and Sunderland respectively, apparently to give them some chance to prepare for the Junto's predictable exploitation of the incident. On 24 February William himself revealed to Parliament the full scope of the planned coup.[27] In a mood of shock and indignation the Commons, on ministerial initiative, drew up a Statement of Association whose voluntary signatories were to declare William 'rightful and lawful' king and undertake to defend or, if necessary, revenge him against King James. For the Tories the Association amounted to a variant of the abjuration theme and, as its devisers hoped, many refused to bind themselves. Over ninety members of Parliament, including Harley's friends Musgrave and Bromley refused to sign the offensive document.[28] But for most members any reservations of conscience were overcome by a sense of outrage at the plot, and the ministry had no difficulty in rushing through a bill setting a date after which non-subscribers would be excluded from office and Parliament.

A political crisis of unrivalled proportions was now at hand, and those Old Whigs and Tories who had signed the voluntary Association now entreated their more scrupulous colleagues to save themselves by abandoning any further resistance; signature under duress, it was urged, was no disgrace to those who had adhered to their principles by refusing to join the Association originally. Foremost among those who urged compliance on such grounds were the Old Whigs, who had themselves found no difficulty in signing. Their most potent argument against further re-

---

26. Kenyon, *Sunderland*, p. 278.
27. Horwitz, p. 175.
28. *Parliamentary History*, v, 987–93; Bonet, in Ranke, v, 120–1; Add. MSS. 17,677QQ, f. 296.

fusal was that used by Harley in an urgent letter to Bromley; the chief object now, he wrote, was 'keeping the nation from the power of a party who can have no strength but what is given them by such a refusall'. The necessity of keeping the new alliance together, as well as the doubters' instinct for self-preservation, were sufficient to prevail; but the names of those who had refused the voluntary Association were published in lists, and those concerned were marked out as extremists for the rest of their careers.[29]

The Association proved to be a major setback for Harley's schemes. In its confused aftermath the Junto had no difficulty in jettisoning the Board of Trade proposals, and the Commission of Accounts was unable to continue its business for several months until some of its members could be persuaded reluctantly to join the Association. Worse still, any chance the Land Bank might have had was lost when the ministers obtained parliamentary approval to adopt a project for replacing the much-clipped national currency with new milled coins. The new coinage was needed, but the Land Bank's sponsors had rashly undertaken to raise a large proportion of their subscription in cash, and it was in vain that they petitioned the Treasury to accept this in unmilled currency.[30] With the newly-minted milled coins being hoarded as soon as they were issued, the government itself was hard pressed for specie. Not even the issue of interest-bearing securities of the type soon to be known as exchequer bills could do much to ameliorate the situation immediately, though in the longer term their relative liquidity was to be valuable as a partial substitute for normal currency. Government credit was too low for any remedial measures, however well-based, to take immediate effect, and the Land Bank did not have time on its side. When its subscription lists were opened the extent of the failure was visible in a derisory take-up of less than £40,000. The bank's failure was complete and final, from its unfortunate timing and the failure of the financial community to lend its support to a political rival of the Bank of England. When Harley came to deal with the financial crisis of 1710 he proved that he had learned the lesson; he never again underestimated the value or the strength of the new force that had entered English life, the organization of the financial resources of the City in the Bank of England as a public creditor.

With the disruption of national life by the Assassination Plot's aftermath and the great recoinage, the summer of 1696 saw little diminution of Harley's activity. In June the assassination affair took a new turn with the arrest of a principal plotter, Sir John Fenwick, who succeeded in removing from the English scene witnesses necessary for his conviction under the new treason legislation. In the absence of direct means

29. H.M.C. *Portland*, iii, 575.
30. Godolphin to Portland, 22 May [1696], Portland (Nottingham) MSS., PwA 504; Hill, p. 69.

of prosecution, the ministry decided to proceed against Fenwick by the arbitrary process of attainder by parliamentary vote. Harley's alliance with the Tories was now at a critical point, for if he were to pursue the undoubtedly guilty Fenwick he would be aiding a constitutionally undesirable process which might well be turned against the ministry's political opponents at some later date. He and his friends had little hesitation in deciding to vote against the attainder as a matter of principle. Before Parliament assembled in the autumn, however, Fenwick himself again succeeded in confusing his opponents by making a 'confession' which purported to implicate as his fellow conspirators several prominent men including Godolphin, Russell and Shrewsbury. Shrewsbury, the least tough of those accused, was deeply disturbed by the charge. Only with difficulty was he persuaded by his colleagues not to resign, for such a move might have been construed as an admission not only of his own but of Whig guilt. Godolphin, on the other hand, was tricked by the Junto, with the help of Sunderland, into offering his resignation under the impression that it would be refused and the King's confidence thereby demonstrated. But his offer was accepted with alacrity, thus accomplishing his Whig colleagues' longstanding desire for his removal. The whole manoeuvre appears to have owed its success to the part played by Sunderland; if so, it was one of his last attempts to conciliate the Junto and one which he may have later regretted.[31]

The ministers' decision to proceed against Fenwick by means of attainder was carefully concerted to forestall any possible objection from Sunderland, who was known to be unenthusiastic. In a private meeting on the morning of 31 October, they agreed their tactics for a larger meeting in the afternoon, and at the second meeting the deliberations of the morning were broken by degrees to the great man without his apparent objection.[32] The Junto were convinced that Fenwick's accusations must be countered by a show of united force, and for this purpose the support of the King's adviser was essential. On 6 November the subject of Fenwick's confession was raised in the Commons by Russell, and he and the other accused ministers were easily exonerated from the charges. The Attainder Bill itself, however, met vehement opposition. Harley forthrightly described it as a party contrivance to circumvent justice for political ends. 'Tis hard', he is reported as telling the House, 'to pervert the methods of common justice without any necessity'. Without the two witnesses required by the Treason Act, Tory oratory observed sarcastically, Fenwick's accusers had little to go on except 'the help of the light within them'. But more dangerous than such expected opposition were abstentions and defections on the ministerial side by those who doubted

31. *Shrewsbury Corr.* pp. 411–15, 419–20.
32. *Ibid.*, pp. 415, 417–20.

the wisdom of trial by attainder. Secretary Trumbull and Harley's old school friend Attorney-General Thomas Trevor absented themselves from key debates. Worse still, the voters against the attainder included two usually dependable leading Whigs, Thomas Pelham and Sir Richard Onslow, both respected and well-to-do country members like Harley himself, men of a type the ministry could ill-afford to lose. But despite such defections there was enough residual resentment among members at Fenwwick's actions to allow the ministry to carry the majority, and at the decisive vote on the third reading on 25 November the bill obtained a sufficiently comfortable majority of 33 votes.[33]

Fenwick went to his death the victim, though not an innocent one, of the ministry's political tactics. In one respect at least the victory was pyrrhic, for government solidarity was weakened by an increased distancing between the Whigs and Sunderland, while Shrewsbury was by no means re-assured that his own vindication followed from the parliamentary repudiation of Fenwick's allegations. Russell might assure him 'the party will not hear of any body's talking of your quitting', but Shrewsbury remained an invalid or hypochondriac passenger in the ministry. His duties as Secretary were increasingly carried on by Under-Secretary James Vernon,[34] whose regular letters to him form a valuable source for Harley's activities in the next few years.

Other parliamentary business during 1696 to 1697 reflected the uncertain outlook. On 3 November Harley reported from the Commission of Accounts on the national financial problems caused by deficiencies in several tax funds and by the substitution of new for clipped money. Subsequent debates saw him and Foley defending themselves desperately on the score of the Land Bank's failure to achieve its promises to raise needed government loans. By this failure the commission itself was, unreasonably, doomed for a time. In the shattered state of country morale the ministers succeeded in packing the membership with their own supporters at the time of its annual renewal, and Harley and his friends were obliged to use the ensuing reaction in the House to vote down the enacting bill and thus abandon the institution which had served their ends so well. Their cause reached its lowest point when Montagu obtained a bill protecting the Bank of England against future rivalry from other joint-stock institutions, in return for the Bank's consent to add some unfunded govenment debts to its existing capital. Harley's future financial expedients would be forced to respect this provision, even when apparently designed not to do so.[35]

For Harley the events of 1696 closed some political vistas and opened

33. *Vernon Corr.*, 46–50, 52–3, 73 and 82; Add, MSS. 17,677QQ, f. 596; *Shrewsbury Corr.*, pp. 426 and 429; *Parliamentary History*, v, 998–1149; Oldmixon, p. 158.
34. *Shrewsbury Corr.*, p. 454.
35. Chandler, *Debates*, iii, 29–30; Clapham, i, 46–50; Horwitz, p. 191.

others. The Old Whigs' separation from the Junto was almost absolute. Juncture with the Tories, though in some ways never complete, was further strengthened by joint opposition to Fenwick's attainder. When financial problems induced King William to set on foot a peace negotiation with the equally indigent Louis XIV the way was open for the fortunes of the country alliance to take a better turn. In a peacetime situation there could be no further governmental excuse for large military supplies and high texation. The miserly pre-suppositions of the late Commission of Accounts could spread to an ever-widening body of members, including even such ministerial Whig supporters as those country gentlemen who had recently opposed the use of attainder. Over the next four years Harley was to turn the House of Commons itself into a macrocosm of the former commission, leading an allied country party in a relentless campaign against court expenditure and ministerial Whig aspirations.

CHAPTER 4

Opposition Leader

IN THE SUMMER of 1697, while Harley paid an unusually extended visit to Brampton to enjoy his first rest for several years from the Commission of Accounts, Portland was negotiating peace with Louis XIV's emissaries at Ryswick near The Hague. Meanwhile, at the court of William III, a bitter power struggle between Sunderland and the members of the Junto took place. As soon as Parliament rose in April Sunderland was given official standing as Lord Chamberlain and as one of the Lords Justices appointed to act in the King's stead during his absence abroad. But this setback for the Junto was softened by promotions for Somers, who was given the higher legal standing of Lord Chancellor, and for Montagu who took the place of First Lord of the Treasury, vacant since Godolphin's resignation. The New Whigs now controlled most important offices except those held by Shrewsbury, his friend Under-Secretary Vernon, and the followers of other protected peers such as Sunderland and Leeds.

The independence of these and other grandees, and their jealousy of the Junto, offered Harley his best chance of splitting the ministry to his own advantage. These men of wealth and title had little love for the abrasive and and grasping tactics of self-made lawyers and younger sons. Such was the attitude even of the wealthy Lord Ashley, later third Earl of Shaftesbury, a scion of the first family of Whiggery who criticized Montagu for having a grant from the crown held in trust for him by his brother.[1] Harley was on good terms with several men critical of the Junto's pretensions, including Somers' subordinate law officer Trevor, currently drifting further towards the Tory camp like Harley himself, and Vernon who ran Shrewsbury's office and held himself at a cool distance from his colleagues. At a time when these and others were showing increasing signs of repeating the independent stance some of them had displayed over Fenwick's attainder, the Junto's control of the Commons

---

1. Anthony Ashley Cooper, styled Lord Ashley, sat in the Commons for Poole from 1695 to 1698.

was being further eroded by the removal of several of their number to the House of Lords; Wharton a year earlier by succession to the barony of Wharton, Russell by his recent acceptance of the earldom of Orford, and Somers by his elevation as Baron Somers at the time of his acceptance of office as Lord Chancellor. All these considerations occupied Harley as he received the frequent letters of his friends in London or at court during his relatively idle vacation, while the diplomats made peace at Ryswick.

As the autumn opening of Parliament approached, and peace was proclaimed in London on 19 October, political intrigues came to a head. Harley had already been approached by Sunderland to come to an accommodation over the King's desire to retain a large standing army despite the cessation of hostilities, and perhaps also with a view to Harley's admission to office as Secretary of State.[2] The Earl was apprehensive of the Junto ministers' latest attempt to improve their ministerial position. Their aim was to obtain a secretaryship for Wharton by removing Trumbull; and Wharton in that office would undoubtedly by his fierce energy dominate the lethargic Shrewsbury and subordinate Vernon. In order to obtain Trumbull's resignation he was subjected to harassment by his colleagues. It appearing likely, however, that Shrewsbury might resign first, as he had long wished to do, the Junto were careful to withdraw their former objections to such and event. But the King's continued aversion from admitting Wharton strengthened Sunderland's hand. The other members of the Junto were given a clear hint that if they pushed matters too far their own services might no longer be found indispensable. On 1 December Trumbull resigned, complaining of mistreatment by other ministers since his part in the attainder debates. On the same evening the King sent for Harley, and this was probably the first to two occasions when the monarch is known (on the testimony of Edward Harley and others) to have offered him the Secretaryship. If this is so, Harley refused the offer because of his determination to dismantle the royal army, writing to Sir Edward that he hoped he had said 'what became an honest man, with all decency'.[3]

James Vernon was promoted the following day, and Shrewsbury was dissuaded by Portland and Sunderland from following Trumbull's example and thereby leaving a vacancy for Wharton. The Junto, chagrined at the transaction, met Shrewsbury's disclaimer of any part in it with disbelief; Somers remarked ironically that he would not fail to pass on to Wharton 'how much your Grace was surprised at the news, and how absolutely ignorant of the thing'. But for the moment Shrewsbury was less vulnerable to the Junto's anger than was Sunderland, whose notor-

---

2. H.M.C. *Portland*, viii, 50 and iii, 588–92.
3. *Ibid.*, iii, 594 (Harley to Sir Edward Harley, 4 Dec., mistakenly described by the editor as from Sunderland to Harley).

ious position as the King's chief adviser while holding only a court appointment aroused much antagonism in Parliament. Harley was an interested spectator, when Parliament assembled in December, of a concerted attack by Junto supporters on their great rival and of Wharton's open refusal of the King's personal request to call off his dogs. At the end of the month Sunderland resigned as Lord Chamberlain, and any hopes he may have retained of ever recovering the responsible office he had held under James II were now lost. 'Lord Sunderland's retiring', commented Harley tersely to his father, 'will leave the managers very naked'.[4]

Parliament's main business, however, concerned the King's desire to keep intact, or almost so, his carefully constructed professional army. The average Englishman's (and even more Englishwoman's) abhorrence of a 'standing' army in time of peace, with the examples of Cromwell's rule through major generals and of James II's use of soldiery to intimidate London, was much in evidence even before the session, and Harley wrote from the capital: 'the argument against a standing army has raised a great heat in the town. There is very little prospect of moderate councils'.[5] A brisk literary controversy which was conducted on the subject began with a pamphlet challengingly entitled *An Argument, Shewing that a Standing Army is Inconsistent with Free Government* written by two extreme Whigs, one of whom, Walter Moyle, was a member of the Lower House, and the other, John Trenchard, a kinsman of his namesake the late Secretary of State. Harley supplied material for this or other similar tracts, of which the standing army controversy spawned a large number, though he appears to have been critical of the more extremist arguments put forward by near-republican writers. The crisis called forth several ministerial replies, including one of Somers' ablest tracts, the *Balancing Letter*. In addition, strenuous efforts were made by the ministry to win over their recalcitrant supporters before the session.[6] The King himself, in his opening speech, strongly repeated his supporters' message. But on 10 December Harley, in a speech of great technical detail, successfully proposed that all troops raised since September 1680 should be demobilized. In the succeeding weeks the court's efforts failed to obtain more than minor concessions, the size of the surviving force being fixed at only 10,000 men. Many of the ministry's usual supporters, including Pelham and Onslow, followed Harley's lead rather than the Junto's. As a partial sop to William, Harley did not object to a ministerial proposal

---

4. *Shrewsbury Corr.*, pp. 499–500, 502, 505–7; H.M.C. *Portland*, iii, 494; H.M.C. *Buccleuch*, ii, 587; 2 and 4 Dec., *Vernon Corr.*, i. 359, 379–80, 391, 399, 411, 432–3 and 438–47. See Dorothy H. Somerville, 'The Dates in the Vernon Correspondence', *E.H.R.* xlviii (1933), 624–30, whose corrections are followed in the present work.
5. H.M.C., *Portland*, iii, 593.
6. Lois G. Schwoerer, 'The Role of King William III in the Standing Army Controversy 1697–1699', *JBS* 5 (1966), p. 80; [John, Baron Somers], *A Letter, Balancing the Necessity of Keeping a Land Force with the Dangers that may Follow on it* (1697); Downie, p. 32.

to raise the Civil List sum granted by Parliament to the monarch by £100,000 to a total of £700,000 per annum, granted for life, but this necessary sum for the maintenance of the court in peacetime by no means compensated the King for the loss of supplies for the army.[7]

When Parliament was reconvened early in 1698 after the Christmas recess Harley's prophesy that the Commons 'managers' would be 'very naked' was fulfilled. Sunderland's resignation left them little real contact with the King. Moreover, the Earl's resentment at his downfall found vent in an attack upon Montagu by his friends Guy, Trumbull and the rich Tory goldsmith banker Charles Duncombe for profiteering on the already-depreciated new exchequer bills.[8] Montagu responded with a vicious but credible attack on his tormentors' weakest member, successfully demonstrating that the alleged form of fraud had been carried on by Duncombe, a longstanding critic of the Bank of England. Duncombe was sent to the Tower on 25 January, but the matter did not end there, for Harley with his usual persistence and dislike of financial mismangement, took up the investigation of the Treasury itself. Montagu, in an effort to lower the discount rate at which the bills were passing, had accepted them at face value in discharge of debts. On 22 February this proceeding was criticized by Harley, Musgrave, Seymour and even Pelham, but the First Lord defended himself as ably as usual, convincing the House of the soundness of his attempt. Later in the session Montagu confirmed his financial ascendacy, raising a £2 million loan by chartering the New East India Company which would act as a useful rival to the older, Tory-backed Old East India Company. If Harley were to press the ministry further it would have to be no more secure ground than the management of the Treasury.[9]

The last months of Parliament were overshadowed by a general election due in 1698 under the Triennial Act. Few members of the Commons were willing to take extreme positions which might have been interpreted unfavourably by their rivals at the polls. Moreover, the international situation was clouding again, with a new danger to peace arising from the poor health of the Spanish King Carlos II, and a likely dispute over the succession to his numerous possessions in America, Italy, the Netherlands and Spain itself. In these circumstances Harley appears to have agreed privately with Montagu, the only member of the Junto with whom he kept up good personal relations despite their political animos-

7. Bonet, in Ranke, v, 173–4; Bonet, 7/17 Jan. 1698, Add. MS. 30,000B, f. 8; H.M.C., *Portland*, iii, 595; *Vernon Corr.*, 439–42 and 445–6.
8. *Shrewsbury Corr.*, pp. 521–2, 560 and 526–7; *Vernon Corr.*, i, 455, 461, 463–6 and 468–70, 477–8.
9. Bonet, 15/25 Feb. and 15/25 March, Add MSS. 30,000B, ff. 41 and 71; *Shrewsbury Corr.*, pp. 528–31; CJ xii, 125; Blathwayt to Unknown, [22 Feb. 1698], Add. MSS 21,551, f. 7; *Vernon Corr.*, i, 77 and ii, 18–19; 'Notes of Proceedings...' CSP. Dom. 1698, pp. 102–3 and 105.

ity, to accede to a general feeling that the dismantling of the army might
to some extent be postponed; William was encouraged to keep 16,000
men in England, paid for out of Montagu's new loan.[10] At the same time
the King concluded a secret treaty with Louis XIV for the peaceful partition of the Spanish empire, apportioning relatively small parts of the
spoils to the French and Imperial candidates and the largest share to a
minor third contender, an infant Prince of Bavaria.

For the election, which took place in July, William gave little support
to his ministers after their continued pressure to exclude Sunderland
from his counsels. On the contrary, his appointment of Princess Anne's
friend Marlborough as a privy councillor and as governor to her son, the
Duke of Gloucester, was taken as a mild gesture in favour of the junior
court's faction of Tories. William's refusal otherwise to 'declare himself'
resulted in a general election in which few could see any advantage for
the ministers. Harley and his border friends suffered no major setbacks,
and Edward Harley was able to obtain a seat at Leominster which he
retained until 1722; a distant cousin Thomas Harley, befriended by Sir
Edward, was successful at Radnorshire, which he continued to represent
until 1715, swelling the inner circle of Harley relations in the Lower
House. The failure of New Whig attempts to halt Harley gains was repeated in similar ministerial setbacks elsewhere. Montagu prudently prepared a bolt-hole for himself in case of dismissal by placing his brother
James, *pro tem*, in the lucrative Auditorship of the Receipt, which fell
timely vacant.[11]

The behaviour of new members would be difficult to assess, as always,
until their views emerged in Parliament. In Harley's opinion, 'if there be
any alteration, it will not proceed from the new members but from the
change of opinions in some of the old'. For the moment patterns which
had emerged in the old House of Commons were the best guide to the
new, and they indicated a continued strong criticism of government.
The standing army controversy had produced a situation in which many
Whigs otherwise loyal to the court had sided with the Tories and Old
Whigs in what the contemporary historian John Oldmixon called 'an
unnatural coalition'.[12] In the debates of January and February 1698 in
which the court had striven unsuccessfully to reverse the reduction of
William's army, the term 'opposition' or near variants such as 'adverse
party' had become common in describing the new groupings.[13] Count

10. Horwitz, p. 235.
11. *Vernon Corr.*, ii, 106, 111, 139, 141–3, 147–8, 152 and 165–7; *Shrewsbury Corr.*, pp. 540–1,
    550–1, and 560.
12. Horwitz, p. 240; Oldmixon, p. 170.
13. James Vernon wrote to Shrewsbury of 'the opposite party' or 'the opposing party'. *Vernon Corr.*,
    i, 463 and 466; Bonet had 'those opposed to the court' 5/15 Feb. 1698, Add. MSS. 30,000B,
    f. 41; Blathwayt had 'the adverse party', [22 Feb. 1698], Add. MSS. 21,551, f. 7.

Tallard, newly arrived in England as Louis XIV's ambassador, was quick to point out to his master, that opposition which arose over the army was not directed against William's person or rule; for 'it must be observed that those persons who are opposed to his will are not opposed to his government; not wishing for commotion, and only desirous of hindering him from becoming master'.[14] The ambassador was right in pointing out most parliamentarians' basic loyalty to their Protestant monarch but if anything he underestimated their resolve to hinder him from becoming master. It was this resolve that Harley was to weld into the most formidable opposition ever seen in a basically peaceable Parliament.

During the life of the newly elected Parliament, Harley is everywhere seen at the forefront of the combined opposition, or, as he preferred to call it, 'New Country Party'. He stood unrivalled as the spokesman of his immediate circle; even Paul Foley, distracted and weakened by his exertions as Speaker and now within a year of his death, was content to take second place to his younger kinsman. An opponent of party pretensions, Harley was never happy either with the party of his birth or with that into which his fortune drew him. It is not without significance that he never associated better with the Tories than in the years from 1698 to 1700, when he could ride beneath the banner of country sentiments which he and his friends currently held in common with their Tory associates. Apart from getting the Junto out of office his aims were probably not clearly formed and thus were hard to divine, least of all by the King who often attempted the task. Certainly it was not Harley's intention to replace the New Whigs by another party; ideally he wanted the King to be surrounded by a non-party ministry acceptable to the landed interest, the 'patriot' monarchy of later mythology. A tract of 1698 written from the Old Whig point of view treated parties as anathema and called for 'a real popularity' of the crown as the only acceptable political situation.[15] But in the prevailing ethos Harley could no more make a popular monarch of William III than he could prevent the continued forging of the Tories, by his own attacks on the ministry, into a true party contrary to his own instincts. His main hope lay in the future; from 1698 he cemented a brilliant association with Godolphin, and through him ultimately with the circle around the Princess Anne, which was to bear fruit when Anne succeeded to the throne. Until he found a monarch near his ideal, however, he had to make do with the material at hand, and bring the King to see the wishes of the majority in the Commons.[16]

14. Grimblot, i, 355.
15. A *Letter to King William III* by Will. Stephens, B.D., in *State Tracts* ii, 631–7. Another tract of later date asserted that in William's reign Harley 'kept both parties and interests in an equilibrio and such an exact mean between them that the one could not, nor did not preponderate the other', anonymous MS entitled 'The Fate of Favourites', Bodleian, Rawlinson MS, D. 37, p. 7
16. Thus Harley reminded Godolphin on 21 July 1705 of the 'seven years that I have enjoyed your protection', H.M.C., *Bath*, i, 73.

Harley was in Herefordshire from July, for his election at Radnor and to assist his brother's return for Leominster. While still there in September he suffered a severe fall which gave some concern to his friends, and he was bled on the advice of his practitioners. But by late in November he was ready in London for the opening of Parliament, and the prospects for success were good. A portent of the Junto's weakness in the Commons was the behaviour of Montagu. Despite the importance of his contribution to the common cause, the First Lord of the Treasury was the least reliable of the Whig leaders as a party man. His abrupt acquisition of the Auditorship of the Receipt had been without the knowledge or approval of his friends, who were even uncertain for a time as to whether the action might pressage immediate resignation from the Treasury.[17] Nevertheless the Whigs had an initial success in the election of a Speaker. Foley, who had done too much in aid of the voting of supplies to please many extremists, no longer commanded a sufficient following among the government's opponents. Several possible candidates were mentioned. Harley himself still lacked the seniority to command a wide following for so august a post, though his claim was considered indirectly by at least one tract and his name was perhaps mentioned more directly in the preliminary jockeying for position.[18] Of the several other possible opposition members mooted the experienced Seymour seemed at first to have the best chance; but he was discredited by a damaging tract setting out his record of courtierly activities, and by his own injudicious action in giving rise to fears that he would be willing to join the court again. Thus, when the Whigs' candidate, Sir Thomas Littleton was nominated on 6 December no rival appeared, and he was elected without difficulty.[19] But the ministry's victory was a misleading one, arising from the country gentlemen's initial inability to pull together in support of a single candidate. Harley now worked to retrieve the situation, and on his suggestion the House brushed aside the usual immediate discussion of supplies and turned at once to the army. On the 17th he successfully moved a further reduction of the English establishment to 7,000 men, aided by the ministry's failure to put up an effective case. Montagu's need to protect his own position left him scant time to defend the King's interest; Vernon reported to Shrewsbury that he had himself received no support in the Commons from his colleagues concerning the army and that 'at Court they are blamed for giving it up'. The country leaders hurriedly brought in a disbandment bill which received its second reading on the 23rd and was committed without a division.[20]

After Christmas, such criticisms as Vernon's produced some response,

17. H.M.C., *Portland*, iii, 599; *Shrewsbury Corr.*, pp. 553, 560 and 569–70.
18. *Considerations upon the Choice of a Speaker*, printed in *Parliamentary History*, v, appendix, cli-cliv.
19. H.M.C., *Bath*, iii, 302; *Vernon Corr.*, ii. 223; the King, Kramer, *Archives* ii, 246.
20. *Vernon Corr.*, ii, 235–6; H.M.C. *Portland*, iii, 600; *CJ*, xii, 359 and 368.

and on 4 January 1699 the ministerial Whigs made their most vigorous attempt to obtain an augmentation of the proposed army numbers, with Montagu now reinforcing Vernon. Even so they again failed, 'upon the cry of the House' as the latter reported, even to force the matter to a division in face of the mastery maintained by Harley, who produced military establishment figures from Charles II's reign showing that the English garrisons had then amounted to fewer than the 7,000 men he how suggested. The King's case appeared hopeless when those speaking against his wishes were seen to include not only such Dissidents as Pelham and Onslow but even Lord Hartington, heir of the influential Duke of Devonshire and lately Littleton's proposer for the Chair of the Commons. At the third reading of the Disbandment Bill on the 18th the government speakers were brushed aside by Harley, assisted by his friend and former schoolfellow Simon Harcourt, and the bill was passed by a majority of 67 votes. Along with English regiments went the King's brigade of Dutch Guards, which had been retained by England since the Revolution.[21] In response William threatened, from anger and for tactical reasons, to quit the kingdom once and for all. His bluff was called, however, he had little further re-course but to blame his ministers. These, it was generally agreed, had been of little assistance against the assaults of the New Country party.[22]

After the army and the placemen, whose discomfiture was this year entrusted to Edward Harley, the next objects of attack were the ministers. Robert Harley and Paul Foley jointly conducted an enquiry into naval accounts with such vigour that even before Christmas Orford was talking of resigning his place at the Admiralty. A parliamentary committee set up to investigate charges of malversation and mismanagement took some time over its enquiries, but after being urged by Harley to complete its work before the end of the session presented a report to the House on 15 March. The report matched the expectations of Orford's opponents, and on the 27th the Commons agreed to address the King complaining of malversation in the Admiral's secondary function of Treasurer of the Navy and the inexpediency of his tenure of two offices at once. The addition of a request that Orford should be removed was rejected only by the narrow majority of four votes.[23] And if the King retained any confidence in the ability of the Junto to control the House he was provided with further evidence to the contrary by the setting

21. *Shrewsbury Corr.*, pp. 572–4; Vernon. to Sir Joseph Williamson, *CSP Dom*, p. 5; Hoffman, in Gaedeke, i, appendix, p. 150; *Hatton Corr.*, ii, 238; *Vernon Corr.*, ii, 245–6, 253, 263 and 269; C.J., xii, 440. Cf. D.W. Hayton, 'Debates...1697–1699' in RHS *Camden Miscellany*, xxix, p.383.
22. Burnet, iv, 400; draft speech by William in Dalrymple, ii, (*recte* iii), 130; William in Kramer, ii, 275; Tallard in Grimblot, ii, 224; Evelyn, *Diary*, v, 309.
23. Tallard, in Grimblot, ii, 230–1; H.M.C., *Portland*, viii, 57–8 and iii, 603; *Vernon Corr.*, ii, 238–9, 241m 270–1, C.J., xii, 618.

up of a commission to investigate another long-standing parliamentary grievance, namely his grants to Portland and other friends of lands which had fallen to the crown by forfeiture after the rebellion in Ireland. 'A majority in opposition', complained Vernon, 'is a great weight.'[24]

Despite the narrow defeat of the onslaught on Orford, Harley's aim was fulfilled shortly after the prorogation of Parliament. Orford resigned his post as Treasurer but pressed for a strengthening of his position on the Admiralty Board by the dismissal from it of his chief Tory opponent, Admiral George Rooke. On the King's refusal, Orford resigned as First Lord and was replaced by a little-known and innocuous politician, the Earl of Bridgewater. The blow to the Junto was a severe one, and worse was to follow. Further months of fruitless negotiation ensued, during which Harley retired to the country and refused to be drawn by either Sunderland or Shrewsbury into any ministerial arrangement which might include the Junto. And at the end of the summer Montagu, who desired some such arrangement, gave up hope and resigned, rather than face a session in which he might be the principal victim of country rancour.[25] The appointment as his successor of the Earl of Tankerville, an even less known figure than Bridgewater, accentuated the ministry's weakness. With Shrewsbury contemplating the travel abroad which was to take him out of politics for several years, there was no fit government team with which to meet a Parliament whose members were again whipping themselves into indignation at Junto rapacity and the further royal grants of forfeited Irish estates. On 11 November, Harley was summoned to a meeting with Shrewsbury but appears to have remained unwilling to compromise his position with the Tories by accepting any appointment while Somers remained in office.[26] On the other hand he remained in close touch with Godolphin, as also with Seymour and Rochester, possibly in the expectation of a summons from William to the Tories to form a new government. In the event such a summons was deferred for a further year while the King continued to resist the logic of dropping ministers who had long since lost control of the Commons.[26]

Parliament assembled without the presence of Paul Foley, who had died three days earlier at his Herefordshire home. Robert Harley wrote to his father: 'This is a sore blow to the Church and State, to Hereford-shire and to all relations. It is a public loss.'[27] Sir Edward himself re-mained at Brampton, as he had for much of the past two years, with declining health. Robert's and Edward's letters to him provide a com-mentary on the New Country Party's aims which now centred upon dis-

---

24. Vernon to Shrewsbury, 27 April, *Vernon Corr.*, ii, 277;
25. H.M.C., *Portland*, iii, 607–9; *Shrewsbury Corr.*, pp. 590–5; Kenyon, *Sunderland*, pp. 312
26. Horwitz, p. 260; H.M.C. *Portland*, iii, 613 and 619; Kenyon, *Svnderland.*, p. 314
27. H.M.C., *Portland*, iii, 611.

gracing Somers, *primus inter pares* of the Junto but a difficult target to bring down on grounds of corruption. An opportunity was presented, however, by rumours concerning the activities of Captain William Kidd. The Captain had been financed by a syndicate, including Somers, Orford and Shrewsbury, to capture pirates and their booty in the East Indies. Among the many extraordinary commercial undertakings of the day this would not have appeared reprehensible had not Kidd discovered that there was more profit in turning pirate himself. On 4 December the House witnessed a full-dress enquiry into Kidd's commission, set on foot by Harley, Jack Howe, Musgrave and Seymour, in the course of which it became evident that Somers was the chief objective. The attempt failed, for the Whigs had no difficulty in showing that the commission was a legal and valid one, and that the parties to Kidd's venture were themselves innocent of piratical intention. Disappointed, the opposition turned their attention to a more vulnerable if less important New Whig, Bishop Gilbert Burnet, once a friend of the Harleys but increasingly since 1695 their *bête noire*, calling for his removal from the post of preceptor to the Duke of Gloucester; but the usual preference of the House for fair play in the case of individuals attacked for party reasons resulted in the defeat of this attempt too.[28]

After these sorties the House turned its attention to the main business of the session, a bill to resume the King's grants of forfeited lands in Ireland. Harley was in the forefront, writing to Sir Edward at one point, 'It has pleased God to lay a great load upon me...I think I have not exceeded four hours sleep'. The attack was prefaced by an able tract, *A Discourse of Grants and Resumptions* by Harley's close associate the polemicist and economist Charles Davenant. A parliamentary commission of investigation was divided as to its conclusions, but the four members who constituted its majority presented a report strongly condemnatory of the grants. Vernon, who was called upon to bear the brunt of the assault on behalf of the court, correctly forecast that the respite gained by the ministry would be frittered away if they were forced to defend the unpopular grants. On commitment of the bill on 18 January 1700, Vernon tried to save one third of the resumed estates for the King's use but was unable to make headway against a great speech from Harley, who intended that the sums realized from the grants should go towards paying off national debts and wondered aloud that 'anybody had confidence to demand only a part [for the King] for we intended to give him all'. One member remarked that 'Mr Harley now manages the whole business of supply, and the House hath hitherto entirely approved of his scheme.' Harley was sounded again about the possibility of his taking office as

28. Prior to Manchester, 15 Nov., *Court and Society*, ii, 52; Vernon to Shrewsbury, 5, 7 and 14 December, *Vernon Corr.*, ii, 375–6, 378–81, 388.

Secretary of State, and Vernon expressed himself willing to yield up the position; but again Harley refused to consider serving with the Whigs, and for the moment negotiation lapsed.[29]

On 2 April 1700 the Resumption Bill received its final reading including 'place' clauses from the Harley brothers, welcome to most country gentlemen, for excluding excise officials from the Commons. A tax provision was tacked to the bill to make its rejection difficult in the House of Lords, where the King's wishes were still expected to receive attention. Even at this stage, however, the Court evidently thought that an accommodation might be reached, and Vernon reported that 'the Tories would be pacified, though their bill were thrown out, upon condition that the Whigs be discarded'. But if this belief was correct as to the opposition leaders' intentions, country opinion was too aroused to permit such a transaction. Wrecking amendments made in the upper House on Wharton's initiative, especially the rejection of the place provisions, caused fury in the Commons. Amid scenes of excitement rarely seen before, Harley is reported as rising to state 'that it was time to think of England and that since that was the last time probably they were to sit there, to show that they were not quite insensible'. The King's advisers were subjected in the House to violent criticism and even threatened with impeachment. Worse was averted only when William surrendered and persuaded some of the bishops to vote in favour of the bill. Even so, country opinion called for the punishment of William's advisers, presumed to be Somers and Portland. Somers was sufficiently popular to survive the new attack, and a motion from Musgrave calling for his removal was fairly easily defeated. Portland was less lucky, and in the Lords an Address to the King to remove foreigners from his counsels passed without a division. The following day, 11 April, William hurriedly approved outstanding measures, including the Resumption Bill, and prorogued Parliament without the courtesy of the customary speech from the throne.[30]

Soon after this event the King took the point, however, and dismissed Somers at last. But though this removed one obstacle to Harley's acceptance of royal favour he had, in full measure, the average country gentleman's reluctance to bind himself by taking an executive post. There is some evidence that Montagu, with whom he remained in friendly contact, wanted him employed and would have been willing to serve with him. Harley may have unwittingly given some ground for hope of this outcome in February when he had diverted the Commons from a new

29. Vanbrugh in *Court and Society*, ii, 54; *Vernon Corr.*, ii, 393–4, 412–13, 435, 439–440, 444, 446, 267–68; Horwitz, p. 263; H.M.C., *Portland*, iii, 614.
30. *Vernon Corr.*, iii, 3–4 and 17–25; newsletter, 11 April, Add. MSS. 28,053, f. 402; Horwitz, p. 267.

attack on Montagu, much to the annoyance, it was observed, of at least one 'Churchman' present, who was provoked to leave the House exclaiming his disgust. But even four years later, with the Tories in office, Harley was to show genuine reluctance to abandon his independence by taking office as Secretary of State; his protection of Montagu was probably no more than was due on grounds of fair play. But Harley's moderation on this and other occasions did not go unnoticed, and helped to pave the way to the King's better favour. Vernon remarked to his mentor Shrewsbury of the recent session:

> What your Grace observes of the behaviour of the Whigs, that even while they were discountenanced, the success of affairs in Parliament was in a great measure owing to them, since it was in their power to obstruct them if they would; may of late, too be said of the Tory party: particularly of Mr. Harley, who for these two years past, has given what turn he pleased to the taxes, and could have made things worse than they are.[31]

Even so, the King's final retraction did not come immediately. Instead he turned to the 'court undertakers' Shrewsbury and Sunderland once again, seeking a new ministerial arrangement and basis for Commons management, perhaps combining Old with New Whigs. But Shrewsbury was no longer prepared to act as broker, intimating to William that he was no more minded to put himself 'between the two parties than between two millstones'. Sunderland was more helpful, but with the Junto Whigs, whom he sounded first, he met little success. Even Montagu, who was approached by the King himself with a similar purpose, replied that 'he hoped nothing would be expected from him that was not consistent with his friendship and obligation to my Lord Somers'. Turning from such stubborn solidarity to Harley and the Tories, Sunderland met more willingness to negotiate, but having little to offer the Tories had little more success than with the New Whigs. To ensure the reversal of Somers' blatantly partisan ejections of justices of the peace the Great Seal was proffered to Trevor, whom Harley tried to pursuade to take it, and on the lawyer's modest refusal it went to a less distinguished lawyer, but more rigid Tory, Nathan Wright.[32] Here, however, the royal concessions ceased for the moment. Until William was ready to negotiate with Harley's Tory allies as a party, government staggered on with a caretaker ministry into the spring and summer of 1700. Meanwhile, the truce of Europe continued fitfully and the nation prepared quietly to renew quarrels unsolved in or after Ryswick.

---

31. *Vernon Corr.*, ii, 444 and iii, 67.
32. H.M.C. ,*Portland*, iii, 618; *Vernon Corr.*, iii, 39, 52–4, 67–8 and 94–5; *Shrewsbury Corr.*, p. 620; H.M.C., *Portland*, iii, 619.

CHAPTER 5

Speaker: the Act of Settlement

FOR TWO YEARS Harley had virtually dictated the course of politics from the opposition side, and secured the Junto ministry's removal. But the Tories who provided his voting strength had, as yet, little reward for their pains. For a short while in April 1700 the Harleys were hopeful that the appointment of Wright to the Woolsack would be followed by the concession of one of their primary objects, a dissolution of Parliament; but the decision was put off until after the King's usual summer visit to Holland when, as they were given to understand, it would be determined 'according to the prospect there should be of being assisted by one or the other party'. Harley, for his part, continued to refuse office; he still had no intention of deserting his friends and therefore took refuge in prevarication. 'Mr Harley', commented Vernon acidly, 'professes himself to be of no party, and yet finds fault with the new reform of the Commissions of the Peace, as if it were done by halves.'[1] At the beginning of July of King, on the eve of departure, made a further gesture of conciliation by summoning and giving audience to Harley and the Tory war-horse Rochester on separate occasions. The outcome of these meetings was probably indecisive: no public announcement followed. Up to now Harley had been 'under a [royal] command' to stay in London, but he was anxious to get to Brampton where Sir Edward's condition continued to worsen gradually. At the end of July he was further delayed by his own state of health and, after his recovery, by measles contracted by his daughter Betty, at first feared to be smallpox. He set off finally at the end of August.[2]

In Herefordshire he was given little peace from public affairs, for correspondence with other politicians passed thick and fast. During William's absence abroad a tragic development helped to confirm his

---

1. Edward to Robert Harley, 3 May, Loan 29/143/2; H.M.C. *Portland*, iii, 619; *Vernon Corr.*, iii, 49–50, 55 and 91; 'Memoirs of Edward Harley, 1688–1715', Add. MSS. 34,515, f. 7.
2. *Vernon Corr.*, iii, 104–5; H.M.C. *Portland*, iii, 621–2 and 624–5.

signalled move towards Harley and the Tories. This was the death on 30 July of the young Duke of Gloucester, leaving no recognized heir to the throne after Anne. In William's view it now became imperative that legislation should be passed during the forthcoming winter to settle the further succession on the line of the Princess Sophia of Hanover and her descendants. Such a project, however, was by no means certain to be fulfilled if the House of Commons remained in the mood of the last session. Harley was sounded both by personal letter from the King and through the mediacy of Sunderland and Guy; from the latter came the hint that a dissolution of Parliament was now attainable. This news Harley lost no time in communicating to the Tories. In addition to the main body of these, it was essential to secure the participation of the Princess's clique, and her uncle Rochester was therefore brought to an agreement to work with his old rival Godolphin, a concession which required some tactful persuasion by both Harley and Sunderland. Thus, the King's return to England on 20 October was immediately followed by a meeting with Rochester, Godolphin and Harley, the later urgently summoned during the last illness of Sir Edward Harley. A later meeting took place between Willam and Harley alone, with the King demanding to know his terms for the Commons' acquiescence in the proposed new order of the royal succession. Harley had had years to think about the conditions needed to prevent, under a future royal house, many of the activities which had been found unacceptable with William. It was agreed to incorporate in a new act of succession further limitations upon the monarchy such as those embodied in the Bill of Rights in 1689, though Harley was able to reassure William that these new restrictions would not take effect in his own reign or that of the heir apparent, Anne.[3]

Upon this basis a bargain was struck, and within days new appointments began. Vernon was given a Tory, Sir Charles Hedges, as his fellow Secretary, Godolphin assumed his old place at the Treasury, and Rochester was appointed Lord Lieutenant of Ireland. Harley himself was still not willing to accept a ministerial post, but he had no objection to the offer of the royal nomination as Speaker of the House of Commons, a place to which he now had a considerable claim by reason of his continued personal ascendancy in the House and the respect of his fellow members. The dissolution of Parliament followed a few weeks later, though by that time Harley was back at Brampton for his father's death, writing many a melancholy letter announcing the event to his own and the old parliamentarian's friends.[4]

The new ministerial arrangements were made just in time to meet a

3. H.M.C. *Portland*, iii, 265–6 and 638–9, and *ibid.*, iv, 4; Edward to Robert Harley, 28 Sept., Loan 29/143/2; 'Memoirs of Edward Harley', Add. MSS. 34,515, ff. 10–11 and 13–14.
4. H.M.C. *Portland*, iii, 638–9.

European crisis. In October there arrived news of the long-anticipated death of King Carlos II. William had recently concluded a second treaty with Louis XIV for partitioning the vast Spanish Empire between the French and Imperial candidates, replacing the partition treaty of 1698 which had been made defunct by the death of the Bavarian claimant to whom most of that Empire had seen assigned in the earlier Treaty. But these arrangements left out of account the intentions of Carlos himself, who in the event left a will in which he bequeathed his possessions intact to Prince Philip of Anjou, Louis's grandson. By November it was known that the French King had overthrown the new treaty and accepted the terms of the will. William was aghast at Louis's action, fearing that it was the prelude to aggression and to an eventual juncture between the French and Spanish thrones which would threaten the balance of Europe. Harley and the Tories had other views. They regarded William's treaties as unlikely to have avoided hostilities, since the Emperor in Vienna had not been a party to them despite being one of the interested parties; moreover, they believed that William's assignment of states in Italy to the Dauphin, the heir to the French throne, was an immediate danger to the British 'Levant' trade. On the other hand, several lives stood between the Prince of Anjou and his succession to the French crown, and such a contingency appeared a remote one. Harley's reaction was that the French King's renunciation of the Partition Treaty was 'better than we could expect'. This view was soon shown to be over-optimistic, and was perhaps due to distrust of William rather than to naive trust in Louis. William lamented in private that his English subjects should remain apparently unaffected by the French King's bad faith, but he had advanced too far to back away, and the Tory appointments continued as agreed.[5]

General preparations for the election were already in hand. Matthew Prior the poet wrote '. . . there never was so much work, as at present, in securing Parties, and bribing elections: Whig and Tory are railing on both sides.' Other reports of greater-than-usual bribery were common. The number of candidates in the field was claimed to be without precedent, possibly as high as three thousand. As results became available, from the second half dof January, most accounts agreed that there were substantial Tory advances, with up to thirty seats gained. Harley was reported to 'approve well enough' of the results. And when the new Parliament met in February 1701 his claim to the Chair was recognized by 249 votes against 125 for the moderate Whig Sir Richard Onslow. Within twelve years of Harley's first entry into Parliament he was Speaker of the House of Commons.

5. H.M.C. *Portland*, iii, 634 and 636; Hoffman, in Gaedeke, i, Appendix, p. 124; William, in Kramer, iii, 249.

Already, however, Harley's optimism concerning the Prince of An-jou's accession to the Spanish throne was dampened when news arrived that Dutch troops manning the 'barrier' fortresses in the Spanish Nether-lands were being ejected by Louis XIV's forces, nominally on behalf on his grandson. One of Harley's first tasks as Speaker was to urge the Com-mons to support an appeal from the States General that England should honour treaty obligations by providing ten thousand men and twenty ships in defence of the United Provinces. Members decided unanimously upon a resolution to provide the required forces. He also directed them to take up the settlement of the royal succession, as agreed with William, and in committee on 1 March he obtained further resolutions to set the matter in motion and to make concurrent provision for 'the rights and liberties of the people'. But parallel with these proceedings the first cri-ticisms were raised against the King's two partition treaties. The new Tory ministers did nothing to restrain their followers, and when the veteran Jack Howe rose on 15 February to presage the coming attack the only minister who defended the treaties was Vernon.[7]

The main assault began on 12 March, when it soon became clear that angry as the Tories were at the King, their main object was to inculpate the Junto in the negotiation and secure their destruction. But when the King was called upon for his instructions on the subject to his former ministers he was unhelpful, replying that no documents existed because the instructions had been delivered orally. Thus frustrated, the attackers turned upon William himself and his Dutch associates. On the 29th Portland was voted guilty of high crimes and misdemeanours for help-ing to negotiate the second treaty. During the debate Harley, out of the Chair during a Committee of the whole House, denounced Somers' action in affixing the Great Seal to a blank commission. But when Howe proposed a motion against Somers the former Chancellor's friends rallied and won the support of moderate opinion by arguing that he had sealed the treaty only as a matter of formal duty to the King. By the narrow margin of 189 to 182 votes Somers was again saved from censure. One observer who failed to rejoice, however, was the King, justly incensed at the Whigs' failure to oppose the motion against Portland, in their attempt to divert attention from the part played by their own leaders. Seeking swift revenge William now ensured that the Tories in the Com-mons were given details of the 1698 treaty, in which several ministers were involved. Vernon was reluctantly forced to yield up his letters, and the House soon established that not only Somers but also Orford and Halifax had been aware of the treaty's details. On 14 April all three men

6. Prior, in Cole, Memoirs, p. 269; H.M.C. Portland, iv, 14015; Evelyn Diary, v, 446; Burnet, iv, 476; Bonet, 7/18 Jan., Add. MSS. 30,000E, ff. 3 and 34; Hoffman, in Klopp, ix, 193.
7. Vernon, in Cole, pp.319 and 323; Bonet, 18 Feb./1 Mar., and 21 Feb./4 Mar., Add. MSS. 30,000E, ff. 44 and 48 and 67–8; Horwitz, p. 283.

were impeached, with Harley giving his support from the Chair. Partly
as a result of his exertions in these tense debates Harley was taken ill
shortly after, with an inflammation of the throat, and the Commons
stood adjourned for a week until he recovered.[8]

While the King's favourite and his former ministers were under attack
the House of Commons also turned to the bill for the settlement of the
succession. When a court spokesman rose on 5 March to propose the
succession of the Princess Sophia and her descendants, Harley as Speaker
suggested that devising limitations on the future monarchs should, as
in the case of the Declaration of Rights, take precedence over consideration of the succession itself. The House then went on to resolve that
under the new settlement of the crown no foreigner might be a Member
of Parliament, Privy Councillor, holder of office or grantee of crown
lands. More restrictions were added later: future monarchs must join the
Church of England, and might not involve the realm in war to aid their
foreign possessions, pardon impeached persons, or dismiss judges except
by the request of both Houses of Parliament. Other clauses were added
in the heat of debate but were later repealed as unworkable or imprac-
tical. Together the restrictions which proved permanent were of the
utmost signifiance for the development of British government, equalling
in importance those contained in the Bill of Rights. As in the case of the
previous measure, the support of the new limitations cut across both
parties. Harley, whose practice was to take a leading part of the debates
in committee when he was out of the Chair, led the Tories in support of
limitations but many Whigs too were, as on the earlier occasion, equally
eager to restrict the future monarchy.[9] Harley exulted in what he saw as
national unanimity in the healing of the constitution, and was reported
to have said on the occasion of the passing the Act of Settlement that
'he hoped in a little time our infamous distinctions and parties, but particularly Jacobitism, should be wholly abolished and extirpated'. His
desire was not destined to be fulfilled except in the case of Jacobitism,
and not even that in his lifetime.[10]

While the partition treaties and settlement of monarchy were still
under discussion the House of Commons found little time to provide
monetary supplies to implement its proposal to aid the Dutch. The delay
caused much disquiet both to the King and to those, outside Parliament
as well as within, who feared imminent aggression by Louis XIV. On 8

---

8. Bonet, 17/28 Mar., 1/12 and 15/26 April, Add. MSS. 30,000E, ff. 89, 120–1, 144; 'Memoirs of
   Edward Harley', Add. MSS. 34,515, f. 20; Burnet, iv, 488, Dartmouth's note; Hoffman, in
   Klopp, ix, 217; *Vernon Corr.*, iii, 144; newsletters, Add. MSS 7074, ff. 5 et. 899.
9. Bonet, 8/18, 11/22 and 14/25 Mar., Add. MSS. 30,000E, ff. 67–9, 73 and 77. Bonet's detailed
   account corrects the later Whig interpretation.
10. (John Toland), *Anglia Libra, or the Limitiations and Succession of the Crown of England Explained
    and Asserted*, (1701), p. 50.

May the Speaker received a petition from the Grand Jury of Kent, urging that action should be taken to provide the necessary assistance. But despite the genuine disquiet behind the Kentish petition, and others like it, there were grounds for suspicion that feeling in the country was being orchestrated by the Whigs in Parliament to justify the partition treaties and to divert the Commons from their leaders' impeachment. After an acrimonious debate the five Kentish gentlemen who presented the petition were taken into custody. A week later Harley read from the Chair an open letter which he had received purporting to threaten the vengeance of the people upon those members who endangered the national safety by abetting French designs. This was Daniel Defoe's *Legion's Memorial to the House of Commons*. The response of an angry majority of Tories was to agree to address the King on the subject of the prevalence of efforts to stir up opinion against Parliament. But in the weeks which followed there was every sign of a further organized campaign directed by Somers and his friends to encourage constituents to protest against lack of support for William's treaty commitments.[11] With successive reports from abroad of renewed conflict their cause gained ground. They were aided too by the attitude of the House of Lords, which was much disturbed by the vindictive way in which the impeachments were being conducted. The peers accordingly refused to co-operate with the Lower House even to the extent of setting up a joint committee to settle procedural difficulties. When the Commons, equally disturbed at what they saw as the Lords' partisan protection for the impeached peers, delayed in sending members to appear against Somers and Orford, both men were formally acquitted, and dismissal of the impeachments of Halifax and Portland followed.[12]

Despite the Tories' disappointment over the outcome of the impeachments, Harley assured the King at the prorogation of Parliament on 24 June, in a concluding address on behalf of the Commons, that they would give him their support if the coming summer brought a 'necessary war'.[13] His first session as Speaker had been one of the most eventful and important of modern times. Until October, when he paid a brief visit to Brampton as its new owner, his responsibilities kept him in London against his inclination longer even than in the days of the Commission of Accounts – a pattern often to be repeated in coming years. The King was wrathful with the Tory ministers who had urged on attacks upon his supporters, delayed aid to his Dutch compatriots and even (in Rochester's case) lectured him on constitutional propriety.[14] Harley was un-

11. Bonet, 9/20 and 16/27 May, Add. MSS. 30,000E, ff. 178–9, 193 and 235; *The History of the Kentish Petition*, in *Somers Tracts*, 2nd. Collection, iv, 300; *Parliamentary History*, v, cols. clxxiv – clxxxviii; Ranke, v, 163, citing a Bonet report; *Vernon Corr.*, iii, 151–2.
12. J. Ellis to Stepney, 20 June, Add. MSS. 7074, f. 32; Bonet, 24 June/5 July, Add. MSS. 30,000E, f. 291.
13. Bonet, 27 June 1701, Add. MSS. 30,000E. f. 297.
14. Hill, p. 86.

certain as to whether the ministry would be changed and a new general election called, throwing his continued occupancy of the Chair into question. The King hesitated for months before deciding to make these changes so soon after the last, but his decision was precipitated by the worsening situation in Europe. In September James II died in exile and his protector Louis announced France's recognition of his son as 'James III'. Marlborough, whose action as army commander had eased James II off the throne, was now selected to sign on William's behalf a Treaty of Grand Alliance between Louis's opponents in Europe. In such circumstances war could hardly be averted as soon as the next spring brought campaigning weather. When William returned to England early in November 1701 he immediately dissolved Parliament in the hope of reducing the number of Tory opponents to war preparation. Godolphin resigned the Treasury in protest, but no further changes were made for the moment, a fact which pointed to a desire on the King's part to avoid causing further antagonism by precipitate action. In pursuance of this intention, William attempted to retain Harley as court nominee for the Chair in the forthcoming House of Commons. But Harley, if he wished to retain his connection with the Tories, could not afford to give such retrospective sanction to the dissolution, and refusing the King's customary gift of silver plate to an outgoing Speaker he retired again to Herefordshire to prepare for his re-election at Radnor.[15]

Though the Harleys' seats were now secure the King's appeal to the country was on the whole successful, with a net gain of about thirty for the Whigs. The most judicious opinion was that the results 'seem pretty equal on both sides, so that to which of them the King inclines, that will be the predominant'.[16] The new Parliament began with a closely contested tussle for the Chair between Harley and a court challenger, sometime Speaker Littleton. Both sides made every effort in the crucial test of strength. Godolphin called upon Harley to appear early in London for the 'decisive stroke', while Sunderland likewise urged upon Somers the importance of securing the ascendancy for Littleton. On 29 December, the eve of Parliament's assembling, Hedges was dismissed for refusing to undertake the support of Littleton and was replaced as Secretary of State by a Whig diplomat, Halifax's kinsman the Earl of Manchester. And on the following day Littleton's nomination by Sunderland's son Lord Spencer was seconded on behalf of the court by Vernon. Nevertheless, any hope William may have had that he could force or persuade all the government officeholders to act as a body on behalf of Littleton, as they had against Paul Foley in 1698, was disap-

15. Bonet, 9/20 and 16/27 Dec., Add. MSS. 30,000E, ff. 416 and 420; 'Memoirs of Edward Harley', Add. MSS. 34,515, f. 26; Hoffman, in Klopp, ix, 428.
16. Hill, p. 89; Ellis to Stepney, 16 Dec., Add. MSS. 7074, f. 72, *cf.* Hoffman: 'Both parties find that the King has the whole matter in his hands', Klopp, ix, 499.

pointed, for the support of some 'false servants', of whom the most prominent were the Princess Anne's group, ensured that Harley carried the day, though only by four votes. The bulk of his support was noted by a pamphleteer as 'the best and most honourable (the landed) Interest and the Country Party'.[17]

William in his opening speech, written by Somers, reminded Parliament of the danger to Europe of Louis XIV's activities, asked for the necessary financial assistance, and adjured his hearers to 'lay aside parties and divisions'. He was little heeded. Under Harley's guidance, war supplies, indeed, were put in train, and the Speaker also exerted himself to obtain an extension to funds to pay for past as well as anticipated war debts. But the King further alienated the Tories by dismissing Rochester on 25 January, 1702 to follow Godolphin and Hedges, and by bringing in the Duke of Somerset, a Whig of noble lineage but little ability, as Privy Seal. Such moves did not amount to a return to a Whig ministry, for mone of the leading Whigs had yet been given responsibility; but Harley and the Tories might have been forgiven for thinking that the presence in office of Whigs of the second rank, such as Somerset and Manchester, indicated a caretaker government which would be replaced in due course by the Junto.[18]

Some such fear probably lay behind a bill brought in by Hedges early in the session providing for the taking of an oath, by Members of Parliament, officeholders and clergy, to accept William as 'lawful and rightful' monarch and to abjure the Pretender. The bringing of an Abjuration Bill by the Tories themselves arose out of a need felt by responsible leaders, in the new circumstances brought about by Louis XIV's recognition of 'James III', to forestall any further Whig attempt to make party capital out of Louis's action. The key issue proved to be whether the oath should be imposed or taken voluntarily. The Tories' position, which was in favour of enforcement, was based upon the same reasoning as had been used by Harley at the time of the Association of 1696, that no violation of conscience was involved in subscribing to a compulsory, as distinct from a voluntary, oath. The Whigs struggled hard to make the new oath voluntary, and were defeated by the narrowest possible margin, 188 votes to 187. So far Harley had been able to follow the Tory line, but when an extremist attempted on 19 February to add a provision directed against the Dissenters' practice of occasional conformity to the Church of England, to qualify themselves for office, the Harleys and Foleys joined the

17. H.M.C. *Portland*, iv, 28; 'Lord Sunderland's advice to Lord Somers', Hardwicke, *Miscellaneous State Papers*, II, 458–9; Ellis to Stepney, 19,23 and 30 Dec., Add. MSS. 7074, ff. 73, 75, 77; iii, 199; Shaftesbury, in *Locke Letters*, pp. 120–1; 'The fate of Favourites,' (MSS. tract), Bodleian Library, Rawlinson, MSS. D. 37, p. 7.
18. *Parliamentary History*, v, 1329–31. For Somers' authorship, Burnet, iv, 546, Hardwicke's note; Ellis to Stepney, 13 Feb., Add. MSS. 7074, f. 89; Horwitz, pp. 300–1.

Whigs to reject a proposal which would have touched their own practices and upset government's relations with the City 'monied interest' on the eve of war.[19] On the other hand, Harley had no scruple in his desire to prevent the Junto from ever taking office again. On the 26th the Tories attempted unsuccessfully to revive the last Parliament's impeachments. The motion was entrusted to Henry St John, first elected a year earlier and already a professed adherent of the Speaker, asserting that the Commons had not had 'right done them' by the Lords. Harley, while out of the Chair spoke vigorously deploring the attitude of the House of Lords in the matter of the impeachments.[20]

Whether he would have been content with this protest without further action against the Junto cannot now be determined; for within a few days of the debate the King was known to be mortally ill from a fall while riding, and on 8 March he died. The return to office of the Junto ceased to be a danger, war was imminent and the Tory Queen Anne came to the throne. Harley stood only to gain in court favour from her accession. His political stance coincided closely with that of her favourite Marlborough and of Marlborough's friend Godolphin. In the Commons Harley already stood pre-eminent among the Tories as well as the Old Whigs, though his recent actions on the occasional conformity question delineated the limit of his attachment to the Tories' High Church element. The more moderate Tories trusted him, and were prepared to take his lead. In the new reign his efforts to keep a balance between Old Whig and Tory interests, as well as between his own backbench inclinations and pressure to take office with its limiting responsibilities, would provide a leading theme in national politics.

19. Burnet, iv, 551–2; H.M.C. *Cowper*, iii, 2; Horwitz, p. 303.
20. Hoffman, in Klopp, ix, 503; Bonet and Spanheim, same date, in Ranke, v, 289–90; Shaftesbury, in *Locke Letters*, pp. 125–8.

CHAPTER 6

Court Manager

HARLEY WAS FORTY when Anne came to the throne. To look at he was 'low of stature, and slender'.[1] A conventional portrait by Kneller some years later shows a calm face, a tight and censorious mouth, and a steady, uninquisitive gaze. In conversation his style was often the same as in his oration: earnest, declamatory and diffuse. He cultivated this manner as especially useful in warding off awkward questions, or requests. But in private he sometimes adopted a lighter vein; at one dinner, Henry St John reported, 'he never laid his banter one minute aside'. He once sat next to Secretary of State Vernon in the House of Commons quipping to that worthy administrator that he did so 'to blast your reputation' with the Junto – a purpose which Vernon feared was successful.[2] Harley's main residence when in London was at York Buildings in Villiers Street, though he also maintained rooms at Lincolns Inn, to which he had transferred from the Middle Temple in 1701. He appears to have resided at this lodging occasionally when Sarah and the children were out of London and business still called for his own presence at Westminster. In religion and politics he claimed to follow a pragmatic *via media*. On public occasions he attended the established Church; in private, down to 1704 at least, he continued to take his family to the nonconformist Meeting.[3] He bragged of his adaptability and scorn of doctrinaire policies, and would say 'we must improve all opportunities and consult about the time present'. The general doctrine of government he upheld was that of John Locke and Locke's imitators; a 'mixed monarchy' based on a division of powers – a pedestrian, middle of the road theory acceptable to most politicians of his generation.[4]

Harley's most valuable political asset, however, was a self-assurance which enabled him to ignore complaints of his opponents and made him,

1. Macky, *Memoirs*, p. 84.
2. H.M.C. *Downshire*, i, part 2, p. 810; *Vernon Corr.*, ii, 220.
3. Woodrow, *Analecta*, i, 324.
4. Cunningham, ii, 304.

especially in his later years, insensitive even to the well-intentioned criticism of his friends. This self-confidence was based firmly on his certainty of his moral mission in politics; he believed implicitly that his own integrity, especially in matters of national finance, was needed in public life. When he became Lord Treasurer in 1711, his brother remarked to him: 'It is very strange when there are so very few instances of statesmen's miscarrying who have adhered to the interest of virtue, so few have thought of securing themselves this way.'[5] Such was the family conviction; but Harley himself had also the practical ability to compromise with the needs of everyday politics. In parliamentary management he was above all a lover of secret and devious ways. To some extent these methods were necessary and unexceptional; but with Harley they were becoming an obsession and were carried to such extremes that the comment they aroused largely neutralized their proper value.

On two or more occasions he might have had the post of Secretary of State but had refused. Now the offer was not likely to be repeated. Anne preferred ministers of proven Church principles. Moreover, the nuisance value which had made William willing to buy his services had disappeared with the death of that monarch, and under the Queen he had no immediate claim to office. For the moment, therefore, it was assumed that the Chair of the House of Commons was the most suitable place for him. As the temperature of party politics rose steadily through the next few years Marlborough would have ample opportunity to test his loyalty, and the Queen would have time to tire of the pretensions of her High Church ministers; while Harley himself would travel further along the path from the strictures of opposition to an awareness of the problems of government from the inside.

Harley's mental transformation had begun before the death of William III, stimulated by the High Tories' attempt to penalize 'occasional conformity' and helped by his association with Marlborough and Godolphin, who now set him the task of preparing the Queen's first speech to Parliament.[6] Though Harley modelled it upon a speech which James II had made a like occasion in 1685, some of its phrases, when it was delivered on 11 March 1702, could be construed as a slight upon the as yet unburied William.[7] Such gestures were necessary to bring home to the Whigs that they could no longer expect protection in high places. Furthermore, some sops of comfort had to be given to the Tory backbenchers, for their beliefs could not be allowed a real outlet in the new ministry's policies. The Dutchman was dead, his policies remained. Marlborough continued to prepare for war, and the newly-revived Tory

5. 13 May 1711, Loan 29/143/3.
6. H.M.C. *Portland*, iv, 34.
7. Burnet, v, 2–3. Cf. *Parliamentary History*, vi, 5.

persecution of dissent would alienate the City, upon which the Treasury relied for war loans. The last war had made clear that the efficiency of Britain's effort depended upon her financial organization. If Marlborough had his way the point of concentration of this effort would be the Low Countries, and strong reliable backing for the army would be needed in the Commons. Marlborough was appointed captain-general five days after the Queen's accession. Harley's continuance in the Chair would, it was hoped, secure the co-operation of the House of Commons. Already his support of war policy had brought bitter complaints from the diehards. One such wrote to him, two days after the King's death: Pray consider, upon the foot you now are, you certainly ruin those that have only land to depend on, to enrich Dutch, Jews, French and other foreigners, scoundrel stock-jobbers, and tally-jobbers, who have been sucking our vitals for many years.[8] So far as Harley was concerned the sooner Parliament rose the sooner he would be free, for the moment, from embarrassing criticisms, so like those which he himself had been wont to make. On 26 March he hopefully wagered a guinea with his brother that both Houses would be prorogued within a fortnight.[9] He underestimated the length of the session, however, by no less than six weeks.

The reason for the delay was bound up with a ministerial struggle to decide who would now occupy the Treasury. Godolphin, Marlborough's candidate, found a well-qualified rival in the Queen's uncle Rochester, who had been at the head of the Treasury in Charles II's reign.[10] This pillar of the Tories was determined to oppose Marlborough's intention of ejecting the French from the Dutch Barrier fortresses. Rochester believed, along with his fellow partisans, that Britain's war effort should be confined to the sea, where the standing force of the Navy would need only modest new financial expense.[11] Not until early May did Marlborough's arguments prevail with the Queen to set aside her uncle's claims and appoint Godolphin as Lord Treasurer. For the moment, however, Anne was not persuaded to avoid other High Tory appointments. Rochester himself became Lord Lieutenant of Ireland, and Nottingham, was made Secretary of State for the southern province. The recently dismissed Hedges returned to the northern office. Nottingham, in the role of new broom, immediately began a purge of the staff in their department.[12] With the Earl of Jersey as Lord Chamberlain and Seymour as Comptroller of the royal household, the High Church element in office seemed strong. Two of Harley's friends, though not of his immediate

8. H.M.C. *Portland*, viii, 96.
9. *Norris Papers*, p. 89.
10. First Lord 1779–84; appointed Lord High Treasurer, 1685, by James II.
11. Rochester's views were set out in his Preface to *The History of the Great Rebellion*, by his father, the first Earl of Clarendon, published in May 1702.
12. R. Yard to G. Stepney, 12 May 1702, Add. MS. 7074, f. 212.

political circle, also took office: they were Simon Harcourt, a strong Churchman, who became Solicitor-General, and Henry Boyle, a politique of Godolphin's stamp, who came under the Treasurer as Chancellor of the Exchequer.

The dissolution of Parliament, due within six months of Willaim's death, took place on 3 July, and in the third week of the month Harley went to New Radnor for his own election. The Queen's preference and the appointment of Tory ministers proved sufficient to sway many results.[13] Harley's own election went without hitch, and reports of Tory victories elsewhere reached him at Brampton Bryan. He rejoiced to Godolphin 'there are many violent Whigs left out', and hoped that more would be excluded in election disputes.[14] He had no doubt of his ability to persuade a Tory House of Commons to vote supplies. A week earlier he had outlined his plan of action for this purpose:

> I doubt not [he wrote to Godolphin] but what is to be done as to supplies and the ways of raising them will be as well thought on as is possible before the actual meeting. Will there not be a party that will find imaginary faults unless they be led to what is real and what is expected to be animadverted upon – I mean some accounts? I fear else they will run at riot and do mischief.[15]

Throughout Harley's career, whenever he needed a means to divert the House of Commons from their course, his thoughts turned to the possibility of finding some financial abuses worthy of investigation. This was the method which had made his reputation in the 1690s and which he was to use again with success in Anne's last ministry. The Tories in the new Parliament of 1702 would vote war supplies for Marlborough's campaign the more willingly if evidence could be shown that government wastage under William was being superseded by vigilant economy under the new dispensation.

In the aftermath of elections, the Tories were threatening that the Indian Summer enjoyed by dissent under King William should swiftly come to an end. This campaign had to be diverted if possible, for it frightened the rich City Dissenters whose co-operation was essential to the Treasury. Harley matured his plans for the programme to be laid before the House of Commons. In the Queen's opening speech to the new Parliament Godolphin drafted the sentence: 'And, that my subjects may the more cheerfully bear the necessary texes, I desire you to inspect

13. Weymouth to Nottingham, 14 Aug., MS. 29588, f. 129.
14. Such, no doubt, was what he chiefly had in mind in a remark about the successful Whig 'hot men, whom I hope the government will take care to prevent by applying proper antidotes', 9 Aug., 1702, Add. MS. 28,055, f. 3.
15. *Catalogue of the collection . . . formed by Alfred Morrison* (ed. A.W. Thibaudeau, privately printed, 1883–92), v, 77.

the Accounts of all the public Receipts and Payments', to which Harley added the words: 'And, if there have been any Abuses or Mismanagements, I hope you will detect them, that the offenders may be punished and others be deterred by such examples from the like practices'.[16] So the scene was set for a new commission of accounts, with the difference that where Harley had once led the Commons' attack on the ministry he would now direct their wrath towards past misdeeds, in the hope of diverting them from present grievances.

The curtain-raiser for Parliament was Harley's re-election, on 20 October, to the Chair of the House of Commons. He had the enthusiastic support of the main body of the Tories led by his friend Bromley; and the government's official backing was indicated by his proposer, Nottingham's brother, Heneage Finch.[17] The chief objection raised to his election, that a new precedent would be created by his holding the position for a third successive Parliament, was overborne by his popularity with the great majority of the members.[18] After the election and the delivery of the Queen's speech the two Houses stood adjourned for a week while stock was taken of newcomers to the House of Commons. It has been estimated that the new House contained a Tory majority of over 130. The Tories' strength was demonstrated on 2 November, when they brought a motion, this time successfully, declaring that the Lords had not given the Commons justice last year over the impeachments.[19] The vote might have heralded a revival of the attack on the Junto; but in fact no further action was taken, and this was largely the work of Harley, in his new role of court manager, insisting from the beginning that 'the enmities of parties ought to be forgotten'.[20]

In other ways, however, party strife was less easily suppressed. The enmities of Tories and Whigs, born in the Exclusion Crisis and continued in hundreds of constituency struggles as each side sought revenge and counter-revenge under James II and William III, were not to be diverted. The new Tory members returned in 1702 were even more eager than their more long-standing compatriots to set the score straight. They had the full support of their constituents, for as Bishop Burnet was to write five or six years later: 'the parties are now so stated and kept up, not only by the elections of parliament men, that return every third year, but

16. *CJ*, xiv, 4. The portion of the speech amended by Harley is reproduced in Sir Tresham Lever's *Godolphin, his life and times* (1952), opposite p. 140. *Cf.* H.M.C. *Portland*, iv, 47.
17. Bromley to Arthur Charlett, 22 Oct. 1702, Bodleian, Ballard MS. 38, f. 137: 'All now approved,or at least acquiesced in, the calling the same gentleman to the Chair that last year we could not have without the greatest struggle and difficulty'; Add. MS. 7078, f. 165.
18. Cunningham, i, 311.
19. Burnet, v, 45; *CJ*, xiv, 12. A modern computation of party allegiances, by Professor W.A. Speck, puts the Tories at 323 and Whigs at 190 before disputed elections were considered – Speck, *Tory and Whig*, p. 123.
20. Cunningham, i, 352.

even by the yearly elections of mayors and corporation-men, that they know their strength; and in every corner of the nation the two parties stand, as it were, listed against one another'.[21] Corporation boroughs in particular were the scene of many party vendettas, often based on sectarian differences.[22] High Tory objections to the Dissenters' habit of taking the sacrament of the Eucharist solely to qualify themselves for a national or local office arose partly out of a belief that the practice was blasphemous. Many Churchmen spoke, like Bromley, of 'that abominable hypocrisie, that inexcusable immorality of Occasional Conformity'.[23] But the Tories' motives in wishing to prevent this practice were clearly political as well as religious. They were determined to cut off the creeping tendrils of dissent where it clung to office and power, and to prevent Dissenters from casting votes in the many borough seats controlled by office holders. To Bromley was given the task of bringing a bill to punish those who resorted to dissenting chapels while ostensibly conforming to the established Church.

The Occasional Conformity bill gave an opportunity to Henry St John, who assisted Bromley in drawing the bill and was already becoming prominent among the Tories in the Commons. Though lacking Bromley's religious motive, St John was determined to lead the Tory pack on every suitable occasion. In later years he was to write: 'You know the nature of that assembly: they grow, like hounds, fond of the man who shows them game, and by whose halloo they are used to be encouraged'.[24] Born, like Harley, into a parliamentary family, but seventeen years later, he typified the cynical outlook of the Restoration generation as Harley in some ways represented the older generation of parliamentary Puritans. St John professed to follow Harley's example and leadership, but though he swiftly mastered the political methods which Harley had developed in the parliamentary in-fighting of the 1690s, he did not share the older man's moral earnestness. He had taken Harley's place as spokesman for the Commission of Accounts and was charged with carrying out his leader's plan of campaign. On 11 November, also with Bromley, St John brought before the Commons a report by the commissioners on financial malpractices alleged to have been committed by the Paymaster-General, Lord Ranelagh. Later, further reports also implicated Halifax, as Auditor of the Receipt of the Exchequer.[25]

Of the two issues thus raised, religious dissent and financial misconduct, Harley found the first a source of deep embarrasment and the

---

21. Burnet, vi, 224.
22. 'I was made a party man very early being baptised' – J. Hooke to Harley, 12 Aug. 1710, Loan 29/147/3.
23. Bromley to Charlett, 22 Oct. 1702, Bodleian, Ballard MS. 38, f. 137.
24. Bolingbroke, *Letter to Sir William Wyndham* (1717); Dickinson, p. 33.
25. *CJ* xiv, 27 sqq. *Parliamentary History*, vi, 97–135.

second not easily controllable, but there was no holding the tide of Tory feeling. In public he made no objection to the Occasional Conformity Bill as it swiftly passed through the House of Commons.[26] As Speaker, however, he was able to avoid committing himself so deeply as completely to alienate the Dissenters. His chief object was to further the passing of supplies, and for this purpose he had to allay the fears of the Whigs, who might prove obstructive as in 1689. Fortunately the depressed status of the Whigs in the House of Commons made them eager to be convinced by his secret reassurances, and he was able to play with good effect on their hope that he might be forced to oppose High Tory religious intolerance if it went further and threatened the Toleration Act of 1689. Already current before the session began, this belief gained ground considerably in the following months. It was expressed by the third Earl of Shaftesbury:

> He is ours at bottom...I believe there is hopes of gaining him. If he who was done so much to divide and break and ruin his own party and friends will but do half as much to piece 'em up and unite them, the thing will be easy and the cause our own. This gentleman and others will then soon come over. God grant that he I mean may be so wise: there is hopes too of this: for great steps are taken, and we are bid to hope.[27]

Such opinions, held by many Whigs who did not understand the extent of Harley's aversion from the Junto or of his ties with the landowning and Church party, did much to assist his clandestine negotiations. He would often say 'men are more apt to be influenced by hopes than rewards'. 'Hope' was all that Shaftesbury and many others ever received from him, and this he gave in abundance. He also found some good to say of William III and, (as Cunningham tells us) 'at his table would launch out in praise of the manner of his death as if it had been above the condition of mortal man, and like that of the ancient heroes. But this was in secret, for in public he took part with the Tories.'[28] Harley's endeavour to convince the moderate Whigs that he was in agreement with much that they held dear was to be a leading theme of his activities for much of his career.

Far more difficult than raising the expectations of the humbled Whigs was the task of restraining the victorous Tories. Apart from the diversionary tactics he had outlined to Godolphin, Harley's main intention was to attach enough Tories to the court to be able, with the assistance of the Whigs, to vote for the essential services of government and war. In

---

26. Cunningham, i, 317.
27. *Locke Letters*, p. 146.
28. Cunningham, i, 369 and 315.

this and the following sessions he laboured to form a party based on the court. To help him he had the vast reservoir of patriotic feeling which was always available to parliamentary leaders who knew how to tap and direct its flow; and for a nucleus of placemen within this group he could rely on crown and Treasury patronage and hope of patronage. Government control of the House by this means, which had conspicuously failed during the burning issues of William's last years, was to be patiently built up by the man who had done most to demolish it.

In one quarter, however, Harley met resistance which considerably hampered his efforts. Opposition came from within the ministry, for though Nottingham's influence was thrown behind Harley into inducing the House of Commons to provide for Marlborough's next campaign, Rochester had withdrawn himself and those who followed his lead in the Lower House into truculent opposition.[29] But on only one occasion were the recalcitrant Tories able to gain enough support to reject a request for expenditure, and this concerned Marlborough's personal income, not the cost of his theatre of war. After a successful campaign Queen Anne raised Marlborough to a dukedom, but government speakers including Harley vainly urged the House of Commons to implement the Queen's suggestion of a permanent parliamentary grant of £5,000 a year; even Harley's usual Tory friends drew back at the suggestion of so great a gift.[30]

On the Occasional Conformity Bill and the pursuit of Whig scapegoats the ministerial speakers had to give the Tories their head, and the session ended in deadlock between the Commons and the Whig majority in the House of Lords. Ranelagh, whose venality was notorious, had to resign his office of Paymastive-General and was expelled from the Lower House. The charges against Halifax were less acceptable to Harley and harder to prove, and with the Junto lords taking the lead in his defence the former First Lord was easily exonerated. The peers also returned the Occasional Conformity Bill to the Lower House with wrecking amendments. In both issues Harley was probably not sorry to see the quarrel develop into a series of angry debates between the two Houses; a good constitutional struggle with the Lords could divert the Commons from other mischief. Furthermore, such a cause increased Harley's popularity; the Tories might accuse him of favouring the Whigs, even of secretly shielding Halifax from justice, but in refutation of such charges he could point to his conduct in the disputes with the Whig House of Lords.[31] Parliament rose on 27 February 1703, with the essential supplies voted for all theatres of war. If Harley could not regard the session with entire satis-

29. *Ibid.*, i, 266.
30. *Norris Papers*, p. 106.
31. See the political squib in Add. MS. 7074, f. 127.

faction, he had achieved his chief purpose and come through with enhanced prestige both in the Commons and in the eyes of Godolphin,
who rewarded him with the lucrative life office of Auditor of the Imprest for his brother Edward. In addition, he had made the beginning
of a court party with which to face the next meeting. In the next two
sessions, while he remained Speaker, the pattern of the first session of
Queen Anne's reign was to be closely repeated, both in issues and in the
quarrels between the two Houses.

As the public stage of Parliament emptied, and the actors dispersed to
their counties and boroughs, the drama was transferred to a private stage.
Throughout 1702 the Earl of Rochester had sorely taxed the patience of
the Queen by his open sponsorship of High Tory policies, despite the
warning implied by his failure to obtain the Treasury. Not only had he
encouraged his supporters to attempt to thwart Harley's efforts in the
House of Commons but he had continued his advocacy of a colonial
and sea war, urging Nottingham to disperse resources by sending a naval
expedition to the West Indies.[32] At the conclusion of the session Marlborough convinced the Queen that Rochester should be forced to take
up his duties in distant Ireland. Rather than do this, Rochester elected
to resign.

The removal of this minister took Harley a step closer to the centre
of power. The leadership of the Tories in the cabinet now devolved
upon Nottingham, who had never been on good terms with Harley and
was on worse with Marlborough. The captain-general assured Godolphin
that Nottingham would follow Rochester if he continued, in collusion
with lesser ministerial Tories like Seymour, to obstruct the Treasurer's
efforts.[33] For the moment Harley formed with Marlborough and Godolphin a leadership already being mentioned as a triumvirate. Harley was
careful to keep Marlborough posted with the threats of the High Tories.
Writing to his Duchess in June Marlborough mentioned: 'The conversa-
sion that was between [Rochester] and [Harley] is noe doubt the langui-
age that [Rochester] entertains the whole party with all; and if they can
once be strong enough to declare which way the warr shall be managed,
they may ruin England and Holland at their pleasure...'[34]

However, Harley's chief task in the summer months was to set about
obtaining as much moderate Tory support for the next session as was
possible while Nottingham remained in office. One way of doing this was
by influencing public opinion. Harley had continued to use the power of
the press late in William's reign when he had assisted Charles Davenant,
author of The True Picture of a Modern Whig and its sequels, with materi-

32. Rochester to Nottingham, 21 Sept., and 8 Oct. 1702, Add. MS. 29,588, ff. 253 and 316.
33. Churchill, ii, 274.
34. 10/21 June 1703, Snyder, i, 203.

cal and in formation. These tracts popularized the Country Party which had assailed the King and the Junto in King William's last years.[35] In the first months of the new reign Harley pointed out to Godolphin the necessity for a regular publication of the government's case by a 'discreet writer', though whether he had Davenant or some other person in mind does not appear.[36] But soon the satire *The Shortest Way with Dissenters* by the Dissenter Daniel Defoe showed that a more effective, as well as more easily influenced writer was available. While Parliament sat, Harley urged the discovery of the identity of the author.[37] But by the time Nottingham had hunted down Defoe and lodged him in Newgate, both Godolphin and Harley were becoming more appreciative of Defoe's views. Harley accordingly visited Defoe in prison and, finding him bitter at his usage by Nottingham and therefore a ripe ally on both private and public grounds, came to terms. Defoe was to receive 200 marks from the Treasury to pay his fine, and in return hold himself ready for any duty the government might require.[38] Thus began the alliance between Harley and Defoe, which resulted in securing the most prolific, and almost the most effective, political writer of the age, as well as an enthusiastic student of public opinion whose reports became increasingly important to Harley by making him constantly aware of the national mood. Defoe's letters to his new master still make fascinating reading on the politics and society of the day.

Some such precautions seemed increasingly necessary in 1703, a bad year for the ministry. In Flanders and the West Indies, British arms had suffered setbacks. But another likely cause of disturbance in the English Parliament in the autumn of 1703, were the affairs of Scotland. While the failure of the recent scheme for a Scottish colony at Darien still rankled bitterly, the Scottish nation had been thrown into further confusion after the accession of Anne by the withdrawal from its Parliament of the Duke of Hamilton, with many of his followers, on the grounds that continued sittings after King William's death were illegal.[39] The northern Parliament had ended in June 1702, and the subsequent policy of the ministry, calling elections in Scotland for a new Parliament in 1703, was attributed to the insistence of Nottingham, who supported Hamilton's stand; whereas Harley threw his influence with those who argued that the war supplies voted in the last session were legal and that it would be injudicious as well as unnecessary to summon another meeting immediately. In his advice to Godolphin, Harley professed 'neither wit nor skill to reason upon these heads myself'; but his adviser was his

35. H.M.C. *Portland*, iv, 5 and 30.
36. Harley to Godolphin, 9 Aug. 1702, Add. MS. 28,055, f. 3.
37. Godolphin to Nottingham [late 1702 or early 1703], Add. MS. 29,589, f. 400.
38. H.M.C. *Eighth Report*, part i, p. 43; H.M.C. *Portland*, iv, 68.
39. *Lockhart Papers*, i, 45.

friend the Reverend William Carstares, Principal of Edinburgh University, a sage political observer whose opinion deserved to have been better heeded.[40] During the winter of 1702–3 the discontent of both nations was increased when their commissioners held an unsuccessful series of meetings in London to discuss the possibility of a Union of Parliaments. And when the Scottish Parliament met in the following summer, its activities were even more turbulent than Harley had feared. The parties joined to pass anti-English measures, especially a Bill of Security to which the Queen refused her consent, designed to force colonial and commercial concessions from England by threatening to exclude the House of Hanover from the throne of Scotland. When the session ended on 16 September Harley's original advice seemed more than justified.

With all the events of the summer in mind, his assessment of the situation, written to Godolphin on 20 September, was not encouraging:[41]

> I have had much converse of late with the hot people of both sides, they who are come off their progress in the north as well as others are very angry...Their complaints are of the mismanagements of the fleet, the uselessness of an offensive warr in Flanders; and both sides will have it that there is a designe against the House of Hanover, and particularly that it appeared in Scotland and by direction from the English ministers.

Before Harley left London in late September for Brampton he submitted to Bromley a 'scheme' for concerting the government's demands for war supplies. The price of Bromley's help was, no doubt, the government's support for a new Occasional Conformity Bill; he replied 'it is only you can raise a building suitable to this foundation. I hope that work is done.'[42] Harley could now safely promise to raise no obstacles in the House of Commons because he knew that the Queen intended to discourage the bill through her husband, Prince George, in the House of Lords.[43] This in itself relieved Harley of a great deal of anxiety, for it meant that he could co-operate with Bromley in the House and leave the Upper House to deal, in a more direct fashion than previously, with the Occasional Conformity Bill. When Harley returned to London, towards the end of October Hedges was detached from his fellow Secretary Nottingham and showed himself prepared to follow Harley's leadership in the House of Commons. Harley himself met Marlborough and Godolphin

40. Harley to Godolphin, 9 Aug. 1702, Add. MS. 28,055, f. 3; H.M.C. *Portland*, viii, 106.
41. 20 Sept. 1703, Blenheim MSS. B 2–33. The remainder of this letter is printed in H.M.C. *Eighth Report*, part i, p. 43.
42. Bromley to Harley, 25 Sept. 1703, Loan 29/191/93. (The original is slightly fuller than the printed version in H.M.C. *Portland*, iv, 67, and also makes clear that the 'scheme' was Harley's).
43. *Conduct of the Duchess of Marlborough*, p. 166.

twice weekly to decide matters of policy before cabinet council meetings.[44] This arrangement, of which Nottingham can hardly have been entirely unaware, indicated Marlborough's and Godolphin's intention of replacing Nottingham by Harley in the Secretaryship as soon as an opportunity arose.

Nottingham's main difference with Marlborough now concerned war strategy. During the summer of 1703 the Secretary had carried through the 'Methuen' treaty with Portugal (named after its negotiator Paul Methuen) which not only initiated a long-lasting alliance but called for the presence of a British army in Portugal and Spain. The original Grand Alliance had returned to William III's principle of partition of the Spanish Empire; the new treaty bound its signatories to obtain the whole Spanish inheritance for the Habsburg candidate. The Dutch, in particular, dislike the new commitment and agreed to it only with great reluctance.[45] Apart from the attitude of this ally, Marlborough was reminded by the withdrawal of several of his regiments from Flanders for Portugal, late in 1703, of the inexpediency of letting Nottingham have his way.[46]

Within a month of first meeting, the Commons passed the Occasional Conformity Bill and sent it up to the House of Lords, where it was this time rejected outright on the second reading. Thereafter the two Houses were occupied with squabbles based upon Tory-Whig differences. The Commons threatened to re-open the impeachment issue of 1701, concerning the former Whig ministers, and the Lords attacked the present ministry, especially Nottingham who was accused of shielding Jacobites suspected of involvement in a recently discovered plot.[47] The chief inter-House bickering concerned the famous constitutional issues involved in the case of Ashby *versus* White. The stand taken by Harley as Speaker was in favour of the Commons' claim to determine the right of an elector to his vote, but he attempted as far as possible to limit the dispute to a judicial rather than a political plane, and in his speeches he appears, judging by one recorded during the following session, to have insisted on bringing the wide-ranging debates back to the legal issues.[48] The Junto-led House of Lords put the determination of voting right in the hands of the courts. Both sides were well aware that not only the ostensible issue of Wharton's control of Aylesbury borough but also the nature of parliamentary elections was at stake, and Harley's stand for

44. H.M.C. *Portland*, iv, 75.
45. Alexander Stanhope to Hedges, 1/11 [sic] Sept. 1703, P.R.O. State Papers 84/226, part i, f. 30.
46. Churchill, ii, 207.
47. *Vernon Corr.*, iii, 241, 144; Boyer, *Annals*, ii, 190–206.
48. Chandler, *Debates*, iii, 360–2; for a good account of the case, see Eveline Cruickshanks, 'Ashby *versus White*: the case of the men of Aylesbury, 1701–4' in Clyve Jones (ed)., *Party and Management*, pp. 87–106.

the Commons' claim to determine the franchise was characteristric of the generation's most devoted parliament man.

As soon as this wearying session ended, the triumvirs made their move against Nottingham. Harley reported to Marlborough that the secretary had been heard to express approval of a High Tory plan to 'tack' the next Occasional Conformity Bill to a money bill to ensure its passing the Lords: Marlborough, relating the story to Godolphin, added 'the Speaker will be able to let you know how much of it may be true'.[49] Nottingham himself anticipated the expected attack by asking the Queen to demonstrate confidence in him by dismissing two Whigs, the Dukes of Devonshire and Somerset, who had been foremost in censuring his handling of the Scottish Plot.[50] When she refused and responded by dismissing Jersey and Seymour, Nottingham asked on 20 April to be relieved of his office.

By forcing the Queen to choose between himself and Marlborough, Nottingham played into his opponents' hands, for the general was indispensable and the secretary was not. At this point, however, an obstacle arose. Harley was offered the secretary's post, but to Marlborough's chagrin he demurred. His reasons for still not accepting at once, despite the recent indications, are not entirely clear, but several possibilities may be suggested. He may have felt some qualms about his ability to carry out some aspect of the duties required. For conferences with representatives of other states his knowledge of French was inadequate; he could understand the language but not speak it as well as Latin, a handicap when dealing with ministers whose command of English was not good.[51] This difficulty was not, however, insuperable, and another reason for his hesitation was probably the hope of bargaining for places for his supporters. Of the adherents appointed immediately, St John became Secretary at War in place of William Blathwayt, and Thomas Mansell took office as Treasurer of the Household. Yet a further three weeks passed before Harley could be persuaded to take office. During this time Harley was negotiating with Godolphin for the admission of the Duke of Newcastle.[52] The Duke was a Whig landowner of great wealth and moderate political ambitions, and his political allegiance was likely to be obtained by the man who secured him the Privy Seal, at present held by his Yorkshire territorial rival, the Duke of Buckingham. Furthermore, it is probable that Harley was already contemplating the marriage of his son Edward, now at Westminster School, to Newcastle's only daughter. But for the moment Newcastle's aspirations were disappointed.

A final reason for Harley's reluctance to take the post was the knowledge that such a step would cut him off from many ties in the House of

49. Snyder, i, 274.
50. Burnet, v, 134 and 141; Coxe, Marlborough, i, 229.
51. Add. MS. 17,677, WWW, ff. 610. Cf. Vernon Corr., iii, 260.
52. H.M.C. Portland, ii, 184–5.

Commons. Hitherto, he had been able to shelter to some extent behind the theoretical impartiality of the Chair; to take Nottingham's place would commit him irrevocably, in Tory eyes, to Marlborough's policies. Harley was always reluctant to be committed too closely to any political path. But his actions during the last two years pointed to only one logical step; and Godolphin assiduously urged him not to decline again.[53] His last objections were swept away as a *nolo episcopari*, and on 16 May 1704 he took over the northern province of the Secretaries' office from Hedges, the latter moving, by a customary arrangement, to the southern and usually senior department in place of Nottingham. There was no doubt, however, that on this occasion Harley was to be the leading secretary, and in the embryonic cabinet which had achieved a regular standing since Anne came to the throne, he would be one of the most important members, a 'triumvir' along with Godolphin and Marlborough.

53. H.M.C. *Portland*, v, 647.

CHAPTER 7

Secretary of State

THE TWO SECRETARIES of State shared responsibility for home affairs but divided foreign business between them. To Harley fell all duties connected with 'northern' Europe, including the Dutch United Provinces, Scandinavia, Russia, Austria and the states of Germany. With his new appointment, Harley entered upon an unfamiliar stage. He had little experience of administration, less of diplomacy. For all but two years of his parliamentary career he had voiced back-bench discontent against the responsible ministers of the crown; for two years he had co-operated with the ministers without sharing their responsibilities. His whole experience had directed his thoughts to England's constitutional and financial problems, not to continental involvements. It is true that during his years as Speaker he had drawn away from the Tory die-hards in the Commons who would have avoided any entanglement in continental war; it is also true that he had alienated the noble Tory leaders and was to do so still more. But he had not abandoned the beliefs of the lower landed class as fully as had Marlborough and Godolphin, and clashes were to arise from the mistaken belief of these ministers that they had weaned him entirely from his earlier ideas.

Especially was this the case with Godolphin, who of the two was thrown into closer contact with Harley. Down to 1704 Harley's chief service to these ministers had been his touch upon the pulse of the House of Commons, his undisputed territory; and his relationship with Godolphin could thus be founded on the respect each felt for the other's abilities. Nevertheless, Harley's habits of mind had occasionally annoyed the precise and clear-thinking Treasurer, whose letters display a testy sarcasm at Harley's obscurities of expression. In return Harley adopted an exaggerated and sometimes provocative style of deference to Godolphin's wishes. As soon as Harley was translated to an administrative department his vagaries of method increased such mutual irritability, causing misunderstandings and anger which added fuel to the more substantial differences of opinion that later developed between the two men. With Marlborough, Harley was always on closer terms. Even after Harley and

Godolphin fell out over home affairs, the captain-general was to retain
a good deal of sympathy for Harley's outlook. Harley, for his part, was
conscious that he had been appointed to carry out Marlborough's foreign
policy. Yet he brought to diplomacy a habit of mind drilled on the floor
of the House of Commons, and he could not readily lose contact with the
back-bench interpretation of England's foreign commitments. One of his
chief duties would now be to justify the government's foreign policy to
the House. At this point, therefore, it is convenient to consider Harley's
first official contacts with other nations in the capacity of Secretary of
State.

How did he envisage the European situation in 1704? During his
whole lifetime the mighty shadow of Louis XIV had fallen over Europe;
Louis invading the United Provinces, persecuting the Huguenots, de-
vastating the Palatinate, supporting British pensioner kings and pre-
tenders. Harley never went outside the British Isles, so it is not surprising
that his thinking was conventionally insular, or that he saw the wars of
his time as part of a prolonged struggle against Catholicism. Like most of
his generation he was well aware of the economic issues involved, but the
kernel of his conception of the European situation was his Protestantism.
A new factor in this situation appeared to give substance to his point
of view. Within his province fell the Great Northern War involving
Sweden against Peter the Great's Russia, and in the summer of 1704
this conflict impinged upon the War of the Spanish Succession with
the conquest of Poland by Swedish forces led by King Charles XII. One
of the King's objects was the restoration of the civil and religious rights
of Protestant inhabitants of the Empire, and he proposed the invasion of
Imperial territories unless his wishes were granted. Furthermore, Swedish
diplomacy refused to envisage the whole of the Spanish inheritance falling into the hands of the House of Austria, as arranged by Nottingham's
diplomacy.[1] Such views, held by a warlike nation, constituted a serious
problem for the diplomats of Europe when, in July 1704, two months
after Harley's appointment, Charles XII solemnly deposed Poland's
elected King, the Elector Augustus of Saxony.

Harley's training inclined him to sympathize with Charles XII. From
his family he inherited the Puritan's instinctive sympathy with Sweden's
self-imposed role as the Protestant conscience of Europe, a sympathy
which had once moved Oliver Cromwell in similar circumstances. Shortly after his appointment Harley began to draw upon the agile and well-
informed mind of Daniel Defoe on a number of political issues; and
among other matters, they discussed Charles XII's presence in Poland
and a rebellion of the Hungarian subjects of the Emperor. It was with
Harley's views in mind that Defoe drew up afterwards a memorandum on

1. H.M.C. *Portland*, ix, 220.

the topics they had discussed. After dealing with domestic affairs and other aspects of foreign policy Defoe continued:

> ...the whole confederacy [sc. of the Grand Alliance] are bound in consequence to support the Emperor against the Hungarians and the King of Poland against the Swedes. If it be objected why not as well the Swede against the Pole and the Hungarians against the Emperor, since otherwise you fight against the Protestant religion, I return, *This is not a war of religion*.[2]

Thus it appears that Defoe believed the basis of Harley's thinking on these subjects to be religious rather than strategic.

On taking office Harley found England's relations with Sweden already strained. The reason was the status of Sweden as a neutral sea-power in the War of the Spanish Succession. The Navy had frequently interfered with Swedish vessels suspected of carrying naval supplies to France. Harley expressed to Godolphin his fears that the French would succeed in inciting the Swedish King to erupt into Saxony in pursuit of King Augustus; and he was unwilling to risk further friction over the carrying trade. In July a Swedish convoy was intercepted by an English squadron and brought into the Thames. Harley took steps at once to obtain its release.[3] He succeeded so well in mollifying the Swedish envoy, Count Leyoncrona, that the two men remained on the best of terms in the future. Harley's attitude to the northern problem was not in itself contrary to Marlborough's strategy, but his attitude to the Allied powers which stood in danger from Swedish policy did constitute some difference of opinion, a difference which appeared in 1704 only in the degree of emphasis which they placed on the need to conciliate Allies, but widened in the end to a difference in policy.

To the Emperor Leopold, Harley showed little sympathy and much indignation. Having put the Hungarians through a long course of oppression and injustice, the Emperor found himself, in 1704, with a rebellion on his hands. While a series of defeats was suffered by the Allies in Italy for want of German troops, the Emperor fought his own subjects and entertained his allies England and Holland with insincere offers to let them mediate. After Marlborough's brilliant campaign ending at Blenheim had saved Germany from French invasion, the cabinet instructed Harley, on hearing that the Emperor proposed to recall a further 20,000 men into Hungary, to protest 'that is an ill return to her Majesty'.[4] Harley's correspondence with this court was a stream of intermingled com-

2. C.F. Warner, 'An Unpublished Political Paper by Daniel Defoe', *EHR*, xxii (1907), p. 140.
3. Count Leyoncrona's memorandum, 3 July 1704, P.R.O. SP 104/154 f. 6; [Harley to Godolphin], 17 July 1704, Add. MS 28,055, f. 94; H.M.C. *Portland*, viii, 130–1; Harley to John Robinson, 25 August 1704, P.R.O. SP 104/154, f. 17.
4. Harley's minute, 3 July 1704, Loan 29/9.

plaints and threats. Above all, he pointed out that Blenheim could not be repeated and the Emperor must make shift to defend himself against the French next season; and he instructed the English envoy at Vienna, in vivid phraseology at variance with the usual staid language of diplomacy, to intimate to the Court that 'tho' the Devil be now cast out, if he be suffered to enter again he will bring seven worse Spirits with him'. His refrain to this warning, then and later, was: '. . . nor will our Parliament heer be very ready to continue their supplies for carrying on a war to support those who will not (tho they can) help themselves'.[5]

Hardly more auspicious were Harley's first official dealings with the United Provinces. From the beginning of the war the English Parliament had clamoured that the Dutch should give up their considerable trade with the enemy. The Dutch government had agreed, in return for an increase in the quota of English forces in the Low Countries, to prohibit this trading for one year. Harley's first task in the spring of 1704 was to ask for a renewal of the prohibition. But on this occasion the Dutch ministers were unable to persuade the States General to renew a commercially crippling restriction.[6] Another point to which Harley had often to return in his correspondence with this ally was their annual failure to fulfil their quota of one war vessel for every two English vessels in the Allied fleets. In the summer of 1704 the position was even worse than usual, for the Dutch had actually withdrawn six ships from an English squadron. Harley's private correspondent in Amsterdam, the British banker John Drummond, informed him that the reason for this action was '. . . private interest in favour of Vice Admiral van der Dussen, who commanded said six ships. The Pensionary Heinsius is said Admiral's near cousin. . .'[7] Such charges on the British side were frequent; whether they were true or not, Harley found his task made more difficult in the House of Commons, where he was forced to defend the Dutch war effort against the Tory back benches. To one diplomat he wrote, after 'two long toilsome days' spent in shepherding the Land Tax through the Commons: 'many very honest gentlemen are uneasy possessed with a notion that we perform our parts, and the States suffer the common good to languish and our efforts to be fruitless for want of supplying their proportion last year at sea'.[8]

Harley's relationship with the Tories was a problem exercising the minds of many politicians as the time drew near for the meeting of Parliament in the autumn of 1704. James Vernon, who as Secretary of State to William III had suffered many sessions of parliamentary intransigence

---

5. To G. Stepney, 1 Sept. 1704 and 14 Aug. 1705, Add. MSS. 7059, ff. 33 and 77.
6. Harley to A. Stanhope, 30 May 1704, P.R.O. SP 104/72; p. 5; Stanhope to Harley, 7/18 July 1704, P.R.O. SP 84/227, part ii, f. 453/456.
7. 6 Jan. 1705 (N.S.), Loan 29/45x/1 (Drummond).
8. To Stanhope, 7/18 Dec. 1704, P.R.O. SP 104/72, p. 73.

directed by Harley, was an interested spectator of the new Secretary's actions: at present (Vernon noted immediately after Harley's appointment) 'the Tories lay the late changes at his door, and the Whigs hold themselves in suspense, not seeing any advances made towards them'.[9] Since the beginning of Queen Anne's reign, Tory opinion had been capable of regarding Harley as a renegade for supporting preparations for Marlborough's war. Conscious of the intensification of this feeling after the dismissal of Nottingham, he made every effort in the summer of 1704, by forwarding the interests of the Church, to compensate the Tories for his political support of Marlborough and Godolphin. At this time Harley was assisting Francis Atterbury, the leader of the Tory lower clergy, in his struggle to be instituted Dean of Carlisle by the Whig Bishop, William Nicholson, of Carlisle; he also forwarded the cause of Bishop Jonathan Trelawney of Exeter over the right to dispose of a living in that diocese.[10]

By early autumn, however, rumours of Tory discontent were all-pervasive. The ministry, unwilling to risk the election of an intransigent Tory to the Chair of the House of Commons, had decided that Harley must remain Speaker; but there existed no exact precedent for his holding a ministerial post together with this office, and criticism was expected from the House when it met. He received warnings that he was generally classed with Marlborough and Godolphin in the ministry, and that this standing did him no service with the 'country'. The tone of one country gentleman's plaint may serve as an example of the rest:

> others say that no gentleman's interest in England could have been equal to yours, had you accepted of no place at all, but only the Speaker's, which they say would have been constantly entailed upon you, nobody could have stood in competition with you; that then the Court would always have courted and feared you, and the Country been managed by you. . .

Similar country dissatisfaction at Harley's combination of offices was reported to him by Daniel Defoe who had undertaken, on Harley's secret service, the first of his tours to discover public opinion and disseminate propaganda on behalf of the ministry.[11]

It was against this background of political unease that a private as well as the public drama was played out when Harley arrived in London on 20 October 1704 from his autumn visit to Brampton. He found his son Edward ill with smallpox at Westminster School. His troubles he related to his friend the Duke of Newcastle, adding 'as to the quarrel some would

9. *Vernon Corr.*, iii, 260.
10. H.M.C. *Portland*, iv, 127, 129, and 131; *The Miscellaneous Works of Bishop Atterbury* (1789–90), i, 329–35.
11. H.M.C. *Portland*, iv, 119, 147.

have with the Chair, your humble servant would be very glad to be fairly eased of that trouble'. But Edward recovered, and the session opened without opposition to his retention of the office of speaker. His tone became more cheerful. He told the envoy at Vienna, George Stepney: 'We have just entered upon our Parliament campaigne, there are many murmurings and hollow noise of distant winds, but I hope no such storme can rise as will endanger the public.'[12]

This hope was not fulfilled, and there began one of the liveliest sessions of Harley's career. Bromley went ahead with a new Occasional Conformity Bill, spurred by a warning from his constituents at Oxford that he would not be re-elected if he did not introduce the bill as before. He was still supported by some members of the government including Harcourt, who believed 'we shall not fail to do it unless some of our members become Trimmers, which God forbid', and possibly by St John with the reservation that the matter should not delay voting of war supplies.[13] But Harley had no need to fear the bill itself; the urgent problem lay in the Tories' threat to 'tack' it to a money bill to prevent its otherwise certain rejection by the Lords. Numbering his forces for the tack issue, he could count on the Whigs and court supporters and on many moderate Tories who were not prepared to make a constitutional issue of the bill. The Tories could be accused of threatening financial supplies and thus endangering national interest. Against the tackers was thrown every resource of the court, and by an extensive canvass Harley obtained strong support. It was later often asserted that he was so sure of his strength that he brought the matter upon the anvil by secretly encouraging the tackers. In truth, no encouragement was needed, and in public Harley discouraged the tack.[14] On the second reading on 28 November, a motion to consider the land tax at the same time as the Occasional Conformity Bill was defeated by 117 votes. The success of the court's activities was demonstrated by the fact that over one hundred members who usually voted for the bill voted against the tack of the land tax. Both St John and Harcourt deserted the Tories and voted with the court.[15] But in the minds of the tackers the chief author of their discomfiture was Harley, and they nursed long and bitterly the memory of his behaviour. His attempts to conciliate them in later years had little chance of complete success; in their view he had crossed the Rubicon in 1704.

By the Whigs, the outcome of the 'tack' debate was hailed with relief.

12. *Ibid.*, ii, 187; Add. MS 17,677, ZZ, f. 464; Harley to G. Stepney, 31 Oct. 1704, Add. S. 7059, f. 39.
13. L'Hermitage, Add. MS 17,677, ZZ, ff. 497 and 515; Bodleian Ballard MS 10, f. 118; Dickinson, *Bolingbroke*, p. 39.
14. Patricia M. Ansell's 'Harley's parliamentary management', *BIHR* xxxiv (1961), pp. 92–6; Add. MS 17,677, ZZ, f. 497.
15. Boyer, *Annals*, iii, 157; *Somers Tracts* (1814), xii, 469.

For a brief moment the City of London, with its large element of dissent, had feared the worst. A dissenting correspondent wrote to Harley on the morrow: 'Nay had you seen the tottering state of our stocks last night you would [realize] the crisis the apprehended success of our violent men would cast us into.'[16] The vote set a tone of rancour for the whole session. Supplies were passed for the English forces though, in view of the mood of the Tories, Harley had to explain to an English diplomat that it was necessary to defer subsidies owed to some Allies.[17] The two Houses were swiftly engaged again in the dispute over the case of the Aylesbury electors. On one matter, however, both Lords and Commons were agreed, and their unanimity was far from pleasing to ministers. During the last session of the Scottish Parliament a Security Bill had been reintroduced and the ministry had advised the royal consent. For this advice Godolphin was attacked in both English Houses. In retaliation they passed the Alien Act intended, in its turn, to coerce Scotland into accepting the English Act of Settlement. The English Parliament proposed to treat Scots as aliens, mainly for trading purposes, but softened the blow by offering a union of Parliaments with no trade barriers and no Security Act.

As a result of the debates on the Alien Act Godolphin appears to have made up his mind that the Whigs must be represented in the ministry. When the Tory leaders were attacking him in the House of Lords it was noticed that he consulted several members of the Junto, leading to the supposition that their admission to office was the price of their support.[18] But Godolphin, having experienced the recalcitrance of Tory backbenchers over several sessions, had public as well as supposed private reasons for a gradual move in favour of the party which steadily supported his and Marlborough's war policy. He was convinced that only with Whig support could Marlborough's war policies be implemented.

When Parliament rose Harley rejoiced at the reflection that dissolution would follow and his tenure of the Chair cease.[19] A general election was due and the Tories were not likely to be able to overset any ministerial proposal for a Speaker, so that the necessity which had kept him in that office since his appointment as Secretary of State was no longer present. And with Godolphin looking towards the Whigs, Harley moved, or appeared to move, with the tide. In great secrecy he made tentative, and on the whole unproductive contact with Somers for the first time since 1701, though when the move inevitably became public it aroused Godolphin's jealousy. But Harley had no desire to meet the Junto's wish to return to office, planning only to arrange the admission

16. H.M.C. *Portland*, iv, 152.
17. *Ibid.*, ix, 169.
18. Dartmouth's note, Burnet, v, 182–3; cf: *Vernon Corr.*, iii, 279.
19. To A. Stanhope, 16/27 March 1705, P.R.O. SP 104/72, p. 113.

of lesser Whigs. He still had in mind the Duke of Newcastle, a more moderate, or at least a less able and ambitious Whig than any member of the Junto.[20] The session of 1704–5 removed Marlborough's objections, and a week after the prorogation the Queen gave the Privy Seal to Newcastle. Harley, writing his congratulations, added that Newcastle was also to have the lord lieutenancy of the North Riding for good measure, one of several such offices to change hands as an indication of royal favour for moderate Whigs.[21]

There were also other county offices up for redistribution, and at least one sheriff appointed at this time owed his place to a supposed ministerial decision to 'call the Whig party into business'. But to Harley's relief the Queen held out against most changes suggested by Marlborough or Godolphin at a ministerial level. Godolphin campaigned for the removal of the Tory Lord Keeper of the Great Seal, Sir Nathan Wright, and wrote to Harley 'I wish you would think what ought to be done in it, as soon as you can'.[22] So far, the Treasurer had little inkling of the Secretary's reservations on ministerial changes. In Harley's view the removals already made at county level were sufficient to carry the elections. He now wrote to Marlborough announcing his doubts about the Whig gains he anticipated: 'I am more concerned how to deal with them when they are chosen than under doubt of having a great majority for the Queen and the public good, though some people's overzeal does not prove very advantageous.'[23] The hint that he was not Godolphin's puppet was not yet sufficiently appreciated, but in his own mind Harley was already clear that future favour for the Whigs would have to be limited.

In the third week of May Harley repaired to New Radnor for his own election. When he returned to London, on 15 June, he found that the national results had been, as he had expected, sufficiently unfavourable to the tackers; in Somers' view 'the Parliament now chosen may probably prove very good, especially if the Court see their interest which wee are told they begin to grow sensible of'.[24] Harley also disgustedly found that Godolphin had made concessions to the Junto by new appointments. The newest adherent to the group Lord Spencer, now third Earl of Sunderland and Marlborough's son-in-law, had been chosen for a mission to Vienna, and Robert Walpole, a rising Whig, came on to the council of the admiralty as the nominee of Orford.

Harley's view that concessions to the Whigs had now gone far enough

---

20. *Correspondence of George Baillie of Jerviswood, 1702–1708* (ed. Gilbert Elliott, Edinburgh, 1842), p. 26; H.M.C. *Portland*, ii, 186–7.
21. *Ibid.*, ii, 189; 'Calendar of dockets and warrants for Privy Seals and other documents...from 1634–1711', *The Thirtieth report of the Deputy Keeper of the public records*, 1869, Appendix No. 10, pp. 371–5.
22. *Memoirs of the Family of Guise* (Camden Society, 1917), p. 145; H.M.C. *Bath*, i, 67.
23. Harley to Marlborough, 27 April 1705, Blenheim MSS. Al – 25.
24. N. Japikse, ii, 564.

was shared by the Queen, who objected to them on the ground of their religious and supposedly republican views. To Godolphin, who still pressed for the removal of Wright, she wrote 'I wish very much that there may be a moderate Tory found for this employment'.[25] Godolphin was under pressure from the Junto; so much so that Harley represented the Queen's case earnestly to Marlborough: 'The Queen hath wisely and happily delivered herself from a party, and I believe she will not easily put herself again into the power of any party whatsoever.' And this view accorded well enough with Marlborough's own view, which he had expressed to his Duchess two months earlier. Thus, the Queen remained unconvinced of the need for a change, and she was not opposed in her stand by Marlborough, who thereby had to defend himself against the reproaches of the Whigs through their strong advocate, his wife.[26] The matter remained unsettled until Marlborough could be persuaded to approve of the Junto's and Godolphin's candidate, William Cowper, for Wright's post.

Meanwhile, there was the more immediate problem of the Chair of the Commons. Godolphin decided that government influence should go to support a moderate Whig, John Smith. Harley himself vigorously disclaimed any desire to take the post again, but he was unable to persuade the Tory leaders in the Commons to support his own nominee, Harcourt, who had voted against the Tack. To his neighbour of the Welsh border Robert Price he commented bitterly on the Tories' intransigence.[27] For by this time Harley felt that he himself had been forced into a new position by the Tories' attitude. He had little relish for the choice of a Whig for the Chair, but he conceded grudgingly to Marlborough that 'it seems to be for the public service to fix upon Mr Smith'. He may have been present when Godolphin addressed '30 of the principall officers of the Crown' on the subject on 25 July, urging them to support Smith and recommend him to their friends. Godolphin's speech would certainly involve the loss to the government of many Tories who had supported it over the Tack issue; Harley's acceptance of the Treasurer's policy was not easily obtained, though his decision, when taken, was loyally adhered to. It was noted that 'Mr H. solicited earnestly for Mr Smith'.[28]

But the decision did not merely involve the question of who should be Speaker, for Harley had decided, however reluctantly, that it would be impossible to control the Tories and that in consequence he must work and vote with the Whigs. His defence of his stand, written to a

25. *The Letters and Diplomatic Instructions of Queen Anne* (ed. Beatrice C. Brown, 1935), p. 172, from Add. MS 28,070, f. 12.
26. Harley to Marlborough, 29 June 1705, Blenheim MSS. Al – 25; Coxe, *Marlborough*, i, 481 and 376.
27. H.M.C. *Portland*, iv, 223; same letter continued, Loan 29/192/256v, not printed.
28. Harley to Marlborough, 26 July 1705, Blenhein, MSS. Al – 25; F. Eyles to Portland, 27 July 1705, Portland (Nottingham) MSS. PwA 410; H.M.C. *Cowper*, iii, 64.

Tory who threatened him with 'Cassandra's fate' if he supported a Whig
for the Chair, is a good statement of his general political position:

> I have the same principles I came into the House of Commons with;
> I never have willingly nor never will change them. It hath been my
> misfortune for twelve years past almost every session to get the ill word
> upon one occasion or other of both parties; for the good word of one
> side I did not court it; and that of the other I lost it only upon such
> occasions by which they ran into those extraordinary things which
> gratified none but their enemies...[29]

But while he was defending the necessity of carrying on government in
face of untrammelled opposition, the following exchange with Godolphin shows that he did not abandon his fear of further encroachment by
the Whigs into the administration. Godolphin wrote: 'I wish you would
let me know what the "unreasonable things" are which you expect will
be insisted upon by them.' Harley replied heatedly:

> ...since your Lordship commands it I will expose my crude notions to
> your correction, as I shall always submit myself to your direction.
>   I take it for granted that no party in the House can carry it for them-
> selves without the Queen's servants join them; that the foundation is,
> persons or parties are to come in to the Queen, and not the Queen to
> them; that the Queen hath chosen rightly which party she will take
> in...
>   The embodying of gentlemen (country gentlemen I mean) against
> the Queen's service is what is to be avoided. Therefore things which
> another time may be reasonable in themselves may prove dangerous to
> be granted at this time, if they will shock more persons than they will
> gain.[30]

The foregoing represents a fairly typical expression of Harley's ideas
on government and parliamentary management. His notion that the
government could derive its strength in the House of Commons from
a nucleus of 'Queen's servants' supported in all reasonable measures by
'country gentlemen' was the traditional one. Yet Godolphin believed
that Whig discipline was too good, and Tory support too undisciplined
and divided, for Harley to hold together a 'court party' in the Commons
any longer. Whig support, if required, must henceforth be paid for. He
pressed his view insistently upon Marlborough, aided by the Duchess;
and the General finally gave way and added his voice to those pressing the Queen for Cowper's appointment.[31] When Harley returned to

29. H.M.C. *Portland*, iv, 261.
30. H.M.C. *Bath*, i, 74.
31. Coxe, *Marlborough*, i, 483–4.

London from leave late in October, he found that the Great Seal had changed hands. From now on he could expect pressure from the Junto for further appointments, resisted only by himself among the Queen's major ministers.

As the session drew near, many anxious calculations were made of the strength of parties, and there was general agreement that the 'Queen's servants' would hold the balance between Whigs and Tories. Most of these office holders had strong party convictions, as evidenced in the record of their performance in other issues, and it is a tribute to Godolphin's and Harley's powers of persuasion that some nineteen Tory placemen, together with a handful of other Tories, voted for Smith and thus carried the day when Parliament assembled on 25 October. Smith was elected to the Chair of the House of Commons by 248 votes, against 205 for Bromley. But in spite of the government's efforts on behalf of Smith, about seventeen of the placemen voted for Bromley. If these insurgents could be disciplined for the future, the result of this election indicated that the government could expect a workable majority. With this intention one of the rebels, the Tory secretary of the Admiralty, George Clarke, was immediately dismissed as an example; but Godolphin did not remove the majority of the others until after the end of the session.[32]

But the immediate removal of only one rebel provoked protests from the Junto. In the words of Halifax, 'making the Court Tories to act as one party with the Whigs' was 'mixing Oyl and Vinegar'. The chief responsibility for maintaining this alliance, however, was Harley's and he had as yet no doubt of his ability to keep order. In the second important vote of the session, that for the election to the chair of the committee of privileges and elections, he further demonstrated his determination to work with the Whigs by supporting their candidate, Spencer Compton, who defeated a Tory, Sir Gilbert Dolben.[33] The Tories' plan of action, as it was soon unfolded, was to attack the government on the succession question and punish the Queen for allowing her ministers' shift towards the Whigs. Unfortunately for the Tories' plans they made the mistake of opening their campaign in the House of Lords, where the Junto's well-organized phalanx of peers was supported by others who were aghast at any attempt to involve the Queen personally. On 15 November the Tory leaders, Rochester, Nottingham, and Buckinghamshire, brought forward in a debate on the state of the nation criticisms about the military stalemate in the Low Countries, government neglect of the Church of England, and the danger of a Stuart restoration in the case of Anne's sudden death. The last point was the preliminary to a motion to com-

---

32. W.A. Speck 'The Choice of a Speaker in 1705', *B.I.H.R*, xxxvii, (1964), 20–46. Professor Speck writes that by 1707 'only five of the rebels still held their places' (p. 30).
33. Cowper, *Diary*, p. 5; L'Hermitage, Add. MS 17,677 AAA, f. 511.

pose an address to the Queen to invite the heir to the throne, Princess Sophia of Hanover, to England, a step well known to be abhorrent to Anne who detested the thought of a rival in Britain. The attempt failed miserably, and when Somers moved a counter-motion to defer the debate for further consideration the Tories were able to muster only fifteen votes.[34]

This result was as decisive a setback to the Tories in the Lords as had been the Tack to those in the Commons. Nor did the matter end here. The Tories' motion had been in part a bid for the favour of the electoral house, and its defeat threw the Princess Sophia and her son the Elector of Hanover into considerable alarm for their succession. Insensitive to this reaction, Harley made little attempt to set the fears of the electoral court at rest. In his official dispatch to the English envoy at Hanover he mentioned the result of the division perfunctorily, adding no explanation or consolatory advice for the anxious court except the words 'they say there were but two ways to ruin the succession, force and this method'. He used exactly the same stock sentence in a letter to the envoy at The Hague.[35]

The Junto's reaction was, as usual, much more opportunist, and they assured the electoral court at Hanover of their loyalty despite the present need to bend to the Queen's wishes. Somers, not content with explanations, brought in a bill designed to set at rest the fears of the Princess and her son for their succession.[36] The bill proposed to nominate a Regency Council, most of whose members would be chosen by the court at Herrenhausen. This council would act after the death of Anne until the arrival of the new monarch on English shores. Harley was as sincere as the Junto in desiring an unimpeded Protestant succession, but the Queen's jealousy counselled caution in dealing with her successor. Later he must have regretted his casual treatment of Hanoverian aspirations, but his subsequent efforts to obtain the confidence of the Princess and the Elector came too late. The Junto had won over the electoral house, and Harley became an object of its increasing suspicion as the years passed.

Nevertheless, Harley continued to work against Tory proposals in the House of Commons. Here the Tories emulated their noble leaders in bringing a motion inviting Sophia to England. On 4 December, Bromley raised the matter in a committee of the whole house. Harley, believing that the motion would be defeated easily, pressed for a division, but many of the Whigs showed signs of reluctance to oppose on party grounds a measure which at other times they might have welcomed. He was

---

34. Coxe, *Marlborough*, i,489; L'Hermitage, Add. MS 17,677, AAA, f. 521.
35. To Howe, 16 Nov. 1705, P.R.O. SP 104/48 (no folio number); to stanhope, 16 Nov. 1705, P.R.O. SP 104/72, p. 223.
36. For Somers' authorship, see Burnet, v, 235, notes by Onslow and Hardwicke.

therefore forced to persuade the committee to postpone the debate until they were able to consider whether the Regency Bill, sent down from the Lords on the same day, would provide a satisfactory alternative to Bromley's proposal.[37] Four days later, however, the Whigs were rallied to the court in opposition to a Tory motion to go into committee to debate the alleged dangers confronting the Church of England. Remarking that to claim the Church to be in danger under the Queen's government was an 'abominable practice', Harley forced a motion of confidence by a majority of over fifty votes.[38]

While these debates were taking place, Harley was concurrently engaged in ushering through the House of Commons a repeal of the Alien Act which he had helped to pass in the previous session. The Scottish Parliament's repeal of the Act of Security, in the summer of 1705, and appointment of commissioners to negotiate the Union, made a reconciliation possible. There is some reason to suppose that Harley's intervention in Scottish politics in the spring and summer of 1705 helped to turn the balance in the Scottish Parliament in favour of those who were willing to negotiate with England. He had approached the principal leader of the opposition, the Duke of Hamilton, through an intermediary who is found reporting in March 1705 that Hamilton 'insists upon knowing plainly to what point and in what manner his service and assistance are expected'. In May there was a report that Hamilton was awaiting instructions from his 'best friend' Harley. And it is well known that the dramatic volte-face by Hamilton in the debate of September 1705 in the Scottish Parliament gave the Queen power to appoint the Scottish commissioners for the Union, a method which ensured that the negotiations would be in the hands of men who truly desired the union of the two Parliaments.[39] It is clear, nevertheless, that in December 1705 Harley's attitude in the Commons to England's northern neighbour gave Godolphin some concern, and the Treasurer wrote of hearing reports that his colleague favoured only a suspension rather than repeal of the Alien Act. Nevertheless, to the jaundiced eye of the Scottish Jacobite George Lockhart, Harley seemed to have performed his task efficiently despite vociferous opposition, and the repeal became law before the House rose for the Christmas vacation. The recent debates, Harley complained to Marlborough, were 'attended with the foulest Billingsgate language I ever heard'.[40]

Godolphin's reservations arose from his perception of Harley's basic unease at the new direction taken by the ministry. The Secretary failed

37. *Private correspondence*, ii, 233; Coxe, *Marlborough*, i, 490.
38. Speck, *Anonymous Parliamentary Diary*, p. 46.
39. H.M.C. *Portland* iv, 171–2 and 238–9; *Baillie Corr.*, p. 35.
40. H.M.C. *Bath*, i, 79; *Lockhart Papers*, i, 139; Coxe, *Marlborough*, i, 489.

to convince his colleagues that his solution to the problem of party management was the best, or even that his estrangement from the Tories was sincere. Before Parliament rose on 22 December the Commons began to investigate the authorship of the Tackers' chief apologetic tract, *The Memorial of the Church of England*; and Harley again came into the displeasure of the other ministers over this matter. When the Privy Council debated what reward to offer for the author, Harley insisted on £200 instead of the £500 favoured by Godolphin and Cowper. From this there was no need to conclude, as they did, that he was not anxious to discover the author. A point on which he remained consistent throughout his career, in and out of office, was his anxiety to save unnecessary government expense. He had already discovered and obtained the imprisonment of the author of a High Tory tract, *The Case of of the Church of England's Memorial Fairly Stated*, which had defended the Memorial. He also commissioned from John Toland a counterblast, *The Memorial of the State of England, in vindication of the Queen, the Church, the administration*...and sent the tract to his acquaintances.[41] Moreover the author of *The Memorial of the Church of England* was not, as the ministers were first led to suppose, an important Tory. Misled by false information that one or more members of the House of Commons were involved, Harley insisted, against the opposition of Marlborough and Cowper, that the House should be consulted before further action was taken. The permission of the Commons to investigate was duly obtained, but the author was discovered to be the relatively obscure pamphleteer James Drake.[42]

This comparatively trivial cause of dispute with his colleagues had important repercussions in historical interpretation of Harley's character; for Cowper was seething with indignation at the affair when he noted in his diary an account which is often quoted. The immediate occasion was a supper meeting intended to reconcile Harley with the Junto. In the course of the evening Harley called, in his florid way, for a toast to 'love and friendship and everlasting union'. These words caused Cowper's caustic reflection 'that humour of his which was never to deal clearly or openly, but always with reserve, if not dissimulation, or rather simulation, and to love tricks even where not necessary....'.[43] The analysis was perceptive but not impartial. That supper did Harley more harm than good with the Whig leaders.

They were further confirmed in their attitude by the second half of the

41. Cowper, *Diary*, p. 29; T.F.M. Newton, 'William Pittis and Queen Anne Journalism', *Modern Philology*, 33 (1935–6), pp. 84–5; Toland's tract was written, according to Toland himself, 'by your lordship's allowance and encouragement': see *A memorial to the Most Honourable, the Earl of xxx* in *The Miscellaneous Works of Mr. John Toland* (ed. P. Des Maizaux, 1747), ii, 228.
42. Cowper, *Diary*, pp. 35–6; *Dictionary of National Biography, sub* James Drake.
43. Cowper, *Diary*, p. 33.

session, which was occupied in both houses by prolonged debates on the Regency Bill. The chief purpose of this measure, to establish provision for a Regency Council to implement the succession laid down in the Act of Settlement, met little opposition. Discussion turned upon whether certain clauses in that Act limiting the prerogative of monarchy under the House of Hanover should be re-enacted. The limitations which the Country elements had insisted upon in 1701 included the exclusion of all office-holders, from the First Lord of the Treasury downward, from sitting in the Commons after the new dynasty came to the throne. But Harley's experience in building up a court party since Anne came to the throne had convinced him of the impracticability of such legislation. Nevertheless, he found himself opposed not only by the Tories but also by many Whigs who were still, as in 1701, in favour of anti-placeman legislation. Vainly he pointed out to the House that if the clause concerning placemen remained in the new bill not only ministers and minor officeholders but even justices of the peace would be excluded. On 12 January 1706 a government motion to drop this clause was lost by five votes, some of Harley's own circle of 'Old Whigs' voting with the majority.[44] There followed several weeks of close bargaining. In the end government was forced to accept a compromise whereby leading ministers and some other officeholders were allowed the right to re-election if they were appointed while sitting members of the House of Commons.

While the debates centred on the placemen, Harley, with the support of the Junto's followers, was able to gain two important points for the ministry. First, the clause in the Act of Settlement which enjoined that the Privy Council should be the responsible executive advisers to the future royal house was laid aside, so that the cabinet meetings which had been systematized under Anne were given a quasi-official recognition. Secondly, he was able to obtain a provision to allow the Queen's last-elected Parliament to sit for six months after her death, even if it had been dissolved; for he told the House of Commons 'no regency will have heart or courage without Parliament sitting'.[45] Taken together, the new constitutional arrangement were of considerable importance.

During the last month of this session Harley's health broke down, though he dragged himself to the House of Commons for the more important debates. There is no indication that his fellow-Secretary took much part in managing the combined court-Whig group; Hedges sympathized with the Tories. By now Hedges had relinquished parliamentary activity, and even administrative duties, not only to Harley but also to St John, who as a junior minister cheerfully usurped much of the senior

44. Burnet, v, 240; Speck, *Anonymous Parliamentary Diary*, p. 62; L'Hermitage, Add. MS 17,677 BBB, f. 49.
45. Speck, *Anonymous Parliamentary Diary*, p. 68.

Secretary's work in the Spanish theatre of war.[46] Harley certainly found that the strain of carrying the ministry's policies in the Commons, sometimes against the wishes of his personal friends, while at the same time incurring the obloquy of the Tories and the suspicion of the Whigs was too much for even his resilience. But though absence gave a respite it could not solve the incongruities of his situation, much less the tribulations which now beset him in his relationship with Godolphin and Marlborough.

46. Harley to G. Stepney, Feb. – March, 1706, *passim*, Add. MSS. 7059; Dickinson, *Bolingbroke*, pp. 46–7.

CHAPTER 8

End of the Triumvirate

THE DIFFERENCES WHICH were becoming apparent between Harley and his colleagues of the triumvirate were increased by developments in foreign affiars. As a diplomatist Harley was altogether of coarser grain than Marlborough; he plunged into the intricacies of the European situation with an enthusiasm and brusqueness which often had to be restrained by his colleagues. On occasions when the two men differed, Marlborough was usually the better judge of the overall interest of the Grand Alliance, but Harley was more conscious of England's private stake in the war. Above all, he retained a closer knowledge than Marl-borough of how far the House of Commons could be led when the Allies' interests seemed to conflict with those of England.

In December 1704, after the Blenheim campaign, Marlborough was reported to have expressed himself 'confident the Queen might prescribe the terms of peace by next winter'.[1] He reckoned, however, without the obstinacy of the Dutch. Any long continuance of co-operation between the two maritime nations would have required identical war aims, but in 1705 there appeared a major difference of opinion over strategy. The object of the Dutch remained as before, to recover their lost barrier for-tresses, and they continued, also as before, to prefer the slow methods of siege warfare to the hazards of battle. But for the English the destruc-tion of French armies in the field seemed the only way to victory in both theatres of war. Marlborough laboured even more under the crimping authority of the Dutch field deputies than his biographers have sup-posed. In the summer of 1705 Harley complained of their restriction of the general's desire for a pitched battle. With the refusal of the field deputies, a month later, to allow Marlborough, with a superior force, to attack the French army, the matter came to a head. Harley warned him 'the root it springs from I fear will produce worse fruit'.[2] Anxiously the

1. *Vernon Corr.*, iii, 278.
2. Harley to A. Stanhope, 24 July 1705, P.R.O. SP 194/72, p. 172; Coxe, *Marlborough*, i, 440 and 442.

cabinet debated sending a special mission under the Earl of Pembroke to The Hague, 'in relation to the command of the army and to endeavour to unite them nearer to us'. When Marlborough decided against such a step, for fear that it would have an adverse effect, Harley accepted the decision with misgiving.[3]

His irritation with the Dutch was increased in the winter of 1705–6 by their attitude to the diplomatic situation in northern Europe. With the Swedish army still massed threateningly in Poland, he pressed Marlborough for joint mediation in the north by England and Holland.[4] No action had been taken, however, when an incident threatened to bring about conflict between Sweden and Denmark in the last months of 1705. Its cause was the death of the Prince-Bishop of Eutin (Lubeck), leaving a disputed succession. One of the two main claimants, the Administrator of Holstein, immediately occupied the city; whereupon the King of Denmark on behalf of the other claimant, his brother, ejected the troops of Holstein and sent in his own. This action caused an immediate reaction from Sweden, the traditional enemy of Denmark, and the Swedish King threatened to restore the Administrator. Here was a spark to set the North alight. The need became urgent to force the United Provinces to join in buying off the Prince of Denmark and to pacify Sweden. The Dutch took long, as always, to come to a decision, and Harley wrote in despair to Marlborough 'if they will treat this affair thus lightly it can have no better consequence than to encourage the Danish ministers who are on the part of France'. To the envoy at the court of Sweden he was even more emphatic: 'The slowness of the States to come to a resolution about Lubeck hath suffered that affair to run a great length and to hazard a fatal rupture in those parts'.[5] After months of pressure by the English envoy at The Hague, the matter was finally settled by Harley personally. In January 1706 Willem Buys, the powerful pensionary of Amsterdam, came to England and was persuaded by the Secretary that joint mediation by English and Dutch was an urgent necessity. Under this dual pressure the King of Denmark gave up his brother's pretensions in return for a pension to be paid by the two countries to the Danish prince. Nevertheless, a further year of dreary correspondence was to pass before the Dutch consented to pay their one-third share of the compensation.[6]

An even more important task was delegated to Harley by Marlborough during Buy's visit. Buys was the spokesman of the commercial oligarchy

---

3. Harley to Marlborough, 28 Aug. 1705, Blenheim MSS. A 1–25; Harley to A. Stanhope, 11 Sept. 1705, P.R.O. SP 104/72, p. 198.
4. Harley to Marlborough, 10 July 1705, Blenheim MSS. A 1–25.
5. H.M.C. *Portland*, ix, 199–200, 217–19, 222; Harley to Marlborough, 11 Dec. 1705, Blenheim MSS. A 1–25; Harley to John Robinson, 16 Feb. 1706. *Morrison Collection*, v, 78.
6. Harley to A. Stanhope, 5/16 and 15/26 Feb., P.R.O. SP 104/72, pp. 252, 256; H.M.C. *Portland*, ix, 226; for the later correspondence see Harley's letters to A. Stanhope, 1706–7, P.R.O. SP 104/73 and 74, *passim*.

in Holland, and a leader of the party which was clamouring for peace; Harley's task was to persuade him of the need to continue the war until Spain was conquered. Though anxious for peace, Harley was avowedly of the same opinion as Marlborough, that Spain must be wrested from Philip V.[7] The Junto later professed to believe that it was Buys who converted Harley and not the reverse. But it is not likely that Harley changed his mind overnight; only by a long transmutation of ideas did he come to believe that England stood to lose rather than gain by fighting in Spain. His letter to Buys, after the latter's return to Holland in April 1706, was a strong mixture of cajolery and threats of commercial sanctions to keep the Dutch in the war. There was sufficient reason for the English fear that the Dutch had become lukewarm in the prosecution of hostilities. The cabinet had debated anxiously the fact that in 1705 only half the Dutch quota of naval vessels had joined the English fleet. Marlborough's victory at Ramillies, in May 1706, made Holland more anxious to conclude peace without winning Spain now that good terms could be obtained for their barrier, a view which Marlborough strongly opposed.[8]

To prevent their withdrawal, Marlborough pressed on with negotiations promising the Dutch a more generous barrier than France was likely to offer. He chose Halifax to conduct this negotiation, and the nub of Halifax's policy was, as the latter explained it to Somers, that: 'their barrier should be as good as we can get for them; and if they insist upon too much, it will be the greater tie on them, not to make peace till it is procured for them'. Harley had no use for such an attitude. He had spiritedly expressed his doubts to Marlborough about Dutch aspirations, even before Buy's visit: 'If the honest people of Holland will not give way they may have it [sc. peace] quickly, instead of a rotten, whimsical barrier.' And since he was capable of uttering opinions apparently contrary to England's war commitment, it is not surprising that Marlborough and Godolphin kept the negotiation largely in their own hands.[9] However, in one essential matter Harley's opinion, representative as it was of the sentiment of the House of Commons, may have carried some weight. He strongly opposed the inclusion in the Dutch barrier of Ostend and Dendermonde, which the Dutch required as 'communication' towns behind the main line of the barrier fortresses. And despite Halifax's promise to Somers, this Dutch attempt to strengthen their foothold in the Low Countires at the expense of English commerce, was the chief point on which the negotiation broke down in 1706.[10]

7. Coxe, *Marlborough*, i, 456; Harley to Marlborough, 17 July 1705, Blenheim MSS. A 1–25.
8. To Buys, 19/30 April 1706, P.R.O. SP 104/73, p. 2; Cowper, *Diary*, p. 5.
9. Geikie and Montgomery, p. 46, note 2; Coxe, *Marlborough*, i, 490.
10. Harley to Stepney, 24 Dec. 1706, P.R.O. SP 104/73, f. 67v, 'It will be hard for them [the Dutch] to make out that Ostend can be a barrier against any but England'; Geikie and Montgomery, pp. 87–9.

While the different attitudes of Harley and the Junto in foreign policy were beginning to take shape throughout the summer of 1706, the Whigs were also putting pressure upon Godolphin and Marlborough to replace Hedges as Harley's fellow Secretary of State by one of their own number, Marlborough's son-in-law Sunderland. In this attempt to fetter Harley to a hostile colleague they had the strong support of the Duchess of Marlborough; she had been outspoken in criticism of Harley's appointment in 1704. Harley was well aware of her influence against him and made anxious attempts to propitiate her, receiving on one occasion the response that they were 'brother and sister'.[11] However, neither of these two formidable political artists deceived the other, though at the moment the removal of Hedges was a more practical objective for the Duchess and the Whigs. By September the Junto had strengthened their demand by a threat to withdraw their support of the government, with the implied warning that the Whigs in the House of Commons would disrupt parliamentary business. The threat was one which could be enforced. The Whigs' organization was not, it is true, that of a modern party, yet it was no small matter to be 'declared enemy of the juncto', and men knew that 'the Tories are not noted to stick so fast to their friends as the others'. Marlborough would have preferred to satisfy his son-in-law with some lesser post, but the Junto were determined to establish their wedge in no lesser post than the secretaryship, and Marlborough, at his wife's insistence, reluctantly concurred.[12]

Harley heard of the new moves with alarm and poured out all his pent-up frustration and long-felt revulsion for the Junto:

> I am sorry to see the same sort of people incorrigible and endeavouring to act the same follys which overturned them before...If they are endeavouring to destroy those who have supported them, without whom they will be a prey to the other side, and to make other well-meaning men desperate in order to secure power to themselves which they can never hold, it is but the same game they played before.[13]

He had met little sympathy from Godolphin or Marlborough. One mind, however, responded instinctively to his abhorrence of the Whig leaders, and this mind belonged to the Queen. By 1706 Anne came to give the greatest part of her confidence to Harley; they thought alike on many subjects. Possibly the fact that her new favourite, Abigail Hill, was Harley's second cousin also recommended him to the Queen.[14] Increasingly,

---

11. H.M.C. *Bath*, i, 86; Cunningham, i, 411.
12. Coxe, *Marlborough*, ii, 136 and 139; *Wentworth Papers*, p. 156.
13. To Lord Poulett, 21 Sept. 1706, Loan 29/153/5.
14. Abigail's father, Francis Hill, was first cousin to Harley's mother, born Abigail Stephens. The common grandfather was Richard Stephens, who died in 1599; *Notes and Queries*, v (1906), p. 390.

as the Queen grew older, people came to mean more to her than ideas, and in particular she had come to rely on the placid Abigail rather than on the Duchess of Marlborough, whose Whig political ideals and enthusiasm increased rather than declined as the years passed. Moreover, Anne, like Harley, had a liking for the close detail of aministration, and the day-to-day contact which a Secretary of State had with the monarch had entrenched him strongly in her sympathy. The similarity of their ideas, thrashed out in frequent conversations, was reflected in their protests against the appointment of a 'party man'. Anne wrote to Godolphin: 'All I desire is my liberty in encouraging and employing all those that concur faithfully in my service, whether they are called Whigs or Tories, not to be tyed to one nor the other. . .' And Harley pleaded with Marlborough to 'shew the true path to a lasting well-founded settlement, clear of the narrow principles and practice of the heads of both factions'.[15]

In successive audiences, Anne determinedly resisted Godolphin's championship of Sunderland. Godolphin wavered. After the last session he had worked out a balance sheet of parties, calculating that there were 190 Tories, 160 Whigs and 100 'Queen's servants' in the Commons, and concluding 'I take it our business is, to get as many as we can from the 190, without doing anything to lose one of the 160'. Nevertheless, in the face of the Queen's resistance, he again asked Harley's view on how the Commons could be managed without the support of the Whigs, adding that for his part 'the leaning to what I take to be an impossibility will, I think, make them [sc. the Whigs] jealous and uneasy, and at best but passive'. Harley's reply was his usual formula for carrying the government's measures by a combination of placemen, moderate Tories and such Whigs as could be detached from the Junto by kind words, appeals to patriotism, and expectation of reward: 'This I am certain, many of the most staunch Whigs (not whimsical) have, and do frequently lament the fury of their leaders, and have rejoiced when their presumption was humbled.'[16] But less than ever did his vision of moderate Tories and Whigs uniting in support of government seem plausible to Godolphin. In the coming session Parliament was due to ratify the Treaty of Union with Scotland negotiated in the course of the summer. The Tories would oppose it, and if the Whigs chose to make difficulties the Union Bill might have as rough a passage as the recent Regency Bill.

The Queen's resistance to Sunderland was far more serious than her objections to Cowper's appointment a year earlier. But the factor which was bound to overcome her resistance in the end was Marlborough's belated insistence that the appointment was a political necessity. All the same, Marlborough was not aware of the extent of Harley's opposition; he advised Godolphin to win over the Secretary 'and by gaining him you will govern the others without taking any pains with them'. Harley, however, continued until the last moment to remonstrate.[17] But his arguments were ignored by the Treasurer, for by this time the victory was in his grasp. Tension relaxed as the Queen sullenly gave way. For maximum effect on members of the House of Commons, Sunderland's appointment was announced a day or two before the opening of Parliament on 3 December 1706. Queen Anne never made an appointment more unwillingly. The Whigs rejoiced in the triumph of their cause, but the days of Sunderland and even of Godolphin in office were not likely to be more numerous than the Queen could help.

In the struggle for domination which now ensued between the two Secretaries Harley had the support of the Queen, but Sunderland was backed by Marlborough, whose indispensability as a military leader gave him the last word in most matters. Harley, it is true, became senior Secretary, though he remained in the northern, and usually junior department. But in the cabinet his views counted for little. He accordingly began to undermine the authority of his colleagues by surreptitious means on every possible occasion. When a minor diplomatic appointment was made to Vienna, Harley pointed out to the unsuccessful aspirant that the successful applicant was a nephew of the Lord Treasurer. On another occasion he told the Dutch envoy that Halifax and Sunderland were paying court to English opinion by censuring the Dutch barrier proposals.[18] Harley's own views on this question, as has already been said, were far stronger than those of the Junto against Dutch claims.

Such intrigues cannot safely be left out of any account of Harley's methods. Paradoxically they appear to have arisen from the moral inflexibility of his character. His strength as a politician lay in his conviction of his own integrity. Because he had decided that his colleagues were opposing the Queen's known wishes, and the Queen was the centre of government, he felt justified in cutting the ground from under their feet. To Daniel Defoe, who was currently serving as a spy in Scotland, he confided:

> I count on all that impotent malice, inveterate spleen can do by misrepresentation, and notorious forgeries to do me hurt. I am prepared for all; and the wrath is greater against me because their weakness as well as villanous arts happen to be detected. And if God spares me life, I think I shall be able to pull off the mask from the real atheists and pretended patriots — but too much of this now.[19]

17. Snyder, iii, 717–18 and 725–6.
18. Guise, *Memoirs*, pp. 148–9; Geikie and Montgomery, p. 82, note 7.
19. H.M.C. *Portland*, iv, 418.

'The real atheists and pretended patriots' – in this outburst Harley expressed his deepest feelings about his opponents. It is the tragedy of Queen Anne's reign that Harley and the Junto so little understood each other's character. The Junto saw him driven only by ambition, while he regarded himself as an instrument of political morality. Harley equally failed to do justice to the Junto: to him they were simply evil. Black and white he understood, but the grey shades never came within his mental vision. The members of the Junto had the best political brains of their generation, and a fair share of its disinterested patriotism, but in Harley's mind this was no answer to what he considered to be their moral defects. There could be no question of compromise when the circles of his thought scarcely touched theirs at the circumference.

When the session began, however, there was no open sign of dissension in the Ministry. Supplies were voted smoothly, and in the creation of honours at the end of December the balance of forces was represented by the creation of three earldoms for Godolphin, Wharton and Harley's friend Poulett.[20] The greatest issue was the Union between England and Scotland. Throughout the summer of 1706 the commissioners of both nations, had laboured to draw up a treaty to be submitted to their respective Parliaments. Harley and Godolphin together with the five Junto lords were among the English contingent, in a joint conference of commissioners, who held out to the Scots the optimum terms England was prepared to allow, namely that in a joint Parliament Scotland would be represented by forty-five seats in the House of Commons and sixteen representative peers in the House of Lords. In January 1707 the Queen was able to announce that the treaty had been ratified by Scotland.[21]

During the last week of January and most of February Harley was ill: the Queen expressed concern for his health 'in such terms', wrote St John, 'as I am sure came from the bottom of her heart'. During his absence there was Tory opposition to the Union Bill. An attempt by Nottingham in the House of Lords to extend some aspects of the English Test Act to Presbyterian Scotland after the Union, a motion intended to prevent harmony, was defeated.[22] But in the House of Commons the Tories concentrated mainly on the commercial clauses of the Treaty of Union. Since Harley, on his return, decided to support the Tories on this matter, and thereby exacerbated disagreements with his colleagues, some discussion of the technicalities involved is necessary.

Hitherto Scottish customs duties had been levied at a lower rate than in England, but by articles 4 and 6 of the Treaty of Union both countries were to have a uniform system of duties after 1 May 1707, the first day of the Union. By this arrangement it was generally understood that all

20. Harley to Stepney, 13 Dec. 1706, Add. MS. 7059, f. 120v.
21. H.M.C. *Bath*, i, 67; Defoe, *Union*, pp. 106–7.
22. H.M.C. *Bath*, i, 157; *Addison Letters*, p. 69.

goods imported into Scotland before that date from countries other than England might be transferred across the border after the Union without payment of further duty. This expectation provided loopholes for several kinds of commercial sharp practice. Some foreign merchants brought large quantities of goods into Scotland at the lower rate in order to avoid English customs duty by bringing them into England after the Union. Others removed goods already imported into England from overseas, and deposited them in Scotland, thus obtaining an English drawback (or refund of duty already paid) with the intention of re-importing into England after 1 May duty free. These practices, carried out on a large scale, caused considerable agitation in the City of London, and the Tories in Parliament took up the cause of the 'fair traders' as a good opportunity to embarrass the government. Nottingham attempted to present a petition from the City merchants to the House of Lords, and though it was refused admission, found himself unwontedly popular in the City.[23]

In the government's view, however, such agitation was undesirable owing to the proximity of Union day and the indignation of the Scots at possible interference in what they considered to be a legitimate per-quisite, one of the commercial privileges for which Scottish political autonomy had been surrendered. In defiance of Godolphin's wishes, however, Harley put himself at the head of the supporters of the fair traders on the merits, as he saw it, of their case. When a bill to prevent the abuses was hurried through the House, less than a month before the Union would come into force, he even proposed and carried an addi-tional clause to make the bill's effect retro-active to 1 February 1707. But the Whig majority in the House of Lords objected to the bill on the ground that it would be regarded in Scotland as an infringement of the Treaty, and on 8 April Parliament was adjourned for a week to give the Commons an opportunity to bring in a milder bill without the retro-active clause.[24] Nonetheless, the Commons carried the bill again im-mediately they re-assembled, and sent it to the upper chamber. Harley assured Godolphin that he had not supported it on this occasion, but the latter commented tartly 'perhaps your appearing in it before has been the occasion of all this broil'. Godolphin himself, however, is reported to have accepted the bill on the floor of the House of Lords, apparently out of deference to its popularity in England. But two days later, on 24 April, the Queen was persuaded to prorogue Parliament while the Lords were still debating the bill.[25] One week later the Union came into effect.

How far the bill had actually put the Union in danger by the offence it

23. Boyer, *Annals*, v, 478; Shrewsbury to Vernon, 27 April, 1707, Add. MS. 40,776, f. 85.
24. *Norris Papers*, p. 159; Boyer, *Annals*, v, 478–9.
25. H.M.C. *Bath*, i, 169; L'Hermitage, 22 April 1707 Add. MS. 17,677, CCC, f. 92.

gave to Scotland, as the Whigs claimed, is questionable. But there is no reason to suppose that Harley was not sincere in his championship of the English fair traders. Much of his diplomatic correspondence was taken up with the interests of the English commercial community, and his indignation about the unfair trading was greater because he believed that Dutch merchants were the chief offenders.[26] Moreover, if he could gain favour with the English merchants and with the Tories at one and the same time, he was well pleased. As a matter of political tactics he had undoubtedly scored a point against Godolphin, and the only complaint which interested English opinion brought against the bill was that it was not sufficiently severe against the offenders.

After the flurry in Parliament the divided ministers paused warily, considering the ground and wondering whether to take the offensive. Marlborough and Godolphin were not long in learning that their position was less secure than they had thought, for the Duchess of Marlborough now made the terrible discovery that she had been supplanted in the Queen's favour by Abigail Hill, now Mrs Masham, whose wedding in the Queen's presence led to the revelation. The appointments of Cowper and Sunderland were now to be paid for. Malborough urged Godolphin to placate Harley, but the Treasurer replied despondently:

[Harley] does so hate and fear [Somers, Sunderland and Wharton] that he omits no occasion of filling [the Queen's] head with their projects and designs; and if [I] should take with him upon any occasion of that kind, he would either say nothing, or argue against what the other says...[27]

To curb Harley's activities during Marlborough's absence on campaign there was some talk in Whig circles of giving Sunderland charge of all diplomacy and dividing home affairs between two other secretaries responsible for England and Scotland.[28] By this means Harley could have been deprived of all influence in Scottish and foreign affairs. If the idea had been carried out it would have anticipated by seventy-five years the division of the secretaries' office into home and foreign departments which took place in 1782. That it took no root in 1707 was no doubt due to the opposition, or anticipated opposition, of the Queen. Nevertheless, when Marlborough went abroad for the summer he took Harley's duties in his own hands as far as possible, especially by negotiating personally with the King of Sweden at Alt Ranstadt in April and by dealing privately with Sunderland. On one occasion Marlborough instructed his son-in-law, who needed no telling, to consult Somers and Halifax for

---

26. Harley to James Dayrolles (secretary to the envoy at The Hague), 1 April 1707, P.R.O. SP 104/73, f. 100v.
27. *The Conduct of the Duchess of Marlborough*, p. 220; Snyder, ii, 831.
28. L'Hermitage, 11 January 1707, Add. MS. 17,677, CCC, f. 93.

their advice on a matter falling within Harley's department, 'so that you must take care of the directions I must receive from Mr Harley'.[29]

But if Harley's opinions on foreign affairs were effectively neutralized, he could still encourage the Queen to assert her independence of her ministers in domestic matters. In June she announced that she intended to promote two Tories to the vacant sees of Exeter and Chester, an action of considerable political importance for the House of Lords, where the Whigs were in only a slight majority. The members of the Junto apparently suggested a compromise arrangement which would have allowed Offspring Blackall to have Exeter but prevented any other Tory clerical appointments currently under consideration. To reinforce their suggestion the Whigs threatened to attack the ministry for incompetent management at the Admiralty. The Queen refused to sacrifice either of her nominees, and denied that Harley had advised the appointments.[30]

While this dispute dragged on inconclusively throughout the summer Harley himself announced his intention of opposing Godolphin on at least one important aspect of policy. The Act of Regency provided that a number of minor placemen were to be excluded at the end of the Parliament then sitting. The problem now was this: did the Union and the creation of a Parliament of Great Britain render the sitting assembly 'new' even though there had been no general election? Godolphin said yes, Harley no. The latter interpretation would have allowed those placemen who were mostly 'Court Tories' appointed in the early years of the reign to continue in the House of Commons for a further session until the election due in 1708.[31] Harley was anxious to retain potential supporters in the House in case he broke openly with the ministry. But as yet he did not give up hope of persuading Godolphin to declare against the Junto. In an exchange of letters they repeated all their old arguments on party management; but neither would concede an inch to the views of the other. Harley's letters became longer and more figurative: Parliament, he thought, could not be 'transubstantiated; the elements and accidents the same but the substance altered'. Party government makes administration 'like a door which turns both ways upon its hinges'. To the sympathetic Newcastle he wrote that the moderate Whig Duke of Somerset was 'publicly exposing the Junta'.[32] It is clear Harley was hoping that if his quarrel came to a head he would have the support of at least two of the most powerful Whig aristocrats, Newcastle and Somer-

29. Coxe, *Marlborough*, ii, 268–9.
30. G.V. Bennett, 'Robert Harley and the Bishoprics Crisis of 1707', *EHR*, lxxxii (1967), esp. 735–40; Coxe, *Marlborough*, ii, 343–4.
31. H.M.C. *Portland*, iv, 422. The details of this issue are not explicitly stated; that it was what chiefly stood between Harley and Godolphin may, however, be inferred from the division of 10 Nov., 1707, on the status of Parliament, for which see below and Burnet, v, 341.
32. H.M.C. *Portland*, iv, 422; H.M.C. *Bath*, i, 180; H.M.C. *Portland*, ii, 200.

set; and it may be assumed that he was assuring each of these two that he was in full agreement with the other. Nor did he neglect to put his case before Marlborough; before he went on leave to Brampton in the last week of September, he complained 'for near two years, I have seen the storm coming upon me, and now I find I am to be sacrificed to sly insinuations, and groundless jealousies'.[33]

Before Parliament assembled for the session of 1707–8 the European situation altered many political calculations. Marlborough, at his interview with Charles XII at Alt Ranstadt, had come to the conclusion that the King had no intention of attacking the Grand Alliance in the rear. But for several more months Charles continued to negotiate with the Holy Roman Emperor about the rights of the Protestant Churches in Silesia. The Emperor gave way on all points to the Swedish King in the treaty of Alt Ranstadt in the first week of September 1707. Harley immediately asked the English envoy at the Court of Sweden whether the King would be willing to hire out 10,000 men to fight for the Grand Alliance on the Rhine, 'being only my own thought, what I have no orders for writing'.[34] What Charles XII thought of this proposal, and whether it came to the ears of Marlborough, is not recorded. The Swedish troops moved east to try their strength against Russia, and eventually meet defeat at Poltava. But if the King of Sweden had shown some restraint in the cause of the Allies, the Emperor himself showed little. He had decided upon the conquest of Naples. After the Italian campaign he concluded the secret Treaty of Milan which permitted French troops to be released to join the campaign in Spain. There the battle of Almanza was lost by the British forces after their French opponents had been reinforced.[35]

Thus, the first Parliament of Great Britain assembled on 23 October with Almanza, and a further military reverse at Toulon, on everyone's mind. Harley did nothing to rally the government voters in the Commons and arrived in London, as Godolphin was careful to point out to Marlborough, only on 'the night before the Parliament met'. To Harley himself Godolphin wrote in recrimination that parliamentary affairs needed much discussion 'if talking would mend them' but 'must go as they will'. Harley drafted in reply: '. . . the little experience I have had inclines me to think that they [sc. home affairs] never succeed so well as when they are directed. The people will follow somebody, and if your lordship will not think fit to explain your own thoughts, others will make use of your authority.'[36]

---

33. Coxe, *Marlborough*, ii, 361.
34. *British Diplomatic Instructions: Sweden* (ed. J.F. Chance), p. 38.
35. Trevelyan, ii, 294–5, 298.
36. Coxe, *Marlborough*, ii, 366; H.M.C. *Bath*,i, 186. The form of Harley's draft seems to indicate that his answer may not have been actually sent.

Before settling down to prolonged debates on the conduct of the war, the House of Commons had to decide the question of the placemen disputed between Harley and Godolphin. The result of a debate on 10 November was a compromise. The sitting Parliament was resolved to be 'new' and several of the officers whose posts were listed in the Act of Regency for exclusion from the next Parliament were immediately disqualified from sitting, but some whose patents or commissions had been renewed since the Union in May were admitted.[37] A second compromise was reached over the episcopal appointments. At a meeting with the representatives of the Queen, the Whig leaders in the House of Commons were informed that though she intended to stand by the two men nominated as bishops the Whigs might be assured that 'for the future she was resolved to give them full content'. And later the appointments were announced of the Junto's candidate for Norwich and a Whig Regius Professor of Divinity at Oxford.[38]

But the Whigs in both Houses were little mollified. Aided by most of the new Scottish members they turned to the conduct of the war, and especially to the administration of the Admiralty where Prince George, the Queen's consort, presided in genial but inefficient authority as Lord High Admiral aided by Admiral George Churchill, Marlborough's brother. The parliamentary enquiries were directed at the loss of convoys the previous summer. But, as one member wrote, 'one need not be a conjuror to know the design'; the Whigs had decided to put pressure on Marlborough, through Admiral Churchill, and on the Queen by threatening to humiliate her beloved husband.[39]

Such a policy played into Harley's hands, and the Whigs later believed that he was able to make good use of it.[40] At first many of the Tories in the House of Commons, following their leaders in the Lords, joined in criticism of the Admiralty. They changed their minds on hearing that Harley had at last persuaded Godolphin to hold a rallying meeting of officeholders, including several leading moderate Whigs, to declare disassociation from the Junto attacks. In a decisive censure debate on 13 December the withdrwal of the Tories' opposition saved the Admiralty. Harley had his own reasons for wishing to divert this debate; his negligence in failing to report to the Admiralty information brought to him by an agent he employed in France had resulted in the loss of several ships in a Russia convoy.[41] By leading the court group and the Tories

37. Clarke to Charlett, 10 Nov., 1707, Bodleian, Ballard MS. 20, f. 63.
38. Burnet, v, 340; Coxe, *Marlborough*, ii, 381.
39. *Calendar of State Papers, Colonial, 1706–1708*, item 1214; Clark to Charlett, 24 Nov. Bodleian, Ballard MS. 20, f. 64.
40. *Private Corr.*, i, 98.
41. Burnet, v, 343; *Addison Letters*, p. 83; Sunderland's memorandum [no date, but about 16 Jan. 1708] Blenheim MS. C 1–16, Fl. *Cf.* Burnet, v, 357; Bennett, 'Robert Harley and the Bishopries Crisis of 1707', *EHR* lxxxii (1967), 743–4.

together in the Commons he saved both himself and the Prince, and earned the further gratitude of the Queen. At this point the beginning of Anne's determination to change her ministry became apparent. She informed her Tory confidant, John Sharp, Archbishop of York, 'that she meant to change her measures, and give no countenance to the Whig Lords, but that all the Tories, if they would, should come in,' though she added 'and all Whigs likewise that would show themselves to be in her interests should have favour'.[42]

So by the last days of 1707 Harley could fairly expect changes which would not be to his disadvantage. The situation changed overnight. One of the clerks of his office, named Gregg, was discovered to have acted as a minor spy for the French Minister of War Chamillard. The Junto seized their opportunity, and Godolphin was soon persuaded to veer again in support of them.

If no-one succeeded in proving that Harley was implicated in the treason, it was not for want of trying. Francis Hare, Marlborough's secretary, wrote later of the Whigs' 'vain endeavours, which I at the time thought provoking to the last degree, to draw Mr Harley into Gregg's affair, which showed with a witness the spirit of party'.[43] Godolphin and the Junto cannot be blamed for putting this gift of the gods to political ends; they had no way of tearing Harley from office other than by frightening the Queen for his life. The enquiry into Gregg's case dragged on for several months, but everything of value came out before he was condemned to death on 18 January 1708. He was poorly paid in the Queen's service, he had been given the opportunity to make a little extra money by sending newsletters – they amounted to little else – to France. The correspondence had begun in October 1707. Only one letter of importance seems to have been sent to Chamillard, a copy of a dispatch by Harley to the Emperor, which had carelessly been left accessible to junior members of the office. In truth, the main fact which came out about Harley was that he was careless and haphazard in his office routine, sometimes to the inconvenience of the staff, who were often forced to work longer hours than was necessary. The same deficiencies had existed in the secretaries' office before Harley's time, and he had ignored a warning by the perspicacious Defoe of the possible result of leaving important state papers lying about.[44] On the other hand, Harley had done his office staff little kindnesses; and he had reduced his own share of the profits of the *London Gazette* for the benefit of the junior members, even the office cleaner. Such consideration goes far to explain why Gregg refused to save his own life by even hinting that Harley might be implicated, which was

---

42. Sharp, i, 323.
43. *Private Corr.*, ii, 16.
44. Howell, *State Trials*, xiv, especially pp. 1383–4; G.F. Warner, 'An unpublished political paper by Daniel Defoe', *EHR*, xxii (1907), 137.

all his interrogators wanted. Gregg even insisted that undue responsibility had been put upon himself by the Under-Secretary, Erasmus Lewis, without Harley's knowledge.[45]

The weeks which followed the revelation of Gregg's actions were packed with political intrigues on both sides. Harley was even more lavish than usual in promises to potential sympathisers in the House of Commons; he did not hesitate to assure a member for Liverpool that an unpopular tax collector would be removed and compensated by the government. Harley's opponents, for their part, seized upon a minor means of harassing him; in mid-January the Jewel Office discovered that he had not received permission to keep the ceremonial dinner plate with which he had been issued as Speaker of the House of Commons, and demanded its immediate return. It was usual for former officers to keep their plate, but Harley asked Godolphin's permission to keep it only a littler longer, 'the time being very near when I shall deliver up the plate I received as secretary'.[46] Such pleasantries were not intended to be taken seriously; they were merely preliminary sparring for the fight to come.

By the second half of January 1708 Harley is seen negotiating with Tory leaders for the formation of a new ministry, a negotiation of which Godolphin and Marlborough were well aware.[47] Here again, however, events overtook him. He hoped to wait for the effect of the Gregg trial to subside before re-opening the ministerial quarrel on the safer ground of the Queen's closet, where a new ministry could be worked out under his leadership. But this possibility was denied him, for a new parliamentary crisis was now precipitated by the Tories. The cause was an attempt by the Tories of both Houses to defeat the government on the management of the land war. Having been held back in the naval enquiry, they felt little disposed to forego any longer so good an argument as the defeat at Almanza. Their leader in this matter was the Earl of Peterborough, who had been forced to give up his command in Spain just before the battle, and was now anxious to vindicate his own dubious conduct by impugning that of his successor. It was unfortunate for Harley that Peterborough's grudge against the ministry which recalled him was centred upon Harley himself. The gist of the matter was that Peterborough, while in Spain, had taken up a large loan in Italy, on bad terms, for the payment of his troops. This in itself was enough to arouse Harley's antagonism in the interest of the public purse. And when Peterborough returned to England in August 1707, it had fallen to Harley to refuse him admis-

45. J.M. Price, 'A note on the circulation of the London press 1704–1714', *BIHR*, xxxi (1958), 218; Sunderland's minute, 16 Jan. 1707/8, Blenheim MSS. C 1–16, D 31.
46. *Norris Papers*, 161–4; Harley to Godolphin, 14 Jan. [1708], Loan 29/64/1.
47. G. Holmes and W. A. Speck, 'The Fall of Harley', *EHR*, lxxx (1965), 673–98.

sion to the Queen's presence until his misconduct was explained.[48] Thus stood the matter when, on 29 January 1708, the House of Commons was due to debate Peterborough's conduct and the war in Spain.

Harley was in a strait. He was desperately anxious not to antagonize the Tories, on whom he hoped to rely if a new ministry were formed. But previous debates in December and January concerning the Spanish theatre of war had made clear that an 'angry corner' intended to criticize the Ministry. And criticism in the Commons for the disastrous campaign of 1707 in that theatre would be directed at Harley himself or at St John as Secretary at War. The best, though inadequate solution to their dilemma was to defend the ministry on the issue of Almanza but remain silent when Tories criticized the avowed determination of the Whigs to continue the war in Spain until that country was secured for the Imperial candidate. Accordingly, when St John admitted to the House on the 29th that of the 29,000 men provided by parliamentary votes for Spain, only 8,600 had actually been present at the battle, he pleaded a number of reasoned explanations. But when the backbench Tory Sir Thomas Hanmer made a wide denunciation of the government's management of the war, claiming that an opportunity to make peace on favourable terms had existed before Almanza and was now lost, Harley and St John made little or no defence. A government motion for adjournment was carried by only fifteen votes.[49]

By this time, however, Godolphin's patience was at an end. His anger did not arise mainly from this incident. On previous days he had certainly become aware of the extent of Harley's plans to replace him. The evening before the debate Harley had written to Marlborough asking for an interview to answer the latter's dissatisfaction and to make 'one more humble request to your Grace upon two or three words you drop't to me on Saturday. It relates to my Lord Treasurer'.[50] Exactly what Harley did suggest to Marlborough when they met on 30 January does not appear, though a letter Harley wrote the following day to Newcastle indicates that he believed himself to have placated the captain-general: he wrote of 'such a scene of defeated malice as is scarce credible'. But despite this respite he knew that Godolphin was now determined on his removal. During the next few days Harley, together with St John and Harcourt, made a canvass of the leading Tories to see how much support could be obtained for a new ministry.[51] The outcome of their enquiries

---

48. *Wentworth Papers*, p. 138; H.M.C. *Eighth Report*, part i, p. 43; H.M.C. *House of Lords* MSS., vii, 396–7.
49. *Vernon Corr.*, ii, 288, 328–30 and *passim; Court and Society*, ii, 272; Godfrey Davies, 'The Fall of Harley', *EHR*, lxvi (1951), 252; Holmes and Speck, 'The Fall of Harley', *EHR*, lxxx (1965), 673–98.
50. H.M.C. *Bath*, i, 190; Harley to Marlborough, 28 Jan. 1707/8, Loan 29/12/5.
51. H.M.C. *Portland*, ii, 201; *Vernon Corr.*, ii, 345.

was seen when they informed the queen that they could not proceed further while Godolphin continued to appear to enjoy her confidence. Anne thereupon decided to write to Marlborough stating her resolve to remove Godolphin if necessary. This letter was carried by St John to the General on 6 February. But by this time Marlborough had decided that it was Harley who must go. In an audience with the Queen, Marlborough stated that though he was under pressure from the Whigs to obtain Harley's removal he had no personal objection to working with the secretary, but that she would find Godolphin less pliable. And so it fell out: Anne sent Harcourt with a last plea to Godolphin, who replied that if she persisted in her design he would resign. On the 8th both he and Marlborough offered resignations in person.[52]

If Marlborough and Godolphin had possessed no other reason for their obduracy at this stage, one was provided by a Whig counter-plot proceeding along a line parallel to Harley's. The Whigs decided to make a demonstration of strength in both Houses. On 3 February, in the resumed Almanza debate, the Tories were joined by a number of Whigs to pass without division a motion of censure on the government. Harley, perhaps out of a conviction that St John had indeed been culpable in the affair of the missing thousands of troops, did hardly anything to defend the government and thereby earned the wrath of Marlborough and Godolphin. On the 5th the Junto used the same tactic in the House of Lords by voting alongside the Tories to defeat a government attempt to extend the life of the Scottish Privy Council by amending a bill for the abolition of the council.[53] One observer noted 'some people imagine these oppositions in Parliament will oblige the Court more heartily to espouse one or t'other party'. And this was the outcome. The day following the last debate Harley asked the general for a further interview and was told simply 'I have been very exactly informed of all the transactions for some days past. . .'.[54] After offering their resignations to the Queen, Marlborough and Godolphin absented themselves from the usual Sunday cabinet meeting on 8 February, and the meeting broke up after only a few minutes, Harley being the only important member, apart from the Queen, who was willing to carry on without them.[55]

Events had once again moved too fast for Harley. The Almanza debate, coming hard upon the Gregg case, had given him insufficient time to prepare for a new ministry. Of the Whig magnates whom Harley had

52. Reports of De Beyries, 13/24 and 17/28 Feb., 1708, Hanover Staatsarchiv, Calenberg Briefe Archiv, 24 (England) 92; Holmes and Speck, 'The Fall of Harley', *EHR*, lxxx (1965), p. 694. Cf. Appendix, below.
53. *Vernon Corr.*, iii, 335; *Addison Letters*, p. 89.
54. *Court and Society*, ii, 276; Harley to Marlborough, 6 Feb. 1707/8, Loan 29/12/6; Marlborough to Harley, 7 Feb. 1707/8, Loan 29/12/5.
55. Burnet, v, 353–4.

expected to rally to the Queen, Somerset and Newcastle turned against him in the fatal cabinet meeting. In the House of Commons he had failed, in the time available, to win back lost ground with the Tories. Even so the Queen would have tried to form a ministry with Harley at its head, but he had seen enough. On the day following the cabinet meeting the House of Lords decided to take the Gregg case into their own hands. They appointed a committee of 'seven lords of the Whig party' to interrogate the condemned man with a view to obtain evidence to impeach Harley.[56] The warning was a plain one. Two days later he wrote formal letters to the envoys in his province announcing his retirement. The only task that remained was to overcome the Queen's final reluctance to let him go, and he did not give up the seals of office until 11 February. With him, on the following days, resigned St John, Harcourt and Thomas Mansell. Only a week earlier Harley had boasted that he had never been 'safer in favour or employment'; now, he confessed, he had 'laid his neck under their feet, and they trod upon it'.[57]

Aged 46, Harley was worn, despondent, and in fear for his career and even his life. He had need of all the fortitude he had displayed on former occasions, especially at his first wife's death. To help him he had a loyal and unified family in Sarah and her charges, Elizabeth's children. His daughters Elizabeth and Abigail were young women, still at home, and Edward was now at Christ Church, Oxford. All now rallied to the head of the family, as did 'Auditor' Edward and other relations in close-knit Harley fashion. In such circumstances political setbacks could seem minor, and Harley was soon to demonstrate that with his family, his friends, and above all his Queen to back him, he was ready to rally his forces. He had made mistakes, and as a result had now to wait for his opponents to commit even greater errors and give him his opportunity.

56. *Swift Corr.*, i, 75; *Vernon Corr.*, iii, 343.
57. *Swift Corr.*, i, 75–6.

CHAPTER 9

Opposition Again

IN LATER YEARS the Duchess of Marlborough was to assert that Harley saw the Queen regularly after his fall from office in 1708. The truth is less clearcut than her dramatization. There may have been one or two secret meetings, but on balance the wording of the letters of Abigail Masham, who was Harley's chief means of communication with Anne, suggests that he was not in personal contact with her before the spring of 1710. But he wrote to her frequently, and she considered his advice carefully, though she was not always able to take it. For instance, Mrs Masham wrote to Harley on one occasion: 'I can't tell you what use my friend has made of the advice was given her in your letter, but she heard it over and over. She keeps me in ignorance and is very reserved, does not care to tell me anything. . .'[1]

What is more important than his relations with the Queen – which were a foregone conclusion – is his attempted rapprochement with the Tories, its extent and its limitations. At the time of his fall observers were taken by surprise, so firmly had he seemed entrenched in the Queen's good opinion.[2] Even the Junto were taken aback by the ease of their victory, though they shyly admitted that their tactics in Parliament might have contributed to it. As for Marlborough, he had not included in his calculations the resignation of Harley's friends.[3] But if Marlborough saw that his troubles were only just beginning, the Tories might well have thought that their fortunes were reviving. Harley was no longer likely to draw off their own moderate element on every occasion. Now out of office himself, he would have to join them, or at least have their assistance, to remain an effective opponent of the ministry. Within a few days of his dismissal an opportunity for him to show Tory

---

1. *Conduct of the Duchess*, p. 264; 4 Feb. 1709[–10], Add. MS. 34,515, f. 106.
2. Beyries, 13/24 Feb., 1708, Staatsarchiv, Hannover, C.B.A. 24 (England), 92: '. . . une disgrace aussy peu prevue que L'a esté celle de Mr. Harley'.
3. Japikse, I, ii, 566; Somers to Portland, 4 Feb., Add. MS. 34,515, f. 208; Lord Coningsby's 'History of our divisions', Lansdowne MSS. 885, ff. 62–3.

ympathies was presented. The pugnacious Francis Atterbury had been
n dispute with William Nicholson, Bishop of Carlisle, since his institu-
ion as Dean, concerning his claim to be exempt from episcopal visita-
ion. The motives of the dispute were political; most bishops were Whigs
ike Nicholson, while Atterbury represented the Tory lower clergy. The
natter in question had a general application, for Atterbury had dis-
·overed that the statute of Henry VIII's reign upon which rested the
ight of visitation had never passed the Great Seal. His claim might,
f made good, deprive many bishops of their rights. Somers, with the
upport of the Archbishop of Canterbury, introduced in February 1708
ι bill to make the Henrician legislation legally valid, and it passed the
House of Lords against the opposition of the Archbishop of York. Har-
ey spoke strongly against the bill in the Commons on several occasions
naintaining that it would 'put the election of 28 members into the hands
of the Bishops'. And a few days later he also voted with the Tories in an
insuccessful motion claiming that the lack of British troops at Almanza
had been caused by a want of effectual and timely reinforcement from
England. From this time no-one doubted that he had thrown in his lot
with the Tories; whether they would consent to accept his leadership
again was yet to be seen.[4]

His conduct did not pass without attempted reprisal by the Whigs.
The report of the committee appointed to interrogate Gregg put the
worst possible light on Harley's conduct of office and offered Gregg some
hope of reprieve if he revealed anything against Harley; but Gregg obstinately declared that he alone was guilty, and so went to his death.
However, the stigma of the affair clung to Harley for a long time, and
the more so because an attempted invasion by the Pretender in March
1708 gave ground for rumours that 'this was Harley's plot'. The Queen
however refused, then or later, to believe in Harley's complicity in any
treasonable activities, despite the efforts of the Duchess of Marlborough
to persuade her of them. But for the moment Anne refused a request by
Harley that he might see her and vindicate himself.[5]

Baffled in their attempt to incriminate Harley, the Junto turned, as
soon as Parliament was prorogued on April the first, to the task of forcing
their way into the ministry. Harley had been replaced in the northern
office by Henry Boyle, whose promotion, though not a counterweight
against the Junto, could not be considered a success for them. And

4. G.V. Bennett, *The Tory Crisis in Church and State*, pp. 94–7; *London Dairies*, pp. 455–6; *Addison Letters*, p. 93; Downie, p. 105, points out that at about this time Harley was apparently almost ready to harass the ministry over the war in the Low Countries as well as Spain, in an apparently unpublished pamphlet anticipating many of the arguments he later supplied to Swift for the latter's *Conduct of the Allies*.

5. Howell, *State Trials*, xiv, 1385–6, 1391–3; *Vernon Corr.*, iii, 362; *Swift Corr.*, i, 78, *Private Corr.*, i, 110–14; Harley to the Queen, 5 March 1707/8, Loan 29/7/1; Abigail Masham to Harley, 17 April 1708, Add. MS. 34,515, f. 93.

Robert Walpole, who replaced St John as Secretary at War, was no
yet a considerable figure. Few observers doubted that the Junto were i
a good position to press their attack; but such observers underestimate
the timescale of the assault by failing to take into account the Queen'
obstinacy. She had a personal dislike of the leading Whigs, and saw th
question as one of 'whether I shall submit to the five tyrannising lord
or they to me'. Godolphin made every effort; he tried the threat of re
signation but found that it 'seems to make no manner of impression'.
But if Anne was obdurate with the Junto, she was kind to Harley. In Ma
1708 he was informed by the Queen's warrant he was to be allowed afte
all to keep the ceremonial plate he had received as Speaker and Secretar
of State. And the Queen must also have scotched a proposal by Sunder
land, which was not carried out, for depriving Harley of the stewardshij
of the royal manor of Cluntismalenny, an office which was held to b
powerful enough to influence the elections in the shire and borough o
Radnor.[7] Possessing these evidences of the Queen's goodwill, Harle
could retire to Brampton for the elections with an easy mind. Elsewher
the Whigs made moderate gains.

After the general election of May had dispelled any hopes the Torie
may have had of victory, Harley began to look about him for allies. H
could reasonably hope that the Tory leaders in the Commons would no
reject his assistance in their newly depressed state. However, his first an
most illustrious ally in the long, uphill struggle to overthrow the Junt
was not a Tory but one of the most influential of the Whig patricians
King William's former minister and favourite the Duke of Shrewsbury
Though Shrewsbury had spent the early years of Queen Anne's reign ir
Italy, Harley had kept in touch with him and had assisted his proteg
James Vernon, notably by not involving him in the impeachments o
1701. Thus, when the Duke returned to England in 1706 he was on cor
dial terms with Harley. But at that time Shrewsbury still held the con
ventional Whig attachment to 'no peace without Spain', and befor
Harley's dismissal he resisted, or at least did not warmly welcome, at
tempts by Marlborough and by the Duke of Buckingham to explore th
possibility of some kind of government of the centre. At the same tim
he had deplored the results of war stringencies on the English economy
which struck him afresh after his absence abroad, complaining 'it is cer
tain the country wants [peace] much more than they did the last war
money is so scarce that we are almost reduced to barter commodities'
The final triumph of the Junto over Harley appears to have decidec
Shrewsbury that peace would be long in coming if their influence wer

---

6. Klopp, xiii, 26, note 2; Coxe, *Marlborough*, ii, 421, 434 and 517.
7. William Lowndes to Harley, 11 May 1708, Loan 29/150/3; Sunderland's Cabinet Minutes
   Blenheim MSS. C1–16, D5, n.d. [early 1708].

not removed. By May 1708 at the latest he was meeting Harley's friends, and in the following years he acted closely with them.[8]

Among the Tories the overtures of Harley were greeted with more reserve. If Marlborough's information was correct, there was an attempt to reconcile Harley with Rochester. But nothing seems to have come of this at that time. More hopeful was his approach to Bromley. Harley wrote (20 August):

... What the gentlemen of England and the Clergy have to fear is very plain from what they already see. You will presently say what is the remedy? The plain cure is obvious, but how far that way is obstructed by the beseigers with their lines of circumvallation and contravallation a little time will discover. In the mean time I humbly crave leave to offer you my thoughts: we see plainly how this is brought upon us, and how those who are the smaller part of the nation have made themselves formidable and terrible to the greater. They have taken advantage of the mistakes of others, and tho' they hate one another, yet they unite together to carry on their designes. Why may not the same thing be done to preserve the whole and for good purposes which they do to destroy and overturn everything?

Bromley replied somewhat tartly. As to past mistakes, he would 'not enter into a nice discussion of that point'; and as to the future, he wished 'you had pleased to have been something more particular'. However, the general tone of the reply was not discouraging; and three weeks later, in reply to a further exploration, Bromley was warmer: 'I must repeat my assurance that I truly value your friendship and that I will on all occasions use my utmost endeavour to disappoint all arts that may be used to prevent our coming to a good understanding'.[9]

However, it was for Harley to make the first gesture, and in mid-October he announced to his friends that he intended to support Bromley's candidature for the Chair. At almost the same time the Junto announced to Godolphin that they intended to set up a candidate of their own, against both Bromley and the court candidate, Sir Richard Onslow, unless Somers and Wharton were admitted to office and Prince George removed from the Admiralty. As it happened, the last demand might have been omitted, for the Prince had been a near invalid for some time and now conveniently died. His death left Anne with no further strength, for the moment, to make resistance. At the end of the month

. Shrewsbury to Delafaye, 5 Oct. 1706. P.R.O. SP Dom. (Anne) 34/8 f. 70; *Cowper Diary*, p. 43; Buckingham to Shrewsbury, 29 Nov., Shrewsbury to Buckingham, 8 Dec. 1707, H.M.C. *Buccleuch*, ii, 718–9; Shrewsbury to Vernon, 22 March 1706 [–7], Add. MS. 40,776, f. 49; H.M.C. *Bath*, i, 191.

. Coxe, *Marlborough*, ii, 516; 20 Aug. 1708, Loan 29/128/3; H.M.C. *Portland*, iv, 504; Bromley to Harley, 12 Oct. 1708, Loan 29/128/3.

she listlessly agreed to admit Wharton as Lord Lieutenant of Ireland and Somers as Lord President of the council.[10] Her resentment at the treatment of her late husband was saved up for another day.

Parliament was opened by a commission on 16 November, in the absence of the Queen. Onslow was elected, and the government, with the solid support of the Whiggish Scottish contingent, was able to master the disputed elections which followed every general election. Although Harley himelf was in no danger his friends did not come off so well. Simon Harcourt was ejected as the result of an election petition from a defeated rival at Abingdon. Henry St John had not succeeded in retaining his seat at Wootton Bassett, or obtaining another, and was disposed to blame Harley for this, with the result of a cooling in their relationship, especially on St John's part. Harley himself could probably have done little to help at this time, and his bid to regain the Tory leadership now depended on his own skill, without the help of some of his closest allies.[11]

After such a beginning the tactics of the government's opponents remained on a subdued note. No criticisms were delivered until the voting of supplies was complete for the theatre of war in the Low Countries. But Harley found opportunities for worrying the government on the armies in Spain, pressing for full details of the expenditure on the last campaign, and rousing the House by his comments on the expense to the British taxpayer of conquering Spain for the benefit of the House of Austria. His attacks gave much disquiet to the ministers in private.[12] Harley was never very far ahead of public opinion, and when he came into the open on any question, he was likely to have the solid support of the public, both within and outside Parliament. The best that the Whigs could hope was that '[Harley] pretends to be at the head, which will make such men as Lord Nottingham draw off as many as they can from him'.[13] In face of Nottingham's brisk championship of the war in Spain, to which he had committed himself while Secretary of State, Harley had to proceed cautiously at first; but the seed of doubt had been cast and could be left to grow in the fertile ground of Tory doubts about the value of campaigns in a land where British armies were never large enough, and victory never in sight. While Harley looked about cautiously for further means of securing himself in the good opinion of moderate men, an opportunity was handed to him by his opponents. Apparently in revenge for his forthright remarks on the scandalously political vote ejecting Harcourt, a motion was carried to ask the Queen to produce the papers concerning the Gregg case. When they were delivered, Harley rose to point out that

10. H.M.C. *Bath*, i, 193; Sunderland to Newscastle, 19 Oct. and 4 Nov. 1708, printed by Trevelyan, ii, 414 and 416; Holmes, *British Politics*, p. 41.
11. *Wentworth Papers*, p. 71; Dickinson, *Bolingbroke*, pp. 63–5
12. L'Hermitage, 14/25 Jan. 1709, Add. MS. 17,677, DDD, f. 31v; Plumb, *Walpole*, i, 143.
13. *Private Corr.*, i, 197–8.

they included one which none of the members had seen before, Gregg's confession in which he completely exonerated Harley of complicity in his crime. This document was then read aloud, to the discomfort of those who had carried the motion, and Harley was allowed to give his account of the case. After this occasion little further was heard in Parliament of Gregg.[14]

Before the end of the session, Harley was allowed one further opportunity of gaining ground. This concerned the Treasons Bill, which was intended to bring Scottish legal practice into line with English as the result of the acquittal in Scotland of five men implicated in the attempted Jacobite invasion of 1708. When the bill came to the Commons, Harley inserted a clause making the provisions more humane by preventing the disinheritance of heirs of condemned traitors; and though the clause was opposed by the court and rendered ineffective by the House of Lords, he had demonstrated once again his ability to seize upon a cause which would gain the sympathy of all Tories and also some moderate Whig members. On the whole, therefore, he could look back upon a session of modest success, with no ground lost, a little gained, and the prospect of more to come.[15]

During the recess Harley's family circle was augmented, and his political alliances widened, by the marriage of his second daughter, Abigail, to George Hay, styled Viscount Dupplin, the son and heir of the Earl of Kinnoul. The marriage articles were originally intended to have been signed just before Harley's fall from office, though the confused political situation at that time had caused some delay on the part of the groom's family; but, it was reported, 'the young man had a liking to his mistress, and would not leave her'.[16] Dupplin proved to be a staunch political ally too, and was to be of considerable service in organizing the Scottish members in later years. This auspicious wedding, which took place on 11 August, seemed, in retrospect, to mark the beginning of a new rise in Harley's political fortunes. The first break in the clouds came from the ministry's handling of foreign affairs in the summer of 1709. Both in the unsuccessful peace negotiation with France and in a successful second attempt to conclude a Barrier Treaty with the Dutch, British policy was bent towards keeping the Dutch in the war rather than towards the ostensible objects of the negotiation. Marlborough was uneasy in this policy, but he consoled himself with the hope that he could precipitate a battle which would open the way to an invasion of the French homeland. The outcome, however, was the costly stalemate fought out at Malplaquet on 11 September 1709. The battle itself was unusually

14. H.M.C. Portland, iv, 518, 520, 521.
15. Burnet, v, 401–4 and 407–8; London Diaries, p. 495; H.M.C. Portland, iv, 522.
16. Private Corr., i, 208.

bloody, as well as expensive, and proved to be the last of its kind under Marlborough's generalship, a tactical success but a strategic failure which left French defences intact and made a miserable end to his string of major victories.

Harley and his followers did not neglect the opportunity. The argument which could be made out to show that Whig governmental profiteers and their City allies were benefitting from the continuance of the conflict, to the detriment of good Tory taxpayers, may be seen from St John's assertion that: 'We have now twenty years been engaged in the two most expensive wars that Europe ever saw. The whole burden of this charge hath lain upon the landed interest...' Such jeremiads were the stock-in-trade of all Tory politicians, or those who wished to appeal to the hearts of Tories. In conversation, Harley himself 'laid it down for a foundation [wrote Godolphin to Marlborough] that [you and I] were absolutely against [peace], and resolved not to admitt of him on any terms, which he would insinuate was very demonstrable 2 or 3 years since'.[17] Harley was aided by dissension in the other camp. The solid face of the Junto itself was beginning to crack. With the admission of Somers and Wharton to the ministry in 1708, only two of its members remained to be satisfied. One of them, Orford, was later appointed first commissioner of the Admiralty; but Halifax, who was disappointed by Marlborough of the opportunity to conduct the peace negotiations with France, fell out with the ministry, so that Godolphin saw no alternative but to 'let him have his full swing with Mr Harley'. Such a judgment did less than justice to Halifax's Whig loyalty, but it accurately caught his discontent with his Junto colleagues. At the same time, Wharton was reported to be on bad terms with both Godolphin and Somers.[18]

Such was the divided state of the ministry when the process of shattering it into warring cliques was completed by the Sacheverell case. Impeached for preaching, at St Paul's on Guy Fawkes' day 1709, a sermon which carefully blended High Tory political theory with personal abuse of Godolphin, Dr Henry Sacheverell raised a storm which blew the dust out of many a dim corner of politics. Harley swiftly realized that this impeachment was an excellent chance to discredit the ministry. His private opinion is probably reflected in a letter written by his sister Abigail to his son Edward: 'This business in all probability will break the Whigs; my foolish fears are it will raise the Tories to their old madness, the extravagance of every party is to be dreaded.' The attack on a clergyman by a Whig ministry brought about in the Church party an emotional return to the persecuting spirit of the Clarendon code. Harley was obliged to

17. St John to the Earl of Orrery, 9 July 1709, Bodleian MS. Eng. Misc. E. 180 ff. 4–5; Snyder, iii, 1324.
18. Coxe, *Marborough*, iii, 8; H.M.C. *13th Report*, Appendix, vi, 250.

swim with the tide or lose his influence with the Tories. In the crucial debates of January 1710 he voted against carrying the impeachment to the House of Lords.[19] How little at ease he was in putting himself publicly on the side of Sacheverell may perhaps be inferred from a report of his speech on this occasion by Cunningham: 'The members observed, that Mr Harley had in his speech made use of such a *circumgyration* of incoherent words as he himself had before condemned in Sacheverell; so that the House could not certainly discover from his expressions whether he spake for him or against him.' But another source, more nearly contemporary, says definitely that 'Mr Harley and some others spoke long and well upon this occasion in behalf of the Doctor'.[20]

A wave of popularity cowed the Whigs and sustained Sacheverell during his impeachment, which ended with the light sentence of a three-year suspension from preaching. Less easy was the fate of the ministry. In the course of the impeachment two Whig peers, the Dukes of Argyll and Somerset, had favoured the imposition of only a nominal sentence. Argyll was given hopes of a Garter, and Somerset was flattered with the belief that he would replace Godolphin at the head of a new and moderate ministry.[21] Where these noblemen led the way, smaller fry were swift to follow. Harley was zealous, according to Cunningham, in encouraging the expectations of all who could contribute to the downfall of the ministry, '...promising everyone whatever he desired; but at the same time he seemed to discover his most secret designs to those only whom he knew to be more solicitous about the public affairs than their own.' Meanwhile, Abigail Masham had long been pressing the Queen to remove Godolphin. The kind of arguments she carried from Harley may be seen from a note by Harley, dated 10 April 1710:

All sovereigns must of necessity have some screen between them and their people in mixed governments; the constitution places a screen between the Crown and the Commons but that is only as to the legislature. There remains to consider the person of the sovereign: and in this case it is necessary to have a personal screen. This is of daily use what every man has in common degree in his own family, and it is the placing of a favour right that makes a family easy and a kingdom happy.

Godolphin, it was implied, was not acting as a 'screen'.[22]

In the first week of April the Queen felt strong enough at length to

---

19. H.M.C. *Portland*, iv, 537; Oldmixon, p. 441; for a good modern account of the Sacheverell case, see Geoffrey Holmes *The Trial of Dr. Sacheverell* (1973).

20. Cunningham, ii, 286; Hearne, *Diary*, ii, 334.

21. Godolphin to Marlborough, 21 March, and 6 April 1710, Snyder, iii, 1440 and 1456; *Private Corr.*, ii, 420.

22. Cunningham, ii, 282–3. H.M.C. *Portland*, iv, 524; note dated 'April 10, 1710', Loan 29/10/20.

dismiss the Duchess of Marlborough from her presence for the last time. If the account of Lord Coningsby, the Harleys' old enemy, is to be believed, Godolphin was so disheartened that he was again entertaining offers of forming a ministry with his old colleague Rochester and the Tories, while Somers, as well as Halifax, was in similar negotiation with Harley. But only Harley and perhaps Shrewsbury knew the next move. On 6 April the Lord Treasurer went to the races at Newmarket, his favourite sport, feeling contented as a result of two amicable interviews with the Queen. On the 14th while he was still there, Anne dismissed her Lord Chamberlain, the Marquis of Kent, and appointed Shrewsbury in his stead. Godolphin had not been consulted about the appointment, but Harley had warned his friends to expect the change.[23] The appointment therefore, went almost unchallenged, though it proved in retrospect to be the decisive point in the downfall of the ministry. Several weeks passed before the Queen could be convinced that she could safely take the next step, the dismissal of Sunderland, but at last, on 29 May, Harley abandoned any further pretence and sent his friend Newcastle to Godolphin with the message that the Queen was determined to dismiss the secretary and appoint someone more acceptable to herself.[24]

At this moment the ministry might have saved themselves by a threat of resignation; Marlborough had shown them the way two years earlier. That they did not follow this example is the measure of their divisions. Tempted by vague offers from Harley, they decided to hold on to their own offices. At a meeting held in the house of the Duke of Devonshire, the principal members of the Administration, including Godolphin, signed a memorandum advising Marlborough to accept the dismissal of Sunderland without giving up his own command. More effective was the response of City Whigs. Immediately Anne dismissed Sunderland on 14 June some directors of the Bank of England, led by Governor Sir Gilbert Heathcote, procured access to her to request strongly that she would make no further alterations in her ministry. She replied untruthfully, as Paymaster-General James Brydges recorded, that she would make no further changes. Anne also helped to keep other Whigs quiet. It was noticed that the Duchess of Somerset, a rising favourite of the Queen, was at this time given apartments at the palace of Kensington and hopes of succession to the offices of the Duchess of Marlborough.[25]

There was a longer delay than Harley expected before a successor to Sunderland could be found; Earl Poulett, his follower, was offered the post first but refused, protesting 'a porter's life is a better thing'. The need

---

23. *Private Corr.*, i, 295; Coningsby's 'History of our divisions', Lansdowne MSS. 885, ff. 65–6; Godolphin to Marlborough, [4 and 7 April, 1710, Snyder, iii, 239–42; Kinnoul to Harley, 26 April 1710, Loan 29/146/4.
24. Coxe, *Marlborough*, iii, 231–2.
25. *Ibid*, iii, 245; H.M.C. *12th Report*, Appendix, part V. (Rutland MSS), ii, 190.

was for a fairly neutral figure whose appointment would not sting Godolphin and the Junto into violent reaction. After Newcastle and the Earl of Anglesey had been considered and rejected by one side and the other, the Junto reluctantly agreed to the Queen's own selection of a colourless figure, but a Tory, the Earl of Dartmouth. The argument Harley was propogating appears in a memorandum in his hand, dated 20 May: 'graft the Whigs on the bulk of the Church party'. He had half convinced some of the Whigs that he wished to form a mixed ministry, and thus was able to prevent them from taking firm retaliatory measures. Godolphin wrote sadly to Marlborough: '[Halifax, Somers, Sunderland], and generally the rest of [the Whigs] are so uneasy, that they are ready to make their court to [Harley], who appears as ready to receive it, and is making advances and professions almost to everyone that hee thinks our friends'.[26] The principal reason for the Whigs' willingness to court Harley lay in their consciousness of what one writer has called 'a revolution of opinion in the constituencies', consequent upon war weariness and the impeachment of Sacheverell, making a Tory victory likely if Harley advised the Queen to dismiss Godolphin and dissolve Parliament. Harley's apparent willingness to receive Whig courtship arose from a different reason, the strong support of the Bank of England for the minister, threatening a drying up of loans to government at the height of the campaigning season if further charges were made. For the next few weeks, accordingly, Harley continued to proceed cautiously.[27]

The downfall of Sunderland wrought an overnight change at court. 'All the Torys and Jacobitts flock to Kensington every day', wrote the disgusted Duchess of Marlborough. The Duke of Leeds, Charles II's Danby, had emerged from retirement to vote for Sacheverell, and now appeared at court, a spectral portent of returning Toryism to raise the hair of all good Whigs.[28] Every post brought fresh accounts of Sacheverell's almost royal progress to the West Country, amid delerious crowds at every halt on the way. The only expedient that Godolphin, in his desperation, could think of, was to ask Marlborough to urge the Dutch to point out to Anne the danger of changing her ministers. The States General formally resolved to inform the Queen that they hoped there would be no change, and she ordered Boyle to reply that the States should not concern themselves with Britain's domestic affairs and she hoped they would not do so for the future. In the City of London the

26. H.M.C. *Portland*, iv, 524; Burnet, vi, 9, Dartmouth's note; Harley's 'Memo 20 May, 1710' Loan 29/10/19; Snyder, iii, 1509–10; Brydges, 17 June, printed by C. Buck and G. Davies, 'Letters on Godolphin's dismissal in 1710', *HLQ*, iii, (1940), 230.
27. Boyer, *Annals*, ix, 231; Lansdowne MS. 885, f. 24; C. Roberts, 'The Fall of the Godolphin Ministry' *JBS*, xxii (1983), 71–93; B.W. Hill, 'The Change of Government...1710–1711',*Econ. HR*, 2nd. series, xxiv (1971), 395–413.
28. The Duchess to Gilbert Burnet, 29 June 1710, Bodleian, Add. MS. A. 191, f. 4; Browning, *Danby*, i, 564.

election of two Whig sheriffs at the end of June was taken as a further indication that the 'financial interest' was of the same mind as the Dutch.
Godolphin remonstrated with the Queen for seeing Harley, or at least
taking his advice, but the charge came far too late. One of Harley's
memoranda drawn up for an interview with Anne, dated 3 July, contains
the words 'you must preserve your character and spirit and speak to Lord
Treasurer. Get quit of him'. But the Whigs correctly attributed their
respite to 'carrying the merchants to the Queen'.[29] The Bank's directors were indeed threatening to cut off short loans to the Treasury if the
ministry were changed. Throughout July Harley continued to polish his
plans for the Treasury. Shrewsbury was offered the post of Lord Treasurer
– no doubt he could have managed it with Harley to assist him – but fortunately he refused.[30] Harley himself had no intention at the moment
of taking the post, which involved leaving the House of Commons. Instead he began to choose members for a Treasury commission of which
he would be the head.

The final obstacle to the dismissal of Godolphin was the character of
the Queen. Always reluctant to take the last decisive step, even when
the logic of her former actions pointed to it, she needed something to jar
her into action. The process was assisted by news that the States General
had formally broken off peace negotiations renewed with France that
spring at Gertruydenberg. But this event was not unexpected, and the
final stimulus was provided from anotehr quarter. The Bank of England
at last implemented its threat to cease, on a plea of political uncertainty,
the routine loans which government needed for the payment of the
forces. On 3 August the directors refused to make a loan of £100,000
urgently required by the spending departments, unless the Queen would
give them a further assurance that she proposed no change of ministry or
general election. The Queen refused to give a second interview and, no
doubt after consulting Harley on his readiness to take office immediately,
sat down to write a note of dismissal to Godolphin.[31]

Much now depended on the advice Harley gave the Queen on whether
or not to dissolve Parliament. The emotions raised in the Sacheverell
case made a Tory majority virtually certain. Bromley assumed immediately after Godolphin's dismissal on 8 August that an election would
follow automatically. But a Tory election victory inevitably meant that
the Tory leaders such as Rochester would have to come into the ministry,
and they would not easily be persuaded to serve with Whigs as their col-

29. *Private Corr.*, ii, 444; Dartmouth's cabinet minute, July 2 1710, William Salt Library; Klopp,
    xiii, 452; Edward Harley's 'Account', Lansdowne MS. 885, f. 24. 'July 3, 1710, Loan 29/10/19;
    H.M.C. *Portland*, ii, 211.
30. H.M.C. *Bath*, i, 198.
31. H.M.C. House of Lords MSS. xi, 326; Hill, 'The change of government...1710–1711', *Econ.
    HR*, p. 401.

leagues. For though Harley was scathing about the aspirations of Somers, he hoped to retain the services of such Whigs as Boyle and Cowper, who were not definitely associated with the Junto.[32] But if Harley wanted a mixed ministry why did he ultimately advise an election? Firstly, not to have done so would have meant the immediate loss of all Tory support. After tasting the bitter fruits of exile for so many years the Tories were in no mood to be kept from the lush pastures of Parliament, office and sinecure. Latterly they had indicated their feelings to him in a deluge of letters. And secondly, he seems to have been confident that by avoiding changes in the minor central and local government offices and commissions, he could prevent too sweeping a Tory victory.

That a dissolution of Parliament could not be announced immediately after Godolphin's dismissal was mainly due to a financial dispute with the Bank of England which threatened to end Harley's ministry ignominiously within its first few days.* On 10 August he took the office of Chancellor of the Exchequer, which in the absence of a Lord Treasurer was the linchpin of the Treasury. Though nominally subordinate to the First Commissioner, for which post he chose Poulett, Harley acted during his year as Chancellor in every practical respect as if he had been Lord Treasurer. The other three commissioners included one close friend, Sir Thomas Mansell, who had resigned with him in 1708, together with Henry Paget and Robert Benson, Paget was *persona grata* with the Whigs and was to be created Earl of Uxbridge by George I. Benson, son-in-law of Nottingham's brother Lord Guernsey, represented an influential High Tory family whose leader Harley intended to keep out of the ministry at all costs in order to prevent the recurrence of Anglican extremism. The balance of 'interests', the sops to unsuccessful aspirants, and the need to keep a majority of his own men in key positions came naturally to Harley. But first one powerful figure had to be conciliated, or at least neutralized, and Harley now made the first steps towards a reconciliation with Marlborough. For this task the most suitable approach was deemed to be through Shrewsbury, who accordingly at the end of August assured James Craggs, Marlborough's political intermediary, that the Queen had no intention of appointing a new Captain-General. One month earlier Anne had, on Harley's advice, instructed a newly appointed envoy to Hanover to offer the Elector the command-in-chief of the Allied forces in the event of Marlborough's resignation. But James Cresset, the envoy chosen, died on the point of embarkation.[33] His sudden death gave Marlborough time to demonstrate that he did not intend to resign in

---

32. Bromley to Charlett, 12 Aug. 1710, Bodleian, MS. Ballard 38, f. 150; H.M.C. *Portland*, ii, 213.

33. Coxe, *Marlborough*, iii, 339; H.M.C. *Portland*, ii, 214; *Wentworth Papers*, p. 127.

*See next chapter.

mid-campaign. The General was quick to respond favourably to Shrews-bury's approach, and, as later events fell out, was not unwilling to come to terms.[34]

Less certain was the attitude of Rochester. By the middle of August a usually accurate observer wrote: 'Lord Rochester is certainly highly dis-gusted against Mr Harley...he, Buckingham and Nottingham being left out of this new scheme'.[35] Of the three Tory peers mentioned, Notting-ham was unacceptable and the Duke of Buckingham was incom-petent, which made Rochester's support, or at least his neutrality, a necessity for Harley's attempt to control the rank and file of the Tories. These, by the beginning of September, with no dissolution of Parlia-ment announced, were beginning to grow restive and more suspicious than ever of Harley's intentions. They probably hoped that Rochester might still lead the government and perhaps even take the Treasury, of which he had been the head when Harley was still of Foubert's academy. But despite persistent reports that Rochester was not anxious to play second fiddle to Harley, he seems at last to have become resigned to the fact that the Queen did not intend to supplant her favourite. In the first week of September Rochester replaced Godolphin as Lord Lieutenant of Cornwall, and within the next few days several other Whig lord lieu-tenants were displaced.[36]

By the 12 September the financial situation, and the Queen, per-mitted dissolution. Harley had hoped until the last moment that Boyle could be induced to remain in the northern department, but the secre-tary was firm in his determination to quit. Harley jotted:

Much to be done in a few days.

If the Queen will reform her Cabinet the rest will be easier afterwards.

Present hands are necessary to carry on the affair. Most of the members of the House of Commons which are immediately necessary should be provided for before their elections.

There was the gist of his problem: the cabinet must be 'reformed' but 'present hands are necessary'. As to the first, the new men, Harley noted several names. St John's appeared first; the Harley family feared this am-bitious politician's impetuous temper, but he refused to be fobbed off with such places as secretary to Marlborough, or possibly Treasurer of the Navy, and would have to be given the secretaryship of state he desired.[37]

34. Coxe, *Marlborough*, iii, 342.
35. *Wentworth Papers*, p. 135.
36. H.M.C. *Dartmouth*, i, 297; Klopp, xiii, 485.
37. 'Memorandum, Sept. 12, 1710', Loan 29/10/19; Harley to the Duke of Newcastle, 12 Sept. 1710, H.M.C. *Portland*, ii, 218; another memorandum dated 12 Sept. 1710, Loan 29/10/19; H.M.C. *Portland*, vii, 12; Dickinson, *Bolingbroke*, pp. 71–2.

Similarly Harcourt's name went down as Attorney General. Both were very acceptable to Tories such as Rochester. The difficulty lay in carrying out the second half of the plan, retaining the 'present hands'. There is a report by the Imperial resident Hoffman that Rochester went to the Queen to tell her that any scheme of forming a government independent of parties would be impracticable, and that he and other High Churchmen were not inclined to serve with those who did not share their principles. But indeed the Whigs in high places were determined not to remain in office after the announcement of the dissolution of Parliament. Lord Cowper's diary shows that the writer resisted several strong attempts by the Queen and Harley to persuade him to retain the Great Seal. The tides of party instinct were moving strongly against a government of the centre.[38]

These were full days for Harley. His levées were crowded with office seekers and country gentlemen looking for pickings at a county level. Peter Wentworth, who decided that this was the time to push the Wentworth family fortunes, found him surrounded by such company: 'He received me very civilly among a crowd of old fashioned gentlemen. . . and asked me I had any commands for him, so I began my speech concerning you [i.e. Wentworth's brother] but before I had done he stepped away to another, which discouraged me a little; and so I saw him dispatch half a dozen. . .'[39] But if the old-fashioned gentlemen got little but fair words from Harley, his own followers were appointed according to plan. Between the 18th and 23rd of September Harcourt's appointment was announced, in place of Halifax's brother, Sir James Montagu; St John took Boyle's office as Secretary of State in the northern department; and a commission led by Harley's old schoolfellow Trevor took custody of the Great Seal. Somers and Orford were replaced as Lord President and First Lord of the Admiralty by Rochester and Admiral Sir John Leake, while Walpole lost the post of secretary at war to Harley's friend of long standing, George Granville. Finally, the Duke of Ormonde took, by hereditary custom, the lord lieutenancy of Ireland, in place of Wharton. Of the old ministry there remained in high office or cabinet only Newcastle, Somerset, and the Duke of Queensberry, who continued as third secretary for Scotland. During the three weeks which elapsed between these appointments and the elections there were no further major changes. Arguably there had already been too many for the successful implementation of Harley's hope for a court ministry with moderate Tory leanings, and once again he was caught up in the strong tide of partizan government. But Whig judges remained in

38. Klopp, xiii, 486; Cowper's *Diary*, 42–3, 45–6.
39. *Wentworth Papers*, p. 142.
40. H.M.C. *Portland*, iv, 598 and 610.

office, protected by the Act of Settlement embodying Old Whig policy, and leading Whig magnates remained on the old and dignified Privy Council (a fact which was to be of great help to a smooth change of dynasty in 1714); while enough ministerial Whigs remained in the lower offices, headed by Sir Robert Raymond as Solicitor-General, to testify throughout the life of the incoming ministry to Harley's desire for moderation despite the incessant complaints of the Tories.

CHAPTER 10

Chancellor of the Exchequer

HARLEY'S HOPE OF retaining a substantial element of moderate Whigs in his ministry, to offset pressure from the High Tories, was nowhere better evidenced than in his attempts to control national revulsion from the Whigs in the impending general election. Recent policies, embodied in the Townshend treaty and the wrecking of the negotiations at Gertruydenberg, were not widely known in detail, but the press had made clear the general tenor of the late ministry's warlike intentions. Of even more immediate concern to the voters, however, was the recent trial of Sacheverell, widely construed as an earnest of Whig intentions towards the whole establishment of the Anglican Church. Harley's alliance with several well-known Whig peers like Shrewsbury served, among other things, to show the electorate that the Queen's displeasure extended only to the dismissed ministers, not to the Whig party as a whole. At the Treasury board the new Chancellor steadily refused to use its patronage solely in favour of the Tory party, or to permit the widespread dismissals of existing minor officeholders demanded by the Tory hotheads. The clerks and officers of the customs, excise, salt, and post offices were ordered by the treasury commissioners 'to be very sure that they do not unduly meddle in elections contrary to law'.[1] Nonetheless, it became clear as soon as the election results were available that the Tory candidates had been returned with a majority over the Whigs of nearly two to one, with many Whig patrons losing control of closed borough seats.[2]

In the mind of the public there now remained only one question, which was formulated by White Kennett, a Whig, as 'who is, or who ought to be, the prime Minister, the Earl of Rochester or Mr Harley'. Harley, as the Queen's most trusted minister, was known to be the

---

1. H.M.C. *Portland*, vii, 22; *Lockhart Papers*, i, 319 and 323; *Calendar of Treasury Books*, (hereafter referred to as *CTB*), xxiv, part ii, p. 85, Treasury minute, 29 September 1710.
2. L'Hermitage, 17/28 Oct. 1710, Add. MS. 17,677, DDD, f. 618; *Wentworth Papers*, p. 149; Speck, *Tory and Whig*, 110 and 123.

architect of the new govenment. But the more extreme Tories had as little cause to trust him as had their opposite numbers of the Whig party. Their strategy was therefore to make use of his talent, and the favour he found with the Queen, until it was safe to discard him.[3] Harley was aware of their distrust but confident of his own strength. To deal with the problems of leadership he drew up a 'plan of administration' which was submitted to the Queen at the end of October, as soon as the results of the last elections were known. The majority of the House of Commons, he wrote, must be won over by 'hopes of places after'; all wavering or independent peers must be gained by the Queen herself to reduce or reverse the Whig majority in the upper chamber; the Allies must be forced to fulfil their treaty obligations, in order to bring efficiency to the Grand Alliance and popularity at home to the British government. These policies, Harley felt confident, were adequate to deal with the situation. By such means, he had written to the Duke of Newcastle, 'as so on as the Queen has shown strength and ability to give the law to both sides, then will moderation be truly shewn in the exercise of power without regard to parties only'.[4] The next four years were to revolve largely on his attempt to 'give the law' to those he had led out of the wilderness.

But before Harley met the new Parliament he was already at grips with a major crisis in government finances, the roots of which were found in the activities of the staunchly Whig City of London, especially the Bank of England.[5] Before his intricate manoeuvres to keep control over the newly elected Tory extremists can be fully understood it is necessary to turn to the state of national finances at the time of Godolphin's fall from office. The new ministry maintained the existence of a conspiracy in which, according to Harley's brother, 'the Bank, stock jobbers and moneyed men of the City all engaged to sink the credit of the government'. Its opponents laid stress rather upon the administration's initially uncertain political basis and on its lack of financial expertise, as the reasons for its failure to inspire the same confidence which Godolphin had enjoyed among the financial community; they argued that the uncertain political outlook put the Bank of England into difficulties which made it unable to lend to the government.[6]

Much of the confusion which Harley found on taking office was caused by the unfamiliar economic phenomena which were the result of

3. Bennett, *White Kennett*, p. 112, from Lansdowne MS. 1013, f. 134; H.M.C. *Portland*, iv, 574.
4. Hardwicke, *State Papers*, ii, 485–8; H.M.C. *Portland*, ii, 219.
5. L.S. Sutherland, 'The City of London in eighteenth-century politics', Pares and Taylor, pp. 52–3.
6. H.M.C. *Portland*, v, 650; Burnet, vi, 16. *Cf.* the earlier and fuller version given by H.C. Foxcroft, Burnet, *Supplement*, p. 432; B.W. Hill, 'The Change of Government and the 'Loss of the City', 1710–1711', *Econ. HR*, 2nd series, vol. xxiv (1971), 395–413.

financial techniques developed since he had entered Parliament. By 1710 the struggle with Louis XIV, which had lasted with one intermission since 1689, was in its eighteenth campaigning season. Britain's first major continental war in modern times was financed by the willingness of the House of Commons to guarantee the interest on vast public loans on behalf of a government of which it approved. But important as was public confidence, the new institutions of public credit were more important yet. The future of the Bank had been confirmed by Godolphin in 1707 when it undertook to circulate interest-bearing exchequer bills, another post-Revolution fiscal device, in return for the prolongation of its charter for as long as the bills should remain at large. To pay the interest on an accumulating burden of national debt, taxes, customs, and excise revenues had been vastly expanded. The land tax imposed since 1693 had become the main revenue, and it has been calculated that 'more branches of duties were imposed between 1702 and 1714 then had been levied during the preceding three reigns together'; but these did not meet the growing need and were subject to diminishing returns in a nation impoverished by war. The land tax fell in yield year by year.[7] Godolphin's straits had forced a resort to illegitimate methods, especially payment of government employees in arrears, if at all, and the issue of a vast mass of unfunded and unredeemable securities which never realized their face value from the day of issue. Navy and victualling bills, army and ordnance debentures, tallies and orders and even seamen's pay tickets all passed at a heavy discount. Navy bills – the Navy ran a debt of between four and five millions – had by the end of 1709 been discounted at 20 per cent, and were to fall lower yet. The paymasters rarely received cash from the exchequer; they borrowed in the open market for the best terms they could obtain on the security of the tallies, for most of the specie which came into the exchequer went to the bank to repay the frequent short term loans.[8]

'Public credit' was popularly associated with the value of the huge and indigestible mass of government securities which were sometimes a few months, sometimes, as in the case of the Navy bills which made up more than half the whole, years overdue for payment. At the time of Godolphin's dismissal these miscellaneous unfunded debts amounted to over eight million pounds, while the amount of cash found by Harley in the exchequer was a little over £5,000.[9] Observers often attributed the

7. E.E. Hoon, *The Organisation of the English Customs System*, p. 26; W.R. Ward, *The English land tax*, pp. 20 and 27.
8. Table of discounts, P.R.O. Treasury Papers, T1/143, f. 160. (For the important of the discount rate of Navy Bills as an indicator of crisis in government borrowing, see D. A. Joslin's 'London bankers in wartime, 1739–84', *Studies in the Industrial Revolution presented to T.S. Ashton* (1960), pp. 156–77); Loan 29/291, 'Tallies in Mr. How's hands', 9 Sept. 1710.
9. P.R.O. Treasury Papers T1/123, ff. 199–202, 'Abstract of a representation to Her Majesty', 31 August 1710.

government's troubles to the activities of 'stock jobbers of the nation's credit' or, as one peer put it, 'that damned tally trade'.[10] But the profitable trade in all forms of government scrip to the detriment of the nation's employees and creditors, who had to take payment in bills, tallies and pay tickets, was a sympton, not a cause, of the breakdown of war finance. However, Harley's immediate problem was the Bank of England's refusal to continue making loans. Fortunately, competition could be expected for its monopoly of favour. In 1707 the existence of rival groups of bankers had forced the Bank, in order to secure the renewal of its charter, to lower the terms of its tender for circulating exchequer bills. the renewal of this rivalry might soon be expected; in the words of Daniel Defoe, now acting as Harley's financial publicist, 'money will come in as naturally as fire will ascend, or water flow; nor will it be in the power of our worst enemies to prevent it'.[11] The directors of the bank needed neither the warning nor the reprimand; they were not unpatriotic, and their instinct, as well as their interest, was to support the government of the day. On the other hand they were cautious men, believing that the smooth functioning of short term loans could only be maintained by the guarantee of stable government. The alternatives before them were clear: they could help to make the new ministry secure by financing it in its hour of need, thus appearing to betray old friends for the sake of winning new ones, or they could continue to refuse credit in the hope of swiftly bringing Harley to the position of admitting that he could not carry on the administration.

The difficulties which the Treasury board had to surmount were sufficient to deter more experienced men. Halifax, the godfather of post-Revolution finance, wrote to Harley on the first day of the new commission: 'Your great abilities and your knowledge of the Revenue, will soon make you master of all the business, but how you will restore credit, and find money for the demands that will be upon you exceeds my capacity'.[12] The success of Harley's efforts is testified by the fact that Godolphin's fall, unlike the invasion scare of 1708 and the later alarm at the Queen's illness early in 1714, and despite the gloomy prevision of the directors, did not cause a run upon the bank.[13] Signs indeed that heavy withdrawals were in preparation, especially among Dutch investors, had not been lacking before the change. Some Bank directors who had visited the Queen in June had, it was believed, made the point that any

10. Loan 29/285, No date, but between June 1711 and June 1714; *Memoirs of Thomas, Earl of Ailesbury* (ed. W.E. Buckley, Roxburgh Club, 1890), ii, 634.
11. Clapham, i, 58; Daniel Defoe, *Essay upon Loans* (1710). H.M.C. *Portland*, iv, 584, makes Defoe's authorship clear.
12. H.M.C. *Portland*, iv, 560.
13. A single assertion of a run, cited by Clapham, i, 228, was written over half a century later and is almost certainly an error; the many panics of this period led to much later confusion.

domestic political change in favour of the peace party would alarm the foreign holders of stock into selling. A month later Marlborough had anxiously informed Godolphin 'I hear from Amsterdam that they are taking measures to draw their effects by degrees out of the several funds'. But such selling of stock as occurred seems to have been chiefly the speculative practice of bears anticipating a fall upon the announcement of the dissolution of Parliament.[14]

The most urgent need facing Harley was the upkeep of the forces in Flanders and Spain. The remittance overseas of commercial bills of exchange with which the paymasters could obtain local services or currency was usually put into the hands of a private bill contractor, and for the Flanders theatre of war this contract was allotted by Godolphin almost entirely to Sir Henry Furnese, an important City broker. At the same time as the bank's refusal to lend, at the beginning of August, Furnese ordered his agents in Amsterdam to accept no further bills from the British paymaster there until his outstanding account was settled at the Treasury. The whole situation of the British army in this theatre was in jeopardy, and Marlborough wrote that 'our troops were already beginning to desert for want of pay'. Faced with this situation, Harley repeated Godolphin's last request for a loan from the bank. The bank deputation, summoned to attend the board, agreed to ask their court to reconsider their decision. After some hesitation the bank offered £50,000 for two months instead of £100,000 for four months as requested; and further, though the loan was to be made in exchequer bills, the bank specified repayment in gold, which was to be withdrawn for this purpose from an emergency reserve held in Portugal for the British and Allied troops.[15]

The Treasury board had no alternative but to agree to these stiff terms. But the fortunes of the new regime were not entirely dependent either on the Bank or on Furnese. A month before Godolphin's dismissal various financiers had been sounded as to whether they would support a new administration. Several now came forward. The remittance business of Furnese was a plum worth securing, and the prospect of taking over part of the Bank's business was even more enticing. Harley and his colleagues accepted an offer to remit £350,000 to the forces in Flanders made by

---

14. L'Hermitage, 16/27 June 1710, Add. MS. 17,677, DDD, f. 524v; Marlborough to Godolphin, 17 June 1710 (N.S.), Add. MS. 9109, f. 176; H.M.C. *Portland*, iv, 559; Charles Davenant, *Sir Thomas Double at Court* (1710), p. 83.
15. Vryberge, (15–)26, August 1710, Add. MS. 17,677, YYY F. 104; B. Sweet to Marlborough, (4–)15 August 1710, Add. MS. 9110, f. 51; Marlborough to Godolphin. (Undated covering letter enclosing the last), Add. MS. 9110, f. 50. *Cf.* Furnese's demand for payment, 12 August 1710, P.R.O. T1/123, f. 117, and his account in T1/130, f. 12v; CTB, xxiv, 35, 15 August 1710. Harley's minute of the same date, Loan 29/19/2; Bank of England, Court Book (i.e. of the Court of Directors; hereafter cited as CB), F. 17–22 August 1710.

Messrs. Hoare, Gibbon and Lambert.[16] Repayment was not required until Christmas, by which time a new Parliament might be expected to meet and vote supplies, and so the survival of the new administration seemed more likely. The general effect was immediate in a lessening of tension. The Dutch diplomat Vryberge informed his masters, the States General, even before the deal was concluded, that the new administration was daily gaining strength. Within a few days British stocks had made a complete recovery on the Amsterdam Exchange. And some further unexpected assistance came at the end of August with the news of Stanhope's victory at Saragossa, upon which stocks in London rose as much as 6 or 7 per cent.[17]

At this point, however, Harley encountered a new financial problem when the Bank raised a fresh difficulty by objecting to the further issue of exchequer bills in loans to the home paymasters, on the grounds that they were being heavily discounted and fresh issues would depress them still further. Fundamental to the new administration's ability to keep its head above water was the circulation of these securities at or near par. Even a comparatively small discount would swiftly efface the advantage which their liquidity gave them over the deadweight of the mass of interest-bearing government obligations already under such a burden. Harley had a scheme for reducing the discount on exchequer bills with profit for the Bank, which he produced a month later, and of which he may have hinted on this occasion. At all events, he persuaded them to make a further two-month loan of £100,000, buoyantly claiming that he could have had even more. An observer caught a glimpse of him about this time being 'joious with the rich men', and there is no doubt that he could exert great personal charm, even on cautious bankers.[18]

By this time he had another reason for optimism, for as has been said, the Queen had agreed at last on or about 12 September, to the dissolution of Parliament. As a prelude to the general election the annual City of London election for Lord Mayor became the focus of attention, for here the Bank's Governor Heathcote, who was next in line for the honour, was opposed by Sir Richard Hoare, leader of the Tory banking combine.[19] Over the issue of Heathcote's policy towards the ministry the usual drone of tracts rose to a shriek. He sent one of them to the Duke of Newcastle: 'Enclosed is another paper. You see by this and the

16. *CTB* xxiv, 39, 22 August 1710; L'Hermitage, 7/18 July 1710, Add. MS. 17,677, DDD. f. 541; for a tender by Francesco de Caseras see Loan 29/290 and Loan 29/45f. Other offers are mentioned by James Brydges to Harley, 21 August 1710, Loan 29/291; *CTB*, xxiv, 42, 25 August 1710.
17. Vryberge, (18–)29, August 1710, Add. MS. 17,677, YYY, f. 105; H.M.C. *Portland*, iv, 577–8; L'Hermitage, (29 August-) 9 Sept. 1710, Add. MS. 17,677, DDD, f. 589.
18. CB F. 31 August 1710; *CTB* xxiv, 53; H.M.C. *Portland*, ii, 219; *Wentworth Papers*, p. 151.
19. When Abigail Masham became keeper of the privy purse in January 1711, she brought the privy purse account to Hoare's Bank. H.P.R. Hoare, *Hoare's Bank*, p. 15.

other I sent what is my crime...If we err'd, t'was in failure of our judg'-ments, and God of his mercy grant that that may be the case, but I cannot help being still of the same mind.' Heathcote was elected Lord Mayor, as was his due, but he was an unsuccessful candidate a few days later when the City of London elected Hoare and three other Tories as its parliamentary representatives. This result in a Whig stronghold was part of the national trend which swept the Church party into power, and it went far towards strengthening the Chancellor of the Exchequer's position.[20]

But though several slips had been averted, Harley's ministry was still insecure. Now that the immediate problem of Flanders had been averted by the Hoare loan, there remained the greater difficulty of supplying the British forces in the Iberian peninsula. Throughout the war Spain and Portugal had presented special problems of supply owing to the difficulty of obtaining commercial bills of exchange to remit to a theatre of war where trade languished. During Godolphin's last months the situation had deteriorated rapidly. His last, unsuccessful request for a loan from the Bank had been partly to meet bills drawn on behalf of Stanhope's forces in Spain.[21] Owing to the Bank's refusal the bills were probably not met, for either these or some others connected with the supply of Spain and Portugal were shortly afterwards protested in Lon-don. By a standing arrangement some business houses in Genoa remitted the value of £20,000 monthly in cash to the paymaster in Barcelona, accepting payment in London by means of bills drawn on the paymaster general of the forces abroad by the British resident minister in Genoa. In August these houses threatened to break their engagement because they had not received payment since May. One month later they suspended the contract.[22]

Such a portent could not be ignored, and Harley made shift to answer some of the bills. The Bank, however, again intervened. Taking advan-tage of the absence through illness of one of the leading moderate Whig directors, who would have opposed him, Heathcote obtained a resolu-tion that foreign bills of exchange should be discounted by the Bank only in the depreciated exchequer bills for the time being.[23] From this posi-tion of safeguarding the Bank's reserves at all costs his opponents could not subsequently shake him. The matter was of the gravest consequence to the Treasury, which immediately pressed the Bank to reverse its decision. Many of the loans made to the Treasury by the Bank took the

20. H.M.C. *Portland*, ii, 222; Abel Boyer, *Quadriennium*, i, 9–10.
21. Burnet, v, 248; CTB, xxiv, 33, 28 July 1710.
22. Boyer, *Annals*, ix, 248; John Chetwynd to Dartmouth, (28 August-) 8 Sept. 1710, P.R.O. SP 44/110, p. 96; William Chetwynd to the same, (1-) 12 Oct. 1710, P.R.O. SP 44/110, p. 129.
23. William Lowndes to William Chetwynd, 10 Oct. 1710, CTB, xxiv, 478; CB F., 4 Oct. 1710. *Cf.* Francis Eyles to Robert Harley, 6 Oct. 1710, Loan 29/290.

form of discounting bills drawn abroad on the paymaster general. Bills like this were bound to suffer from the Bank's decision, through the inability of the paymaster general to dispose of all such bills unaided. 'So severe a blow to the public credit could not have in any other manner been contained', wrote the Amsterdam banker John Drummond to Harley. Certainly any attempt by the Bank to preserve its own margin at this juncture automatically weakened the Treasury, and the measure was one which should have been taken only after other expedients to cope with the influx of bills had failed. A few days after their resolution the directors decided to make a call on 10 per cent of capital, which in the event, came in more easily than expected.[24]

One effect of the credit crisis, and especially of the difficulty which was experienced in meeting bills drawn in Spain and Portugal, was the reverse of what the Whigs intended. Immediately after the victory at Saragossa the Allied forces had advanced and occupied Madrid, there to await reinforcement from Portugal. It never came.[25] In vain the British ambassador at Lisbon, the Earl of Galway, pressed his home government to remit the subsidies due to the Portuguese troops, lest they should 'follow their inclination of doing nothing'. Instead the paymaster's reserve of gold in Portugal was shipped to England in October at the insistence of the Bank of England.[26] From Spain a British colonel reported that 'our army not having been pay'd since our coming into the country and as ill provided with bread was fallen into great disorder beyond the remedy of the Generals'.[27] The Allied army was forced to retreat from Madrid and the British force obliged to surrender at Brihuega, with decisive result for the war in the Peninsula. It is hard to see that the Chancellor and the Treasury board could have adopted for the Spanish theatre of war any other course than they did; under pressure from the Bank and inheriting a situation beyond their control, they failed to retrieve a situation already lost.

The arrival of the news of Brihuega in London on 23 December 1710 was the lowest point in the ministry's fortunes, for Harley had already taken the first steps towards retrieving the general financial impasse. He seized upon the problem which was fundamental to the whole structure of national credit, the problem of the exchequer bills. Under the first agreement of 1707 the Bank had discounted all exchequer bills for cash, but with the second issue in 1709 it reserved the right not to discount any bills until they had passed, after issue from the Bank, through the

24. J. Taylour to the Bank of England, 6 Oct. 1710, CTB, xxiv, 475; H.M.C. *Portland*, iv, 617; Clapham, i, 66.
25. Trevelyan, iii, 83.
26. Galway to Dartmouth, (22 Setp.-) 3 Oct. 1710, P.R.O. SP 44/110, p. 112; J. Taylour to the Bank, 4 Oct. 1710, CTB, xxiv, 474.
27. Trevelyan, iii, 334.

exchequer, usually in payment of taxes, and had been reissued by the exchequer. By the end of 1710 it was estimated that £975,000 of the bills in circulation – about one third of the whole – were still 'non-specie', that is to say they had not been reissued.[28] The original purpose of the bills, that of supplying the government with credit, was supplemented by their negotiability at a time when bank notes were still a comparative novelty and metal currency was in short supply.[29] It was in the subsidiary function, as transferable paper, that the bills were falling short of full usefulness in 1710.

Thus, if exchequer bills were to circulate as a substitute for specie the need to make them cashable at sight by the Bank was clear. In mid-November Harley submitted to the Bank a scheme to reimburse it for any losses sustained during the coming year by discounting the depreciated bills at face value.[30] The method proposed was to allow the Bank to take up a maximum subscription of £1,000,000, its interest guaranteed by Parliament. After much deliberation the directors offered to adopt the scheme if, among lesser alterations, the permitted subscription were increased to £1,500,000. At this the vials of wrath overspilt at the Treasury. The Queen, 'having had the goodness to offer so great a sum of money to remedy the mischief...but the Court of Directors having by their alterations expressed their unwillingness to comply with the proposal, thinks it will be very preposterous to press them to do what they declare themselves unwilling to undertake'.[31] More ominously, a government pamphleteer immediately remarked that 'the Bank should be called upon either to make all the said bills specie, or to yield up the Circulation of 'em to such as will undertake it'. Harley's assiduous cultivation of rival banking interests might yet yield further fruit.[32]

Despite this unveiled threat to oust the Bank from its most profitable undertaking, the negotiation ceased throughout December, frustrating the genernally high hopes which had been entertained that a strengthening of exchequer bills would restore government credit.[33] But in the same month the Parliament had met and strengthened the ministry's chances of survival. This was by no means a foregone result of the elections. After a stalemate campaign in Flanders during the summer of 1710 it was necessary to persuade Parliament that at least one more campaign must be fought in order to obtain as good terms as France had offered in 1709.

28. Clapham, i, 66.
29. For the reasons for the notable deficiency of specie, see Ashton, pp. 110–11. On the profit to be made by smuggling English coin to Holland, see the 'Letter from Rotterdam', 23 Sept. 1710, in P.R.O. State Papers 44/110, pp. 95–6.
30. CBF., 14 Nov. 1710.
31. CTB., xxiv, 100–1, 22 Nov. 1710; Treasury to the Bank, 23 Nov. 1710, *ibid.*, xxiv, 516.
32. Charles Davenant, *New Dialogues upon the present posture of affairs* (1710), an imaginary conversation supposed to have taken place on 18 Nov. 1710.
33. L'Hermitage, 14/25 Nov. 1710, Add. MS. 17,677, DDD, f. 645v.

The Tories disliked the Dissenters in the City of London, and they were anxious to bring the war and the land tax swiftly to an end. A phrase in the Queen's opening speech in Parliament had been taken as inimical to dissent and had lowered the quotation for Bank stock by 3 per cent. Harley had striven hard, with some success in the elections, to reassure the Dissenters that Tory persecution would not be renewed.[34] Now he had a difficult task; while he drove the Bank hard he was obliged to hold the Commons on a close rein.

Above all, his political measures had to take account of such difficulties as that presented by the negotiations over the exchequer bills; finance was an administrative problem, credit a political one: but the two were mutually dependent. A clause in the land tax bill to give priority of payment out of the income for 1711 to some deficiencies of 1706, 1707 and 1708 brought down the discount rate of the tallies from 30 per cent to 3 or 4 per cent.[35] On the security of the same tax a government loan of £200,000 was raised in the City on the day the bill received the royal assent, and the loan was taken in exchequer bills at face value, although they stood at 3 per cent discount on the market, in order to revive confidence in the bills after the Treasury's failure to come to terms with the Bank.[36] In the first days of the new year there arrived a victory for the Treasury in the dispute over the exchequer bills. On 10 January 1711, the Treasury asked the Bank if they would consider discounting the non-specie bills on demand in return for a sum of £45,000 a year, to be guaranteed by parliament as a fund for the payment of interest on a subscription raised by the bank. The subscription itself was to remain at the original figure of £1,000,000 suggested by the Treasury. The proposal was approved by the directors on the 11th and by the House of Commons' committee of supply on the 12th. Clearly the matter had been thrashed out and carefully prepared behind the scenes, both in the Bank and in the House, before it was rushed through the stages of formal approval. Such harmonized management was an area in which Harley excelled, as all acknowledged.[37]

Even as it stood, the transaction was very profitable to the subscribers, whose number included many of the Bank of England's own directors. Only £83,210 needed to be raised, being the initial 10 per cent paid up of £832,100 subscribed; and since the interest of 6 per cent on the total paid up was supplemented by 3 per cent on the nominal capital, the

34. Boyer, *Quadriennium*, i, 31–2; M. Ransome, 'Church and Dissent in the election of 1710', *EHR*, lvi (1941), 76–89.
35. L'Hermitage, 19/30 Dec. 1710, Add. MS. 17,677, EEE. f. 1.
36. Boyer, *Quadriennium*, i, 42.
37. On 1 December 1710, the Treasury had asked the bank to 'consider of some methods for reducing the discount of Exchequer Bills', *CTB*, xxiv, 108. For the submission of the scheme by the treasury, see *CTB*, xxv, 4, 10 Jan. 1711; for the court's acceptance, *CBF*. 11 Jan. 1711; and for the approval of the committee of supply, see: *Bolingbroke Corr.*, i, 69.

subscribers reaped a total yield of 36 per cent.[38] The bribe was a considerable one, but the benefit to the Treasury through the stabilization of exchequer bills was correspondingly great. On the day the House of Commons agreed to the scheme the discount rate fell from 3 to 1½ per cent. In March 1711 the Bank began to accept non-specie bills, and the first problem of the crisis was solved.[39]

The next problem to be attacked by the Treasury board was the government's short-term debts to the Bank, some of which had several times been extended by one or two months, and which by December 1710 amounted to about £600,000.[40] The efficiency in parliamentary technique which Harley had displayed in obtaining a fund for settling the exchequer bills could not but make an impression in the City, and he was not slow to follow up the advantage. With the facility of a conjuror who produces the rabbit after due intimation that the hat is not devoid of content, he now unveiled his proposition. He had often hinted of his plans for restoring public credit. Now he produced his first scheme: it was the lottery loan.

The importance of the lotteries of 1711 can only be mentioned here, though they played the major part in restoring government credit. They were the best and easiest way of raising loans, and they restored the government to solvency. In the spring of 1711 two lotteries brought in £3,500,000. Weeks before the books were opened for the first lottery in March the million and a half expected to be subscribed was already mortgaged to various government contractors and creditors. By extracting an assurance that the Bank would receive priority for payment out of this imcome, the directors agreed in the middle of February that they could recommence the discounting of foreign bills.[41] The lottery was oversubscribed on the day of its opening, and preparations immediately went forward for another. And when the second lottery opened its books two months later it was so well received that the subscription was increased from one and a half to two million pounds.[42] The thaw in relations between ministry and Bank became assured when, after a two year period of office, Heathcote's term as governor expried in April 1711. The elections for a new governor and directors were conducted with unprecedented acerbity on the issue of whether the outgoing officers had misused their authority in regard to the government. But the notoriety given to Dr Sacheverell's purchase of a voting share of Bank stock brought more prominence to the Tory attempt to storm these elections than was justified by the outcome. All the Whig candidates were return-

38. Clapham, i, 68–9.
39. Luttrell, vi, 677, 13 Jan. 1711; CTB, xxv, 32, 23 March 1711.
40. CBF. 2 Jan. 1711.
41. CBF. 15 Feb. 1711.
42. Boyer, *Quadriennium*, i, 178 and 295.

ed with handsome majorities – governor, deputy, and directors. Just as the Bank had failed to oust the ministry, so the Tories had failed to find a lodgement in the citadel of the Bank.[43]

To set a seal on Harley's success in the financial situation he still had to deal with its best known aspect, the unfunded debts. His solution was the South Sea Company, which evolved out of a scheme drawn up by a City financier, John Blunt, in the autumn of 1710 for a form of holding company for government securities.[44] The South Sea scheme, as presented to Parliament in May 1711, was a later development apparently designed by Harley himself.[45] Unlike the Bank of England and the New East India Company, the South Sea Company was not founded in order to raise a share capital; such an expedient was rendered unnecessary by the success of the lottery loans. Instead, Harley designed it to amalgamate in its capital stock the government debts which stood at the highest discount in the market. The interest payment on such securities would now be assured, in theory, by a government annuity to the Company of 6 per cent of the capital thus converted from old debts. The fabled wealth of the 'South Seas' (that is, for the most part, Spanish Central and South America) which the Company proposed tap, was sufficient attraction to bring most government creditors into the company.

Harley's ability to balance rival interests in his own favour, to synchronize apparently incompatible activities, is rarely better displayed than in the foundation of the South Sea Company. Though he encouraged the Tories in Parliament to consider the company as a prestige rival to the Bank, he was too well aware of the Bank's usefulness to attempt any real infringement of its privileges; indeed, he leaned backward, to avoid giving grounds for further fears. The directors were able to inform the shareholders that they had secured the insertion in the South Sea Act of a clause preventing the company from either issuing notes or keeping cash deposit accounts for its customers. At each stage of the formation of the company, Harley gave the Bank's directors opportunity to state their views. By this means the new court of directors was convinced of the constructive and conciliatory intentions of the government.[46] Though acclaimed by the Tories as a panacea for all the evils of deficit finance, the South Sea Company was chiefly important as an administrative convenience. It anticipated the later principle of the

---

43. *Ibid.*, i, 264–5.
44. George Caswell to Harley, 6 Oct. 1710, Loan 29/28;
45. It is sometimes attributed to Daniel Defoe, though his role must have been limited to suggestions.
46. Bank General Court Book 2, 26 May 1711. *Cf.* Clapham, i, 81; for an example of Harley's anxiety to conciliate the directors see *CTB*, xxv, 84: 'My Lord [*sc.* Treasurer, as Harley became on 29 May] says the Bank shall have the Charter for the South Sea Company before the warrant be carried to the Queen, for them to consider'.

'consolidated fund' by making a general parliamentary provision for diverse debts. After the crisis of 1710 some such consolidation was almost an inevitable development, and despite the clumsy facade of a trading company, Harley's scheme pointed the way to Henry Pelham's innovations in settling the National Debt four decades later.

The South Sea Company, unlike Harley's earlier Land Bank, was not a rival to the Bank of England, which, feeling its position now secure, could afford to be co-operative. From April 1711 until the end of Harley's administration the relations between the government and the Bank were apparently amicable. The Tories in the Commons and the Whigs in the City recognized their mutual dependence. Financially as well as politicially this was a far-reaching achievement. Financially because the Bank, though threatened with rivals, was confirmed in its monopolistic position as a private body within the national fiscal system; politically because the outcome of the crisis removed a fear that the government credit system built up since the Revolution could crumble as the result of a change of administration. To Harley must go the chief credit for this outcome, which hardly seemed likely in the first months of his administration. He had learned from the failure of the Land Bank a new policy which determined the future relations between government and its chief financial supporter; each major stage in the recovery of government credit – the establishment of the value of exchequer bills, the lotteries, and the funding of government debts in the South Sea Company – was marked by substantial concessions to the Bank. But at the same time the dominance of the politicians over the financiers was asserted for good. While 'public credit' had been held to be the perquisite of a particular man or ministry, and not of the national government as such, confusion was bound to attend every change of administration.

Harley had himself named as the South Sea Company's first governor, enhancing the apparently political bias of the new foundation, to please the Tories. And it is to these Tories, the High Churchmen and the hard-drinking backbenchers of the newly-formed October Club that this account must now turn for a fuller appreciation of Harley's remarkable achievement in stabilizing his ministry amidst surrounding uncertainties.

CHAPTER 11

Lord High Treasurer

MORE THAN ANY other aspect of his administration, Harley's struggle to restore financial stability caught the public imagination. But he was not only Chancellor of the Exchequer and virtual head of the Treasury. He was the Queen's chief adviser and the leader in the House of Commons of the party which he had brought to power. In both the latter spheres he met repeated challenges to his authority during the early months of 1711. As if the task of conciliating the City and the moderate Whigs was not enough, he had also to control the turbulent discontent of the Tories. At times he came near to failure. From the first days of the session the hotheads called for the impeachment of Godolphin and other former ministers.[1] Such a proceeding would have rendered futile Harley's efforts to convince the City of the moderation of his government; and it would have delivered him entirely into the hands of the extremists by preventing the possibility, which he always kept before him, of bringing back moderate Whigs like Boyle and Cowper into the ministry. At first he resisted pressure without difficulty. Before the Christmas recess, as has been seen, the Tories were sufficiently impressed by the gravity of the financial situation to give support to Harley's emergency fiscal measures. Thereafter, opposition developed rapidly to his policy of retaining all the armed forces at full strength for a further campaign in order to negotiate peace from a position of strength. Furthermore, the best means at hand for coercing him to prosecute the old ministry lay in obstructing the long procedure of voting the apportionment of taxes. The right wing soon discovered their strength. Encouraged by the mass of new and mostly young members elected to revenge the martyrdom of Sacheverell and put and end to the war, they formed themselves, early in the New Year, into the October Club for deep drinking and high politics.[2]

1. *Wentworth Papers*, p. 161.
2. John Cope to Lord Raby, 2 Mar. 1711, Add. MS. 22,231, f. 105: 'The age of most of the members is more suitable to their house of drunken entertainment than to that other august assembly to which they all belong'.

It soon became clear, however, that the October Club was only one aspect of the Tory opposition. The well-spring of intransigence was not in the House of Commons but within the ministry itself. Though Harley's fear concerning St John did not yet appear to be justified while the Secretary retained a cautiously moderate stance, any support that Harley could expect from Rochester was at best lukewarm. It was generally rumoured that the Lord President had been responsible, against Harley's wishes, for the insertion of the alarming promise of 'indulgence' rather than the customary 'toleration' for Dissenters in the Queen's opening speech; though rumour may have been mistaken, for 'indulgence' was a term which came naturally to Harley himself. A month after the opening of Parliament, the new Hanoverian resident in London, Kreienberg, was reporting to his home court 'a perpetual jealousy between these two'.[3] The chief cause of dissatisfaction to Harley's colleagues was his continued refusal to make sweeping changes in the minor personnel of government. His attitude remained the same as when he had protested to Godolphin before Parliament met in 1705 'lest persons who serve without reproach be turned out for not being of a party'. Ability to serve the Queen was more important than political partisanship, and if officials appointed by the previous ministry would support the present one, they should be protected; in his own words, when requested to dismiss certain Scottish officers, his policy was that the government should 'not dismiss them without calling 'em together and asking for a definition of their position and whether they will enter her Majesty's measures'.[4] One concession, indeed, Harley made. George Clarke, a scapegoat who had been dismissed for voting against the election of John Smith as Speaker in 1705, was restored to the board of the Admiralty. But Harcourt commented bitterly in private 'I wish all other offices was filled with as good men. Good God, what a glorious government this we have.' So small was the approval Harley could expect even from one of his closest friends in any attempt to put his ethic of the Queen's service before the demands of party government.[5]

Before the end of the Christmas recess, however, he was able to offer the Tories a more substantial sacrifice in the figure of Robert Walpole, who had been allowed to retain one of his posts, that of Treasurer of the

3. Dickinson, *Bolingbroke*, pp. 76–7; Kreienberg's report s 28, Nov./9 Dec., and 19/30 Dec. 1710, Niedersächsisches Staatsarchiv, C.B.A. 24 (England), 99. Harley was capable of assuring one of the leading Dissenting divines, at the time of the dismissal of Godolphin, that 'there is a resolution to preserve the Indulgence inviolable': Harley to Dr. Daniel Williams, 5 Aug. 1710, Brampton MSS. Lord Raby wrote: Harley 'did govern all till Lord Rochester and the crowd of Tories came in upon him, how I don't yet know', *Wentworth Papers*, p. 132. Another observer speaks of 'Mr. Harley's party' holding back from attacks on Godolphin by 'Lord Rochester's party' during this session: Cunningham, ii, 352.
4. H.M.C. *Bath*, i, 74; a draft written by Harley for the Queen, n.d. Loan 29/12/6.
5. Harcourt to Charlett, 15 Dec. 1710, Bodleian, Ballard MS. 10, f. 123.

Navy, but who had continued to oppose the government in the House of Commons, and was dismissed on 1 January 1711, the day before Parliament was due to re-assemble. And a fortnight later the Duke of Marlborough was prevailed upon to induce his wife to surrender her offices in the royal household.[6] These places were taken by two of the Queen's newer favourites; the Duchess of Somerset became Groom of the Stole and First Lady of the Bedchamber, and Mrs Masham received the custody of the privy purse. As to Marlborough himself, Harley wrote with satisfaction to the Duke's most powerful supporter, the Elector of Hanover, that the dismissal of the Duchess was 'so far from hindering the Duke from continuing his places, that he seems resolved to accommodate himself to the Queen's pleasure and goe on in her service'.[7] By securing the wavering Duke while dislodging the tenacious Duchess, Harley hoped to please the Tories without alarming the City and the House of Hanover. But the effect of the dismissal of Walpole and the Duchess was not so much to sate as to excite the appetite of the Tories. Their aims remained twofold: in Jonathan Swift's words 'to call the old ministry to account and get off five or six heads', and in the words of another Tory 'to have every Whig turned out and not suffer that the new ministry should shake hands as they do with the old'.[8]

While taxes were being voted, Harley resorted to his old devices for diverting the House of Commons. He provided a programme of legislation calculated to meet the approval of the Church and Country interests. To investigate the finances of the last ministry the commission of accounts was revived. And though withholding political advantages from the Tories, he was prepared to conciliate them by retrenchment and even by direct financial aid to a good cause. A bill to provide funds for fifty new churches in the London area passed into law during the session, despite financial stringency. And to prevent the introduction of a Place Bill which would have weakened the government's already tenuous hold on the Commons, Harley supported as an alternative another Tory measure, the Property Qualification Bill.[9] Nevertheless, the Place Bill passed its stages in the Commons during January, with the Tory back-benchers pressing hard for it; even Harley's conciliatory gestures were turned against him, and when he supported a bill to lift the restriction on the import of French wines, in defiance of Britain's treaty obligation to Portugal, the Tories accused him of secretly encouraging the House of Lords to reject the bill. Wrote the Hanoverian resident again: 'It is certain that in no Parliament of which he has been a member has he been

6. Plumb, *Walpole*, i, 165; *Wentworth Papers*, p. 174. Cf. Churchill, iv, 369.
7. Boyer, *Quadriennium*, i, 155; Harley to the Elector, 19/30 Jan. 1711, Stowe MS. 241, f. 142.
8. Swift, *Journal to Stella*, i, 195, 18 Feb. 1711; *Wentworth Papers*, p. 180.
9. H.M.C. *Mar and Kellie*, i, 485–6.

less followed than in this'. The Tories had the bit between their teeth.[10] In this atmosphere of distrust the government's business in the Commons sank into stagnation in February. In vain Harley hinted that he had a scheme to restore the financial situation as soon as supplies were passed.[11] Until he made some concession, the October Club were prepared to dig in their heels, accusing him of hindering their attempt to punish the former ministers; on one occasion, indeed, he was only able to force the House to resume its proper business by threatening that Parliament would be dissolved if the financial estimates were not passed.[12]

In desperation Harley tacked towards the Whigs. In a division on the 20th over a Tory attempt to censure Sir James Montagu, Halifax's brother, for alleged electoral malpractices, he actually voted with the Whigs.[13] Taken with his threat of dissolution, this gesture must be regarded, as it was no doubt intended, as a disciplinary threat to the Tories. It is possible that he seriously considered calling a new Parliament and forming a coalition ministry; the Whigs certainly entertained the hope of some such outcome. Marlborough, when he left England at the end of February for the coming campaign, was convinced that the ministry could not continue on its existing footing: 'At bottom [wrote another Hanoverian observer] my Lord Duke is entirely in agreement with Lord Townshend that the government cannot last long as it is, and that one of the two factions, Rochester's or Harley's, must take entire direction of affairs.'[14] The impasse at which the government had arrived by the first week of March, unable to stave off the creditors of the service departments by further promises, and with the Commons delaying the voting of taxes until measures were set on foot which would have alienated the Bank, was the worst parliamentary situation that Harley had hitherto faced.[15] Indeed, the Tories were talking openly of forcing him to resign 'unless he rewards their labours better or tell them why his predecessors were in fault'.[16] The accumulating problems were

---

10. Kreienberg, 30 Jan./9 Feb. and 9/20 Feb., 1710/11, Niedersächsisches Staatsarchiv, C.B.A. 24 (England), 99. Kreienberg wrote in French, translated here as elsewhere in this work.
11. Thomas Rowney to Charlett, 8 Feb. 1710(−11), Bodleian, Ballard MS. 38,f . 191: 'We go on very slowly with our supply. Mr. Harley tells us he will pay the debts after we have provided for this years services'.
12. Kreienberg, 20 Feb./3 Mar. 1710/11, C.B.A. 24 (England), 99.
13. *Ibid.*, 23 Feb/6 Mar.
14. Robethon's report, 21 Mar. (N.S.) 1711, Klopp, xiv, 675. In French. Much of this and the succeeding paragraphs is taken from my Cambridge dissertation on 'The Career of Robert Harley, Earl of Oxford, from 1702 to 1714' and was subseqeuntly published in my article in *Econ. HR* (see chapter 9, note 27 above).
15. Clarke to Charlett, 1 Mar., 1710(−11), Bodleian, Ballard MS. 20, f. 67; 'We of this place [sc. the Admiralty] look with longing eyes after some method to lessen the discount of Navy and Victualling bills, but as yet no glimpse of comfort, tho' some still feed us with hopes, which is so thin as yet that many an honest man has starved upon it'.
16. Cope to Raby, 2 Mar. 1711, Add. MS. 22,231, f. 105.

solved for him in an unexpected and dramatic fashion. On 8 March a French spy, the Marquis de Guiscard, while under interrogation by the committee of the cabinet, attacked and wounded the Chancellor of the Exchequer with a knife. He was saved from the worst effects of the blow by the thick gold brocade of the formal coat he happened to be wearing. He withdrew from public affairs, his popularity in the House of Commons rising overnight on a wave of indignation and sympathy. Some observers excited Harley's denial by claiming that the knife was primarily intended for St John.[17] But no reflected glory in which the Secretary might bask could dim the splendour which radiated from the sickbed of the real victim. Before Harley emerged again six weeks were to pass, during which time the inability of the ministry to carry on without him became daily more evident.[18]

Harley was in no hurry to give up the advantage of his unexpected reprieve from parliamentary intransigence, though he continued to call his colleagues to his sickroom for consultation while he put the finishing touches to the South Sea scheme. It was probably during his long absence that he was reconciled with Rochester and his first quarrel with St John came to a head. During Harley's dispute with the October Club the ambitious secretary's position had been difficult and unsatisfactory to both sides. In the Commons he had not hesitated to flay the 'money'd men' while Harley tried to calm them. Among the handful of court voters who followed Harley in defence of Montagu, the name of St John is conspicuously absent. Three years later Harley was to accuse St John, in a paper drawn up for the Queen's eyes, of more than mere sympathy with the October Club. He recalled: 'The beginning of February 1710–11, there began to be a division among those called Tories in the House, and Mr Secretary St John thought it convenient to be listing a separate party for himself.' And it is not likely that Harley would have greatly mis-stated the case to one who knew the facts.[19]

But apart from St John's behaviour in the Commons, there arose another serious disagreement over war strategy. At the time of Harley's wounding, an expedition was in preparation, at St John's insistence, with the object of capturing Quebec. The scheme had first been drawn up during Godolphin's ministry, but was abandoned in the summer of 1710 when the uncertain political situation delayed the expedition until

17. *Swift Corr.*, i, 238–42; Boyer, *The Political State of Great Britain* for April 1711 stated that after stabbing Harley, Guiscard rushed towards St John. Harley wrote a laconic 'false' against this passage in his copy – Loan 29/166/2.

18. *Bolingbroke Corr.*, i, 114; *Wentworth Papers*, p. 189.

19. Dickinson, *Bolingbroke*, p. 78; Kreienberg, 23 Feb./6 Mar., 1710/11, CBA 24 (England).; 'A brief account of the public affairs since August 8, 1710 to this present 8th of June, 1714...' printed in, *Parliamentary History*, vi, appendix iv, column ccxlv.

the season was too far advanced for likelihood of success.[20] After St John
revived the project and obtained the Queen's approval, Harley does not
seem to have offered much opposition to the early stages of preparation.
Nor is it likely that he objected to the selection of Mrs Masham's
brother, Colonel John Hill, as commander of the land forces of the
expedition. Indeed, the appointment of Hill was St John's strongest card.
But Harley could not view the preparation of an expensive expedition
with enthusiasm while his government was struggling to honour existing
financial commitments. His opportunity came at the time of his wound,
when he sent Poulett with his 'dying request' to Rochester that the
expedition should be laid aside.[21] Nevertheless, Rochester's decision to
press the cabinet to abandon the scheme was not taken until five weeks
later and was impelled by a new factor in the international situation. On
17 April there arrived news of the death of the Emperor Joseph and the
consequent succession of the Archduke Charles, or 'King Charles III' of
Spain, to the Habsburg dominions and, almost as certainly, to the
Imperial throne. The Queen immediately called an emergency meeting
of the cabinet for the following evening. The prospect of Charles controlling both the Empire and the territories of the Spanish crown was no
less distasteful to Britain than that of Philip V possibly ruling France and
Spain. Rochester saw an immediate argument for concluding peace
without further trying to obtain Spain for the future Emperor; and he was
prepared to sacrifice St John's project as no longer necessary or desirable.[22] Harley had gone out of his house for the first time on the 16th,
and Rochester urged him to come to the cabinet meeting; but Harley
either was not strong enough or saw no reason for burning his fingers
on the question of the expedition and contented himself with prim-
ing Rochester with arguments for the meeting. As a result, the strong
personality of St John prevailed in the cabinet; Rochester's objections
were swept aside, and the expedition proceeded as planned, with St John
expressing surprise and indignation to Harley at Rochester's intervention.[23] But the episode left Rochester in closer sympathy with Harley.

Despite this setback, the matter which chiefly occupied the Chancellor of the Exchequer during his convalescence, the South Sea project,
achieved his object of satisfying the Commons. Before the presentation
of the scheme itself, Edward Harley, as Auditor of the Imprest, reported
to the House of Commons on 4 April that £35 millions voted by

20. H.M.C. *Portland*, iv, 656; G.S. Graham, *The Walker expedition to Quebec, 1711* (Toronto, 1953).
21. H.M.C. *Portland*, v, 655.
22. H.M.C. *Bath*, i, 200; Kreienberg, 20 April/1 May, 1711, CBA 24 (England), 99.
23. Rochester to Harley, 18 April 1711, Loan 29/197/105, printed in H.M.C. *Portland*, iv, 675 with the omission of Rochester's request to Harley to come in person; *ibid*, iv, 676.

Parliament in Godolphin's time or earlier had not yet been passed by audit. The effect of this report was sensational, as its devisers intended but the deficit was largely a technical one resulting from cumbrous accounting procedure, though it also uncovered numerous malpractices by minor government officials. Its main purpose, to enable the Tories to let off steam against financial abuses as a consolation for Harley's refusal to allow impeachment, showed the same technique that he had used in 1702–3. On the 28th the former ministry was resolved by the Commons to have been responsible only for 'a notorious breach of trust'. Two days earlier Harley had appeared in the House for the first time since his injury, though he stayed only long enough to receive the compliments of members and left before business could be raised.[24] He was not anxious to be involved in the debates over the alleged deficit, especially since St John had unexpectedly complicated the issue by defending one of the defaulting officials, his friend and private banker James Brydges, pay-master general of the forces abroad.[25]

By the beginning of May, however, the stage was cleared for the main play. On the 2nd, in the House of Commons, Harley at last revealed his long-promised scheme to restore public credit. After outlining the plan for a South Sea Company he went on to emphasize the need to vote the remaining war supplies for the coming season so that Britain could bargain from strength to obtain a good peace. This time there was no opposition. For the next three weeks applause swelled as he carried the South Sea Bill and the service estimates together through their stages in the House. On 2 May also, while Harley was unfolding his scheme to the delighted Tories, the Earl of Rochester died suddenly.[26] His initial rivalry with Harley had of late been diminished, if not altogether removed, by the Chancellor's policies as well as by St John's behaviour. On Harley's shoulders, therefore, the mantle of Rochester fell con-veniently. Already it had been decided that, in consideration of his health as well as his importance, Harley should take a place on the earls' bench of the House of Lords. There were rumours during April that he would become a peer and take the post of Lord Treasurer. On 23 May he accordingly received the title of Earl of Oxford, to which he laid claim by reason of a marriage relationship with the previous bearers, the family of De Vere; and he took also the ancient title of Earl Mortimer, lest any other claimant should challenge the former title.[27] With skilful

---

24. Boyer, *Quadriennium*, i. 287; Kreienberg, 27 Apr./8 May CBA, 24 (England), 99.
25. Swift, *Journal to Stella*, i, 252–3, 27 April 1711. For a fuller account of this incident, see: Godfrey Davies, 'The Correspondence of James Brydges and Robert Harley', *HLQ* i (1938), p. 457.
26. L'Hermitage, 4/15 May 1711, Add. MS. 17,677, EEE, f. 193; Boyer, *Quadriennium*, i, 294.
27. An attempt to lodge a caveat in the Chancery against Harley's assumption of the title of Oxford was made on behalf of the Berties a few days before he received it. Peregrine Bertie to the Marquis of Lindsey, n.d. [19 May, 1711?], H.M.C. *Ancaster*, p. 442.

showmanship for the benefit of the Tories he delayed his acceptance of the white staff of Lord High Treasurer until the 29th, the anniversary of Charles II's Restoration, at a date which was still celebrated as fervently by them as was 5 November the anniversary of William's landing in 1688 by the Whigs.[28]

The ancient and dignified office of Lord High Treasurer was the most prestigious appointment in the land. Oxford, as Harley now became, intended to use its weight to the fullest extent, to offset the disadvantage of leaving the Commons. He was to be the last minister to hold this office for any length of time, and his choice of prestige would confirm recent successes. On the day that he became Lord Treasurer he announced his promotion to Marlborough with a phrase which was to set the tone of his future administration: 'I shall be honoured with your commands in every particular of good husbandry'.[29] Good husbandry, or economy, and an attempt to deal with the chaos left by war finance, immediately became intensified in all departments which felt the influence of the Treasury. Already some efforts had been made in this direction by the late treasury commissioners, but their attention had hitherto been chiefly occupied by the problems of keeping afloat on the flood tide of debt. With the most pressing difficulites past, retrenchment became the standing order. As Lord Treasurer, Oxford was now at the centre of government administration in a very real sense. The Treasury was at a crucial stage of its development; it had acquired a large measure of control over other offices germane to finance, but in consequence it was fast becoming too complex internally to be easily supervised, even in its more important departmental functions, by the single person of a Lord Treasurer. The solution adopted in the next reign was to put the Treasury permanently into commission. The method which Oxford adopted to ensure the smooth running of the department under his own control at the lower administrative levels was the immediate appointment of his 'cousin' Thomas Harley as co-adjutor to the experienced William Lowndes as Secretary of the Treasury. With Edward Harley already in the Imprest Office, to be joined in January 1713 by Thomas Foley of Stoke Court when the other Auditor died, Oxford was able to influence many minor procedures as well as dealing with major matters of treasury policy.[30] He made no sweeping changes in organization, content to rely on the existing system and make it operate as efficiently as possible. Above all he examined every item of expenditure. Tardy accountants and peculators swiftly learned from a flood of 'processes' at law that tra-

28. In connection with Harley's showmanship, it has been pointed out that the publication of Thomas Madox's *The History and Antiquities of the Exchequer* was delayed to coincide with his appointment – Douglas, p. 239.
29. Harley to Marlborough, 29 May 1711, Blenheim MSS. B2–19.
30. CTB, xxv, 379, 23 July 1711; *ibid*, xxvii, 89, 22 Jan. 1713.

ditional procedures could be made to serve the purpose of enforcing economical administration in the interest of the taxpayers.[31] Oxford's activities, as displayed in the Treasury minutes, give strong confirmation of the applicability in all departments of Professor Hughes' finding: 'It is clear from the records of the Audit Office that he greatly speeded up the passing of accounts instead of drifting on as Godolphin had done with accounts of eight and more years' standing'.[32]

During Oxford's period of office he was in attendance every weekday when he was in London, dealing personally with a great deal of relatively trivial administrative business of the department. But although his attempt to gear the whole Treasury to a single decision-maker was a considerable stimulus when he was present, his absence tended to cause an accumulation of work awaiting his return; the stock accusation of his critics was that his distrust of subordinates and unwillingness to delegate responsibility clogged the wheels of administration. To some extent this was true, but it was not the whole truth. Despite Oxford's penchant for personal intervention, the Treasury probably gained rather more than it lost by his term of office, especially by his refusal to make changes in the personnel of the departments to suit the Tories.[33] Because of this reluctance to make the Treasury a playground of politics, and because of the lengths to which his zeal for economy drove him, he did not enjoy the political advantages which Walpole and later ministers were to derive from their tenure of the Treasury. Indeed, Oxford's economy drives were capable of alienating rather than conciliating members of Parliament, as when he attempted to prevent their improper use of the privilege of free postage to convey their friends' letters under the official franking; he ordered that every letter was to be endorsed with the members' own signature.[34] This disregard of members' perquisites appeared particularly after 1711 in the House of Commons, where a more wholehearted use of all aspects of treasury patronage would have assisted his control over the Tories. Insufficient control of the Commons, indeed, continued to be his main political weakness.

But in June 1711 this fact was not immediately obvious. To most onlookers Oxford appeared by far the most important member of the government by reason of his exalted office and the immense reputation with which his double conciliation of the City and the Tories had

---

31. For some examples of Oxford's activities in tightening up loopholes in accounting procedure and the outgoings of the spending departments, see *Cal. Treas. Books*, especially xxv, 88, xxv, 532, xxvi, 359, xxvi, 398, xxvii, 51, and the 'Report to the Lord Treasurer relating to the method of issuing process against accountants in default', Add. MSS. 6726, f. 5.
32. Hughes, pp. 276–7. For Oxford's contributions to the organization of the customs service see: Hoon, pp. 8–9, 29–30, 33.
33. Apart from the examples already cited of Oxford's attitude to minor personnel, see the instances mentioned by Ward, pp. 63–4, and Hughes, pp. 247–7 and 289.
34. CTB, xxvi, 402.

invested him.[35] In St John, it is true, he had already begun to find a determined rival who would become more formidable in the House of Commons after Oxford's elevation. But against the possibility of a bid by St John for the leadership of the Tory right wing, Oxford could set the support of Rochester's friends, following that shown by the late Earl, and the confidence of the Queen and most of his colleagues in himself as the man who had first brought into being and then saved the ministry. Nevertheless, St John's behaviour was causing him much anxiety. Jonathan Swift, who had been in receipt of the confidence of both men since he began to write *The Examiner* for the ministry in October 1710, witnessed the displeasure of the Harleys by the following April:

> ...I easily saw that they take things ill of Mr St John, and by some hints given me from another hand that I deal with, I am afraid the Secretary will not stand long. This is the fate of Courts. I will, if I meet Mr St John alone on Sunday, tell him my opinion, and beg him to set himself right, else the consequences may be very bad; for I see not how they can well want him neither, and he would make a troublesome enemy.[36]

Swift assessed Oxford's difficulty correctly. St John's great abilities not only made him hard to replace, but if he were once dismissed and joined the Tory dissidents there would be few men capable of standing up to him in the Commons on behalf of the ministry. A better solution than dismissal, and one which Oxford considered, would have been to set up a strong Chancellor of the Exchequer as rival to the Secretary in the Lower House. Court rumour maintained that he was planning to bring Boyle back in some capacity.[37] If so, Boyle must have again refused. Next, Oxford approached Sir Thomas Hanmer, who had refused a place on the treasury commission in August 1701, and whose watchful leadership of the Tory back benches is comparable with Harley's role in King William's Parliaments. The comparison between Hanmer in Queen Anne's reign and Harley in King William's might be further extended, for when Hanmer at last agreed to take office, in 1713, it was as Speaker, like Harley himself in 1701. But in 1711 Hanmer again refused to be tempted, though expressing himself, in the words of Bromley as intermediary, 'satisfyed with the measures taken'. Accordingly Robert Benson, one of the late Treasury commissioners, became Chancellor. Rumours of possible action against St John died down after the prorogation of

---

35. Cf. the impression received by the Earl of Shaftesbury from his correspondents in England: 'We are now at the mercy of one single man, who has all power in his hands and every secret in his breast', *Shaftesbury Letters*, p. 512.
36. Swift, *Journal to Stella*, 27 April 1711; HMC *Portland*, v, 684.
37. Arthur Maynwaring, n.d. [early May, 1711], *Private Corr.*, ii, 70.

Parliament on 12 June removed, for the moment, one area of friction.[38]

Others remained, however, and particularly an attempt by St John to curry favour with Marlborough at Oxford's expense. This attempt concerns a committee of high-ranking officers set up by Harley early in 1711 to exercise a measure of control over Marlborough, especially in making army appointments. St John appears to have deliberately prevented the working of this committee.[39] The final demise of the committee was also no doubt due to a more conciliatory policy towards Marlborough by Harley himself. After the experience of this session, Oxford intended less than ever to close to door on the possibility of some kind of coalition if future need arose. He too was to pains to avoid offending the General, and throughout the summer intermediaries ferried to and fro between the two men. Apart from general assurances, it is true, Oxford was evasive in discussing the political future, but on the other hand he acceded to all Marlborough's reasonable military schemes. At the end of the campaign he had the satisfaction of Marlborough's testimony to 'your punctual remittances for the Troops'.[40] Nor were the remittances only to the troops, for in August, Oxford allowed the building work of the General's monumental Blenheim Palace at Woodstock to recommence by ordering the payment of £20,000 in weekly instalments for the purpose.[41]

Unfortunately for any assurances he might hold out to Marlborough and the Whigs, three deaths in the summers months made clear that Oxford intended for the moment to remain in a Tory posture. The Lord Presidency left vacant by Rochester's death was filled, not indeed by the obvious candidate Nottingham who remained, Poulett advised, 'party sense in person' but by Buckingham, an unimportant Tory whose chief qualification for the office was that he could be quietly dropped without offence to any but himself if need arose.[42] Buckingham was replaced as Lord Steward by Poulett. On 6 July a second death, that of the Duke of Queensberry, appointed by the late ministry in 1709 as third secretary of state dealing mainly with Scottish affairs, posed a more difficult problem. No fewer than four powerful Scottish magnates aspired to the post, and to appoint any one of them would be to alienate the remaining three, a disaster for the government's strength in the House of

38. Bromley to Oxford, endorsed June 1711, Loan 29/128/3.
39. The committee became ineffective in July, and I.F. Burton writes: 'There can be little doubt that St John sabotaged the working of the committee, both by his own absenteeism and through his joining with Marlborough to circumvent its recommendations by the direct approach to the Queen' – I.F. Burton, '"The Committee of the Council at the War Office": an experiment in Cabinet Government under Anne', *HJ*, Vol. 4, (1961), p. 83.
40. Churchill, iv, 415–16, 451; Thomas Somerville, *The History of Great Britain during the Reign of Queen Anne* (1798), p. 646.
41. *CTB*, xxv, 86.
42. H.M.C. *Portland*, iv, 684.

Lords. In the outcome, no-one was appointed and the post lapsed for the time being. This was evidently the solution which Oxford had favoured. To Marlborough he wrote: 'Third Secretary is so new a thing in England and so much out of the way of doing business here that it ought to be put on some other foot, if the Queen should think fit to have anyone succeed him.'[43] The Queen agreed that Queensberry's duties should be apportioned between the other secretaries. Time was to show that this was a mistake, involving the strengthening of St John's position against Dartmouth, particularly by allotting the Spanish Netherlands, among other countries, to the former's province.[44]

A third death, that of the Duke of Newcastle on 15 July, touched Oxford more pesonally. It delayed for two years the marriage arranged between his son Edward and Newcastle's only child, Lady Henrietta Cavendish Holles. The bulk of the Duke's vast estates went by his will to his nephews, especially Thomas Pelham Holles, eldest son of Baron Pelham, though enough remained to his daughter to make her the greatest heiress of her day.[45] In one of the most famous lawsuits of the age the Duchess of Newcastle challenged the will, advised and often restrained in her enthusiasm by the Harley brothers. The law, however, proceeded slowly, and Oxford's caution and unwillingness to indulge in illegal short cuts was to estrange the Duchess. Before the question of the marriage was taken out of her hands, two years later, it had become a political issue of importance to the fate of the ministry.[46]

Meanwhile the immediate problem set by Newcastle's death was to find a successor to hold the privy seal. Oxford was determined to have no-one strong enough to challenge his own authority. His first choice was a political nonentity, the Earl of Jersey, who had recently helped him to open a peace negotiation with France; but Jersey himself died on 26 August.[47] The appointment therefore went to John Robinson, Oxford's old friend, the former envoy to the court of Sweden, whom he had advanced to be Bishop of Bristol in the autumn of 1710. At one stroke he promoted a follower and gave some pleasure to the Church party.[48] Any further changes Oxford continued steadily to refuse. In August Jonathan Swift, who remained closely in touch with him, wrote 'I know particularly that he dislikes very much the notion of people that everyone is to be turned out'.[49] All the same, Oxford had done enough by the new ap-

---

43. *Private Corr.*, ii, 76; Oxford to Marlborough, 6 July 1711, Blenheim MSS. B2–19.
44. *Bolingbroke Corr.*, i, 269. For the other changes, see: Thomson, *Secretaries of State*, p. 32.
45. H.M.C. *Portland*, vii, 40; Swift, *Journal to Stella*, ii, 406–7, 8 Nov. 1711.
46. The best account of the lawsuit is given by A.S. Turberville, i, 296–327.
47. Oxford to the Queen, 17 Aug. 1711, Loan 29/12/4.
48. Sykes, 'Queen Anne and the Episcopate', EHR 50 (1935), p. 42; Weymouth to Charlett, 7 Sept. 1711, Bodleian, Ballard MS. 10, f. 79.
49. *Swift Corr.*, i, 279–80.

pointments to scotch the Whigs' hope that they would be taken into the ministry on equal terms. It remained for them to be disillusioned still further by his foreign policy. He remained basically at one with the Tories in believing that the long and expensive war with France should not be further prolonged, and the time had now come to execute a new policy.

CHAPTER 12

Peacemaking – the Preliminary Articles

WHILE ENGAGED in struggles with the October Club and the Bank, Harley had secretly re-opened peace negotiations with France. In the course of an investigation carried out by the Whig ministry during and after 1715, in the hope of finding evidence for his impeachment, several of his friends were to deny that he took any active part in the preliminary articles of peace signed between Britain and France on 27 September 1711.[1] In fact, he and Shrewsbury began to communicate with France in 1710, without knowledge of the secretaries of state, through the agency of François Gaultier, a French Chaplain of the Earl of Jersey's household. The use of Gaultier gave the transaction a Jacobite flavour which did not necessarily displease Oxford, so long as it came to nothing, since it smoothed the way to obtaining peace.[2]

The first definite step had been taken by Harley and Shrewsbury in December 1710. The event which decided them was the evacuation of Madrid in November by the Allied forces, soon to be followed by the British defeat at Brihuega. Any remaining hope of wresting Spain from its Bourbon king now vanished, and the war of the Spanish Succession lost its rationale. Through Gaultier the two ministers informed the French court that Britain would no longer insist upon obtaining the Spanish Empire for the House of Habsburg but would be content with good sureties for the unmolested commerce of British subjects in the Spanish dominions. In the existing situation of the ministry, Harley was not prepared to open negotiations officially and add the immediate hostility of the Emperor, and perhaps the Dutch, to his other difficulties. In the first week of January, therefore, Gaultier was dispatched to

1. Notably Matthew Prior and Lord North and Grey. See: *The Miscellaneous works of Matthew Prior* (ed. Adrian Drift, 1740), i, 427, and North and Grey's memorandum on his interrogation, 16 June 1717, Bodleian, North MS. B2, ff. 99–100.
2. B.W. Hill, 'Oxford, Bolingbroke, and the Peace of Utrecht', *HJ*, xvi (1973), 241–63. For the 1710–11 negotiation see: G.M. Trevelyan, 'The Jersey period of the negotiations leading to the Peace of Utrecht', *EHR* xlix (1934), 100–5.

Paris with verbal instructions; he was to say that if the French would make the first approach to Holland for re-opening the peace congress, British plenipotentiaries would this time be sent and would, if necessary, act in secret collusion with the French to force the Allies into step. When the Dutch reply was received it was to be sent to Harley, under the alias 'Christopher Bryan' via his agent John Drummond in Amsterdam.[3] The decision by Harley and Shrewsbury to keep this correspondence secret from St John cannot adequately be explained by the fact that they first contimplated it before he took office. The main reason for St John's continued exclusion was his violent antipathy to the Allies in general and to the Dutch especially. The Whig Barrier Treaty of 1709 he loathed. He is later seen urging the conclusion of a separate peace between Britain and France, and this was probably his first wish as early as 1710; thus while Harley still hoped for Dutch co-operation, prudence counselled that St John's explosive personality should not intrude on the delicate negotiation.[4]

It soon became clear that France too would welcome an opportunity to make peace but would also endeavour to divide the Allies. The reply which Gaultier carried to Britain from the French Foreign Minister Torcy was that in view of the attitude of the Dutch during the congress of the preceding summer, the French government was not prepared to approach them again but would open a separate negotiation with Britain. The British ministers properly rejected the latter suggestion; instead they suggested that France should draw up preliminary articles which could be offered to Britain and sent on from there to The Hague. In reply, Torcy sent a paper of general propositions which Harley and Shrewsbury rejected as being insufficiently explicit; they demanded that the terms now offered should be not less favourable than France had been prepared to give in 1710.[5] In the last week of March 1711, therefore, Gaultier returned to Paris primed with their verbal suggestions as to the general form these terms should take, with territorial and commercial concessions for Britain and a defensive 'barrier' for the Dutch against the possibility of future French invasion attempts. Gaultier glossed up the demands for the benefit of the French government; the British ministers would not, he said, support a Dutch claim for all the barrier towns allotted to them in the Anglo-Dutch Barrier Treaty of 1709 but would

3. Gaultier to Torcy, 23 and 30 Dec. (N.S.), 1710, Trevelyan, 'The Jersey Period' 347–56, Jan. 21 (N.S.), 1711.
4. *Bolingbroke Corr.* i, 156; Gaultier certainly received the impression that Harley and Shrewsbury conducted the negotiations behind the backs of their colleagues to keep St John in the dark as long as possible – 'Memorandum du Marquis de Torcy', 21 July (N.S.), 1711, P.R.O. 31/3/197, f. 349.
5. Legrelle, iv, 585–7. P.R.O. 31/3/197 ff. 328–9: 'Mémoire envoyé en Angletere', 2 Mar. (N.S.) 1711, and 'Memoire apporté par le Sieur Gaultier', 25 Mar./5 April 1711.

allow only such a barrier as seemed necessary for Holland's safety; furthermore, though they insisted that the Allied claim to the Spanish possessions for the Archduke Charles must be placed before the peace congress. France shold stand firm for the claims of Philip V. The French reply, received about the third week in April, offered preliminary articles which closely followed the British suggestions.[6]

On receiving the new French proposals, Harley's first impulse was to send them to the Grand Pensionary Heinsius; Shrewsbury, however, on whom the burden of this negotiation fell during Harley's enforced retirement after his stabbing, urged that the cabinet should first be informed, since the other members would get wind of the affair soon enough after it had been communicated to the Dutch. The news of death of the Emperor also made the time ripe for a revelation of the peace negotiation, and Shrewsbury's view prevailed. On 26 April, therefore, the Queen informed the cabinet of the French offer, and it is not surprising that, as Shrewsbury reported to Harley, some of the members assumed that 'the whole is concluded'. Having kept their colleagues in the dark so long, they achieved the same effect of surprise and admiration which Harley was to obtain a few days later with the South Sea Bill.[7]

The articles suggested by France were therefore communicated to the Dutch through the official channel of St John and the British envoy at The Hague. But Harley did not thereby give up his participation in the matter. He intended to keep the negotiations closely under his own supervision throughout. The Pensionary's agent Willem Vanhuls was dispatched to Holland with a personal communication drawn up by Harley suggesting that the Dutch and British together should consider the procedure to be adopted and take no step without each other's knowledge. Harley wrote:

> As proof of her good intents, the Queen has communicated France's first offers of treating for peace. You are therefore to mention this to the Pensionary as a mark of her Majesty's confidence. The paper is looked upon here only as an offer to treat, without any regard to the articles expressed in the paper.

The Dutch understandably hesitated to accept this vague basis for the preliminary articles of peace. In 1709 the Whig ministry had kept them in the war only by promising them a share of commercial concessions in the West Indies and a barrier in the Low Countries strong enough not only to resist French aggression but to reduce the territory to commercial dependence on the United Provinces even at the expense of British

6. 'Mémoire pour l'Angleterre', 16 April (N.S.) 1711, P.R.O. 31/3/197, ff. 330–4; proposals dated 22 April (N.S.) are in P.R.O. SP 78/154, ff. 103–4.
7. H.M.C. *Bath*, i, 201–2.

trading interests. The Dutch now refused to be manoeuvred into a general congress where, as Harley hoped, France and Britain acting in collaboration would obtain a reduction of the excessive concessions to Holland and better terms for Britain than the 1709 treaty envisaged. The British ambassador was informed by Heinsius that the proposals were 'very dark and general' and needed a more precise explanation.[8]

It was at this point that Harley abandonded his intention of bringing the Dutch into the signing of the preliminaries. To explain why he did so, it is necessary to glance aside, for his policy from May onwards was influenced by his plans for the South Sea Company. Much of the initial support which the scheme received was due to the general belief, which he was careful not to deny, that the expedition generally known to be in course of preparation was intended for an attack on the West Indies to take a foothold for the Company. That its real destination was the St Lawrence was a closely guarded secret. The popular delusion was helped by encouragement given by the ministerial press to the traditional English desire for pickings on the Spanish Main.[9] Though Oxford intended to swivel British demands on the Spanish Empire from political to commercial concessions, he was to find it necessary until the middle of 1712 to encourage the Company to hope for a military expedition. But when the belief which eased the foundation of the Company was discovered to be false, he would be bound to obtain monopolistic concessions in the peace treaty for the Company's trade. The most obvious concession was the Spanish Assiento, or slaving contract; but in June 1711 he was also optimistic for the establishment of permanent general trading posts, perhaps even British colonies, in Central and South America, and he commissioned a report from the resourceful Defoe on the possible location of such posts. However, as Drummond privately reported from Amsterdam, the passing of the South Sea Bill and the question of obtaining commercial concessions from Spain had immediately excited the jealousy of the Dutch, and threatened to pro- voke their opposition unless they were allowed a share.[10] This demand Oxford was by no means prepared to admit, and there was thus a very good reason for his desire not to go into details with the Dutch over the concessions which he intended to demand for Britain in the peace preli-

8. Harley's draft instructions for Vanhuls, 30 April 1711, in Loan 29/10/18; Geikie and Montgomery, 188; Raby to St John, 25 May (N.S.) 1711, Add. MS. 22,205, f. 98.
9. L'Hermitage, (4–)15 May, 1711, Add. MS. 17,677, EEE, f. 194. Cf. *Swift Corr.*, i, 266: 'Our expedition under Mr. Hill is said to be toward the South Seas, but nothing is known'; Charles Davenant's *Sir Thomas Double at Court*... (1710): 'And as to invading the West Indies, the reign the Queen Elizabeth shows how easy and profitable those expeditions were, and what Masses of Gold and Silver were brought from thence'. Cf. Defoe's *Review*, 28 and 30 June 1711.
10. Defoe's report took the form of three letters to Oxford, H.M.C. *Portland*, v, 50, 58, and 66. The latter is printed out of order and was clearly written between the other two, that is to say between 17 July and 23 July 1711; Drummond's letters, *ibid.*, v, 1, 24 and 28.

minaries. He accordingly determined to go ahead with a negotiation with France and present the Dutch with a *fait accompli*.

The path of deception being once determined, the way was made easy by two fortuitous events. The first was t he death on 3 July of the Dutch envoy Vryberge; and second was another death a few days later, that of the young Prince of Nassau Friesland, giving rise to internal dissensions in the United Provinces which helped to delay the sending of a successor to London. The British ambassador at The Hague, the Earl of Strafford, was withdrawn for consultations in London in June, and remained in England throughout the summer months, nominally to complete his wedding preparations.[11] Thus, during the crucial period Oxford was able virtually to ignore the Dutch, except for sending reassuring messages through unofficial channels. As soon as Parliament rose on 12 June he drew up instructions for a British messenger, the poet-diplomat Matthew Prior, to carry to Paris fuller suggestions for peace terms, covering the South Sea Company's interests, and to obtain written French observations on them. The terms fell into two sections; demands on behalf of the Allies and demands for Britain. The first, couched in general terms, included stipulations that the crowns of Spain and France should be kept seaparate and that Holland, and other Allies, should have 'barriers' sufficient to their needs. The second section demanded recognition of the succession of the House of Hanover, the cession by France of Newfoundland and Hudson's Bay, and by Spain of Gibraltar, Port Mahon and of the Assiento contract. Prior was verbally instructed to demand territory in Central and South America, with a minimum of four settlements, together with their immediate hinterlands, nominally in connection with the slave trade but actually as a foothold for general trade; and it was to this demand that Torcy raised the greatest objections when Prior reached Paris, on the grounds that the King of Spain could never be induced to concede the territorial privileges required by Britain.[12]

Prior therefore concluded no agreement, but returned to London in the second week of August accompanied by a French diplomat, Nicolas Mesnager, who was to take up the negotiation. Mesnager's instructions, however, forbade him to promise the concession of territory on behalf of Spain. Thus, when Mesnager and Gaultier met Oxford, Shrewsbury, the two secretaries of state and Prior on 15 August, there arose an altercation of several hours duration; and in the end the British ministers, refusing to

11. L'Hermitage, Add. MS. 17,677, EEE. f. 255; *Bolingbroke Corr.*, i, 229.
12. Oxford's instructions for Prior is dated 16 June 1711, in Loan 29/10/17; The accounts of the negotiation differ slightly. See: Matthew Prior's 'Journal', H.M.C. *Portland*, v, 36, and 'Torcy's account of Matthew Prior's negotiations at Fontainbeleau in July 1711', *EHR*, (1914), 531–2. Torcy gave a shorter account in the *Memoirs* ii, 132–3. *Cf.* Wickham Legg, *Matthew Prior*, p. 153.

discuss anything but the demands on behalf of Britain, told Mesnager to inform his court that there must be territorial concessions in connection with the commercial concessions.[13] They also refused to consider a separate final treaty between Britain and France. Oxford reported to the Queen stressing this point, for he had no intention of abandoning the Allies to their fate:

> Last evening the lords your Majesty appointed met the two Frenchmen at Lord Jersey's house. The conversation was very long; it was [made plain?]* at last that the French had a mind to draw into a separate treaty, which was rejected with great firmness...He [Mesnager] pretended to write to France for further instructon, tho' I believe he needs it not and that he will comply.[14]

But if a general treaty was essential the territorial concessions in South America were not. Within five days of the first meeting Oxford offered to give up his territorial claims together with any hope of obtaining a permanent foothold for Britain in South America. In return, Mesnager undertook to obtain an extension of the period of the Asseinto from ten to thirty years together with associated tariff concessions and to obtain for Britain certain tariff privileges in Spain. Why Oxford so easily gave up his original claim; with its obvious possibilities for illicit trading throughout the Spanish dominions in America, may be explained in two ways. Firstly, a footing in South America never played so great a part in his calculations as he made the subsequent directors of the South Sea Company believe. But the immediate cause of his concession is probably to be found in an incident which made haste necessary in concluding the preliminaries between Britain and France; for, owing to the attentions of a zealous customs official, the return of Prior with Mesnager to England had become widely publicized. To explain Prior's mission, Oxford found it necessary to give a guarded and incomplete account to Vanhuls for the Grand Pensionary. The Dutch were extremely suspicious of the British negotiation, fearful that their interests were being entirely abandoned. Oxford could not admit that the Whig promises of 1709 were not to be kept, but he endeavoured to resasure this only ally that they would· be represented in the main treaty negotiations. He did not add that he now had no intention of admitting the Dutch into the nearly-concluded preliminary treaty.[15]

13. Mesnager's instructions, 3 Aug. (N.S.) 1711, Legrelle, iv, 597–600; Mesnager to Torcy, 28 Aug. (N.S.) 1711, *ibid.*, iv, 601–2.
14. Oxford to the Queen, 16 Aug. 1711, B.L. Loan 29/12/4.
15. Mesnager to Torcy, (23 Aug.) 3 Sept. 1711, and Torcy to Mesnager, (7–) 18 Sept. 1711, Legrelle, iv, 602–4. Wickham Legg. *Matthew Prior* p. 160; Oxford to Vh [Vanhuls], 17 Aug. 1711, Loan 29/10/17.

*Writing illegible

His assurances were clearly intended only to stave off enquiries until the preliminaries were signed. On the 29th fresh proposals, embodying the new arrangements put forword for the South Sea Company, were handed in form to Mesnager, despite a belated protest from Shrewsbury that there was 'something in them looks so like bargaining for yourselves apart, and leaving your friends to shift at a general treaty...'. Such a procedure was precisely Oxford's intentions. In a letter to Torcy, he asked that full powers to sign the preliminaries should be sent to Mesnager as soon as possible.[16] A few days later he told Hoffman, the Imperial resident in London, that Great Britain would take the lead in the peace negotiations, though he added that a general peace would be signed on the continent of Europe. He also gave the Duke of Marlborough, who still possessed the confidence of the Dutch, an account of the peace negotiation. Its wording was disingenuous; and it failed to add that the intention was to send the preliminary articles to Holland as a signed agreement which the Dutch might accept or reject but could not haggle over.[17]

Not the least reason for Oxford's anxiety to conclude the preliminaries was the Queen's eagerness to obtain peace. As soon as Mesnager's new instructions had arrived, and before they had been revealed to the British ministers, she was urging Shrewsbury to abandon his doubts. On 20 September Mesnager conveyed his new instructions to the assembled British ministers. After he had read out all the articles, he reported to Torcy, there was a long silence, with Shrewsbury in particular looking 'pensif et inflamé', and the meeting broke up without much further discussion.[18] Apart from Shrewsbury's dissatisfaction with the whole method of separate negotiation, the chief British objection to Mesnager's proposals was the continuance of a previous demand that French nationals should be allowed to fish off the coast of Newfoundland, and dry their fish on part of its shores, after the island was ceded to Britain. But Oxford, at least, did not consider the French objections to the British articles insuperable. On the 22nd Swift found him 'as merry, and careless, and disengaged as a young heir at one and twenty'.[19] The Queen, in her anxiety to see the preliminaries signed, authorized St John to concede the important point concerning the Newfoundland fishing rights, but on the other hand, Oxford otained from Mesnager some last-minute alterations including explicit French recognition of the Hanoverian succession and agreement to demilitatize the privateering port of

16. *Bolingbroke Corr.*, i, 337; Oxford to Torcy, 29 Aug./9 Sept. 1711, P.R.O. 31/3/197, f. 391.
17. Report by Gallas (the Imperial envoy), 18 Sept. (N.S.) 1711, Klopp, xiv, 133; Oxford to Marlborough, 5/16 Sept. 1711, Blenheim MSS. B2–19.
18. H.M.C. *Bath*, i, 210; Mesnager to Torcy, 20 Sept./2 Oct. 1711, P.R.O. 31/3/197.
19. Torcy, *Memoirs*, ii, 171–62 (sic: nos. 161–72 occur twice in the 1757 edition); Swift, *Journal to Stella*, 22 Sept. 1711.

Dunkirk.[20] Shrewsbury's scruples forbade him to sign the articles, and after anxious consultation it was decided that only the two secretaries of state should sign on behalf of Britain and Mesnager for France. On 27 September two documents were signed, both based on Oxford's draft of 16 June, one containing a general statement of terms required on behalf of the Allies, including Britain, and the other detailing specifically the concessions to be made to Britain.[21] The second was to remain a secret from the other Allies. The signing of the preliminary articles by Britain and France was a first step. The conflicting interests of the members of the Grand Alliance, especially the impracticable claim of the Hapsburgs to the Spanish inheritance, had made a private preliminary selttement between France and one or more of the other Allies almost the only means of obtaining peace. Oxford hoped to make use of such a settlement to obtain a general peace congress in which Britain's claims had already been guaranteed by the enemy. But there remained, after the signing of the preliminaries, the problem of forcing the Allies to accept as the basis for a congress the articles Britain chose to communicate to them.

For this task of coercion St John's talents were needed. With the Emperor, the ministry had already taken the offensive. This Secretary's pen flashed, and the court at Vienna was harried with new vigour. A special mission was sent to demand that Imperial occupation forces should be transferred from Hungary to a theatre of war. The inevitable refusal or prevarication would provide ready material for ministerial peace propaganda. Oxford himself chose a more emollient role, and assured the Imperial envoy Gallas that a league between the Allies would be continued after the war.[22] But neither threats nor promises staved off the indignation of the Emperor at what he rightly considered to be the abandonment of his hopeless pursuit of the Spanish succession. Gallas did not wait to obtain his court's reaction; as soon as the open preliminaries were communicated to him, he published them in the Whig *Daily Courant*, where they appeared on 13 October.

Oxford viewed the resulting uproar in the Whig press without dismay, telling Marlborough (who would be sure to pass it on) that if the Allies held back from a treaty they had only themselves to blame.[23] The ministry could reckon on strong support from the House of Commons and from the war-weary country. When a crowd recognized Prior, whose

---

20. H.M.C. *Bath*, i, 212; Torcy, *Memoirs*, ii, 164–5 (second occurrence of these number); *Bolingbroke Corr.*, i, 368.
21. Shrewsbury to Stanhope, 15 July 1715, P.R.O. State Papers, Domestic, George I, 3/32, cited by D.H. Somerville, 'Shrewsbury and the Peace of Utrecht', *EHR*, xlvii (1932), 646–7; the articles are printed in *Parliamentary History*, vii, App. cvii-cx and cxii-cxiv.
22. *Bolingbroke Corr.*, i, 295; Gallas's report, 18 Sept. (N.S.) 1711, Klopp, xiv, 133.
23. Oxford to Marlborough, 19 Oct., 1711, Blenheim MSS. B2–19.

part in the negotiations was now generally known, they are reported to have 'gathered about him as they used to do about Dr Sacheverell'. It was therefore decided to take a strong line. Gallas was immediately forbidden to come to court, and his government was requested to withdraw him from England.[24] It is characteristic of Oxford's desire to give no more offence than he considered necessary, however, that he thought of a point his colleagues had overlooked and ordered a yacht to convey Gallas, thus sparing the Imperial envoy the further indignity of travelling in a mail boat.[25]

The Emperor's opposition had been foreseen. The only way to force his hand was to detach the Dutch from his cause. They, at least, had no objection to abandoning Spain if their own interests were served. Until the last moment Oxford had continued to assure Heinsius that the preliminaries would be communicated to Holland as soon as they were submitted by France, without mentioning that they would first be signed by Britain and France without Dutch participation. When this pretence had served its purpose, he relied on massive threat drawn up by St John. When Strafford at last set off for The Hague with the articles at the end of September, he carried also instructions to put the strongest possible pressure on the Dutch to submit to a revision of the Barrier Treaty and to enter a peace congress, with the alternative of being abandoned to fight on with no more than nominal support from Britain.[26] The reaction of the Dutch was first indignation, then despair lest they should be left to fight on for the Emperor, and finally, in November, an unwilling agreement to the British ultimatum.[27] With their consent, that of the Emperor, however reluctant, became certain, and arrangements for a peace conference began.

A third ally to be encountered, and the most difficult because of his influence on British internal politics, was the Elector of Hanover. The open preliminary articles were carried to the Princess Sophia and her son the Elector by Earl Rivers, who had been employed on a similar journey a year earlier to announce the change of ministry. On that occasion Rivers had received little encouragement from the Elector, who, primed by Marlborough, had been prepared to refuse an offer of the supreme command of the Allied armies. The offer was not made, and Rivers had been received with no more enthusiasm than courtesy and expediency dictated.[28] Harley, in return, had given the Elector nothing more than

24. G. Clarke to A. Charlett, 3 Oct. 1711, Bodleian Ballard MS. 20, f. 73; Klopp, xiv, 682.
25. L'Hermitage, Add. MS. 17,677, EEE. f. 374v.
26. Weber, p. 409; Strafford's instructions are printed in Bolingbroke Corr., i, 398–404, together with the open preliminary articles.
27. Geikie and Montgomery, pp. 219–29.
28. Private Corr., i, 364; Robethons Bericht, 21 Sept. (N.S.), 1710, in R. Pauli's 'Aktenstücke...' Zeitschrift des Hist. Vereins für Niedersächsen (1883), 8–9.

fair words, including the remark 'I know your Electoral Highness has an English heart' – a thoughtless compliment to a prickly German prince.[29]

Throughout the Oxford ministry, the question of the royal succession bulked large. In Oxford's 'plan of the administration' drawn up for the Queen in October 1710, he had called the succession question the 'one weak place where the enemy may attack'. The Whigs, for their part, did not overlook the advantages which might be derived from the Elector's Whig sympathies. Sunderland wrote to Marlborough: 'that affair of Hanover is, and must be our sheet anchor, and if it be rightly managed, you will be effectually revenged of all your enemies'. Townshend went so far as to suggest to the Elector that he should press for the title of Duke of York, come to England, and take the place in the cabinet once occupied by the Queen's late consort.[30] But at that time, the end of 1710, the Hanoverian court had no immediate fear for their right of succession. The Pretender would stand little chance if Queen Anne died while Britain was still at war with the country which sheltered him. From this point of view, Hanover stood to gain from the continuance of the war. Furthermore, George Louis hoped to see his electorate raised, with the assistance of the Emperor, to the status of a kingdom, and this ambition depended upon Hanover's continued support for the Emperor's own design on the Spanish crown. It is not surprising that early in 1711 the Elector laid it down as the fundamental purpose of his foreign policy that Spain must be won for the Habsburg candidate, and that this could only be achieved by the abasement of France.[31]

Thus Rivers' second mission, in October 1711, met even less success than the first. The Elector felt no confidence in Oxford's assertion, conveyed by Rivers, that though the preliminaries had ensured France's recognition of the British succession this was 'without any reciprocal obligation or promise from her Majesty to France'.[32] Like the Emperor, George Louis felt sure that the claim to Spain had been abandoned by Britain. He determined to ignore Rivers and send his protest to London by his own representative, who could choose the best moment for its presentation. This dignitary, Baron Bothmer, waited a month in London before presenting his credentials early in December. At the same time he handed over a memorandum from the Elector accepting the principle of a peace congress but flatly refusing to consider the abandonment of the Emperor's claim to the Spanish empire.[33]

The opposition of the Elector was certain: could the opposition of the

29. Macpherson, *Original Papers*, ii, 197.
30. Coxe, *Marlborough*, iii, 297; Baron Bothmer (Hanoverian envoy at The Hague and special envoy to England) to the Elector, 20 Dec. (N.S.), 1710, in Felix Salomon p. 90.
31. Electoral Rescript, 25 Jan. (N.S.), 1711, in Salomon p. 123.
32. Macpherson, *Original Papers*, ii, 255.
33. Klopp, xiv, 217. For the text of the memorandum, *ibid.*, xiv, 687 sqq.

House of Lords be overcome? Oxford foresaw storms when Parliament met, but had little opportunity to avert them. From the middle of October he lay ill at home, when Swift found him feverish but 'with a thousand papers about him'. Towards the end of the month he went to the Treasury for a day, but retired suffering from attacks of gravel and rheumatism which lasted through most of November. At the same time St John was in a bitter and unco-operative mood; the news of the failure of the Quebec expedition left him 'much mortified', though Oxford was reported 'just as merry as usual'. St John was further disgruntled by the Queen's coolness to him. Amid these disruptions there was not much hope of ministerial unity during the forthcoming session, when the Whigs would carry their attack on the peace negotiation into the public forum.[34] Oxford made desperate attempts to bring sympathetic peers up to London, but they trickled in very slowly.[35] The meeting of Parliament was put off by periodic prorogations in November. Meanwhile St John was busy arresting the publishers of the flood of Whig anti-peace tracts, and Swift did his greatest service for the ministry by publishing their case in *The Conduct of the Allies*, which sold out and had to be reprinted, a few days after its publication on 27 November, with some minor alterations by Oxford.[36]

In this dilemma, Oxford's gyrations between the leaders in both Houses become hard to follow. He was probably negotiating with Walpole's brother-in-law Townshend.[37] He was also sounding Halifax about the opposition's intentions. On 14 November Halifax wrote to him:

> I received the honour of your Lordship's letter in company of my lord Somers to whom I was then giving an account of what your Lordship commanded me. And I do assure you that neither he nor I know, or ever heard of such a design as your Lordship mentions: I find my Lord as much disposed to wait upon your Lordship as you can desire and leave the time and manner entirely to your Lordship's convenience.

And the following day Halifax added: '. . . tis plain we shall never be at quiet till a better understanding is begun between those who have most prudence and temper'. On the 21st Oxford visited Marlborough, who had been ostentatiously absenting himself from the cabinet.[38] The forthcoming session would see both Oxford and the House of Lords in

---

34. Swift, *Journal to Stella*, 6, 20 and 24 Oct. 2, 14, 27, 30 Nov. 1711.
35. Bromley to Oxford, 15 Nov. and 3 Dec. 1711, Loan 29/128/3; Lexington to Oxford, received 5 Dec. 1711, Loan 29/158/9.
36. Swift, *Journal to Stella*, 24 Oct. 27 and 29 Nov. 1711; Dickinson, *Bolingbroke*, p. 89.
37. Oxford to (? Townshend), 26 Nov. 1711, Cambridge University Library, C(H) MSS. 652, quoted by Plumb, *Walpole*, i, 176.
38. Halifax to Oxford, 14 and 15 Nov. 1711, Loan 29/151/6; L'Hermitage, Add. MS. 17,677, EEE, f. 374.

key roles, for that House had a very fine balance of parties and Oxford would be sitting there as governmental leader for the first time. His efforts to deploy his forces, especially the office holders and Scottish elected peers, have been shown to be Herculean, given his physical indisposition for much of the time.[39]

At the same time, he met the Tory leaders in the Commons. Bromley, as Speaker, arranged the meeting: 'Since your Lordship desires it I will give notice to Sir Tho Hanmer and the other gentlemen that they may wait upon your Lordship at my house at the time appointed.'[40] The main purpose of this conclave was apparently no less than a desire on the part of Oxford to intimate that he was now prepared to countenance a measure against the practice of occasional conformity, if this would obtain the support of a few Tories in the Lords such as Nottingham, known to oppose the abandonment of Spain to the Bourbon; on the day of the meeting a rumour was spread that the court would concede such a measure. According to one report Oxford also approached Nottingham himself with a proposal to permit on Occasional Conformity Bill if Nottingham would support the peace preliminaries.[41] But, if the report was true, Oxford was spared the need to come out openly against the Dissenters, for on 4 December, the day of the meeting, Nottingham made known that he would vote with the Whigs on the question of Spain.[42]

The Junto, while negotiating with Oxford, had come to terms with this highest of the High Churchmen, still omitted from the ministry. As the price of his support they too were prepared to abandon the Dissenters. Lady Cowper ascribed Nottingham's reason for joining the Junto to 'hatred of Lord Oxford'.[43] But indeed Nottingham's private and public motives coincided; since he had initiated the war in Spain eight years earlier he had unswervingly maintained that Spain and its possessions must go to the House of Habsburg. The Whigs followed his announcement on 6 December, the day before Parliament was due to meet, by publishing in the Daily Courant the Elector of Hanover's protest against peace without Spain. Any peer or Member of Parliament who hoped for future favour from the House of Hanover now knew where his long-term interest lay.

Thoroughly outmanoeuvred, Oxford could only await defeat. It was not long in coming. On the opening day of the session the Queen asked

---

39. Clyve Jones, '"The Scheme Lords, the Neccessitous Lords, and the Scots Lords": the Earl of Oxford's management and the "Party of the Crown" in the House of Lords, 1711–14', in Clyve Jones (ed.) Party and Management in Parliament 1660–1784 pp. 123–67.
40. Bromley to Oxford, 3 Dec. 1711, B.L. Loan 29/128/3.
41. Kreienberg's report, 4/15 Dec., Niedersächsisches Staatsarchiv, C.B.A. 24 (England), 107a; Salomon, p. 126, apparently on the authority of Bothmer's report, 4/15 Dec.
42. Bothmer's report, 4/15 Dec. 1711, Salomon, p. 126.
43. Lady Cowper, Diary, p. 18.

for the support of both Houses in making peace. In a tense debate which followed in the House of Lords on a motion of thanks for the Queen's speech, Nottingham moved an amendment to add 'that no peace could be safe or honourable to Great Britain or Europe, if Spain and the West Indies were allotted to any branch of the House of Bourbon'. Oxford then endeavoured to persuade the House that this issue was one which should not be dealt with in a motion of thanks; but this opinion, given by a new peer on a point of order, was portrayed by Wharton, who spoke next, as disrespect for the traditions of the assembly. Wharton concluded by threatening that any minister who attempted to conclude a peace without first securing Spain 'might answer for it to the House with his head'.[44] At the conclusion of the debate the House decided by a majority of one vote in favour of Nottingham's request to bring in his amendment, and two later divisions passed the amendment against the government with larger majorities. To add a final measure to Oxford's cup, the Queen allowed herself to be conducted from the House by the Duke of Somer-set, who had voted against her government; Oxford quoted bitterly to Swift on this instance of royal disloyalty: 'The hearts of kings are unsearchable'.[45]

On the day of the defeat, Oxford seems to have considered accepting the verdict of the House of Lords, even though a similar motion to Nottingham's had been defeated in the Commons by 232 to 106. It was clear that the Lords could not be relied upon to ratify any treaty concluded on the basis of leaving Philip V in possession of the Spanish dominions. But a little more reflection by Oxford and a more sober view of the affair by the Queen brought a more hopeful mood. Soon he was writing to Heinsius that the ascendancy of the Tories would be main-tained.[46] What brought about this change of tone was the Queen's deci-sion to adopt his celebrated expedient of creating twelve new Tory peers. Oxford and his followers put about a story that he had deliberately en-gineered his own defeat in the Lords in order to provide an excuse for the creation of the peers. St John told Swift that Oxford had 'suffered all that had happened on purpose, and had taken measures to turn it to advantage'.[47] This, however, is not likely. Oxford had made every effort to bring ministerial supporters in the Lords up to London in time for the session. Moreover, he had no guarantee that Queen Anne, the most conservative of monarchs, would accede to an unprecedented device which was bound to raise serious opposition from the Whigs and mis-giving even within the ranks of the ministry.[48]

---

44. L'Hermitage, Add. MS. 17,677, EEE, f. 389; [Unknown] to Dr. Colbatch, 11 Dec. 1711, Add. MS. 22,908, f. 87.
45. Swift, *Journal to Stella*, 8 Dec. 1711.
46. *Bolingbroke Corr.*, ii, 50, footnote; by Geikie and Montgomery, p. 236.
47. Swift, *Journal to Stella*, 9 December 1711. Cf. *Wentworth Papers*, p. 222.
48. Burnet, vi, 94–5, Dartmouth's note.

For a fortnight most of the ministry remained ignorant of Oxford's intention; he gave words of encouragement without details, but feeling remained despondent. Nottingham's Occasional Conformity Bill passed through all its stages in the Upper House, and was sent to the Commons on 19 December. The following day it passed the second and third readings there. The bill's easy passage, compared with the disruption engendered by its predecessors in 1702–5, caused widespread and caustic comment. Oxford drew his own moral concerning the Dissenters' betrayal, in the short term at least, by their Whig allies. He wrote, in a letter to a dissenting clergyman, Dr Daniel Williams: 'They [the Dissenters] are epicureans in act, puritans in profession, politicians in conceit, and a prey and laughing stock to the deists and synagogue of the libertines, in whom they have trusted...All they have done or can do, shall never make me their enemy.' The 'deists' would number several of the Junto and 'libertines' included Wharton. There is no record, however, that Oxford himself raised his voice in public against the bill, which passed into law before the Christmas recess.[49]

On one matter, however, Oxford did speak out. The Dissenters were not the only group whose interests were sacrificed by the Whigs in December. Other victims were the Scottish peers. On 20 December the constitutional case of the Duke of Hamilton, a Scottish peer who had recently been created Duke of Brandon in the peerage of Great Britain was heard. To much Scottish indignation, Hamilton was judged by the Lords on this occasion to be ineligible to sit in the House by right of his new title rather than as one of Scotland's sixteen representative peers. Oxford, claiming to speak from a judicial standpoint, urged the House on Hamilton's behalf not to 'consider of the convenience or inconvenience now, but whether by right his patent was not good'. Afterwards he signed a protest against the decision.[50] The opponents of the court clearly considered the Duke as the thin end of a wedge of potential government supporters, Scottish lords with new titles, who might be brought in to ratify the Tory peace treaty. This vote probably contributed to the Queen's decision to create new English peerages, a not entirely new idea which had been canvassed and rejected at the beginning of Harley's ministry in 1710.[51]

During the last week of December, Oxford approached a number of

---

49. The letter, dated 21 Dec. 1711, is printed in *Swift Corr.*, i, 391, where the name of the recipient is given as the Reverend John Shower. But a draft in Oxford's hand in B.L. Loan 29/160/8 indicates that he intended it also for Williams.

50. *Wentworth Papers*, pp. 226–30; *Lords' Journal*, xix, 347.

51. Boyer, *Annals*, ix, 252, mentions a 'strong report' at the time of the general election in October 1710 that the Queen intended to create several new peers to obtain a majority against the Whigs, but suggests that this was found to be unnecessary at that time in view of the entirely 'Church Party' return of Scottish peers to the House. For a similar report, see: *Wentworth Papers*, p. 150.

rich commoners and eldest sons of members of the House of Lords with the offer of peerages. Most of them accepted. Twelve in all, including Mrs Masham's husband, Oxford's son-in-law Dupplin, and four other close supporters, Mansel, Trevor, Granville and Thomas Foley of Witley Court, were gazetted as barons on 31 December 1711.[52] At the time of their promotion there fell a greater man. Even before Marlborough had voted for Nottingham's motion on the 7th, Oxford had marked the General for dismissal.[53] Though the relations of the two men had been outwardly good, since based on a mutual need for each other's services, Oxford had not neglected to warn Marlborough that he retained his post on sufferance, during good political conduct; when the Commons, in the previous session, had appointed commissioners to investigate the accounts of the armies in Spain and Portugal, Oxford had informed Marlborough that 'Flanders was left out of the address by your well-wishers'.[54] The time had now come to include Flanders. A report was drawn up by the commissioners for accounts, and before Parliament rose on 22 December every member was in possession of a copy of this document, which accused both Marlborough and Walpole, as former Secretary at War, of peculation in the army accounts. The charges were largely trumpery, but had great value to the government in that they placed the case before Parliament without giving the accused an opportunity to reply until after the recess. And before Parliament re-assembled, Marlborough had been dismissed; while the Whig leader was sent to the Tower by the Commons as soon as they re-assembled.[55] The tables had been turned in a manner worthy of the greatest political tactician of the day. A formal peace congress could now take place thanks to the clandestine negotiation which, if agreeable to Oxford's love of secrecy, had been necessitated by the obduracy of the Allies and the Whigs in attempting to continue a war in Spain which could not be won. There now remained an even greater task; that of obtaining a final treaty, despite continued resistance from the same quarters, without succumbing to the Tories' hot-headed disregard of the Allies' genuine interests.

52. *London Gazette*, No. 4946.
53. Gregg, p. 345.
54. Coxe, *Marlborough*, iii, 404.
55. Churchill, iv, 501–2. Plumb, *Walpole*, i, 178–81. 'Report of the Commissioners for Examining and Stating the Public Accounts', 21 Dec. 1711, *Parliamentary History*, vi, cols. 1049–1056.

CHAPTER 13

Peacemaking II: the Treaty of Utrecht

OXFORD WAS PRESENT at every meeting of the House of Lords during the critical month of December 1711, and his political victory was not won without taking its toll. Gone was any hope of obtaining the sympathy of the future royal house; the most he could expect was that after peace was concluded the court at Hanover would in its own interest side with the government of the day. If Hanover continued in its implacable opposition, however, there remained the threat of future impeachment with its extreme punishment of beheading. The spectre raised at the time of the Gregg case was grimly resuscitated by the Whigs at the time of Nottingham's motion and danced puppet-like before his eyes; from this time neither his enemies nor his friends would let him forget it.[1] All were aware that the last word would remain with whoever possessed the sympathy of the future ruler; for even by the most optimistic calculation Queen Anne's health did not leave her a long span of years.

In this situation the Jacobites saw some hope of gaining Oxford for their cause. George Lockhart, their leader in the House of Commons, saw that the Whigs 'would certainly squeeze him if ever he again fell into their hands' and believed that Oxford would not put himself at the mercy of his old political enemies the Junto under a German monarch.[2] Nor did the Lord Treasurer omit to give grounds for optimism to the court at St Germains. Gaultier, in the course of his mission to France in April 1711, had visited the Pretender with a verbal message from Oxford. If James would follow closely the directions of the British ministry there was every hope that his restoration could be accomplished as easily as that of Charles II in 1660; three conditions, however, must be observed: the first was, typically, secrecy, even from the rest of the Jacobite court; secondly, the 'Princess Anne' must continue to enjoy the crown undisturbed for the remainder of her life; and lastly, the Church of England must be

---

1. Macpherson, *Original Papers*, ii 271; *Swift Corr.*, i, 324.
2. *Lockhart Papers*, i, 345.

preserved: on these conditions Oxford would obtain a restoration. As the Church could no more be held to be preserved under a Catholic king now than in 1688, and as James Edward was known to be devoted to his father's faith, this condition was unlikely to be met.[3]

How far Oxford was sincere in his professions to the Pretender must be judged by his actions. He never took any step which might have led to the return of the House of Stuart; he refused to present the Pretender's letters to the Queen or to envisage the plan desired by the Jacobites that James himself might secretly visit England. The policy which Oxford pursued, as must all much-solicited politicians, was that of giving hope in return for services. From the beginning of 1712 the Jacobites in the Lower House, acting on instructions from the court in exile, always voted for the government.[4] It is not surprising that the exiles could be raised to wild optimism by a few easy promises; their correspondence concerning Oxford's motives had an air of unreality, sometimes of hysteria, which precluded cool political calculation. The Pretender was eager to clutch at any straw offered, to believe Oxford's assurances and continue to hope even after belief had vanished. On the other hand, it is difficult to believe that Oxford himself ever let any motive of sentiment warp his sense of reality in this matter; and if he ever dreamed in moments of despondency of the return of a pliable young prince under his own tutelage, rather than the succession of a vengeful German warrior, the dreams vanished in the strong light of his awareness of British feeling, his strongest political asset.

If the events of December 1711 raised the likelihood of retribution in the future, they made no difference to Oxford's present plans. The preparations for the peace congress went on. At the end of the month the bishop politician John Robinson, Oxford's close supporter in the cabinet, set off for Holland bearing instructions for himself and the Earl of Strafford as British plenipotentiaries to the forthcoming peace conference. According to these instructions they were to insist, in conformity with the resolution of the House of Lords, that the Spanish crown should not be allotted to Philip of Anjou. On 3 January 1712, Oxford assured the House, on behalf of the Queen, that such instructions had been given.[5] But already the first step had been taken to circumvent an instruction impossible of achievement. On the day following Oxford's assurance, the *London Gazette* announced that Marlborough's successor as Captain-General was to be the Duke of Ormonde, a Tory, some said a Jacobite. Ormonde would follow faithfully the ministerial line by not

---

3. *Berwick Memoirs*, ii, 182. The date of the interview is given by Torcy, *Journal medit*, p. 426.
4. *Berwick Memoirs*, ii, 187–91; 'G.W. Cooke's Memoirs of Lord Bolingbroke', *Edinburgh Review*, lxii (1835), p. 17; *Lockhart Papers*, i, 369. Szechi, pp. 182–91.
5. *Bolingbroke Corr.*, ii, 96, footnote; Luttrell, vi, 710, 4 Jan. 1712.

prolonging a war in Flanders which, even if successful, could not hope to remove Philip from his people's affection or from Spain. And a few days later Oxford wrote to Torcy that the Queen's determination for peace was unaffected.[6]

Oxford was now certain that he could carry the peace in both Houses of Parliament. In the Commons he had regained control after the storms of last session, a remarkable achievement as it was to appear to one foreign observer when the House had been sitting several months. He was not, indeed, able to prevent the routine passage of a place bill in the Lower House, and he endeavoured unsuccessfully in the Lords to turn the bill to advantage by postponing its effect till after the Queen's death, an attempt which possibly indicated that he did not consider the survival of his ministry likely after that event.[7] It was, in fact, the Upper House which gave him most anxiety, despite the presence of the twelve new barons; indeed these gave him only a bare majority which in certain easily-conceivable circumstances might turn into a minority.[8] On more than one occasion in the next few months he saw the House pass motions directed against his peace policy and did not venture to try his strength. Such strength as he had lay not in the existing situation but rather in the implied threat that more peers could if necessary be created; and he conserved his forces for the real struggle which would come after peace had been concluded and its terms communicated to Parliament.

Nor did he neglect to make conciliatory gestures, however futile these might prove to be, towards the Whigs and the House of Hanover. By the beginning of January 1712 he was again negotiating with Halifax. The latter wrote to him on the 10th: 'I have this morning given a full account of what your Lordship commanded me to the two persons, who are very desirous to serve your Lordship and promote the good of their country...'[9] And at the same time he out-bid the Whigs, for once, at Hanover. Just before the Christmas recess the Duke of Devonshire had proposed a measure giving precedence of all peers to the Electoral Prince of Hanover as Duke of Cambridge; Oxford went one better and brought in a bill to give precedence to the whole electoral family. The Act was carried to Hanover in March by Thomas Harley, and in an accompanying letter to the Princess Sophia, Oxford expressed a warning against the family's participation from a distance in the game of British politics. He wrote plainly, though not as servilely as most of the German court's British correspondents: 'The bulk of the nation centre in your succession,

6. Salomon, p. 140.
7. Kreinberg, 28 March, 8 April 1712, Niedersächsisches Staatsarchiv, C.B.A. 24 (England), 107A; Ibid., 4/15 March, 1712.
8. Swift, 4 March 1712, *Journal to Stella*, ii, 504 '...In short, the Majority in the H. of Lords is a very weak one, and he has much ado to keep it up'.
9. Halifax to Oxford, 10 Jan. 1711(−12), B.L. Loan 29/151/6.

and there cannot be anything more unhappy than to have an opinion take place that your serene family were attached to any party. They are to reign over the whole nation and not to be the sovereign of a party only.'[10] At the same time, having removed Marlborough by means of an insubstantial charge, Oxford was willing to make a show of letting him off lightly. On 25 January the Commons passed a vote of censure on the former Captain-General for the offences alleged in the report of the committee of accounts. But a day or two earlier Oxford had taken Marlborough aside in the Upper House and in sight of others, whispered confidentially to him, an action which was taken as a truce overture.[11] The charges were not easy to press home, and Oxford was aware that if a measure cannot be carried, the next best thing is to give way gracefully and acquire the credit for refraining. The mere threat of further prosecution some months later was sufficient to remove Marlborough from England.

Another statesman whose absence from England would have been desirable was Shrewsbury, owing to his qualms concerning the peace negotiations. Oxford pressed him to take Ormonde's place as Lord Lieutenant of Ireland, an arrangement which would also have had the advantage of quelling fears that a possible Jacobite *coup d'état* might begin in the predominantly Roman Catholic island. But though Shrewsbury was to accept the post the following year, he demurred in the spring of 1712 on the plausible grounds that his policy would be too Whiggish to please the English Tories.[12] For the moment, therefore, Ormonde retained his old post. But though Shrewsbury could not be removed from the scene, there was another difficult member of the government who could expect no further forbearance. Somerset's retention of the post of Master of the Horse after his opposition to the dissolution of Parliament in 1710, after attempts to interfere with subsequent policy, and after voting for Nottingham's motion in December 1711, had been made possible by the favour which his wife found in the Queen's eyes. But at last the Queen, assured that she could retain the services of the Duchess, consented in the New Year to remove the Duke, and thus mark her confidence in her government's peace policy in time for the opening of the negotiations at Utrecht.

10. L'Hermitage, Add. MS. 17,677, FFF, f. 29v; Oxford's draft, Loan 29/12/5, no date [early 1712].
11. CJ, xvii, 37–8; Kreienberg, 25 Jan./5 Feb. 1712, C.B.A. 24 (England), 107A; 'on a vue que le dit Comte a donne beaucoup de preuves de bonne volonté au Duc et que ces jours passés encore il le tiroit à coté dans La Chambre Haute et luy parloit à l'oreitlle en presence de beaucoup de gens, marque certaine de son Amitié et de son affections particuliere'.
12. Shrewsbury to Oxford, 4 April 1712, B.L. Loan 29/159/1: [Excuses himself] 'because I hear it is one of the Grievances of those angry gentlemen who are labouring a separation among their own friends, that I am to be sent to Ireland to revive the Whiggish party there;...others in whome the Tory party have a more entire confidence might affect that with ease, which if I attempted would give great offence, not only against me, but perhaps against your Lordship too'.

The congress met for the first time in January 1712. Oxford's plan to conduct the real business behind the backs of the plenipotentiaries had been long premeditated and was now put into action. He had held out against an embarrassing French suggestion that the congress should be held in London, for this would have given him far less opportunity to manoeuvre, to use for advantage the delays in communication between London and Utrecht, and to avoid the footlight glare thrown on the actors in the conference centre.[13] His intention to continue the negotiation by means of a secret settlement betwen Britain and France was not without a good precedent, for he cannot have been unmindful of the Peace of Ryswick, when the chief points at issue were settled in Brabant by the Earl of Portland and Marshall Boufflers, two men who thereby, in Macaulay's words 'very nearly accomplished the work of restoring peace to Christendom while walking up and down an alley under some apple trees'.[14]

Such was the role which Oxford intended to assume. A few days before the congress was formally opened, he informed Torcy that he wished to carry on a correspondence which was to remain secret not only from the Allies but even from St John in whose hands, as Secretary of State, the negotiation formally rested.[15] The French minister readily adopted the arrangement with its golden opportunities for taking advantage of differences within the British ministry. It has often been supposed that St John was responsible for the secret negotiation with France. In fact, until Oxford lost the confidence of the Queen, which cannot be dated before the conclusion of the Peace of Utrecht, he retained a firm control over his colleague, who often complained of the fact with bitter sarcasm. But although the Secretary's other colleagues might fear his caustic tongue and pen, Oxford cared out. On one occasion St John wrote to him: 'I enclose the draught of a letter to the States together with theirs to the Queen. You will please to correct what may be amiss. It is a little more flourished than usual, but I hope on this occasion that may be allowable.' Few men have written abler state papers than St John; and the rancour on which his heart fed while Oxford corrected his prose style before the Queen can only be imagined. For it is clear that Anne expected Oxford to see and approve everything of importance that St John wrote for transmission overseas. On one occasion she wrote to Oxford:

> Not knowing whether Mr Secretary has consulted you about the enclosed I send it for your approbation before I would copy it. Mr St Johns known nothing of the little alteration there is made in the

---

13. Torcy, *Memoirs*, ii, 191.
14. Thomas Babington Macaulay, *The History of England* (1855), iv, 798.
15. Gaultier to Torcy, 27 Jan. (N.S.) 1712, cited by H.N. Fieldhouse, 'A note on the negotiations for the Peace of Utrecht', *AHR* xl (1935), 275–6.
16. St John to Oxford, no date [late 1712], B.L. Loan 29/156/1.

letter, therefore take no notice of it to him. He proposes the Secretary of the Embassy that is now at the Hague should cary this letter to the Emperour, I should be glad to know whether you think him a proper person to do it.

Another time St John wrote to the Queen: 'I have the honour to transmit to your Majesty, at the same time, a draught of my letter to Mr Scot, which I have shown this morning to my Lord Treasurer; and which, with your Majesty's approbation, is to be sent. . .'[17] The Cabinet usually saw St John's more important drafts, and Strafford's reports kept Oxford in touch with the situation at Utrecht. St John's correspondence with the plenipotentiaries was copied, with marginal epitomes, for Oxford's benefit, and is still to be seen among the latter's papers.[18]

Nor is it true that Oxford at any stage voluntarily relinquished his part in foreign affairs. Indeed, he frequently interfered with St John's work, and in addition maintained a wide correspondence with many foreign governments besides France, often through his own messengers; and these governments, not slow to realize his importance in the conduct of British foreign policy, did all they could to gain his ear. His own account of the part he played in obtaining peace was written for the Queen in June 1714. In this paper he was to claim: 'That during this whole negoiation, the Treasurer was obliged by his own hand, and his own charge, to correspond in all the courts concerned in the negotiation; and very often he had the good luck to set right several mistakes, and to obtain some things very little expected.' He added diplomatically: 'But the only merit of this belongs to her Majesty'.[19]

At the outset of the congress the two most pressing problems which faced British diplomacy were, firstly, the Dutch claim to share the commercial concessions demanded of Spain, and secondly, the demands which the French felt entitled to make on the Allies by reason of concessions made to Britain.[20] The Dutch argument was parried by a British counter-claim to share Dutch commercial control of the Spanish Netherlands. In 1709 the 'private and additional' instructions given by the British government to Marlborough and Lord Townshend as negotiators of the Barrier Treaty had permitted the Dutch to levy revenues in the Low Countries generally, and not simply in the barrier towns. Unease felt among Whig ministers concerning the inclusion of these commercial privileges in the Barrier Treaty of 1709 was concealed from the Dutch at

17. H.M.C. Bath, i, 215; Bolingbroke Corr, i, 352.
18. See St John's letters to the Plenipotentiaries, 16 Feb., 19 March 1712, Add. MSS. 37,272, ff. 29 and 51, and same to Strafford, 31 May 1712, Add. MS. 31, 136, f. 352v, for instances of St John delaying to write until the committee of Cabinet had been consulted; H.M.C. Portland, ix, 290–402; Loan 29/309 for copies of St John's diplomatic correspondence.
19. Oxford's 'A brief account of public affairs. . .8th of June, 1714', Parliamentary History, vi, appendix iv, column ccxlvii.
20. H.M.C. Portland, ix, 324.

the time and, by reason of Whig opposition tactics, for several years thereafter.[21] This concession St John in particular was determined to revoke. Oxford, for his part, was similarly determined not to yield to Holland any share in the Assiento. He wrote to Buys, in a letter carried by a private messenger, Thomas Harley: 'I told you Sir plainly all that England asked. Envy us not the Assiento which we are like to purchase with a hundred millions laid out in two wars'. But at the same time he soothed the Dutch witht he hope of some undetermined 'equivalent' for the Assiento.[22] This bait did much to soften Dutch complaints during the coming months. While they were busy devising schemes for such an 'equivalent' the British ministers continued to undermine any sympathy which might remain for the Dutch claims. Oxford supplied Swift with material for the most effective of all anti-barrier tracts, *Some Remarks on the Barrier Treaty*, though he provided it, Swift remarked, 'as he always does, too late'. The pamphlet did not come out in time for a Commons debate concerning the treaty on 14 February, which was nevertheless concluded with the resolution that the Barrier Treaty was dishonourable to the Queen and nation. Thus strengthened, the ministry could be assured of their ability, if necessary, to coerce the Dutch.[23]

The second problem was the excessive French demands, of which the most exceptionable were that several key fortresses, the most important being Tournai, should be returned to France and that the Spanish Netherlands should fall to the Elector of Bavaria rather than to the Emperor.[24] On these demands were centred the main rifts in the ministry, St John and the Tories favouring a quick settlement by means of concessions to French demands, Oxford still being determined to bargain on behalf of the Allies' more reasonable requirements. During the discussions of August and September 1711 the British had carefully staved off any attempt to discuss the French claims. In the months which elapsed between the signing of the preliminary articles and the opening of the peace congress, the French had continued to press their claims and those of the Elector, while the British had countered by putting forward more specific claims on behalf of the Allies; but despite several journeys by Gaultier no satisfactory agreement was reached before the congress opened, and Oxford was careful to keep his correspondence with Torcy non-committal, though conciliatory.[25]

Soon after the opening of the congress, however, these problems were

21. *British Diplomatic Instructions: France*, p. 12; After 1714 the Whig government refused the Dutch claims in which they had formerly acquiesced: Geikie and Montgomery, p. 189.
22. Oxford to Buys, 8/19 March 1711/12, Add. MS. 20,985, f. 17iv; John Drummond to Buys, 25 Jan. 1711/12 Geikie and Montgomery, pp. 250–1.
23. Geikie and Montgomery, pp. 250–1; same pages; Swift, *Journal to Stella*, 12 Feb. 1712; *Wentworth Papers*, p. 266.
24. Trevelyan, iii, 211.
25. Torcy, *Memoirs*, ii, 188–190, 210–12, 216–17.

again set aside, for there occurred in the French royal family a misfortune which threatened to destory all previous calculations for the peace negotiation. This was the death in February of the two members next in line to the French throne, leaving the future Louis XV, a child of two, as heir and only bar to the succession of Philip of Anjou. It became at once imperative to provide some safeguard against the unification of the Spanish and French inheritance in the hands of one man, and until this could be done all other questions were virtually suspended. In officially notifying the deaths, Torcy stated that Louis XIV would take measures to prevent a union of the crowns; to Oxford he offered to give any sureties that Britain thought necessary.[26] The British reply, which was carried to France by Gaultier, demanded that Philip should completely renounce his claim to the French succession; but Torcy responded with a lengthy memorandum showing that in French legal theory such a renunciation would be invalid. To this assertion, both Oxford and St John replied that the renunciation must be made, with the alternative of breaking off the peace conference altogether.[27] Torcy, in return, offered a scheme by which Philip would be compelled to chose between the two crowns in the event of the death of the young prince. There was, Torcy added, no reason to suppose that Philip would in such a case choose to remain in Spain. As a seasoned diplomat, however, the French minister can hardly have expected this hollow assertion to be taken at face value.[28]

The obvious danger of this plan for the future peace of Europe impressed the British ministry and the Queen, anxious though they were to press on for peace. The result of their deliberations was a scheme which envisaged something like a return to the principle of the Partition Treaty of 1689, in that it proposed that the major part of the Spanish inheritance might go to a minor European prince unconnected with either the Bourbon or the Habsburg families. Philip must make his choice immediately; should he choose to retain Spain, he must renounce his right to France, otherwise he must immediately hand over Spain and Spanish America to the Duke of Savoy, ruling instead Savoy-Piedmont, Mantua, Montferrat and Sicily. That this reapportionment of the European cake was Oxford's idea rather than St John's may be seen from a letter which the Secretary sent to Strafford at Utrecht:

> The whole event of our treaty turning on this article of the reunion [*sc.* of the crowns], I should not think our affairs in a very good situation, had I not reason to believe that the Treasurer knows, that this

26. *Bolingbroke Corr.*, ii, 204; the same to Oxford, same date, P.R.O. 31/3/198, f. 20.
27. 'Reponse au Mémoire apporté par le Sieur Gaultier le 23me Mars, 1712', included in Torcy's letter to St John, 28 March (N.S.) 1712, *Bolingbroke Corr.* ii, 221–6 and footnote; Oxford to Torcy, 23 March 1712, P.R.O. 31/3/198, f. 36. *Cf. Bolingbroke Corr.*, ii, 229.
28. Torcy to St John, *ibid.*, ii, 246. Also Torcy to Oxford, 8 April (N.S.) 1712, P.R.O. 31/3/198, f. 42.

expedient, or something very near to it, will be closed with by the French Court. I may tell you, in the utmost confidence, that the first hint was given by him, in the Committee of Council, and, by several expressions which dropped from him, when alterations were started, I could plainly find, that he knew what would be most, and what least agreeable at Versailles.

As the Secretary rightly concluded, the negotiation was being orchestrated by the Lord Treasurer well before it took official channels. And indeed, Oxford's confidence in his scheme was such that he communicated it to the court at Vienna, through the devious mediacy of the Palatine resident in London and Prince Eugene, without St John's knowledge, while the French reply was awaited.[29] On the strength of Torcy's assertion of Philip's preference for France, Oxford unwisely assumed, in a letter to Torcy dated 1 May, that the acceptance by France of his proposition would settle the matter; he dilated on the advantages of frustrating the ambitions of the Hapsburgs, of setting at rest the fears of the other Allies, and of having Spain remain unconnected with a naval power. These advantages were, perhaps, theoretically compatible with Philip choosing to remain in Spain, and in the outcome Oxford had to accept such a choice; but the tenor of that letter, and of his actions generally, seems to be that while he did not absolutely exclude this possibility, he believed that Philip would give up Spain. Two days later he informed Thomas Harley, then waiting in Holland to be ordered to Hanover, that Torcy's reply was expected within a week, and without any question of waiting longer than this until the plan had been considered at Madrid, added 'I believe you will carry the best peace that has been made these 200 years'.[30]

This belief did more justice to Oxford's fervent desire for peace than to his usual caution. On 9 May, Torcy's reply duly arrived, stating that a messenger had been sent to Madrid to pose before Philip an immediate choice on the lines suggested by the British. On the following day St John dispatched the celebrated 'restraining orders' to the Duke of Ormonde, ordering him to avoid contact with the French forces without acquainting the Allied commanders with his instructions, and entertaining the hope that an armistice would be 'as good as concluded in a few days'. At the same time St John revealed Ormonde's orders to Gaultier for communication to Torcy.[31]

29. *Bolingbroke Corr.*, ii, 299–300; Salomon, p. 146, citing Oxford to Eugene, 17 April; Steingens (Palatine resident), to the same, 19 April; Eugene to Oxford, 30 April; and Eugene to Charles VI, same date (all N.S.), 1712, in *Feldzüge Eugen*, ii, series v, Supplement, pp. 114–16.
30. Oxford to Torcy, 1/12 May 1712, P.R.O. 31/3/198, f. 66; Oxford to Thomas Harley, 3/14 May 1712, Add. MS, 40,621, f. 70.
31. Torcy to Oxford, 13 May (NS) 1712, P.R.O. 31/3/198, f. 74; *Bolingbroke Corr.*, ii, 314, 317 & 320–1.

The question arises, how far Oxford shared responsibility for this last treasonable step. During the proceedings of his impeachment in 1715 he denied foreknowledge of the restraining orders. He was fortunately not called upon to defend himself against a charge of communicating them to the enemy. According to Gaultier's account to Torcy, Oxford and St John together took the French message to the Queen and she ordered St John 'on the spot' to dispatch the restraining orders to Ormonde. Both ministers later put the blame on her impetuousity.[32] But it is not likely that she came to the decision without advice and premeditation. In previous days there had been ample time to decide on the next step, supposing that the French agreed to the British proposition; and Oxford's optimism in the letter to Thomas Harley makes it likely that he had encouraged the Queen to expect a cessation of arms. Some illumination may be shed on Oxford's attitude by a coeval statement by St John. In a brief letter to Torcy, saying that Gaultier was informed of Ormonde's orders, the secretary added a postcript which did not appear in the office copy. The addition reads: 'I send this courier without giving the Lord Treasurer time to write to you, but he orders me to assure you that no-one could honour your more or be more your devotd servant'. Discounting the flowery civilities, usual in concluding correspondence at this time, this would seem to indicate that Oxford was also aware of the betrayal of Ormonde's orders. If so, the fact that be absented himself from Gaultier's briefing suggests his unease.[33] That St John forged Oxford's compliments for some purpose of his own is also possible, since the postcript was omitted from a copy which would be under the eyes of Oxford's friends in the secretaries' office. But there can be no question of St John concealing from Oxford the gist of the message to Torcy. At most, it is possible that by order of the Queen, Oxford was not consulted before the message was sent if he was known to disapprove. More likely, however, is that Oxford knew of the action taken but did not intend to implicate himself in writing.

In short, it is probable that Oxford was responsible jointly with the Queen and St John for the restraining orders and that he also knew of their communication to Gaultier, whether he approved or not. He was anxious, by immobilizing the British and French forces, to avoid a further

32. 'The Answer of Robert, Earl of Oxford', 3 Sept. 1715, Article 8, *Parliamentary History*, vii, 175; Gaultier to Torcy, 21 May (N.S.), 1712, Trevelyan, iii, 230; St John's testimoney to the First Earl of Hardwick in *Miscellaneous State Papers*, ii, 482.

33. St John to Torcy, 10/21 May 1712, P.R.O. 31/3/198, f. 71. The postcript does not appear in the version printed from the copy, already cited, in *Bolingbroke Corr.* ii. 317. The evidence given here for Oxford's involvement in the restraining orders, and probable cognizance of their betrayal to France, does not, of course make him the 'real author' of the former, as Professor Gregg's biography of Queen Anne claims on the strength of 'Gaultier's letters between November 1711 and May 1712' (Gregg, p. 354). Gaultier's letter of 21 May, cited above and printed by Trevelyan, makes the Queen's personal rôle clear.

campaign's bloodshed and expense. He hoped that as soon as Philip of Anjou's acceptance of his scheme arrived, the Emperor and the Dutch would submit to an arrangement not unlike that which the Empire had been prepared to accept in 1689, and would agree to a ceasefire. Not less responsible than either of the ministers, however, was the Queen herself, never a mere figurehead to her ministries. She was in a fever of anxiety for peace; special prayers for the war had ceased in the royal chapel three weeks earlier. But the brutal advice which went with the communication of Ormonde's orders to the enemy was characteristic of St John; when Gaultier asked him what the French commander should do if Prince Eugene attacked, the secretary replied, 'fall on him and cut him to pieces'. If Oxford felt any qualms about the betrayal, St John felt none. [34] Nevertheless, Oxford's share in one of the most discreditable episodes of British history cannot be discounted. Miscalculation of Philip of Anjou's intentions, over-credulous acceptance of Torcy's smooth professions, over-anxiety to cease bloodshed and save national expense, and failure to resist, on this occasion at least, the importunities of the Queen and St John, all contributed to error engendered by his necessary but inexperienced diplomacy. He was to do better later.

The gist of Ormonde's instructions soon became generally evident from his military inactivity. Marlborough and the Whig leaders, wrote Kreienberg to his master of Hanover, insisted that the ministry had 'torn off the mask', and they urged in the strongest terms that the Pretender would be in England within two months unless prevented by the 'great project', which was doubtless the dispatch of the Elector's heir, as Duke of Cambridge to England. On 28 May the matter was raised in the House of Lords, where the ministers were pressed to reveal Ormonde's orders. Oxford admitted that the captain-general had been forbidden to fight a battle, though claiming that the orders permitted the undertaking of a siege. In any case, he added, an advantageous peace would be announced within a few days. After this assurance, a motion by Halifax proposing an address to the Queen in which she should be asked to instruct Ormonde to act in conjunction with the Allied forces, was lost by 28 votes. Two days later Oxford blandly assured Kreienberg that Ormonde would fight if necessary and that the supposed restraining orders were a fiction invented in Holland. [35]

Oxford's hope of an arrangement of the Spanish succession which would be acceptable in Vienna was due to be shattered as a major miscalculation. In the first week of June the British government received from Torcy the unexpected news that Philip had chosen to remain in Spain and renounce his right of succession to the French crown. The

34. L'Hermitage, Add. MS. 17,677, FFF. f. 166; Trevelyan, iii, 230.
35. Kreienberg, 27 May, 7 June and 3 May, 10 June 1712, CBA 24 (England), 107A, L'Hermitage, Add. MS. 17677, FFF, f. 220.

effect of this communication was little less than staggering, especially to Oxford, but the ministry put the best face possible on the development. On 6 June the Queen announced to Parliament that Philip had agreed to make a solemn renunciation of his claim to France; she spoke in confident terms of a peace soon to follow. Despite the efforts of Wharton and Marlborough in the House of Lords, motions of thanks were voted in both chambers. During the following weeks, the ministers abandoned hope of Emperor's participation in peace, but tried desperately to obtain at least Hanoverian and Dutch agreement to an armistice. The House of Hanover, as well as being closely tied to the policy of the Emperor, hoped that Britain would still be at war with France when Queen Anne died, thus facilitating the exclusion of the Pretender. On the refusal of the electoral court to join a ceasefire, Oxford wrote indignantly to Thomas Harley of Bothmer, the Hanoverian Envoy:

> It is now given as a reason by Toland and the associates of Baron Bothmer hear (and they quote the Baron for it) that the Succession is not secure without an army, and therefore they are against a peace now because it must be disbanded; should people once believe this to be the sentiment of that family we are all undone, but I will never believe it.[37]

For the moment the Dutch, in the absence of a guarantee of their political and commercial interests, also preferred to fight on. With disastrous military consequences for the Allied forces, the British withdrew their troops early in July.

But despite the obstinacy of the Allies, Oxford was determined to obtain a formal treaty for Britain and as many of the Allies as would accede to it as soon as France would yield on some of the matters which had been outstanding since the beginning of the congress. He greatly exaggerated but did not mistake the national desire for peace when he wrote to one of the Imperial plenipotentiaries at Utrecht: 'At length the body of the nation awakes and 200 to one declare for peace, approve all the Queen had done, are impatient all is not finished'. Nevertheles, Oxford did not give up the Allies' justifiable claims. Concerning the French demand that the Spanish Netherlands should go to the Elector of Bavaria, the ministry remained firm for the Emperor's claim, and Torcy showed signs of desisting; furthermore, when he suggested in the middle of July that the Elector should have Sicily instead, both Oxford and St John insisted that this should go to a loyal ally, the Duke of Savoy.[38]

At this point it was decided to speed up the slow process of wrangling

36. *Bolingbroke Corr.*, ii, 356. Torcy to Oxford 8 June 1712, P.R.O. 31/3/198, f. 83; Cobbett, *Parliamentary History*, vi, 1141–4.
37. Oxford to Thomas Harley, Aug. 12/23, Aug. 1712, Add. MS. 40, 621, f. 112.
38. *Welbeck Letters*, p. 64; *Morrison Collection*, v, 79; *Bolingbroke Corr.*, ii, 474.

at a distance by sending St John to Paris to negotiate in person. At the beginning of July, after the prorogration of Parliament, St John had been granted his desire of being raised to the peerage with the title of Bolingbroke, though he did not conceal from Oxford his chagrin that his new rank was viscount and not earl. Nor was St John alone honoured, for Oxford himself was given the wardenship of Sherwood Forest, a post last held by the Duke of Newcastle. In a later account, Oxford summed up the situation as follows: 'This discontent continued until there happened an opportunity of sending him to France, of which there was not much occasion, but it was hoped that this would have put him in a good humour, which it did...'[39] However, the immediate occasion of the decision to send Bolingbroke was a letter received from Torcy on the last day of July asking for the conclusion of a general peace between France, Spain, Britain and Savoy. Against this proposal Oxford stubbornly set his face, though Bolingbroke would willingly have accepted it and abandoned the Dutch and Austrians in the treaty as well as in the field. On 1 August therefore, Bolingbroke announced to the British plenipotentiaries at Utrecht that he was to go to Paris to clear up the remaining points at issue, including the formalities of King Philip's renunciation, though he claimed to be 'very indifferently instructed upon this head'.[40]

Nevertheless, Bolingbroke set off with a light heart on 2 August, taking as companions Prior, who was to remain in Paris as unofficial envoy, and Gaultier. And within two days of his arrival he had fulfilled his instructions; he obtained the assurance that the Emperor would receive the Netherlands and the Duke of Savoy acquire Sicily; he professed himself satisfied with Philip's renunciation, and he signed the document proclaiming a cessation of hostilities between Great Britain, France, Spain and Savoy. He lingered in Paris a few days, basking in the warm hospitality of the Hôtel de Croissi, enjoying the receptions and entertainments which Torcy arranged for his benefit. Deft was the flattery of the French minister; and it was not long before Christian names were being used for 'Harré' Bolingbroke, and even of 'Robin' back in England.[41]

In Bolingbroke's absence, Oxford became increasingly useasy. The period lengthened into three weeks, whereas the secretary had been expected back in England within twelve or thirteen days. He feared that Bolingbroke would overstep a cessation of arms, and Torcy's account leaves no doubt that Bolingbroke would have concluded an immediate

39. H.M.C. *Portland*, v, 198; William Levinz to Oxford, 8 July 1712, Loan 29/149/6; 'A brief account of public affairs, 8th of June 1714', Cobbett, *Parliamentary History*, vi, appendix iv, column ccxlvi.
40. *Bolingbroke Corr.*, ii, 492; Torcy *Memoirs*, ii, 347; Bolingbroke to the Plenipotentiaries, 29 July, continued on 1 Aug. 1712, Add. MSS. 37, 272, ff. 155–6.
41. *Bolingbroke Corr.* iii, 1–23, 53 and 57; Dickinson, *Bolingbroke*, p. 101.

peace had he dared to override his superior's instructions. According to Torcy:

> [Bolingbroke] had counselled the Queen to prefer a separate peace to a suspension of hostilities, and to secure to her subjects as soon as possible the enjoyment of those advantages which the king consented to grant them [but] Bolingbroke's advice was opposed by the lord treasurer, cautious of offending the duke of Hanover, and apprehensive of being called to an account, whenever that prince ascended the British throne. It was therefore resolved to abide by the project of a cessation.[42]

Bolingbroke was more skilled than his colleague in the labyrinth of diplomacy, but he was matched against an even greater user of its ways in Torcy. To Bolingbroke negotiation was not simply a national necessity, it was an end in itself, a game of wits to be played with zest: Torcy had all Bolingbroke's bravura, but in addition he possessed the cool experience of a professional diplomatist as against a gifted tyro. It would have gone hard with British honour, and ultimately with British interests, if Oxford had not exercised restraint.

As soon as Bolingbroke reached London late in August Oxford took him on to Windsor for audience with the Queen. The result of what must have been a heated conference was, as Bolingbroke reported without comment in his first letter to Prior in Paris, that the negotiation with France was handed over to Dartmouth, in whose province it fell. Henceforth, Prior would receive only 'now and then a letter of friendship'.[43] Nevertheless, within a fortnight Bolingbroke was writing to Prior, concerning the outstanding problem of the Dutch barrier, in a thoroughly Francophile letter (the substance of which would undoubtedly be communicated to Torcy) that 'in my own opinion, and I believe I speak the Queen's upon this occasion' the French should insist on the Dutch giving up Tournai, and he added that 'we shall go on to ripen everything for a conclusion between us and Savoy, and France and Spain'. But Oxford was advised by Strafford, who cannot be suspected of pro-Dutch sympathies, that Tournai was a strategic necessity to the Dutch Barrier. Throughout September Strafford had become more and more convinced that the Dutch were about to give up their attempt to act independently of Britain. By the 24th he reported his certainty that with Tournai secured they would give up all their other claims.[44] It was perhaps this opinion which enabled Oxford to win his point in the cabinet dispute which now exploded.

42. HMC. *Fifteenth Report*, appendix, part ii. 213; Torcy, *Memoirs*, ii. 347–8.
43. Kreienberg, 22 Aug./2 Sept. 1712, C.B.A. 24 (England), 107A; *Bolingbroke Corr.*, iii, 23.
44. *Bolingbroke Corr.*, iii, 66–7; H.M.C. *Portland*, ix, 344, 346, 349 and 352.

In September a series of cabinet meetings revealed that Bolingbroke was not without his supporters. Unfortunately none of the participants left a record of the dispute, though it was widely reported at third hand. On domestic policy Oxford was under pressure to dissolve Parliament immediately instead of waiting for a dissolution in the normal course in 1713. A new election, before the conclusion of peace, would undoubtedly have returned the Tories more strongly than ever on the peace issue alone. On the side of Bolingbroke for a dissolution were Harcourt, Buckinghamshire and, more surprisingly, Shrewsbury. Against an immediate general election stood Oxford, Poulett and Dartmouth. Over Bolingbroke's desire for an immediate peace, excluding the Dutch and Austrians, there was a similar division in the cabinet meeting on 1 October. Kreienberg reported: 'that in the Cabinet Council last Sunday it came to very rude expostulation, and I add that I know from an authentic source, who knows nothing otherwise of the subject, that the Queen cried copiously that evening'. Oxford was joined by Harcourt on this occasion and the two argued that since the Dutch appeared prepared to be reasonable and had made a just proposition, Britain would put herself in the wrong to ignore them. In the course of the argument Oxford is reported to have upbraided Bolingbroke for overstepping his instructions during his visit to Paris.[45]

The upshot was that the participants of this quarrel separated in anger or dismay, each expressing his feelings in his own manner; Bolingbroke left for some hard hunting, and Oxford retired to his chamber with rheumatism, refusing for several days to see any visitors.[46] But his views prevailed: no general election was called, nor was peace signed at once or without the participation of the Dutch.

It is clear that the Queen had been more than inclined to listen to Bolingbroke's argument for immediate peace, though she eventually came down on Oxford's side. When the ministers returned to their duties a general reconciliation was patched up and she poured oil on the troubled waters. In the course of October Oxford received the Garter and Bolingbroke was compensated, though scarcely to his satisfaction, with the Lord Lieutenancy of Essex.[47] But while the surface ruffles were smoothed, disturbances continued in the depths. Bolingbroke kept up unconcealed his correspondence with Prior, giving advice on all material points of the peace negotiation. Dartmouth, visibly unhappy at the position of competition with his caustic colleague into which Oxford had

45. Kreienberg, 26 Sept./7 Oct., 3/14 and 7/18 Oct., C.B.A. 24 (England) *Loc. cit.*, 107A; L'Hermitage, Add. MS. 17,677 FFF. f. 361; *Private Corr.*, ii, 82
46. H.M.C. *Portland*, vii. 93 Kreienberg, 3/14 Oct., 1712, C.B.A. 24 (England) 107A.
47. G.E. Cockayne, The *Complete Peerage* (1945); Oxford was nominated on 26 October 1712 and installed in the order of the Garter on 4 August, 1713; for Bolingbroke's appointment see P.R.O. SP 38, Docquet Book 27.

forced him, was barely persuaded by the Queen to refrain from resignation. And outside ministerial circles, feeling ran as strongly as ever on both sides. The Duke of Hamilton was killed in a duel – the Tories said assassinated – on the point of taking up the embassy to Paris, and Oxford himself escaped a similar fate at the hands of a booby trap which arrived by post on King William's birthday.[48]

Before the month of October was out, the wisdom of Oxford's more patient diplomacy was justified. The French suddenly yielded up their claim to Tournai.[49] This was the first break in the clouds over Utrecht, and a few days later there came a second. Since Bolingbroke's return from Paris, Dartmouth had laboured, at Oxford's instigation, to produce a more stringent form of King Philip's renunciation of his right to succeed to the French throne than that which had satisfied Bolingbroke; indeed, the alleged inadequeacy of the previous form, particularly by not naming the new order of succession to the French throne, would seem to have been a material charge which Oxford levelled against Bolingbroke.[50] When the new renunciation was received from Madrid in the second week of November, Oxford publicly expressed himself well satisfied with it. The Queen wrote to Louis XIV in her own handwriting of her desire to speed the conclusion of peace. But before her last great desire was fulfilled, five more months were to pass while the plenipotentiaries of all the combatant nations, except the Empire, undertook the slow task of putting into proper form the decisions which had been taken elsewhere.[51]

One of the most important consequences of the long postponement of a peace which Oxford had confidently expected in June was its effect on his plans for the South Sea Company. By his own choice he was its first governor. Much of the acclaim and initial success which greeted the company's foundation arose, as has been said, from the general belief that the 'South Sea' trade was to be opened to British merchants by the expedition which was actually intended for Quebec. In fact, any possibility of using force to open this trade passed away when the signing of the preliminary articles seemed to make peace imminent. In the course of the negotiation of the articles, Oxford had also given up his plan for obtaining permanent settlements which would permit a far wider trade than that envisaged in the Assiento. But when he addressed the directors of the company at their first meeting on 14 September 1711, he was no position to reveal these facts, though he discoursed generally and opti-

48. H.M.C. *Bath*, i, 222; Swift, 15 Nov. 1712, *cf.* Swift, *Journal to Stella*, 26 January.
49. Bolingbroke to the Bishop of Bristol, 28 Oct. 1712, Add. MS. 37,272, f. 232.
50. Prior to Dartmouth, 16/27, Sept. 1712, and Dartmouth to Prior, 25 Sept. 1712, P.R.O. SP 78/154, ff. 166 and 174. Sir Nathan LLoyd to [Dartmouth?], 4 Sept. 1712, P.R.O. SP. Dom. 34/19, f. 103.
51. L'Hermitige, Add. MS. 17,677, FFF. f. 410; Anne to Louis xiv, 14/25 Nov. 1712, *Morrison Collection*, i, 24.

mistically on trading prospects.[52] Nor could he do so after the articles were signed. For one thing, the existence of separate articles concerning Britain's claims was a closely guarded secret; and for another the Treasury at once began to use its South Sea stock for all purposes of debt payments to which the constituent securities had been put. The first use of stock for this purpose was ordered by Oxford in October, 1711, and he later obtained a royal warrant to cover the practice, which henceforth became common, of depositing South Sea stock as security on short term loans. But any revelation of the insecure basis of the hopes of the Company would immediately have lowered the value of all stock, of which the government departments were the chief holders.[53]

Thus it was, that in January 1712 the directors informed Oxford, without a quiver of doubt as to their reception, that in the coming summer they would need an expeditionary force of four thousand soldiers, forty transport ships, twenty men of war, and an appropriate number of store ships, hospital ships, and bomb vessels.[54]

Oxford prevaricated. He stayed away from the directors' meetings. This in itself was not exceptionable; it had never been intended that he should play the part of an active governor, and for this purpose a subgovernor. Sir James Bateman, was appointed. But he corresponded with them at infrequent intervals, and through Bolingbroke, whose letters were evasive. The first of these letters held out some ill-defined hope of a royal force, and the directors thereupon resolved to purchase goods to the value of £200,000 to send to the South Seas.[55] Because of the state of the peace negotiations early in 1712, the ministers put off the scheme until, at the end of May, the directors felt constrained to write direct to Oxford that should there be any further delay 'they may not without difficulty be induced to believe that any trade is intended'. By September they announced that they now had 1,200 tons of merchandise in London warehouses awaiting dispatch to the South Seas.[56] They were by now aware that any idea of a warlike expedition must be abandoned, but were assured that the commerical treaty with Spain would obtain facilities for general trade as well as the slaving contract. Like ministerial quarrels, the fate of the South Sea trade waited upon the signing of peace, and upon Oxford's ability to emerge successfully from the even more complicated web of his closely interlinked political and diplomatic projects.

52. L'Hermitage, Add. MS. 17,677, EEE. f. 311.
53. CTB xxv, 100 and 569, Treasury minute, 2 Oct. and royal warrant, 30 Nov. 1711.
54. The Company to Oxford, 31 Jan. 1711(−12), Company Memorials Book, Vol. 1, Add. MS. 25,559, p. 14.
55. St John to Sir James Bateman, 13 March 1712, P.R.O. SP 44/111; Court Minute Book 1, Add. MS. 25,494, p. 121, for the court's desision.
56. Robert Knight to Oxford, 23 May 1712, Loan 29/45c/8; The directors to Oxford, 3 Sept. 1712, Add. MS. 25,559, p. 21.

In many ways, in both his public and his private life, the turn of the year was a trying time for Oxford. After the assurances of early peace given to Parliament in June it would be injudicious to summon the members until the peace was actually signed. And because of the political situation, he failed in the autumn of 1712, for the third successive year, to find time for his once customary holiday at Brampton. Nor, when he surveyed the affairs of his family, was he much consoled for the cares of his public life. The Duchess of Newcastle's lawsuit dragged on, and in the meantime she would by no means consent to her daughter's marriage with Oxford's son. And while Lord Harley waited upon the slow course of English legal proceedings, his sister Elizabeth was in scarcely better case. She was engaged to the Marquess of Carmarthen, who had been left a considerable fortune by his grandfather, the first Duke of Leeds. But Carmarthen had fallen out with his father, the second Duke, concerning a disputed portion of the inheritance, and was also forbidden to marry. Early in October the young man, with the aid of a letter drafted by Oxford, attempted to heal the breach. This failing, Oxford decided that the marriage should go forward, since the groom was of age. Happily the Duke allowed Oxford to reconcile him with the young couple at the last moment, and the ceremony took place on 15 December.[57] This was, for Oxford, the one bright spot in a disturbing year.

With the new year of 1713 came the long-awaited treaties. For the last stage, Shrewsbury was sent to France as ambassador extraordinary, despite his lachrymose protests, and perhaps as a punishment for his support of Bolingbroke, or to prevent a repetition of it. Arriving in Paris in the first week of January, he immediately began to assail Oxford with complaints of his own inadequacy for the duty, especially in regard to the negotiation of the forthcoming commercial treaty with France. Oxford was obliged to accept an arrangement by which others, with Bolingbroke's assistance from England, took over responsibility for this aspect of Shrewsbury's task.[58] The result of Shrewbury's weakness was that this last stage of peace making, especially that for the commercial treaties associated with the main negotiation, fell more under Bolingbroke's influence, with disastrous consequences which were seen later.

The conclusion of the general treaties at Utrecht followed a settlement between Britain and Holland. The British plentipotentiaries had been instructed to leave the Dutch in no doubt that British support in obtaining Tournai was conditional not only on co-operation in obtaining peace, but on giving up the Townshend treaty for another more favour-

---

57. 'For Lord Carmathen to the Duke of Leeds', 6 Oct. 1712, Loan 29/152/4; Leeds to Oxford, 10 Dec. 1712, Oxford to Leeds, same date Loan 29/152/4; L'Hermitage, Add. MS. 17,677, GGG, f. 13v.
58. H.M.C. *Bath*, i, 228; Prior to Dartmouth, 19 Jan. (N.S.), 1713, PR.O. SP 78/154, f. 412.

able to Britain.[59] The second Barrier Treaty, signed in January 1713, gave the Dutch the right to garrison a line of fortresses which, though curtailed from that permitted by the Townshend Treaty, represented a considerable advance on the provision of the Treaty of Ryswick; and this advantage they owed, after Marlborough's victories, to Oxford's restraint. At the same time the tariff privileges enjoyed by Dutch merchants in the Netherlands since 1709 were reduced in order to allow the British an equal share of its commerce, a reasonable amendment of the exessive concessions of that year. This settled, the peace treaties were signed on 31 March 1713 at Utrecht between the main participants, except the Emperor and the Elector of Hanover, who both preferred to fight on against France and Spain until they were forced to conclude a separate peace at Rastadt in March 1714. Oxford's stock with the heir to the throne had never been lower, but his popularity with the Tories and above all with the British general public rose briefly almost to its level of 1710 as the nation breathed a sigh of relief after nearly two and a half decades of war or uneasy truce.

59. Instructions to the Plenipotentiaries, 11 Nov. 1712, *British Diplomatic Instructions: France*, pp. 29–33.

CHAPTER 14

Postwar Problems: Commerce and Succession

THE NEWS OF the settlement at Utrecht reached London on 3 April 1713. But while the church bells rang out for peace, there was little immediate prospect of tranquility for Oxford. To have carried the treaty, in face of all opposition, was a considerable achievement; to have held the ministry together would have been even more remarkable, had he managed to do so. Such an achievement, however, eluded him.

In preparation for the submission of the peace terms to Parliament, he made an attempt to conciliate the Whigs. The acidulous former Lord Chancellor Cowper, whose moderation Oxford over-estimated, has left a record of a conversation in which Oxford tried to re-assure him concerning the safety of the Hanoverian succession and the advantages obtained in the peace treaty. 'He had written down Head[ing]s on a Paper', wrote Cowper, 'yet spake, as always, very dark and confusedly.' Oxford assured him that the Highland clans had been bribed by the government to favour the Protestant succession in Scotland, that Marlborough was in close touch with St Germains, and that as soon as peace was concluded, the Queen would take measures to demonstrate that she was for the House of Hanover. As to Cowper's pointed remark that one more campaign would have brought a better peace, Oxford replied earnestly that 'if we were at the Gates of Paris, we could not have a better Peace than what we were now to have'. As a result of this and another meeting with '4 principall whigs', Oxford was forced to tell the ever-inquisitive Jonathan Swift that his overtures to the moderate Whigs had been without success and he was 'resolved to begin a Speech against them when the Parliament sits'.[1] All the same, he did not entirely give up hope, for a few days later he hinted to Richard Steele, the ardently whiggish writer, of the possibility of a scheme comprehending both Tories and Whigs in government. Nothing, however, appears to have come of this.[2]

1. Cowper, *Diary*, p. 54; Swift, *Journal to Stella*, 21 March 1713; *London Diaries*, p. 602.
2. H.M.C. *Seventh Report*, part i, appendix, p. 238.

In fact, there was no real alternative to reliance on the Tories, for the Whigs were determined to oppose a parliamentary ratification of the peace treaties. And even the Tories, despite the achievement of their great desire to end the war, were reported by Bromley to be restive after repeated prorogations of Parliament. The last of these prorogations took place on 26 March, and the date set for meeting was 9 April: there could be no further delay. Oxford set himself to rally all the Tories. He had already summoned the Jacobite George Lockhart to bring up his friends, at the same time not scrupling to hint that as a reward some of the present justices of the peace in Scotland might be replaced by men more in sympathy with the House of Stuart.[3] And on the eve of the first meeting new ministerial changes favoured the Tories, with Harcourt raised from Lord Keeper to Lord Chancellor; while a Whig, the Earl of Cholmondeley, was removed from the royal household.

At first all went well. The Queen's opening speech to Parliament on 9 April 1713 announced the signing of peace, though without communicating the terms. In the House of Lords, Halifax accordingly opposed the ministerial address of thanks, which congratulated the Queen on the treaty, on the tenable grounds that terms not yet disclosed ought not to be endorsed by Parliament. Oxford replied that the treaty would soon be shown to Parliament, and that the more its terms were examined the better they would seem; the Whig motion was defeated by 75–43.[4] For nearly two months the session passed fairly smoothly; the peace terms were communicated and debated enthusiastically in the Commons, and without disaster in the Lords. In the Lower House, however, Bolingbroke noted growing opposition to certain commercial articles which he hoped would bring good relations between Britain and France but which appeared to favour the latter country. In the words of two modern authors the most-favoured-nation provisions alarmed 'that small but determined group of Tories which had for more than eighteen months suspected the whole drift of the government's peace policy', the Hanoverian sympathizers. The Secretary put the blame on Oxford for taking insufficient measures to hold the Tories together:

> We act [he wrote to Shrewsbury] as if we had nothing to do, but get this session over any how. No principle of government established and avowed, nobody but my Lord Treasurer, and he cannot be in every place and speak to every man, able to hold out hopes and fears, or give a positive answer to any one question.[5]

3. Bromley to Oxford, 18 Feb., 1712(−13), B.L. Loan 29/200; Oxford to Lockhart, 9 Feb. 1712/13, Loan 29/150/3: '. . .I beg you will hasten up all your friends both Lords and Commons and that you will come fully instructed about Justices of the Peace and all other matters requisite for the repose of your country'.
4. Add. MS. 17,677, GGG, f. 126; *Parliamentary History*, vi, 1171–4.
5. *Bolingbroke Corr.*, iv, 139; Geoffrey Holmes and Clyve Jones; 'Trade, the Scots and the Parliamentary Crisis of 1713', *Parliamentary History*, i (1982), p. 62.

There was a good deal of truth in this statement. Oxford's attempt to control government business as closely as possible often led to delays and disruptions. This was seen particularly in Scottish affairs which, for patronage purposes, he had put mainly into Dartmouth's listless hands after the death of Queensberry; in the session of 1713 the Scots in both houses were unanimous in condemning the government on a formidable score of mismanagement and neglect. Since many Scots in both houses were reckoned solid government voters, their discontent at this time was unfortunate. The Whigs were not slow to take advantage of the situation. Despite Oxford's efforts to stay this agitation, the blow nearly fell on 1 June in the House of Lords, when the Scottish peers, supported by the Junto, discoursed long on their real and imagined grievances and came close to defeating the ministry with a bill to repeal the Union.[6]

It is questionable, however, whether the main disaster of this session, which occurred three weeks later, can be attributed to Oxford. This concerned commercial articles 8, 9, and 10, negotiated by Bolingbroke's associate and friend Arthur Moore, providing that subjects of Britain and France should be entitled to the same trading status that those of the most favoured other nations enjoyed, though with exceptions of some commodities, such as tobacco, thought to be detrimental to Britain and with a high French tariff on British woollen produce. The outcome was the defeat of the government's bill to ratify the commercial treaty of Utrecht. The Whigs were against the bill on the opposition principle; what ensured its defeat was the desertion of the government by a number of Tories. How far the bill's opponents argued correctly that it was against Britain's interest is still debated by economic historians. The first serious contribution was partisan; Charles Davenant, inspector general of revenues and a government publicist, prepared the way for the bill in 1712 by the publication of figures purporting to show that Britain was not, as was commonly supposed, a loser on balance of trade with France. However, the established view died hard.[7] Throughout May and June both houses heard petitions for and against the new policy, and those against were the more numerous and vociferous. What turned the scale against the ministry, however, was the desertion by Sir Thomas Hanmer. After supporting the bill in its early stages, Hanmer lobbied against it before the third reading on 18 June and carried over with him a large number of other Tory members, thus ensuring its defeat by nine votes. He claimed to have been converted by public opinion, though many observers believed that Oxford was behind Hanmer's *volte-face*. There is no evidence for the suspicion but, true or not, it serves as a reminder of his reputation for political chicanery. Bolingbroke appears to have

6. Riley, p. 242 sqq.; L'Hermitage, Add. MSS. 17,677 GGG, ff. 202–4.
7. Charles Davenant, *A report to the honourable the commissioners for…the public accounts*, 1712; for the opposing argument see Sir Theodore Jansen's *General Maxims in Trade* (1713); Chalmers, *Treaties*, pp. 396–8; Dickinson, *Bolingbroke*, 107.

suspected Oxford of choosing this devious method of defeating a policy negotiated by himself.[8] But it is probable that Hanmer was telling the truth; he was member for Suffolk, a county where the declining cloth trade was likely to suffer from French competition, and an election was due within a few months. More importantly he was to emerge as leader of a 'Hanoverian Tory' wing of his party over the next year, dedicated to rejecting any measures smacking of favour to France and hence to the Pretender.

The session was drawing to a close, and the decision of the House of Commons had to be accepted for the moment. To soften the blow, Hanmer agreed with Oxford to carry an address asking for the appointment of commissioners to give further consideration to the terms of the commercial treaty. Unlike Bolingbroke, Oxford did not feel that his diplomatic strategy was at stake over the commerical clauses, and he was probably not displeased at the Secretary's embarrassment, confiding to Swift that he did not care whether or not commercial arrangements passed in their present form.[9] Before Parliament rose, Oxford again broached with Hanmer the possibility of his taking government office, or perhaps becoming Speaker in the next House of Commons, with Bromley becoming a Secretary of State. Much of the difficulty of controlling the Commons this session had arisen from the want of a secretary in the House; moreover, some encouragement had to be given to the Tories before the next meeting, and Hanmer was more than ever the obvious leader. To encourage him, Oxford wrote: 'The Queen has determined in her thoughts to do all that is possible to assist her true friends in the next election.' And he suggested a meeting to discuss ways and means. But at the subsequent interview it seems that Oxford was not prepared to make sufficient concessions, for Hanmer is reported to have gone off to the country 'much discontented'.[10] Did Oxford remember wistfully his own days of independence in 1699, when he had gone off similarly discontented at King William's offer of office?

As soon as the session was over, a ministerial crisis erupted, Bolingbroke leading a strident chorus of dissatisfied Tories demanding a purge of Whigs still in office and aiming, as Lockhart thought, 'at nothing less than being prime minister of state'.[11] In this ambition Bolingbroke was

8. For example, William Bishop to A. Charlett, 20 June 1713, Bodleian, Ballard MS. 31, f. 104: 'Whether they did so with the consent of the Lord Treasurer or not is variously reported...however it is certain the Lord Treasurer might have carried it through the House 3 weeks, nay but 3 days before'; *Bolingbroke Corr.*, iv, 166.
9. T. Edwards to Lord North and Grey, 22 June 1713, *loc. cit.* '...Sir T.H. has been with him since the debate, and this day the Commons will order an address to the Queen to appoint commissioners to transact the commerce, which is designed to soften the loss of the bill...'; Swift, *Ford Letters*, p. 12.
10. *Hanmer Corr.*, p. 143; *Swift Corr.* ii, 55.
11. *Lockhart Papers*, i, 412.

encouraged by a slight coolness on the Queen's part towards Oxford since the cabinet controversy of the previous September. On one occasion she had written to the Lord Treasurer, more sharply than was her wont:

> I have just now received your letter for which I give you many thanks, and am very sory anything I said on Teusday morning should make you think I was displeased with you. I told you my thoughts freely as I have always and ever will continue to do on all occasions. You cannot wonder that I who have bin ill used soe many yeares should desire to keep myself from being againe enslaved; and if I must always comply and not be complyed with, is I think very hard and what I cannot submit to, and what I beleeve you would not have me.

And as an example of the Queen's occasional independence of Oxford, Bolingbroke took heart from the nomination of Francis Atterbury as Bishop of Rochester in June, at Harcourt's insistence, after Oxford had conspicuously failed for three years to prefer this pillar of the High Church party. Together Bolingbroke and Harcourt decided to ask for more.[12]

Circumstances favoured their scheme. Throughout July Oxford had been unwell, and as soon as Parliament dispersed on the 16th he retired to his bed. Bolingbroke, who took a malevolent interest in his colleague's health, reported the symptoms with grim relish. He told Drummond: 'My Lord Treasurer is now confined very closely by a severe fit of the gravel, an inflammation in his eyes, and a falling of the same, or some other humour, into his knees.'[13] In Oxford's absence, the administration of the Treasury came to a virtual standstill. The situation was made worse by the raising to the peerage of Robert Benson, the Chancellor of the Exchequer, on 24 July, a measure which was taken on Bolingbroke's initiative as a first step towards the appointment of his friend William Wyndham, since Benson as a peer could not continue to hold his post. Oxford immediately composed a letter to Bolingbroke which, according to the sender's later paraphrase 'put Lord Bolingbroke in mind of the several particulars which than required dispatch and were solely belonging to his province'.[14] After this rebuke Oxford suggested a new arrangement for the ministry, relieving Dartmouth of his duties, at his own longstanding request, and bringing in Bromley as Secretary. Bolingbroke's reply was not enthusiastic about Bromley, and after thanking Oxford for discussing matters of policy 'with so much appearance of

---

12. H.M.C. *Bath*, i, 223; Burnet, vi, 176, Dartmouth's note; Bennett, *The Tory Crisis*, pp. 168–9.

13. *Bolingbroke Corr.*, iv, 208.

14. Franics Ellison to Strafford, 24 July 1713, Add. MS. 22,233, f. 286: in Oxford's absence, Ellison complains, 'noe direction is made, or ordinary, or extraordinary'. The charge is borne out by the treasury minutes; H.M.C. *Portland*, vii. 160; 'A brief account of the public affairs...', *Parliamentary History*, vi, appendix iv, column ccxlviii.

openness', reiterated his usual arguments: 'want of encouragement' to Tories, and 'drones who clog the administration', pressing for the dismissal of those Whigs who were still protected in their offices by the Lord Treasurer.[15]

It was not likely, however, that the Queen would submit to so complete a Tory administration as Bolingbroke desired. Oxford went out for the first time after his illness on 30 July. From his bed he had drawn up a scheme for the re-arrangement of the ministry and he now presented it to Anne. For a moment the matter seemed to Oxford's followers to hang in the balance.[16] But the Queen acceded; if Bolingbroke had succeeded in impressing her with the unsatisfactory nature of the existing situation, she was not prepared to cast off Oxford in order to sumbit to another, and possibly more dictatorial minister. Bromley was duly appointed to the northern department in place of Bolingbroke, thus taking over correspondence with Hanover, while Bolingbroke moved to the southern department and Dartmouth took Robinson's place as Lord Privy Seal. Robinson was not forgotten, and was compensated with the Bishopric of London in place of the deceased Henry Compton. Lord Lansdowne, Oxford's old friend George Granville, who had been on distant terms with Bolingbroke for two years, took the post of Treasurer of the Household, vacant since Cholmondeley's dismissal in April. Bolingbroke's only distinct success was the appointment of William Wyndham at the Exchequer, but even this was not so useful as it seemed, for in a post directly subordinate to the Treasurer, Wyndham could be rendered politically ineffectual. On the other hand Oxford at last persuaded Hanmer to accept the government's nomination as Speaker in the next Parliament, thus ensuring that an influential 'Hanoverian' Tory would hold that key post whatever the outcome of the election. On the whole, Oxford's friends thought that he had exerted himself successfully. One such, the Oxford Tory Dr William Stratford, wrote complacently if prematurely to Oxford's son: 'I expected no other of Lord B's management, I wonder it has lasted so long. He is a sad warning to gentlemen of how little use the greatest parts are to one void of all sense of honour and religion.'[17] And three weeks later, early in September, Oxford secured three further appointments. The posts of third Secretary of State and Lord Chancellor of Scotland were revived in the persons of Scottish peers, the Earl of Mar and Earl Findlater, appointments which are setbacks respectively for Bolingbroke and his recent sympathizer Harcourt, both of whom suffered some loss of authority and patronage north of the border. A few days later

15. H.M.C. *Portland*, v, 311.
16. *Swift Corr.*, ii, 57, H.M.C. *Portland*, vii, 161.
17. *London Gazette*, 5145 and 5147: For Oxford's visits to Hanmer, see L'Hermitage, Add. MS. 17,677, GGG, f. 309. For Hanmer's acceptance, see *Hanmer Corr.* p. 148; H.M.C. *Portland*, vii, 164.

it was announced that the Duke of Shrewsbury, his duties completed in France, was posted to Ireland in place of Ormonde, where his uncertain loyalties would do no harm.[18] By these means Oxford kept Scottish patronage out of Bolingbroke's hands for the general election due in the autumn, and reestablished the ministry on a predominantly Harleian basis.

But the appointments represent Oxford's last success with the aid of Queen Anne, for soon after he secured them he made one more demand which was not acceptable, and with this began the last phase of his ministry. His standing, like that of all Queen Anne's ministers, depended much if not entirely on the delicate balance of mutual trust in his relations with the Queen herself. Oxford's real offence in the eyes of the Queen occurred in September over a personal request, nor over the ministerial changes in which she backed him in July. The cause of her annoyance would seem venial, if not trivial, were it not remembered that Oxford had taught her to look for disinterested service among her ministers. Bolingbroke she expected to aggrandize himself by office; but when Oxford tried to do the same, she was angered. When Oxford later, for public consumption, antedated his loss of power by two months, he did so because the Queen enjoined secrecy over the cause of their quarrel, and because this touched upon his pride, so that he did not wish it to be generally known. The humiliation he felt was considerable, especially as the case was one of the rare instances when he acknowledged himself in the wrong.[19]

The occasion of the Queen's displeasure was Lord Harley's marriage. His engagement to the daughter of the late Duke of Newcastle had already been the subject of a negotiation of several years' standing when the Duke's death in July 1711 prolonged it indefinitely. The widowed Duchess made her daughter's marriage conditional, firstly on the Harleys' support in her lawsuit against the Duke's will leaving the bulk of his vast estates to his nephew Thomas Pelham*, a cause which she pursued with high disregard for either the spirit or the form of law, and secondly on Oxford's persuading the Queen to bestow the title of Newcastle on Lord Harley. By August 1713 the suit was seen, by all except the Duchess herself, to be heading for defeat.[20] It was therefore decided by the young couple, with Oxford's support, that despite the continued opposition of

---

18. Oxford's accounts, H.M.C. *Portland*, v, 466–7; H.M.C. *Dartmouth*, i, 318.
19. *Swift Corr.*, ii, 198.
20. A ruling against the Duchess's petition took place in the court of Chancery on 9 December 1713, and her appeal was dismissed by the house of Lords on 19 May 1714, *Lords Journal*, xix, 542. *Cf.* Edward Harley, 'Memoirs of the Harley Family', H.M.C. *Portland*, v, 658.

*Later Thomas Pelham-Holles (adopting his uncle's name), created Duke of Newcastle by George I in 1715.

the Duchess the marriage should be delayed no longer. On 13 August
Oxford wrote to his brother: 'Now as to the Title of Newcastle the case is
this. A year since (when the Dutchess made it one of her Demands) I
ask'd it of the Queen, who said she would make him first Earle, and then
Duke as soon as the marriage was over.' He went on to argue that it
would be better to obtain the titles after the marriage in order to allow
them to be entailed upon the bride's heirs; otherwise the honours would
go only to Lord Harley's heirs. He added that the graduation of the titles
'is the best and truly honourable way'. He showed, at this stage, no doubt
of the Queen's compliance.[21]

The last days of August were spent by Oxford at the bride's house,
Wimpole Hall in Cambridgeshire, preparing for the ceremony which
took place on the 31st. Arriving at Windsor on 5 September, he spent
a few days settling the problem of the Scottish appointments and
Shrewsbury's transfer. On the 15th he brought the married couple to an
audience with the Queen, and the next day he broached with her the
question of the titles.[22]

By this time, however, Anne had repented her promise. In the
eighteenth century peerages were conferred only upon those who enjoyed
a sufficient income to maintain the title with the necessary splendour; a
dukedom was not lightly to be conferred on someone whose wealth
seemed likely to be insufficient even for a lower rank in the peerage. If
the greater part of the estates which had hitherto supported the title of
Newcastle were to be granted away from Lady Henrietta, it was not
advisable to bestow the title on her husband because the younger Harley
was, except in his father's eyes, a man to squander away the finances of
an inherited earldom rather than rebuild the broken supports of a
newly-confirmed dukedom. It is to Oxford's credit that the one occasion
on which he was blind to the subtleties of a human situation was when
his son was involved; and he made the capital blunder of trying the
Queen's goodwill beyond the bounds of reason. Her displeasure at being
forced to make the refusal was accentuated by the unfairness of the
situation in which he placed her, and by her awareness that she was
breaking a promise, even though it had been made in different circumstances. Both Oxford himself and Bolingbroke privately dated the
beginning of the former's misfortunes from this incident. According to
Oxford:

> I had the Queen's leave to go into Cambridgeshire. After my return
> from thence, advantage was taken of my never enough to be lamented
> folly in mentioning to her Majesty the titles? I never did this to anyone

21. Turberville, *Welbeck Abbey*, ii, addenda, p. 452.
22. Itinerary of Oxford's movements, Aug. – Sept. 1713, Loan 29/10/12. Oxford's account, 1 July
    1714, H.M.C. *Portland*, v, 468, for the date of the request.

else except Lady Masham, and have kept my word never to speak of it since directly or indirectly, not to the nearest relation I had, but this was made my crime.

Bolingbroke's more oblique reference was made to Swift in 1719: '. . . a certain lord whose marriage with a certain heiress was the ultimate end of a certain administration. . . '.[23]

If Oxford's request was distressing to the Queen, her refusal was even more so to him. By assiduous courtiership he might still have regained much of the ground he had incautiously lost. Instead, he allowed himself to sink into despair and self-pity. His mood may be gauged by a paper he drew up for an interview with the Queen, one month after the last episode, though it is not clear whether the confused reproach was actually delivered:

> This is the question. Is it for the service either of the public or Queen that Mr H. [i.e. Oxford himself] should continue to be employed? If no, justice requiring that you should tell him so.
>
> If you act otherwise he is not so blind as not to see that and will find a hole to creep out hoping rather to [stay?]* out of court than to be thereabout. And he seems sensible of the circumstance against him. He was always indifferent but now is more earnest to get rid of a service where his fellow servants cross him and his sovereign is either weary of him [and considers?]* him not worth or is ashamed to own him. He desires no protection from faults.
>
> The whole is easy to be cured [if] it is worth while to keep him in then let the world see that he is to be in.[24]

While Oxford became estranged from the Queen, he was giving continued offence to the Tories. In the general election he saw no more reason than in the 1710 elections to forward their cause and thereby earned the expostulations of many of their number, including his friend Lansdowne. As the returns came in most observers thought that the Tories had again obtained a large majority, though this time weakened by a division among themselves between those who were in favour of a new bill to carry out the treaty of commerce with France and those who were against. Thus, the results gave promise of a House of Commons which would vote heavily Tory on such traditional issues as support for the Church of England against Dissent, but less decisively on the Commerce Bill or any other measure apparently favouring France or France's protegé the Pretender. Significantly, the election campaign

23. H.M.C. *Portland*, v, 466; *Swift Corr.* iii, 113.
24. Paper in Oxford's hand, 20 Oct. 1713, Loan 29/10/11.

*paper torn

brought into widespread use the comparatively new term Hanoverian
Tories for a group of up to seventy or so members loosely to be equated
with Hanmer and his followers in commercial policy. In these circumstances a nominal Tory majority of over 200 members was more proble-
matic than it appeared.[25]

Until the ministry could decide what kind of programme it would put
before the new members, a decision was taken to postpone the meeting
until the new year, following the precedent of the last session. But, far
from coming to any compromise between Bolingbroke's advocacy of
satisfying the Tory extremists and Oxford's preference for a pragmatic,
middle-of-the-road administration, they drifted ever further apart. Before
the end of 1713, moreover, the quarrel had been enlarged by two
domestic misfortunes. The first was the death, on 20 November, of
Oxford's eldest and favourite daughter Elizabeth, the Marchioness of
Carmarthen. In his grief and despair he stayed away from public functions and duties for several weeks, thus allowing an opportunity for
Bolingbroke to pay assiduous court to the Queen almost every day.[26] The
Queen, indeed, returned a friendly and sympathetic reply to Oxford's
continued reproaches. After an audience on 7 December she wrote
desiring him:

> . . .when you come next, to speake plainly, lay everything open and
> hide nothing from me, or els how is it possible I can judg of anything. I
> spoke very freely and sincerely to you yesterday, and I expect you should
> do the same to her that is sincerely your very affectionate friend.

But Oxford was not to be comforted while his rival remained in the royal
favour and boasted the support of Lady Masham. Herein Oxford's judgement was in error, for what he lost in the Queen's eyes, Bolingbroke
never gained.[27]

The second event, which followed hard upon the first, was the almost
fatal illness of the Queen herself, on Christmas Eve and Christmas Day.
For over a month Bolingbroke was constantly with her while Oxford was
himself unwell and unable to attend upon his royal mistress for much of
the time.[28] On 17 January 1714, she was well enough to attend a cabinet

25. H.M.C. *Lonsdale*, p. 246; Add. MS. 17,677, GGG, f. 347: H.M.C. *Dartmouth*, i, 319: *Hanmer Corr.*, p. 153; *Lockhart Papers*, i, 438–9; Speck, *Tory and Whig*, p. 123; Holmes. *British Politics*, p. 283 and note.
26. Schutz the Hanoverian envoy wrote on 4/15 December, British Museum Stowe MS. 225, f, 321: Md Bullinbrook a esté fort assidu auprez de la Reyne depuis quelque temps, et il n'a esté que deux jours absent de Windsor pendant prés de trois semaines que le Grand Tresorier n'y a pas esté'.
27. H.M.C. *Bath*, i, 243; H.M.C. *Portland*, vii, 174.
28. *Bolingbroke Corr.* iv, 417 and 444. Oxford's neglect was not, however, as great as Bolingbroke hinted, for he appears to have been with the Queen on 27 December at least, and satisfied her by a letter that he had not been able to come earlier. See: Lord Masham to Oxford, received 26 Dec. 1713 (endorsed), Loan 29/45.

meeting, but suffered a serious relapse in the last week of the month. On this occasion a panic in the City ensued, for fear that the Pretender might benefit from her death, until the announcement of her recovery.[29] Parliament had been prorogued at frequent intervals, but could be put off no longer, and to allay public fears and rumours the date was set for 16 February. By this time there had long been a general opinion, in Britain and in the courts of Europe, that Oxford and Bolingbroke were irreconcilable and that Lady Masham had gone over to the latter.

In order to explain the position taken by Lady Masham in the political triangle which had its corners in the Queen, Oxford, and Bolingbroke, it is necessary to return to the affairs of the South Sea Company. These affairs, by occupying the stage as soon as Parliament assembled in February 1714, were to play an increasingly important part in national politics during the session. Since the Company's foundation Oxford had sought by Fabian tactics to save his face with the directors until trading concessions were obtained from Spain. Not unmindful of the merchandise which the Company had been encouraged to gather, and which was beginning to rot on the quays, he sought to make amends. By the commercial contract signed in Madrid in March 1713, Britain obtained not only the Assiento slaving contract and permission to send a merchant ship, other than slavers, to the annual 'fair' at Vera Cruz, but also special licences to send two merchant ships at once. These 'license vessels' were permitted to take 1,200 tons of goods, exactly the amount which the Company had in stock, and the concession was confirmed in the Anglo-Spanish treaty signed at Utrecht in July 1713.[30] As soon as the Company were informed, in June, that they were to have the licences, they requested Oxford to provide two large warships to carry their goods, since the vessels already provided were not large enough to take full advantage of the concession. The request was granted and ships were lent at government expense.[31] Oxford also did his best to smooth the path of the South Sea Company in other matters, such as a dispute with the Royal African Company, in his capacity of governor to the former, a gesture for which the South Sea directors were not ungrateful.[32]

But Oxford's efforts on behalf of the Company were negated by a development which he was powerless to stop. The Spanish concession of the Assiento was assigned to the Queen as head of state and, with the

29. H.M.C. *Seafield*, p. 226; Add. MSS. 17,677HHH, ff. 54–7.
30. Chalmers, *Treaties*, ii, 85.
31. H.M.C. *House of Lords MSS.*, x, 438–9. Much, though not all, of the Company's correspondence was copied for the Houses of Parliament during a public enquiry into its affairs in June-July, 1714.
32. CTB, xxvii. 351; J. Pym to Oxford, 23 Sept. 1713, S.S. Company special letters book i., Add. MS. 25,559, p. 37.

prompting of Bolingbroke, Anne was persuaded to reserve a portion of the profits of the trade nominally to herself, actually to her court favourite and the Secretary's new ally Lady Masham, while re-assigning the remainder to the Company. Lady Masham, according to Edward Harley's account:

> ...thought nothing ought to be done without her privity and consent, and finding the Treasurer could not be brought into those corrupt measures that might fully gratify her avarice, she set herself with all the malice that passion could inspire to prejudice the Queen against the Treasurer. Lord Bolingbroke and others...contrived to gratify her avarice in obtaining for her a share in the Assiento contract.[33]

The directors of the South Sea Company protested vigorously when informed of this arrangement, and they asked that the Company should immediately be granted the sole enjoyment of the trading profits, as had been Oxford's original intention when he devised the South Sea Bill.[34] The distaste of the Company for one or more sleeping partners was enhanced by the justified belief that these beneficiaries did not expect to share the initial expenses of the trade. Oxford was forced to accept the *fait accompli* of his ailing Queen's foolish gesture, but he attempted to find a compromise. As soon as he resumed his duties in the second week of December he informed a deputation of directors that their demand could not be granted, but offered that the Queen's share should be placed in the hands of responsible trustees who would advance a proportional share of the cost of commerical undertakings.[35] After anxious debates and after taking legal advice, the directors raised, early in January 1714, the question of the extent of liability under Common Law of an (although they dared not say it) unknown partner. At a meeting of the board on the 11th Oxford endeavoured to persuade them that there was adequate safeguard in case of default on the part of the trustees, and it was agreed to put before a general meeting of the shareholders the question of whether the Assiento should be accepted by the Company on the Queen's terms.[36] Despite Oxford's anxiety to get the sordid affair settled, this could not be arranged before Parliament met. But in a ballot taken during the third week of February, the General Court endorsed a motion that the Queen's offer should be accepted if the other assignees were effectually obliged to secure the payment to the Company of their proportions of the cost of carrying on the trade.[37]

33. 'Memoirs of the Harley family', H.M.C. *Portland*, v, 661.
34. Court Book 2, 10 Nov., 2 Dec. 1713, Add. MS. 25,495, pp. 197 and 213. J. Pym to Oxford, 2 Dec. 1713, H.M.C. *House of Lords*, x, 446.
35. Court Book 2, 11 Dec. 1713, Add. MS. 25,495, p. 217.
36. Ibid. 11 and 13 Jan., 1713(−14), Add. MSS. 25,495, pp. 234–6. Bolingbroke to Bateman, 11 Feb. 1713(−14), H.M.C. *House of Lords*, x, 447.
37. Court book 2, 26 Feb. 1713(−14), Add. MS. 25,495, p. 267.

Thus, at the opening of the parliamentary session on 16 February 1714 the future of the South Sea trade was still in doubt, and the ministry highly vulnerable to criticism. One thing only was certain; whoever won the tussle between the Queen and the directors, Oxford would incur odium. If the company won, he would further antagonize the Queen: if the Queen won, he would see the corporation he had planned and fostered doomed from the outset to internal strife. To add to his discontent in February, he discovered that Bolingbroke and his friend Arthur Moore had involved the Queen in further shady dealings, this time with the trade to Old Spain. Moore, one of the commissioners of trade and plantations, had accepted a bribe from the Spanish court to accept less favourable terms for British merchants in Spain than had been laid down by the plenipotentiaries in a commercial treaty signed between the two countries the previous autumn.[38] Bolingbroke persuaded the Queen to accept the amended or 'explanatory' articles required by Spain. When Oxford heard of this affair from Bromley, at about the beginning of the session, he seriously considered immediate resignation in protest but was persuaded by his old friend Trevor to continue in office.[39]

It is not surprising that Oxford considered resignation: why he allowed himself to be persuaded to remain in an intolerable position is subject to several explanations. In the first place, loyalty to the Queen's wishes cannot be discounted. It is clear that she did not wish to lose him; she had just been ill and was not well enough to face another ministerial crisis before a session of Parliament. A second reason for his remaining in office was his fear for national security if Bolingbroke took control. The Secretary would have supported the Pretender in a succession dispute if the latter had been willing to make even a nominal rejection of his Catholicism. Two years earlier John Arbuthnot, the Queen's physician and pamphleteer, in *The History of John Bull*, had written a shrewd estimate of Oxford's attitude to his role in politics: 'Sir Roger [i.e. Oxford] shook his ears and nuzzled along; well satisfied within himself that he was doing a charitable work in rescuing an honest man [John Bull] from the claws of harpies and bloodsuckers.'[40] Oxford believed that the longer he stayed in office the safer the nation would be. There was certainly an imminent risk of the Queen's death after her illness over the New Year; and Oxford's fondness for her and desire to prolong her days was probably a motive for retaining his office, in addition to his fervent desire to frustrate Bolingbroke's ambitions.

Oxford's own explanation of his motive, given to the Earl of

---

38. The disadvantages of these amandments for British merchants lay in the tariffs they permitted to be levied on exports to Spain. In Mrs Lindsay's words, the treaty 'proved so actively hurtful to trade that within two years another had to be negotiated to make good its shortcomings': J.O. McLachlan, p. 46. See below for the parliamentary enquiry of June 1714 into Moore's conduct.
39. *Bolingbroke Corr.*, iv, 452; 'Memoirs of the Harley family', H.M.C. *Portland*, v, 661.
40. Dickinson, *Bolingbroke*, p. 118; John Arbuthnot, *The History of John Bull*, part 3, 1712.

Peterborough after the Queen's death, was that about the beginning of 1714, realizing that the Queen's attitude had changed towards him, he had intended to go into opposition on behalf of the Hanoverian cause, but that the Elector thought it better for him to stay in office and act as a check upon Bolingbroke and others. Peterborough told this to the French ambassador with a view to doing Oxford harm with the Pretender, but despite the malicious turn given to the story there may be some truth in it; at least it may reflect Oxford's attitude to the situation in February 1714.[41]

That the Elector ever actually gave Oxford such advice is unlikely. Oxford was certain of his own devotion to the Protestant cause; the Elector was less certain, and would probably have preferred to see Oxford withdraw into opposition and affix the stigma of Jacobitism firmly to a Bolingbroke administration. Oxford's relations with the House of Hanover were anything but happy. While sending frequent assurances of the safety of their succession, he had done little, in their eyes, to prove his fidelity. He had not been able to obtain a parliamentary pension for the Princess Sophia or permission for any of her family to set foot in England. In May 1713 he had refused a bribe of £200,000 for himself and £1,000,000 for distribution in useful quarters, on the grounds that the succession was already safe and that the further requests by the electoral family were displeasing to the Queen.[42] Nor had he always been able to curb his impatience at the Elector's domestic aspirations. Thus, the Hanoverian envoy Schutz reported to his court in December 1713: '. . . when I spoke to the Lord Treasurer about the interests of the elector with regard to his rank, and to his office of Arch Treasurer of the Empire, he answered that they were but inconsiderable things, and that his Electoral Highness ought to have much more considerable ones in view. . .'. This callous dismissal of a valued honour was not well calculated to endear Oxford to his German future master however much it reflected the frank British point of view.[43]

Despite his dubious standing at Hanover, his hope for the future lay in the Hanoverian succession. It is true that at the time of the Queen's relapse into illness, at the end of January, he asked the Pretender for a declaration renouncing Catholicism and the use of force to obtain a restoration, terms impossible of acceptance; and by the beginning of March he was aware of the young man's indignant refusal. Of this approach a recent historian of Jacobitism, Dr Szechi, writes: 'Oxford was in no danger of James's accepting his "terms". James had been under

---

41. Iberville to Louis XIV, (3–)14 Sept. 1714, *Revue Nouvelle*, iii (1845), 48.
42. Paper in Oxford's hand, dated 10 May 1713, half past twelve at noon, Loan 29/10/13. Cf. Edward Harley's account, Add. MS. 34,515, ff. 36–7.
43. Schutz to the court at Hanover, 18/29 Dec., 1713, (translated copy) Stowe MS. 242, f. 32.

constant pressure to convert from within the Jacobite movement ever since he came of age. He had always courteously refused, and showed no signs of changing his mind – as Oxford was well aware.'[44] Oxford's correspondence with the exiled court, though generous of promises, had the limited purpose of persuading the Pretender to move further from England during the parliamentary session. The Whigs played upon the danger of James's continued presence in Lorraine, and every postbag which left London for Hanover carried their letters urging the presence of a member of the electoral family in England.[45]

Oxford's policy was, as always, to take advantage of events as they arose. Certainly he hoped to play a part under the next monarch without Bolingbroke; but while the Queen lived, Lady Masham and Bolingbroke were secure, and Oxford could only hope to foil them by keeping in touch with the Whigs and the electoral house, however tenuous this connection might be. Bolingbroke, on the other hand, was too anxious for a completely Tory ministry to compromise his power in the party by dalliance elsewhere. His aim, failing a Jacobite restoration, for which he could hardly have hoped unless the Pretender changed his religion, was to build up a party hegemony so strong that not even a Hanoverian successor, if she or he came to the throne, would dare to challenge it.[46] With Oxford determined to keep out the Pretender and willing, as always, to deal with selected Whigs, the ministerial struggle resolved itself into a clash of conceptions of government as well as a clash of wills.

Bolingbroke's chief overt charge against his colleague was indolence and apathy. So far as departmental duties were concerned, this charge was not true. In the Treasury, Oxford's last months leave no trace of the deterioration and drunkenness with which he is often charged; indeed in all branches of the financial administration he appears to have continued active and watchful down to the day of his dismissal. It is true that Oxford's several long absences in the summer and autumn of 1713 threw the Treasury into temporary disorder, but this was soon retrieved. In the sphere of economy his zeal continued unabated. A curious example occurred early in 1714, when he objected to the cost of lighting the two Houses of Parliament and ordered an investigation.[47] The following

44. Gaultier to James III, 26 Jan., 6 Feb. 1714, *Edinburgh Review*, lxii (1835), 24; Salomon, pp. 335–7; G.V. Bennett,' English Jacobitism, 1710–1715; Myth and Reality', *T.R.H.S.*, 5th series, xxxii (1982), 144–5; Szechi, p. 186.
45. Gaultier to Torcy, (8–)19 March 1714, *E.H.R.* xxx (1915), 516; H.N. Fieldhouse, 'Oxford, Bolingbroke and the Pretender's place of residence', *E.H.R.* iii (1937), 289–95; Szechi, p. 190.
46. Sir Edward Knatchbull's Diary, Braborne MSS: '[April] 11, A.N. Newman, 'Proceedings in the House of Commons, March-June 1714', *BIHR*, xxxiv (1961), 214.
47. *CTB*, xxviii, 142. Oxford's continued assiduity at the Treasury is evidenced by the day-to-day business record in the *Calendar of Treasury Books* and in the Treasury papers; it is borne out by Hughes, especially pp. 280 and 288.

opinion by a later head of the Treasury, recorded by a Lord Chancellor, appears to apply to the end as well as to the beginning of Oxford's administration: 'Mr Pelham (who cannot be supposed to have any partiality to the earl of Oxford) has said frequently, that, in his administration of the treasury, he was the most exact and attentive minister that ever presided at the head of it.'[48] This must throw a good deal of doubt on the theory which explains Oxford's last months in office in terms of a maundering and flagon-stayed decline. If he was dilatory and obstructive in affairs of policy, it was mainly because he deliberately set out to act as a restraint upon Bolingbroke until the Queen became disillusioned with the Secretary. Once the choice was made to remain in office, no other course was easily available, and his waiting game does much to explain Oxford's stance.

48. Hardwicke's note, Burnet, vi, 69.

CHAPTER 15

Brief Whig Ally

THE LAST FIVE months of Oxford's ministry, and of Queen Anne's life, gave rise to a more tense political scene than any other period since 1688. The spectre of a resumption of violence over the Succession was present in the minds of all participants, most of whom could personally remember the events of the Revolution. That Anne's death did not, in the outcome, result in civil war should not obscure the dangers which were very real to contemporaries; and if the dreaded lapse of the nation into a new struggle over the House of Stuart was eventually avoided this was in large measure because of Oxford's stubborn retention of office until the last days of the Queen's life. His approach to the Pretender at the height of her illness in January, with a project for the young man's conversion to Protestantism, was made at the same time as Boling-broke's similar and possibly more sincere overture, but Oxford acted with little risk in view of James Edward's well-known devotion to Roman Catholicism. Both ministers may have behaved, at a time of emergency, in conformity with what they believed to be the Queen's deepest and dying wish. Months later Sir David Hamilton, one of those closest to Anne, was still not sure whether she was 'for the Pretender'. Unlike Anne, whose closest living relation was now her half-brother, and unlike Bolingbroke who was later to serve the Pretender in exile, Oxford was committed by both family history and public career to the succession of the Protestant House of Hanover, whose claim he had done more than anyone to establish in the Act of Settlement of 1701. Oxford's occasional secret assurances to Jacobite representatives need be taken no more seriously than those of practically all political leaders, including Marlborough, Godolphin and most of the Junto, who made similar professions as an insurance against a Stuart restoration. From March until July 1714 Oxford's remaining energy was reserved, in a situation of declining influence, for obtaining the legal succession and beating off Bolingbroke's challenge to his authority. To these ends he was now almost ready to play his last card, open alliance with the Hanoverian Tories or even with the Whigs.

Parliament duly met on 16 February 1714, and the House of Commons chose Sir Thomas Hanmer as Speaker according to Oxford's arrangement. After preliminary business both Houses were then adjourned for a further fortnight until the Queen was able to make her opening speech. On 2 March she told them, after announcing the conclusion of the treaties with Spain that: 'There are some, who are arrived to that height of malice, as to insinuate that the Protestant Succession in the House of Hanover is in danger under my government'.[1] Her vehement denial, which had the ring of Oxford's phraseology and was almost certainly written by him as usual, prepared the way for his first important action in Parliament, two weeks later.

The occasion was a speech by Oxford in the House of Lords on 17 March. This provoked an incident which threatened to bring his ministry to an abrupt conclusion before any of the major issues of the session had even been raised. After agreeing readily to a request by the Whigs that copies of all the recent treaties of peace and commerce should be made available to Parliament, a first essential to exposing Boling-broke's machinations, he asked for leave to bring in what Professor Holmes has reasonably called 'a strange bill' making treasonable any attempt to carry foreign troops into the country without the permission of Parliament. This measure, Oxford added, would set at rest some recent tales of foreign soldiers coming over to Britain secretly. Wharton and others immediately rose to point out that such a measure would exclude not only the Pretender's supporters but Dutch troops, if these were required to support the Protestant Succession under the terms of the Barrier Treaty. Oxford replied, but too late to prevent an unfortunate impression, that he did not intend his bill to exclude such treaty troops.[2]

Some light is thrown on his intentions in this speech by a letter he had written three days earlier to his cousin Thomas Harley, in which he mentioned:

> ...a rumour spread by the Whigs that there was a design to bring over foreign forces here in the Queen's sickness; this I treated as a malicious invention – a great lord among the Whigs was so weak as to own it and said that M. Bothmer was treating for four thousand Danes and also for vessels, since Holland could not be depended upon; the revival of this story will do mischief...[3]

Thus, the explanation of Oxford's proposal, which puzzled many contemporaries, seems to be that he wished to exclude any foreign

1. *Parliamentary History*, vi, 1257; Bennett, 'English Jacobitism', *loc. cit.*, 137–49; D Szechi, 'The Duke of Shrewsbury's contacts with the Jacobites in 1713', *BIHR*, lvi (1983); *London Deiaries*, p. 61.
2. L'Hermitage, Add. MS. 17677HHH, ff. 127–8; Holmes, *British Politics*, p. 86.
3. Oxford to Thomas Harley, 14 March 1714, Add. MS 40, 621, f. 176.

mercenaries whom the Elector might choose to send at the time of the Queen's death. Unlike Dutch treaty troops, such forces might be little under Oxford's control. It is now known that the proposal to use other foreign troops was also favoured by Marlborough, and in a letter to his ally Prince Eugene in December 1712, of which a copy found its way to Hanover, the Duke had mentioned that he was trying to persuade the Grand Pensionary of Holland of the need to have a large body of Imperial troops in the Spanish Low Countries which could join forces with those of the Republic to prevent any attempt by the Pretender.[4] Another reason for Oxford's desire to exclude foreign troops other than the Dutch was the need to set at rest rumours that the Pretender's followers were seeping into England and Scotland.

These motives make clear why he brought the subject of foreign troops up, not why he abandoned it. The explanation of the latter seems to be that he was startled by the ferocity of the criticisms, particularly one from an unexpected quarter. During the debate Bolingbroke had risen to say that if the bill was intended only in case of an invasion by the Pretender, then the contingency was already covered by existing legislation. Oxford could not openly own that his bill was also intended to exclude foreign troops supporting the House of Hanover, and he was thus neatly silenced in the House by his own colleague and made to look as though he opposed the Barrier Treaty provision designed to protect the Protestant Succession. Such opposition, or at least correction, from the government side could not be tolerated. Oxford threatened resignation the same day. Bolingbroke and his associates were quite unprepared for such an explosive reaction, and Harcourt wrote hurriedly asking Oxford to defer any such action till they met, arguing: 'should your Lordship give way to your resentment, consider how the Queen will be affected by it, what confusion in every part of the public service must inevitably follow'.[5] However much Bolingbroke may have wished to be rid of Oxford, the ministry was in no position to carry on without him in mid-session. Bolingbroke was clearly in the wrong over the incident, and if Oxford went into retirement he might well carry with him several of the uncommitted ministers. As well as firm supporters like Dartmouth and Poulett other friends like Bromley could well follow him on such an issue. And an exodus like that which Bolingbroke and Harcourt themselves had joined in 1708 would be a serious blow to any ministry that Bolingbroke might aspire to lead.

Oxford made the most of his opportunity. For several days he continued to waver on the verge of resignation. Parliament was adjourned on 19 March for Easter, and on the same day he wrote a carefully phrased letter to Harcourt:

4. Marlborough to Eugene, 20 Dec. (N.S.) 1712, Copy, Niedersächsisches Staatsarchiv, C.B.A. 24 (England) 113.
5. *Parliamentary History*, vi, 1330; H.M.C. *Portland*, v, 400.

I have found myself a burden to my friends and to the only party I ever have or ever will act with. For many months, ever since this was apparent, I have drawn myself from everything but what neglect [of] would be inexcusable.

When a retreat happens to be desirable to one's friends and agreeable to one's own inclination and interest, it must be sure to be right. I think the opportunity is very near, and as I desire to have your approbation, so I shall desire to have the advantage of your advice when I may the most decently withdraw myself.[6]

Despite its outward form, this is not the letter of a man who intends to resign at all costs; it was in fact an invitation to the minister who currently stood closest to Bolingbroke to be a guarantor of the Secretary's future behaviour. And this is probably what happened. Bolingbroke later told Gaultier that the quarrel was carried to the Queen, who ordered her ministers to compose their differences, refusing to accept Oxford's offer of resignation; and he added that she would now take steps through himself, Harcourt, and Ormonde, to purge the government and armed forces of Whigs.[7]

So the ministry straggled on, each faction taking its own path. Oxford kept up his overtures to Cowper and Halifax, offering reassurances concerning the succession and feeling the way to reconciliation. The Whigs, for their part, leapt at an opportunity to make so important an ally. Halifax is found writing to the Lord Treasurer: 'I can't help saying I think in this juncture much good might be done, and I am so zealous to do my part, that I will be so impertinent to desire to know if I could no way assist in making your Lordship the happy instrument of saving our country, which I think on the brink of ruine'. But Oxford was still cooperating with Bolingbroke at a whipping meeting held for Hanmer and about thirty other members of Parliament on 4 April, when the members were exhorted to 'not let a majority in Parliament slip through our hands'.[8] During the following days there took place a series of strenuous debates in both Houses, with narrow government victories on motions of confidence concerning the peace treaties and the alleged inadequacy of measures protecting the Succession. On the 9th Oxford took advantage of an ill-advised attack in the House of Lords led by Townshend on the government's policy of distributing small bribes among the Highland clans to keep them passive; a practice which, as Oxford demonstrated, had begun under the Godolphin ministry. In this debate, one eyewitness

6. Oxford to Harcourt, 19 March 1714, Loan 29/138/5.
7. Gaultier to Torcy, (1–) 12 Apr. 1714, *Revue Nouvelle*, iii (1845), p. 47.
8. Cowper to Oxford, 30 March 1714, Loan 29/132/3; Halifax to Oxford 21 Apr. 1714 Loan 29/151/8; A.N. Newman, 'Proceedings in the House of Commons, March-June 1714', *BIHR*, xxxiv (1961), p. 213.

reported, Oxford spoke 'much bolder and clearer than I ever heard him before', and Bolingbroke made amends for past mistakes by proposing and carrying a motion expressing confidence in the Lord Treasurer. But in spite of this accord, the minister averted defeat four days later by only the closest of margins – two proxies after an equality of 61–61 votes – in a debate on the safety of the Succession.[9] Ministerial unanimity was not to last, however. Bolingbroke had no intention of following Oxford's lead and, as if to emphasize this, told a group of Tory MPs on 11 April that Whigs still in office would be dismissed by the end of the session, adding that should even one remain 'he would give any one leave to spit in his face' if he remained in office himself a further two months.[10]

As if in reply to this hard line there arrived, the next day, a request by the Hanoverian envoy Schutz for a writ to the Elector's son Prince George August, as Duke of Cambridge, to take his place in the House of Lords and establish his family's presence in Britain, a development dreaded by Queen Anne. This démarche was the prelude to a full-scale Whig attack in the Commons on the 15th when the ministry were able to reject the proposition that the Hanoverian Succession was in danger by only 48 votes in a full House, with Speaker Hanmer leading over 50 Hanoverian Tories over to the Whig side on this issue. Nevertheless, in view of the Queen's strong objection to having a member of the House of Hanover on her doorstep, Oxford had to bow to her wishes. The Queen would not contemplate having the Duke in England, and though she could not refuse the writ, she took every step to ensure that it would not be used. Latterly, Thomas Harley had been sent again to Hanover with orders to dissuade the court from any such project, and to offer the Princess Sophia a pension from the Queen and any reasonable safeguard for the Succession.[11] After the demand for the writ, Oxford wrote in a private letter to his cousin that the Prince should be urged in the strongest terms not to take advantage of the writ, adding 'I never saw her Majesty so much moved in my life'. This message certainly throws strong doubt on the suggestion that Oxford was anxious to prevent the Prince's presence in England for some Jacobite purpose of his own, rather than at the Queen's earnest desire.[12]

It was, indeed, frequently suggested in the next two months that Oxford himself clandestinely promoted Schutz's demand. The argument may have been used by his friends, who were anxious to assert that he

---

9. *Wentworth papers*, p. 374; L'Hermitage, Add. MS 17,677, HHH, f. 179v.
10. H.M.C. *Polwarth*, i, 19 cf., H.M.C. *Portland*, v, 422; Newman, 'proceeding in the House of Commons'., p. 214.
11. 'Memoranda for the journey to Hanover', January 1713(−14), Add. MS. 40,621 f. 163. Harley's instructions from Bromley, dated 11 Feb. 1714, Add. MS. 40,621 f. 169. Harley did not actually leave The Hague for Hanover until the first week of April.
12. H.M.C. *Portland*, v, 417; Gregg, p. 383. See also next note.

had refrained from tesigning in order to protect the Protestant Succession. The story was certainly spread by the Whigs with the purpose of persuading the Electoral family that the scheme had a powerful supporter within the ministry. Schutz, however, did not take this view, and regarded Oxford as chiefly instrumental in obtaining his expulsion from England.[13] Oxford himself wrote to a correspondent close to the Elector, the Baron Wassenaer Duvenworde, that the only way to endanger the Succession was to send a member of the Electoral family to England, and such was the Queen's emotional state of mind on the issue, Oxford may well have feared that such a step would push her towards negotiation with the Pretender. Nevertheless, both the Baron and, a month later, the Elector himself replied that in Hanover the presence of the Electoral Prince in England was regarded as essential.[14] Oxford served his royal mistress loyally, but at the expense of further alienating the heir to the throne.

As it was impossible to satisfy the Electoral House in their chief desire, Oxford set about finding emollient measures. Early in May he was reported to be seeing the Whig chiefs nightly. Their knowledge of the Queen's personal role in keeping every member of the Hanoverian family out of Britain led them to overlook his necessary support for her prejudice, and accept his assurance of his true, if concealed sympathy for the Electoral request.[15] The first result of these conferences was a motion brought by Edward Harley in an estimates committee of the House of Commons on the 10th proposing that the arrears of pay due to the Hanoverian troops who had left the Duke of Ormonde's command in June 1712 should now be undertaken by the British government. The effort was thwarted by the Tories on the advice of Bolingbroke, who assured them that the Queen knew nothing of the matter. Bolingbroke's action reinforced the unfavourable reaction of the House of Hanover to the vigorous purge of Whig army officers, as well as civilians, that he was conducting in pursuance of his recent vow.[16]

In their dangerous contest, Oxford and Bolingbroke now appeared to

13. *Swift Corr.*, ii, 137; Macpherson, *Original Papers*, ii, 604; Schultz to the Electoral Prince, 20 April, 1 May 1714, C.B.A. 24 (England), 119. Leading Whigs would hardly have spread this story if they had not been convinced of the sincerity of Oxford's continued devotion to the Hanoverian succession. It is difficult to see how Queen Anne's biographer judges the Elector's continued attempts to establish a member of his family in Britain to be inimical to Oxford's real wishes, rather than Anne's, or as shaking 'the entire basis of his scheme for continued power' (Gregg, pp. 379 and 384). Professor Gregg's basic premise that Oxford was for the Pretender produces many distortions in his interpretation of Oxford's actions.
14. Sir Henry Ellis, *Original letters illustrative of English History*, 2nd series, iv (1827), p. 269; Macpherson, *Original Papers*, ii, 616. Ellis, 2nd series, iv, 279.
15. Gaultier to Torcy, (10–) 21 May 1714, *Revue Nouvelle*, iii, 46.
16. Kreienberg to Robethon, 14/25 May, 1714, Stowe MS. 227, f. 46, *cf. Lockhart Papers*, i, 469, and Bolingbroke's own account, *Bolingbroke Corr.*, iv, 531.

have reached a stalemate; Bolingbroke could take no further step for the moment to secure his own ascendancy, and Oxford was unable to dislodge him from his entrenched position with Lady Masham. From among the memoranda which Oxford was in the habit of jotting down in preparation for a conversation or speech, three, together with a letter written at this time, illustrate his state of mind and supplement his well-known 'Brief Account of Public Affairs'.[17] The first, dated 11 May, began as two columns of 'arguments for Hanover' and 'arguments for the Pretender', though the latter column was left blank:

Arguments for Han, viz
1. Security of our religion which cannot be under a Papist.
2. Securing our ancient rights which cannot be under one bred up in French maxims and who comes with the [intention?] to revive his father's quarrels.
3. Hazarde of the Queen's health.
4. Designs of any *in power* against the Succession.[18]

The second paper, written three days later, seems to be an *aide-memoire* for a straight talk with Lady Masham:

You cannot set any one up. You can pull any one down.
The first point is to support the Queen.
The enemy make advantage of your coldness to L[ord] T[reasurer].
What views can you have in it?
It is the pretence (to wise people) for their jealosie
Has it not done hurt enough to the Queen already?
If you hate him however counterfeit indifference for the Queen's service.[19]

Thirdly, there is a note of a conversation which Oxford held with the Queen on 8 June, in the course of which he demanded the removal of ministers of Jacobite tendencies.[20] The appeal fell upon stony ground. The following day he penned a letter intended to be sent to Anne with the 'Brief Account of Public Affairs' written as an apologia for his administration. In this letter Oxford wrote:

17. *Parliamentary History*, vi, appendix iv.
18. 11 May 1714, Loan 29/10/8.
19. 14 May 1714, Loan 29/10/8.
20. 8 June 1714, Loan 29/10/8. Professor Gregg (pp. 382–3) cites this document but dismisses it as evidence of Oxford's Hanoverianism on the ground of the Treasurer's concurrent revelation to the Queen of evidence of suspected Hanoverian military plans to secure the succession. But Oxford, though he supported the Protestant succession, would hardly have viewed with favour any activity which appeared to call for premature invasion by German troops, as he had shown in his contribution to the debate of 17 March.

Madam,

Godolphin is out, Harley is out. Who will [you] trust after that? Who has any credit to lose?

In order to keep your affairs quiet I have retired myself. I do not quarrel – I do not set people to approach you. Nobody will believe you act by yourself.

You manage so as to be for niether Hanover nor the Pretender. Nobody would joyne in their scheme.

He concluded: 'Has Hanover any credit but what your conduct gives them?'[21]

But by this time there was a strong possibility that the parliamentary situation would force the Queen's hand, one way or the other. Bolingbroke had been nurturing a plan to unite the Tories behind himself on a religious issue which would reveal the Treasurer's lack of sympathy with High Church extremism. In May, Sir William Wyndham, on Bolingbroke's behalf, carried through the House of Commons a Schism Bill to destroy the Dissenters. Proposing to tear out organized Protestant dissent at the root, by destroying its educational system, this measure was nicely calculated to rally the Tories on an issue to which they could all subscribe; but it was also intended to invite opposition 'from Oxford and destroy his remaining influence with the Church Party. He was unable or unwilling to prevent his brother from voting with the Whigs in the Commons, though other Harley relations were reported voting for the bill or abstaining, and the bill passed its third reading and was sent to the other House on 1 June.[22] Here Oxford himself, anxious not to offend the Tories further, pursued a similiarly equivocal course, voting for the bill at one stage, and absenting himself at another, though according to some reports he went so far as to speak against the bill's severer clauses. As Bolingbroke intended, Oxford was in a cleft stick.[23] But the Lord Treasurer's real plan did not take the form of opposition to the bill itself. For by 15 June, the day of the last reading in the House of Lords, he had the inkling of a scheme which might turn the tables on Bolingbroke and make the measure a dead letter.

By mid-June the crescendo of rumour concerning the Queen's quarrel with the South Sea Company had reached its climax. Since February the failure of the government to carry the company's General Court against its Court of Directors had resulted in Oxford's withdrawal from further attempts to coerce the company, leaving Bolingbroke to attempt, by

---

21. 9 June, Loan 29/10/8. The covering letter actually sent was uncontentious. See: *Parliamentary History*, vi, appendix vi, col. ccxliii.
22. Add. MS. 17,677, HHH, f. 238.
23. *Wentworth Papers*, p. 388; *Lockhart Papers*, i, 462. Cf. *The Secret History of the White Staff* [by Daniel Defoe], (1714), p. 33.

every threat and evasion at his disposal, to avoid the rigorous safeguards required to bind the Queen's sleeping partners.[24] By 2 June the directors finally decided that they could not proceed on the basis of the names of the trustees nominated by the Queen, two treasury officials, and demanded that the names of the true assignees of her share should be named. This attempt to force Lady Masham's name into the open is an indication of the despair felt by the company at irregular arrangements over which it had no control.[25] From this point events moved swiftly and the task of coercing the Queen was taken over by the Whigs in Parliament. On the 9th the House of Commons resolved to present an address asking Anne to dispose of her share 'for the use of the public and towards discharging the debts of the nation'.[26] Oxford was probably party to this move before it was made; there is a suggestion in a letter from a correspondent, that he had recently been considering a scheme to use this share as the fund for a lottery loan.[27] The presumption that he may even have been behind the Commons address is increased by Oxford's smooth and immediate reaction, when it appears that he informed the directors on the day following the motion that he was in favour of the summoning of another General Court to consider the new development, though he counselled that the meeting should be deferred until the 18th.[28]

If he hoped that by this time the Queen would be persuaded to accede to the Commons' request, a second new development, hard upon the first, altered his plan. On the 15th the captain of one of the warships still waiting to sail with the company's merchandise wrote to Sub-Governor Bateman complaining that Bolingbroke's associate Arthur Moore had attempted to bribe him to carry and sell goods other than the company's.[29] The following day the directors were convened to examine the captain, whose revelations had a timing which appeared providential for the company. The result of this examination, the directors' indignation at a 'discovery' of proceedings of which they had been cognizant for months, has the air of a stagemanaged drama.[30] The outcome was predictable. On the day after this examination, the 17th, the company re-

---

24. It would be tedious to follow in detail the negotiation which attempted to regulate the legal status of the Queen's trustees, since it ended in failure. See: Court Book 2, *passim*, especially 21 April 1714. Add. MS. 25,495, p. 292, and J. Pym to Bolingbroke, 7 May 1714, Memorials Book 1, Add. MS. 25,559, pp. 48–9, same to same 12 May, and Bolingbroke to Bateman, 11 and 17 May, 1714, H.M.C. *House of Lords*, x, 449–50.
25. Court Book 2, 2 June 1714, Add. MS. 25,495, p. 322. Pym to Bolingbroke, same date, H.M.C. *House of Lords*, x, 452.
26. *Commons Journal*, xvii, 673.
27. Arthur Steventon to Oxford, 24 May 1714, Loan 29/45c/11.
28. Court Book 2, June 10 1714, Add. MS. 25,495, p. 326.
29. Captain Robert Johnson to the Company, 15 June 1714, Special Letters Book, Add. MS. 25.562, p. 17.
30. Court Book 2, 16 June 1714, Add. MS. 25,495, p. 330.

ceived an intimation from Bolingbroke that the Queen had decided to give it her share of the Assiento.[31] The surrender was due to fear of further investigations which would probably implicate Bolingbroke, and perhaps also Lady Masham. Thus, the directors had outwitted Bolingbroke with his scheme for the benefit of Lady Masham, and to this extent Oxford could be satisfied with his revenge, though he too was disappointed by the company in his plan to acquire the Queen's share for the public income. It was still not clear to the directors whether the Queen intended the whole of the Assiento concession to be conceded unequivocally to the company, and Oxford professed an equal ignorance. When a deputation of directors came to him for the elucidation of this, and some other minor points, he replied, as they reported to the court, 'that if the Court of Directors addressed themselves to Lord Bolingbroke, he could better give an answer than himself, who had not intermeddled in the affair for some time'.[32] But despite his chagrin at the failure of his plan for the disposal of the Queen's share, he had achieved his main political object. It was now too late for Bolingbroke to prevent the affairs of the South Sea Company and the Spanish commercial treaty being dragged into the light.

A major concession having been wrung from the government, the Whigs in Parliament widened the scope of their attack. On 18 June the House of Commons ordered the South Sea Company to give an account of all its proceedings in the establishment of a trade, a prelude to a fullscale investigation of corruption. Ten days later the Lords followed suit.[33] Oxford's co-operation was no longer equivocal from this point. Edward Harley organized the investigation in the Commons and advised Townshend on how to proceed in the enquiry instituted in the House of Lords; this much is clear from some notes partly in Edward's handwriting, though partly by the hand of an amanuensis, now among Oxford's papers.[34] On 30 June the Lords called for a report by the commissioners of trade on the commercial treaty with Spain, as amended by 'explanatory articles' of February. With Oxford's support, the House called merchants trading with Spain to testify to the disadvantageous nature of articles 3, 5, and 8; a clerk from the commissioners' office revealed that Moore had been offered a bribe by the Spanish authorities to obtain the revision of the treaty; one of the other commissioners testified that Moore had rushed the articles through the scrutiny of the department and that none of his colleagues had seen them until they were in print. In a debate on the results of the enquiry on 5 July, Bolingbroke did his best

---

31. H.M.C. *House of Lords*, x, 455.
32. Court Book 2, 23 June 1714, Add. MS. 25,495,p. 343.
33. *Commons Journal*, xvii, 689; *Lords Journal*, xix, 733.
34. Brampton MSS. subscribed 'To the Rt. Hon. the Lord Viscount Townshend'.

to defend the treaty, but he was unable to withstand the tide of accusation.[35]

At last Oxford had decided that the time was ripe to come out openly
with the Whigs against Bolingbroke. Three days earlier, he informed
some of their leaders, he had attempted to remonstrate with the Queen
to dismiss the Secretary, telling her that if she trusted him any longer
after the revelations in Parliament she would put not only the Protestant
Succession but even her own person in danger. Obtaining no satisfaction
he joined in the attack on the explanatory articles after Bolingbroke had
defended them on the 5th.[36] The *Journal* of the House of Lords shows his
name at the head of the list of those nominated to draw up an address to
the Queen which, when it had passed the House, remonstrated on the
'insuperable difficulties' imposed on British merchants by the commercial treaty. 'All readily conclude', a newsletter informed its readers, 'that
Lord Treasurer endeavours to sacrifice Lord Bolingbroke.'[37]

The counter-attack on Bolingbroke came very close to success. Of
the leading ministers, only Shrewsbury spoke out for him against his
accusers. There appeared little chance of forming a new ministry, and
even before the storm broke Bolingbroke had despondently informed
the French ambassador that he was only awaiting the end of the session
for an opportunity to resign.[38] Then, at the eleventh hour, the Queen
intervened to prevent further enquiries which would damage not only
the Secretary but herself and Mrs Masham. On 9 July, when the House of
Lords reported to be 'in a flame' had just received the consent of the
Commons to an unusual request to examine several of its members in
connection with the South Sea Company, Black Rod knocked upon the
door with the Queen's message of prorogation.[39]

From this moment all agreed that Oxford had lost his chance – all,
that is, except Oxford himself. He still hoped to make the Queen see
reason. In a sketchy *aide-memoire* drawn up for a further attempt to show
Anne that her favour for Bolingbroke and Lady Masham would be generally interpreted as an intention to favour the Pretender he wrote:

> All the Whiggs and much the greater part of the Church are united in
> a jealousie of some foule play and design for the Pretender.
> There was an obvious reason for the last change [*sc*. Godolphin's fall

---

35. *Lords Journal*, xix, 741 to 749; *Wentworth Papers*, pp. 396–400; Boyer, *Quadriennium*, iv,
    564–73; Dickinson, *Bolingbroke*, p. 127; 'Abstract of parliamentary affairs', 5 July 1714, Add.
    MS. 22,217, f. 58.
36. Kreienberg 6/17 July 1714, C.B.A. 24 (England), 113A; Erasmus Lewis to Swift 6 July 1714,
    Swift Corr., ii, 167.
37. *Lords Journal*, xix, 746; Newsletter, n.d. July 1714, *Wentworth Papers*, p. 403.
38. D'Iberville's reports, (8–) 19 July, P.R.O. 31/3/203, f. 242, and (28 June–) 9 July 1714,
    Salomon, p. 298.
39. *Commons Journal*, xvii, 722; *Swift Corr.*, ii, 174.

in 1710]. This will have a bad reason for it. And the Queen alone charged with it.

As for Lady Masham, he noted for the Queen: 'It is for your service that you reconcile L[ady] M[asham] and O[xford]. Tell them both so, have them together. O will own himself in the wrong.'[40] But the Lady of the Bedchamber remained obdurate. Patiently Oxford allowed himself to be snubbed; he dined with her a few days after the rising of Parliament, immediately after she had told him 'you never did the [Queen] any service, nor are you capable of doing her any'. Swift's comment on this remark, when he heard of it, sadly acknowledged Lady Masham's power: '. . .what she said to the Dragon [i.e. Oxford] a week ago is of so desperate a strain, that I cannot think of her in a temper to be at the head or the bottom of a change; nor do I believe a change accompanied with such fusions can ever succeed.'[41]

But the only reason for the Queen's delay in dismissing Oxford was, apparently, the need to detach his colleagues from him. Shrewsbury's views oscillated violently. On 17 July Bolingbroke told Dr Arbuthnot: 'The Duke of Shrewsbury is taken himself to the Dragon in appearance'. Three days later, another of Swift's correspondents wrote:

> . . .I can guess no reason why matters are delayed, unless it be to gain over some Lords, who stick firm to the Dragon, and others that are averse to the Captain [Bolingbroke]. The D of S[hrewsbur]y declares against him in private conversation; I suppose because he is against every chief minister. . .[42]

Shrewsbury, in fact, may have been working for a compromise, and Oxford too had hopes of some such outcome; a minute in his handwriting taken at a committee meeting of the cabinet on 22 July contains the words 'Try an accommodation. Draw up in writing terms of accommodation.'[43]

Bolingbroke however, was already far past any desire to compromise; he was widely reported to have drawn up a list of Treasury commissioners to replace his rival, and had succeeded at last in turning the Queen's mind to immediate dismissal of Oxford though not, as events proved, to his replacement by Bolingbroke's motley supporters. Any further attempts at accommodation by Oxford came too late for hope of success; he defied intimations that he might retire gracefully, and by the 27th he was aware that he would be dismissed. By coincidence his last formal

40. '4 July, 1714', Loan 29/10/6.
41. *Swift Corr.*, ii, 182 and 190.
42. *Ibid.*, 185 and 189.
43. 'Cockpit, July 22, 1714', Loan 29/10/6.

duty, on the morning of that day, was to present his son's successful rival for possession of the late Duke of Newcastle's main estates, Lord Pelham, to the Queen on the attainment of his majority. Pelham was to become in the next reign successor to the Newcastle title by a new creation of that dukedom. After the audience, Oxford remarked succinctly in the hearing of surrounding ministers and others that he had carried out his last presentation.[44]

At a specially summoned meeting of the cabinet the same afternoon, however, Oxford gave vent to his bitterness more fully and fell into recrimination with Bolingbroke in the Queen's presence. The two men can have behaved little better on this occasion than on previous days, when it had been reported that 'they give one another such names, as nobody but Ministers of State could bear, without cutting throats'.[45] Oxford delivered up the white staff on the same evening. According to the loyal Defoe in *The Secret History of the White Staff*, Oxford's defence of himself and indictment of Bolingbroke determined the Queen 'in a short while to restore it to the same hands again'. But if Oxford had any hope of re-appointment in the longer term his preparations to leave London preclude any speculation that he hoped for an immediate reversal of fortune. The Queen, indeed, came finally to the conclusion that she could not appoint Bolingbroke or his nominees to the Treasury after the recent revelations in Parliament. After three days of acute stress, wracked by indecision, she turned not to Oxford, but to Shrewsbury, once William III's choice for his first Secretary of State and now Anne's for her last Lord High Treasurer. Even before this appointment she had taken to her sickbed and she died the morning of the 1st of August, worn out by longstanding physical ailments and recent mental turmoil. One of her physicians, Dr Hamilton, ascribed her death not so much to medical causes as to her 'disquiet' at recent events.[46]

At a series of Privy Council meetings during Anne's last illness the Whigs Shrewsbury, Argyll and Somerset, whom for four years Oxford had stubbornly refused to dismiss from that body, took their places and joined in taking the measures needed to ensure the undisputed Protestant succession of the Elector of Hanover as King George I, his mother the Princess Sophia having died just three months earlier. Bolingbroke took the defeat of his personal ministerial ambitions philosophically, with the comment 'how does Fortune banter us'.[47] As for Oxford, the sometimes devious, sometimes disconcertingly simple, indispensible statesman of

44. Dickinson, *Bolingbroke*, p. 129; Bothmer to Robethon, 27 July 1714, Stowe MS. 227, f. 243;
45. *Swift Corr.*, ii, 193.
46. *London Diaries*, p. 3.
47. *Swift Corr.*, ii, 214.

his generation, the matter was one which could be summed up in a few lines of doggerel as he prepared to travel to Lord Harley's mansion at Wimpole for a needed rest:

> To serve with love,
>   And shed your blood,
> Approvéd is above
>   But here below,
>   Th' examples show
>   'Tis fatal to be good.[48]

48. *Ibid.*, 199.

CHAPTER 16

Retirement Postponed

AT THE TIME of his dismissal Oxford was fifty-two. For several years he had suffered a partial deafness in his left ear, and he was exhausted after four years of heavy responsibility and many months of quarrels in cabinet and at court. But he had never lost his talent for making staunch friends, and they rallied to him now. Even Bolingbroke had conceded, albeit in 1711 before the worst of their disputes, that 'though he often wants that grace and openness which engages the affection, yet I must own I never knew that he wanted either the constancy or the friendship which engages the esteem'.[1] Thus it was that Erasmus Lewis, diplomat, MP and admirer, wrote in his defence on the day of his dismissal:

> ...it is not the going out, but the manner, that enrages me. The Queen has told all the Lords the reasons of her parting with him, viz. that he neglected all business; that he was seldom to be understood; that when he did explain himself, she could not depend upon the truth of what he said; that he never came to her at the time she appointed; that he often came drunk; that lastly, to crown all, he behaved himself towards her with ill manner, indecency, and disrespect. *Pudet haec opprobria nobis,* * etc.[2]

'It is shameful both that such reproaches should be uttered against us, and that we should be unable to refute them', ran the full quotation from Horace. Apart from quarrelling in her presence, and possibly drinking too much wine to assuage his troubles, Oxford had not deserved the enraged Queen's wrath, and with Lewis we may safely discredit most of her hysterical accusations for what they were; Anne had said hardly less of Nottingham, Godolphin, and Marlborough, upon like occasions. But though the charges themselves must be scanned with care, the fact that

1. *Bolingbroke Corr.*, i, 245.
2. *Swift Corr.*, ii, 199.

* Pudet et haec opprobria nobis
Et dici potuisse, et non potuisse refelli

they were delivered at all represents Nemesis's judgement on Oxford's latterday political methods. He climbed to power with good intentions, but some of his means hindered, and all but defeated, his ends. He had risen by his own talents in the Commons and by the confidence he inspired among many of its members; but he sought to consolidate his influence with the Queen through Abigail Hill and his control of the Tory host through St John. In the end he found that Lady Masham and Bolingbroke could not be laid aside.

Such was the situation in his last year of office. While Bolingbroke and Lady Masham manipulated the Queen, discrediting and saddening the last months of a patriotic reign, Oxford withdrew as far as possible, since neither his leadership nor his resignation were acceptable. Whether it was an act of wisdom to retain office while unable to execute many of its political responsibilities is debatable. Oxford's main justification was that he ensured a smooth Protestant Succession, but his enforced inaction certainly gave opening for accusations of neglect, and induced in Oxford himself an indifference from which he was aroused too late to save himself, though he frustrated the Secretary's plans. Never prone to take action when a waiting game would serve, he patiently waited for his opponent to overreach himself. When at last he was goaded into action, the ground he chose was not entirely favourable. The enquiry into the South Sea Company affected Lady Masham; and the treaty of commerce with Spain, however disadvantageous, was one which the Queen herself had signed. That he miscalculated is not, however, entirely to Oxford's discredit; it demonstrates that the misuse of the public income, even with the Queen's connivance, could still flick him out of cool political calculation and show a flash of the spirit which had made even William III fear him.

Oxford's Fabian tactics gave time for the Queen to realize the extent of her own errors, and of her misjudgment in allowing Lady Masham to persuade her to overlook her Secretary's chicanery. It is difficult to look back past the Bolingbroke of the *Patriot King* (1738) to the Secretary of State of Queen Anne, yet a generation of experience lies between the later political theorist and the earlier minister. The later Bolingbroke would have pleased Anne; the Secretary of State did not. In 1714 he wanted a dominant Tory Party strong enough to impose terms on the House of Hanover, and strong enough therefore, if necessary, to dominate Queen Anne. But the Queen had another conception of politics, a conception in which she played the part of a Queen indeed, a Patriot Queen over parties. And this outlook she shared, not with Bolingbroke but with Oxford. Nor did she admire Bolingbroke's violent methods. During the years he had been first a professed disciple and then a colleague of Oxford, he had learned much from the older man's political stratagems but nothing from his instinctive moderation; it was only later in life, when an older Bolingbroke was prompting from the wings the part he had spurned when on the stage, that he came to believe he had acted it too. In Anne's last years, however, it was clear that the only man who could command the support of moderate opinion in the country was Oxford.

With his retirement he ceased to have any effect on public affairs and became a pawn in the game of Whig politics. He had once told a correspondent 'I can retire with ease every hour in the day to the same plenty and more peace than I now enjoy, and I shall think myself as a great a man in my own bowling green at home, as now in a toilsome office at Whitehall'.[3] He was telling only half the truth: the office at Whitehall had its attractions too, and by his retention of it until July 1714 his fall became the more complete. But it is unlikely that Anne, if she had survived, would have been as remorseless as her successor in depriving Oxford of his remaining offices and honours. His disgrace was made plain not only by King George I's obvious personal dislike but by dismissal from most of the lesser offices acquired over the years. Before 1714 was out Oxford ceased to be Deputy Lieutenant of Herefordshire, an office he had held for over two decades, and Deputy Lieutenant of Radnorshire where he had been in post for more than ten years. He also ceased to be Custos Rotulorum for Radnorshire and was removed from the bench of justices for Herefordshire. The Stewardship of Sherwood Forest, bestowed as recently as 1712, was also taken from him. Such changes mirrored thousands of others taking place as the triumphant Whigs took over from their rivals under the new dispensation.

Deprivation of office brought time for leisure, and for the next few years Oxford was able to pursue his intellectual and literary interests with greater vigour. In 1712 he had become a Fellow of the Royal Society and so could keep himself up to date with matters of scientific and general interest. His main interest, however, lay in literary matters and his large collection of manuscripts and books. This famous library, second only to the Cotton Library in the annals of British scholarship, undoubtedly emerged in the first place out of his personal craving for knowledge, instanced on many occasions by the erudition he displayed in speeches and in conversation. After he became Speaker in 1701 his time for personal research became more limited, but his purchases of documents, rare books and pamphlets increased manyfold after he inherited the Brampton estate together with the financial ability to indulge his taste for collecting. The first of many acquisitions of intact major collections was made in 1705; and with the appointment of Humphrey Wanley as his librarian, Oxford's purchasing policy was set new horizons. Three years later, when he was enforcedly idle after ceasing to be Secretary of State,

3. H.M.C. *Portland*, iv, 261.

Wanley was directed to begin the justly celebrated *Catalogue* of the Harleian Manuscripts, medieval or later, now in the British Library.

By 1715 Oxford already owned about 3,000 books, many illuminated, together with 13,000 charters and deeds, 1,000 rolls and parliamentary journals and a commensurately large collection of letters and other papers, often rare and of priceless value to scholars. The Harleian collection included the former substantial libraries of John Foxe, the martyrologist, John Stow and Sir Simonds D'Ewes.[4] Although the early purchases had been relatively cheap, before he and other collectors pushed the prices up, Oxford continued to collect in retirement, at great expense on both purchase and binding. For all that the library was too vast for most men to have had a comprehensive knowledge of its scope, let alone its content, Oxford kept up his personal acquaintance with both books and manuscripts. A later editor of the *Harleian Miscellany* recalled 'he is said to have acquired so particular a knowledge of them all, as to be able, without a catalogue, to go immediately to the least of them, upon having it named, though his library consisted of more than 100,000 different authors.'[5] He allowed easy access to scholars and to the curious, such as Atterbury's Whig rival Bishop William Nicholson, who recorded that he had had a 'View of Mr Harley's Choice Library, and kind Treatment by the Owner'. A modern historian of English scholarship writes that 'the whole company of scholars looked up to Robert Harley, Earl of Oxford, as the great Maecenas of English medieval learning, and they were right to do so, for he was the correspondent and benefactor of many of them'.[6]

But Oxford's enjoyment of retirement to improve his collection and share the company of scholars and literary men was not allowed to last. As the Whigs took control with the consent of the new King they brought with them a cry for revenge for past impeachments, and in Walpole's case imprisonment, together with a determination that the punishment of members of Queen Anne's last ministry should serve also to crush the Tory party for ever. Bolingbroke was dismissed at the end of August 1714, even before George arrived in Britain, to be followed by Bromley and nearly all Tory ministers. Clearly loyal men such as Bromley and Hanmer were offered subordinate posts, which they indignantly refused. There followed a clean sweep of local offices in preparation for the dissolution of Parliament, due within six months, and the subsequent general election. In the elections Whig patronage worked with great efficiency wherever the new men in office could promise, cajole, threaten or bribe, assisted by a genuine swing in public opinion among those

4. H.M.C. *Portland*, v, 514–16.
5. *Harleian Miscellany* (1808), i, 1.
6. Hamilton, *Diary*, p. 503; Douglas, p. 263.

floating voters who had been alarmed at the danger to the Church in 1710 but were now convinced that the Protestant Succession had been in danger in 1714.[7] The Harleys were strongly attacked in the seats which they usually influenced, their principal assailant being Lord Coningsby, now Lieutenant of both Herefordshire and Radnorshire, who in 1690, as Thomas Coningsby, had helped to unseat Sir Edward Harley for Herefordshire. Oxford's son had represented New Radnor since a bye-election in 1711 but showed little talent for the everyday grind of plitics or electioneering and lost his seat to Thomas Lewis, the more energetic son of a nearby landowner. 'Auditor' Harley narrowly retained his seat for Leominster but saw no point in risking an expensive poll at Bishops Castle on behalf of his son Edward. Throughout the country the news was of disaster for Tory candidates as they were toppled from the seats they had acquired in 1710 and retained in 1713.[8]

In January 1715, with the seizure of Strafford's papers concerning the recent treaties, a new phase in the Whigs' preparations for retribution began. As the meeting of the new Parliament approached, rumours were rife of an intention to impeach not only Strafford and Bolingbroke, whose documents had also been impounded, but also Oxford and Ormonde. Anne's own papers had produced little of an incriminating nature against Oxford, but contained letters from him accusing Bolingbroke of Jacobitism. At the end of March 1715 Bolingbroke ran for protection to France, perhaps fearing that Oxford would be among those who would testify against him. Oxford commented acidly to his brother 'the going away of Lord Bolingbroke is like his other practices. I thank God I was never in his secret, and for late years out of his way of converse but only what was necessary'.[9] He made the difficult journey to London over the soft roads of early April and took his seat in the House of Lords on the 11th. In the Commons the Whig majority approached a two-to-one ratio, and impeachment proceedings began against the accused peers; Walpole chaired the Secret Committee, and Coningsby (a peer of Ireland) continued his vendetta by moving that Oxford be impeached of high crimes and misdemeanours. The cowed opposition did not divide the House. Lady Oxford wrote bravely 'my Lord doth not fear Coningsby nor pack of bloodhounds. I pray God deliver him out of their hands.' But the Whigs pressed on, against the advice of some of their own best lawyers, for political victory was in sight. On 9 July Coningsby, for the Commons, brought sixteen articles of impeachment against the former Lord Treasurer at the bar of the House of Lords.[10]

---

7. H.M.C. *Portland*, v, 503; Speck, *Tory and Whig, passim.*
8. H.M.C. *Portland*, v, 505–6 and 663.
9. *Ibid.*, v, 508–10.
10. *Ibid.*, v, 510–11; *LJ*, xx, 99–111.

Most of the articles referred to Oxford's part in concluding the Peace of Utrecht, but other areas were covered for good measure; article 16 even made his 'unprecedented' advice to Anne for the creation of the twelve peers in 1711 the subject of a charge.* Oxford's defence, delivered during an attack of gravel, was long and detailed. Some charges he denied, as being about matters within the competence of either the Queen or Bolingbroke rather than his own. On the treaties in general he claimed, untruthfully, that France had made the first approach. In the main he relied upon the argument that his own function had merely been carrying out the Queen's own policies, and that he had broken no law thereby. He warned the Lords assembled that: 'If Ministers of State, acting by the immediate commands of their Sovereign, are afterwards to be made accountable for their proceedings, it may one day be the case of all the Members of this august assembly....'.[11] The argument had strong appeal, as testified by the fact that no subsequent first minister has been answerable with his or her life for conduct of office. But the force of the attack was irresistable in the atmosphere of suspicion and confusion created by the flight of Bolingbroke, soon followed by Ormonde, and the concurrent proceedings against the other accused men. On 16 July the motion for Oxford's committal to await trial was carried by 82 votes to 50. By reason of his illness he was allowed to return to his own house under the care of Black Rod, but after two days he was removed to the Tower of London. A fortnight later Coningsby brought up six further articles of impeachment, accusing Oxford of giving evil advice to the Queen and working secretly for the Pretender.[12]

Even in the Tower Oxford was pursued, Auditor Harley believed, by petty spite. While still ill he was moved from his first lodging, with a former dependant, to another where, according to his brother's indignant account, 'taking a fresh cold, his pains grew so very severe, that for many months he was neither able to put on his clothes or feed himself'. His illness included arthritis and rheumatism, accompanied by influenza-type colds and possibly pneumonia. Fortunately Sarah was able to accompany and nurse him, until she herself succumbed. On 23 October Oxford was able to write, after twelve weeks' confinement, 'your mother by her kindness in sitting up and watching me was very ill, but is now much better'.[13] When recovered he turned to the Greek classics for recreation and also followed the accounts of the Pretender's landing and unsuccessful rebellion. These events had the minor effect of turning the attention

11. *Parliamentary History*, vii, 106; Mallet, pp. 308–12.
12. H.M.C. *Portland*, v, 513 and 665–6; *LJ* xx, 136–42.
13. H.M.C. *Portland*, v, 666 and 529–30.

*There was, in fact a recent precedent: Godolphin had advised the creation of five baronies in 1703 for ministerial supporters.

of the Whig ministers and the House of Lords elsewhere so that Oxford's
stay in the Tower was much prolonged, though the delays possibly saved
him from the worse fate which might have befallen him if his case had
been dealt with while it remained a matter for hot contention. Prince
James Edward's rising and defeat was followed by some more urgent trials,
and the executions of rebel peers taken in arms. Oxford's imprisonment,
like his father's confinement during Monmouth's rebellion in 1685, at
least spared him any charge of complicity, though the accused rebels
were questioned on the subject.[14]

As a result of the uprising of 1715 the ministry were emboldened to
pass the Septennial Act the following year, prolonging the permitted life
of the sitting Commons with its huge Whig majority and increasing the
maximum life for Parliament to seven years. Oxford's case continued to
be ignored. His letters to his family at first reflected his bitterness. To his
brother he wrote in March 1716: 'I never had the least view in anything
I did for promoting the Protestant succession for my own private
advantage...I was determined to enjoy myself in a quiet retirement, and
you know I had prepared everything for it, if I might have been suffered
to enjoy that repose I ought'. But as time passed he became more
resigned, writing six weeks later to Sarah, now evidently removed from
the precincts of the Tower, 'I have fully disposed my mind to be easy
under any confinement, and as I look for no favour, so I shall do nothing
towards my freedom, that may not become the character of an English
gentleman, and I will go out of this place with the same honour and
innocence as I came into it'.[15] It was this more philosophical attitude
which sustained him, and often his thoughts were on his family, now
including grandchildren, as the months of his imprisonment grew into a
year and more. To his brother Nathaniel, for many years a merchant in
distant Aleppo he wrote, in the hope of Nathaniel's return, of:

> My children and grandchildren, viz., dear Betty (Lady Carmarthen)
> whom you just saw, and God was pleased to take away, leaving a sweet
> child, Lord Danby. Daughter Dupplin and her husband, Lord Hay of
> Pedwardine and their two sons and three daughters. Your nephew Lord
> Harley and Lady Henrietta and their pretty daughter Margaret Caven-
> dish; and may our good and gracious God vouchsafe a comfortable,
> speedy meeting.[16]

The climax to the Whigs' triumph over their now prostrate rivals,
marked by the Septennial Act, now ushered in party schism and, for
Oxford, the opening needed for his eventual release. In late 1716 the

14. *Ibid.*, v, 667.
15. *Ibid.*, v, 530–1.
16. *Ibid.*, v, 521–2.

Whig Party was torn apart by quarrels made possible by the very certainty of its security from Tory challenge. One faction was led by Walpole and his brother-in-law Townshend, the other by the opposing ministers Sunderland and Earl Stanhope. This internecine quarrel came to a head with the dismissal of Townshend and resignation of Walpole. Oxford's supporters saw the opportunity, with both Whig factions disposed to bid for Tory support, for obtaining his release. But he stubbornly refused advice, even from his brother, to purchase his freedom by some kind of assurance of future good conduct. As he told his sister in February 1717: 'I cannot see that is is my Duty to give way in the least to staine my own Innocency; and therefore I cannot submit to the least thing (no not so little as cocking my hat) that is to be understood as a confession of guilt'.[17] And his stubbornness won the contest. By May he considered the time ripe for a petition that his trial should be brought on. His judgment was correct, for his alleged offences were becoming a more distant memory and secondary to current political events. Trevor presented the petition on Oxford's behalf in the House of Lords. In the Commons Walpole, though now in opposition, resumed his position of chairman of the committee of Secrecy which had brought the charges against Oxford. In the new climate of co-operation against the Stanhope-Sunderland Whigs, Walpole privately assured Bromley that he would do his best to take the impeachment no further.[18] So it turned out. With the first day of the trial set for 24 June another old school fellow, Harcourt, carried a motion in the Lords that the charges of high crimes and misdemeanours should not be dealt with until the more important articles relating to the difficult case for high treason had been heard. This brought immediate disagreement with the Whig managers in the Commons, who had no evidence of value on these charges. Walpole now proved as good as his promise, and saw to it that the managers did not appear in the Upper House on the appointed day to present their objections. Harcourt again took the lead in proposing that Oxford should be discharged, and he was duly cleared of all charges, to the relief of not only his friends and the many who thought him innocent but even the embarrassed ministry, whose success would have forced the Tories and discontented Whigs even further into a working alliance. Oxford's release was accompanied by an immediate, typically unforgiving order from the King that he should present himself no more at court.[19]

Oxford's acquittal was followed by a period of recuperation at Wimpole Hall, his son's Cambridgeshire residence, and in London before he undertook the longer journey to Brampton which he now found increas-

17. Oxford to Abigail Harley, 13 Feb. 1616/17, Brampton MSS.
18. H.M.C. *Portland*, v, 526–7.
19. *Ibid.*, v, 559 and 668–9; *LJ* xx, 512.

ingly irksome. In London he was surrounded by literary friends, headed by Swift and Pope when they were in town, and could continue collecting for his library. At Wimpole he aided his son in the tangled management of the latter's financial affairs, for the large estate which Lady Henrietta had inherited was no match for her husband's talents for spending and mismanagement. Lord Harley's sporadic political ambitions too could be furthered by judicious help and advice; and though Oxford's efforts to woo a Herefordshire seat for his son were to prove unavailing he had the satisfaction of living to see him, as an important landowner, return to Parliament for Cambridgeshire in 1722. Later in Edward's life, however, his weaknesses were not restrained by parental concern, and his undistinguished subsequent career in the House of Lords was accompanied by heavy drinking, early physical decline and the enforced sale of the Wimpole estate in his lifetime. However, the younger Harley was to earn the gratitude of future generations of scholars by enlarging his father's library extensively, though with less financial judgment, and to receive the affection of the *literati* to whom his father was patron and friend.

Oxford's warm family feeling was not limited to his own offspring. As Lord Harley had no son it became increasingly likely that the title would descend eventually to one of Auditor Harley's two sons. The first, Edward the younger, was the more likely. Oxford did not live to see him gain a Herefordshire seat and take a leading place among 'Hanoverian' Tories in the Commons, but his political interests were already visible. In 1717 at Christ Church, Oxford, Edward was already taking the keen interest in parliamentary affairs which Oxford may have wished that his own son would show.[20] The Auditor's younger son, Robert, was less promising than his brother, and Oxford felt called upon in October 1717 to write to the eleven-year-old boy urging him to industry and application, laying before him 'the danger of your continuing in a heedless lazy unthinking, course of life'.[21] Robert responded sufficiently to proceed to a respectable if not outstanding parliamentary career for forty years, during which he, like his brother and cousin, voted staunchly Tory except on the occasion in 1741 when the family voted against the censure of Walpole, thus repaying a family debt for Walpole's help in obtaining Oxford's release.[22]

Oxford's more important later appearances in the House of Lords took place in 1718 and 1719. In February 1718 he felt sufficiently active to take a leading part in debates on the Mutiny Bill, which the Tories objected to by reason of the sanction it gave to the continuance of a

20. H.M.C. *Portland*, v. 553 *sqq*.
21. Oxford to Robert Harley the Younger, Loan 29/166/6.
22. Sedgwick, *House of Commons, 1715–1754*, *sub* Harley, Edward, Lord Harley; Harley, Edward, of Eywood; and Harley, Robert.

standing army. As Trevor pointed out, the army 'if continued now might with a great reason be continued for ever'. Oxford's efforts were based on the Harleys' longstanding dislike of the professional army, dating back to the experiences of Sir Robert and Colonel Edward in the 1640s and 1650s. Oxford spoke, reported Edward Harley the younger from Christ Church, 'very·bodly, clearly, and easily, was answered by Stanhope, who cast several reflections on him which my Lord did not think proper then to answer'.[23] The bill was carried, and Oxford appears to have been content with the alarmed response he had provoked by his first major incursion into Parliament life since his release. In the summer he made a prolongued visit to his home and friends in Herefordshire, but December saw him back in London for the new session of Parliament. The talk of the day was that George I desired a repeal of the Act of Attainder passed in 1715 against Bolingbroke in lieu of impeachment after his flight; for that adaptable politician, having first joined the Pretender as 'Secretary of State', had left him again after the failure of the rebellion and was now loudly proclaiming his dissatisfaction with the court-in-exile while secretly working to buy support at that of George I.[24]

   In the event little came of Bolingbroke's attempts to be allowed to return to England until several years later. Oxford spoke alongside his old rival Nottingham on Stanhope's bundle of measures to repeal the Schism Act and ameliorate the sacramental tests for Dissenters. He gave out-spoken support to Nottingham's clause to prevent the growth of Socini-anism, for he had often inveighed against all forms of the unitarianism which was now strongly affecting the Presbyterian ministry. It is possible that he voted against the bill in its entirety, as did his brother in the Commons, while exonerating the Dissenters of the worst accusations flung against them by the Tories. The Harleys' lack of sympathy with the new leadership of their former favoured Church had been growing for many years, and their view of the proposed measures was shared by many Church Whigs in both Houses, who continued as in 1689 to vote against repeal of the tests.[25] A month later Oxford was active in opposition to the first appearance of the Peerage Bill, this time alongside Townshend. This bill would have prevented any repetition of the expedient in 1711 of creating new peers to overcome opposition in the House of Lords. The proposal to secure a permanent majority of government supporters in the upper chamber, by preventing for the most part the further creation of peers, went against Oxford's wholehearted, if conventional concept of a useful 'balance of the constitution' between King, Lords and Commons – a concept which had by no means been weakened by his own temporary

23. H.M.C. *Portland*, v, 557; *Parliamentary History*, vii, 543–8.
24. G.A. Aitken, *Life of Arbuthnot*, p. 93; H.M.C. *Portland*, v, 573.
25. H.M.C. *Portland*, v, 574–6.

assault on it in the creation of the Twelve. The bill was dropped for the moment after meeting an unexpected degree of Whig as well as Tory opposition.[26]

In 1719 Oxford stayed longer than usual at Brampton, enjoying his favoured pastime of bowls enough to mention it in his correspondence.[27] He did not return to London in December in time for the reintroduction of the Peerage Bill, apparently because some of the Tories were showing signs of responding to Stanhope's blandishments. There was a suggestion from a family friend, Dr William Stratford of Christ Church, that the real reason for Oxford's absence, despite reasonably good health, was 'because those who should will not be directed by him, or put themselves under him again'. Despite some Tory intransigence he put in an appearance in the Lords after Christmas, though his friend Bromley stayed away from the Lower House in disgust. The Peerage Bill was defeated in the Commons when Walpole reached the peak of his opposition career in an impassioned campaign against the measure. Oxford does not appear to have played a prominent part in the Lords' opposition, but he must have been a fascinated spectator of Walpole's omnipresent activities and power, so reminiscent of his own in the 1690s; and he stayed on in London long enough to watch the commencement of events which were to elevate the younger man to the position of leading minister.[28]

Walpole's rising star was the result of both the rejection of the Peerage Bill and the debacle of the South Sea Bubble. Sunderland's South Sea Act, passed in the spring of 1720 was identified by Oxford as having no real relation to his original scheme in setting up the company in 1711, for the earlier scheme was an honest one and the later was principally intended to make its devisers rich. Many ministers and members of the royal court were involved. Oxford later wrote indignantly to Lord Foley of the affair: 'the original South Sea Company was instituted to pay debts (as it did), this to make debts; that to relieve poor suffering tradesmen who had only bread for the day, this to ease rich men of their spareable money'.[29] As South Sea and other stock rose to unprecedented heights on a wave of euphoria, even before the end of the session in which the Act passed, Oxford returned to Herefordshire, where he heard from his brother that 'the madness of stock jobbing is inconceivable'. Oxford instructed Edward to sell his already over-inflated Royal African Company stock in May, three months before the bubble burst. Few, even of those so worldly wise as Walpole, sold earlier.[30]

During the remainder of 1720, while the South Sea Bubble further

26. *Ibid.*, v, 579 *sqq.*: *Parliamentary History*, vii, 589.
27. H.M.C. *Portland*, v, 590.
28. *Ibid.*, v, 590 and 600; H.M.C. *Portland*, vii, 266–7.
29. 20 January 1720 (−21), Loan 29/136/2.
30. H.M.C. *Portland*, v, 597; Plumb, *Walpole*, I, 308–9.

expanded, overstretched, then burst, Oxford remained at Brampton with worse than usual health, including a suspected visitation of smallpox. From Aleppo came a new blow, with the news that Nathaniel Harley had died of a fever without achieving his hope of a return to England.[31] For the following session, when parliamentarians of all political shades united in demanding retribution for the South Sea fiasco, Oxford did not go to Westminster. Few blamed him for the crash, for his foundation plan for the South Sea Company had been stretched almost out of recognition, and he had no solution to offer for those holders who were victims of their own credulity in buying at inflated prices. He wrote:

> To remind anyone that they have been foretold of their danger without offering a remedy is upbraiding and useless...to offer a remedy to a patient who can neither bear the disease nor the medicine is lost labour; and in such a jumble of jarring interests, boundless avarice, necessitous clamours, enterprising quacks, it must and will create confusion, and it must be a head better than mine, who can pretend to talk reasonably upon so perplexed a subject.[32]

In fact no one could solve the problem: restitution to all who had been ruined by their own folly was impossible, and Walpole, to whom all men turned for a solution, hardly attempted the task of compensating even the South Sea stockholders but concentrated on preventing the general thirst for retribution from getting out of hand. Bromley was disappointed that Oxford did not come to lead the Tory peers, at a time when the Jacobite Tories were showing a disposition to join with Bromley's Hanoverian Tories.[33] But the opposition, united for once, did not need Oxford to accuse the guilty men, and despite Walpole's activities as a 'skreen' for the guilty, many succumbed to the ferocity of the attack. Stanhope, the least culpable, collapsed in the House of Lords and died soon after, Sunderland was irretrievably disgraced in all eyes except those of the court, and other ministers committed suicide or fell prey to illness under the strain. By the end of the session Walpole and Townshend were firmly in power.

Little however, now distracted the even tenor of Oxford's life. His political desires were few, for he considered that he had achieved most of them in his ministry or earlier. He wrote to Lord Foley in 1721 'we enjoy liberty, property, and the Protestant Succession'.[34] These were the mundane but deep-seated wishes of most Britons in the eighteenth century; they were the ends Oxford valued and which, at different stages

31. H.M.C. *Portland*, v, 603–4, 611.
32. *Ibid.*, v, 607–8.
33. *Ibid.*, vii, 309.
34. Oxford to Foley, 20 Jan. 1720 (−21), Loan 29/136/2.

of his career, he had done as much as any to attain. The general election due in 1722 called for some activity and resulted in Lord Harley's success at Cambridgeshire, but did little to improve the Tories' general position.[35] Oxford did not neglect to insure against the now-remote contingency of a Jacobite restoration but gave little but words, as always, to the Pretender and his followers. In 1723 Atterbury, imprisoned after an attempt at a coup, wrote to him from the Tower 'I shall preserve to my death a grateful sense of your Lordship's past favours', but the Bishop was not called upon to give his life for his cause, nor to repay favours in the currency of the exiled court.[36]

Oxford's gradually declining state of health did not improve in 1723, not least perhaps because of the traumatic medical treatments he received in accordance with the customs of the day. By autumn, however, he was back at his London house in Albemarle Street, where he heard of a newer and more scientific medication, the practice of inoculation which was to make life easier for the next generation, at least for those who could afford it. It is to be doubted whether he gave a careful reading to Bishop Burnet's newly-published *History of My Own Time*; Bromley looked at it and wrote that it was a 'collection of vile, low scandal'. Bromley also reported that many of their friends in Parliament were 'discouraged, despond, and conclude they can do no service by their attendance'. Politics was at a low ebb, with the Tories cowed by Walpole's propaganda after the Atterbury plot, and even disaffected Whigs unable to make much way against the triumphant minister.[37] Oxford's thoughts turned to the past, and to family history, rather than the present. On 21 October, the anniversary of his father's birthday, he wrote to his grand-daughter Margaret, Edward's child:

> My father had the courage and firmness of my Lord Vere, your excellent mother's great grandfather and my father's uncle. To this may be added, he had the sweetness, gentleness, and piety of my Lady Vere his aunt, godmother, and your mother's great grandmother.[38]

And on such reflections Oxford passed his time at Wimpole and his new London home. His own birthday, in December, brought him to the age of 62, not a great age for those who had survived thus far; but he was weary, under the burden of years of debility, and prey to even minor illnesses. With Sarah's devoted nursing he survived the winter but he died in the spring, at Albemarle Street, on 21 May 1724. His body was taken to Brampton Bryan for burial at the church restored after the siege, close

35. H.M.C. *Portland*, v, 628–31.
36. *Ibid.*, v, 634.
37. *Ibid.*, v, 365–6; and *Ibid.*, vii, 367–8.
38. H.M.C. *Bath*, i, 250.

to the home of his ancestors and to his beloved bowling alley. Sarah survived as dowager countess until 1737.[39]

Many hastened to offer their condolences to Sarah and to the second
Earl of Oxford, including Swift and Pope. Swift offered to inspect the
late Earl's papers to see 'whether there be any memorials that may be of
use towards writing his life'. The new Lord Oxford replied that there was
'a vast collection of letters and other papers' and urged the Dean to come
over from Dublin inspect them. But Swift was involved in Irish politics,
and never wrote the proposed tribute. Politics, like life, moved on.

To assess a man's character and achievements after two and a half
centuries is not an easy task or one which can always profitably be
attempted; but contemporary opinion, both of friends and enemies, as
well as the testimony of his own correspondence, point to certain
characteristics in Robert Harley. From his father he inherited the habit
of conscious rectitude which marked his attitude in later life. He often
censured the conduct of others, but despite conventional self-deprec-
ation, rarely seems to have felt a serious doubt about the probity of his
own motives. He once wrote to Poulett: 'I thank God I have neither
Ambition nor Avarice to overrule me', and he believed what he wrote.[40]
Fortunately Harley's belief in himself was largely justified, but such self-
confidence had its drawbacks. A passage which appears in Swift's *The
History of the Last Four Years*, but which Harley evidently wished to be
omitted when he revised the draft, noted that:

> There is one thing peculiar in his temper, which I altogether dis-
> approve, and do not remember to have heard or met with in any other
> man's character: I mean an easiness and indifference under any impu-
> tation, although he be never so innocent, and although the strongest
> probabilities and appearance are against him; so that I have known
> him often suspected by his nearest friends for some months, in points
> of the highest importance, to a degree, that they were ready to break
> with him, and only undeceived by time and accident.[41]

On the whole, however, Harley's reliance upon his own opinion of
himself, and indifference to that of others, gave him strength when other
men might have been broken by events. Alexander Pope, the author of a
conventional if not downright trite epitaph, caught his subject's virtues
better in a description of his sojourn in the Tower: 'He would have sate
out the storm, let the danger be what it would. – He was a steady man,
and had a great firmness of soul, and would have died unconcernedly: or
perhaps, like Sir Thomas More, with a jest in his mouth.' Harley's often

39. *Gentleman's Magazine*, vii, 371.
40. 21 Sept. 1706, Loan 29/3/7.
41. *Journal to Stella*, ii, 613–14, 3 Feb. 1712–13, and Appendix IV, p. 681.

heavy jokes and his 'trifling verses', delivered in person or sent in writing to the Scriberus Club almost every day 'even when his all was at stake', as Pope described, provide other signs of his determination not to be overborne by problems when he felt himself in the right.[42]

This side of Harley's nature does something to explain his devoted following among those politicians and others who knew him best; and it also explains a more instinctive approbation by those who viewed him from afar and found his actions more acceptable than those of most politicians. He was of the type who reach the top not least by their power to inspire a feeling of security in their followers: Lord Attlee once called such leaders 'stabilisers, rather than propellers, very necessary when big ships are rolling in heavy seas'.[43] Sir Winston Churchill had some similar function in mind when he wrote: 'That Harley was false to every cause and every man was in a certain sense true; but he was not false to himself, nor to his persistent purpose of steering a middle course for England between many alternating extravagant attitudes and perils'.[44] Such a judgment, from one who had also changed party too often to be entirely trusted by any but was nevertheless put in charge of national affairs in difficult times, deserves consideration.

The period of Queen Anne's troubled last ministry provides most of the substance of subsequent criticism of the minister chosen to take the strain. Yet Harley, at the time of his dismissal in 1714, was still widely trusted, though those who knew him best, like Erasmus Lewis, found 'his parts decayed' after four strenuous years of office. Incongruities there were in his character, more perhaps than in that of any other major British statesman. Many of his actions have no obvious explanation; they were instinctive rather than rational gestures. Yet it was obvious to all, even while they cursed his evasiveness, his untruthfulness, his dilatoriness, and his incoherence, that by his own peculiar standards he was consistent to some important if imperfectly understood purpose. Pressures such as many contemporaries thought would lead to civil war 'did not influence him to alter his way [admitted the Jacobite George Lockhart], for he still jogged on at the same rate, from the beginning to the end of his administration'.[45] Distrusting the ability or desire of his colleagues to live up to his misty ideal, he clung to office because he believed that he could thereby save his country.

What was the nature of his appeal to moderate Toryism? He was surely one of the most unusual persons who ever led the Church party. The strongly puritan cast of his mind sometimes led him along paths of thought which have been trodden only by Oliver Cromwell among major

42. Spence's *Anecdotes* (1858), p. 152.
43. *The Observer*, 13 March 1960, p. 18.
44. Churchill, ii, 80.
45. *Lockhart Papers*, ii, 372.

statesmen. Yet he appealed to much that was permanent in the British way of thought. His earnestness and moral stance came at the right moment to appeal to those who disliked the lax morals and laxer talk of the generation brought up since the Restoration. And despite his upbringing, his way of thinking was unmistakably conservative. He told the Tories ·

> there is a spirit which will maintain the ancient government of England in Church and State and will not neglect those opportunities which are like to be presented for asserting that which is so necessary to our preservation, without being bewitched by any false lights of liberty or such pompous names as are used only to amuse the credulous and cheat them of what they have already.[46]

Few could have put the argument with more earnest conviction.

When we turn from Harley's innate conservatism to his part in the development of the Tory party, the picture is less clear. In the later 1690s the lead he gave to the disunited and disoriented Tories in their first, often diffident, attempts at united opposition was certainly crucial to the emergence of a Tory party independent of the Crown. If his career had ended with his election as Speaker, and with the formation of the ministry of 1700 which presided over the passing of the Act of Settlement, his place in party history would be secure. Yet his alienation from the majority of the Tory party from 1704 to 1708 and again in 1714 serves to point to his lack of sympathy with its strong extremist element. His instinct was for moderate government using the most amenable talent of both parties. In this sense he was the exponent of a 'court' tradition later to be advocated (without acknowledgement) in Bolingbroke's *The Idea of a Patriot King*. When the tides of party conflict forced Harley to take sides he chose the Tories, except when they seemed to endanger national interests. Like Sir Robert Peel over a century later he played an important part in developing a party only to see that it did not always adhere to his own concept of patriotism.

One consistent thread in Harley's attitude to parties was his aversion from the new leaders thrown up after 1688 by the Whigs, his party of origin, changing it into what he regarded as the tool of an irreligious clique. The contrast between what he saw as the old Whig party's idealism and the Junto's expediential methods was to have a profound effect on his attitude not merely to the Whig Party but to the Dissenters who were its most loyal electoral supporters. Some of his sharpest denunciations were reserved for the Presbyterian clergy whom he suspected of sharing the Junto's lax theology. Harley never really understood how the successors of the great Richard Baxter and other

46. H.M.C. *Portland*, iii, 634.

divines of the seventeeth century could allow themselves to be guided by what he saw as corrupt and irreligious politicians. His drift from the Puritanism of his youth to a sincere if moderate churchmanship by the reign of George I resulted partly, it is true, from conformity by the Harleys and their kind to religious tests which would otherwise have excluded them from public life; Sir Edward Harley himself had conformed to the Church of England while retaining his preferred religion. But Robert Harley's estrangement from the Dissenters was accelerated by the behaviour of many Presbyterian ministers, who were already on the road which was to lead them and their flocks to Unitarianism in the eighteenth century. The change was a result of the cult of Reason among those who in 1689 had been refused the 'comprehension' which could have given them a place in the established church. But Harley, insulated by office and by social position from their predicament, had little sympathy; by the end of his career his connection with the Dissenters, long strained, was virtually severed. What remained of his puritan inheritance was a strong adherence to religious morality which served to distinguish him from many less scrupulous political colleagues.

Harley played an important part in the development of British government. As an opposition leader in the Commons under King William he ensured that the limitations placed on the crown after 1688 would not succumb to that monarch's confident assertion of royal authority at a time when the national emergency of war favoured the executive. In the brief years of peace after 1697 Harley was able to reduce the royal powers and to enforce new restrictions in the Act of Settlement. During Queen Anne's reign, Harley's governmental activities and his long alliance with the Queen in no way overrode the legislation passed in the foregoing reign. A strong supporter of *limited* monarchy, he saw this as the true and ancient form of English government. His loyalty to Anne, and fierce support for her demands for her rightful place in government against pressure from the Whigs, was by no means hypocritical, and it appears as often in private notes for his own eyes alone, as in his public statements. Yet the legislative restrictions upon monarchy, which he had done more than most to obtain, made first Godolphin then himself more powerful in office than William's ministers. Both men were sometimes called 'Premier' and accordingly played a significant part in the early development of the prime ministerial office, a process to be further developed by Walpole's long and often autocratic ministry.[47]

Harley's tenure of the highest office added to its status by his conduct of affairs. His achievements, both positive and negative, were important.

47. For the early use of the terms 'Prime Minister' and 'Premier Minister', see Holmes, 'Robert Harley, Earl of Oxford, as "Prime Minister"', in *British Politics*, Annendix C. pp. 440–2.

He prevented Bolingbroke from accepting a far less honourable peace then was actually obtained, and he protected the personnel of the administrative departments in a crucial stage of the development of these departments. He obstructed the desire of some of his colleagues for a Jacobite restoration. As Speaker, during the passage of the Act of Settlement, he had helped to give an independent legislature its final form, but in his four last years of office he proved to have learned the necessity of strong government in its new form, based upon the Treasury and the Bank of England. By fusing the two traditions together, and by preventing the 'landed' and 'financial' interests from trying to destroy rather than compromise with each other, he ended a friction which might have permanently embittered British politics. Much of Harley's active life was involved in a search for balance between the legislature and the executive. His search was a reflection of Britain's search after the Revolution, and on the whole it was successful.

But he did not escape the censure of posterity as he expected. He would have been incredulous to know that the Whig vituperation could so convict his administration of treason that half a century after the accession of George I the suspicion of being a 'Tory' was still likely to be fatal to the aspiring politician who incurred it. He would have been amused to hear Macaulay inform his constituents at Edinburgh that it was the Whig Party alone which had 'maintained the constitutional throne of the House of Hanover against the hostility of the rich Catholic nobility and gentry of England and the designs of the Pretender'.[48] He would have conceded that some of his ministerial colleagues were working for a Jacobite restoration, but insisted that even in the last months of his ministry his own role had been essential in obtaining the enjoyment of 'liberty, property and the Protestant Succession'.

48. Quoted by H.A.L. Fisher, 'The Whig Historians', Raleigh Lecture, British Academy (1928).

APPENDIX

Two Reports by De Beyries, * and a Note on the Hanoverian Representatives in London.

MOST OF THE reports of the Hanoverian representatives in London are deposited in the Niedersächsisches Staatsarchiv at Hanover. Down to 1710 these are of little value compared with the well-known reports by the Dutch representatives (British Library Additional MSS. 17677). The surviving Hanoverian reports for 1702–10, of which those of the Resident, Guillaume De Beyries (or Beyrie) form by far the greatest part, show little personal knowledge of British politics, and De Beyries himself was in the habit of supplying his court with information which was a literal translation of English newsletters when at a loss for more original information. The only episode of these years for which his reports became more than marginally interesting is Harley's fall from office in February 1708, a time when the Dutch Resident L'Hermitage was absent from London. Extracts from two such reports are printed below. On the arrival of Christoph Friedrich Kreienberg, De Beyries' successor, in September 1710, the Hanoverian reports immediately become a valuable commentary, for his minister made himself closely acquainted with Harley and thoroughly familiar with the British political scene. The reports of the other Hanoverian representatives (there were no fewer than four special envoys between 1710 and 1714) are better known, since they have often been used in connection with the succession question; but they are generally of less value for English politics than Kreienberg's reports, from which several short passages have been quoted in this volume.

A Londres le 13/24 fevrier 1708:

... [The Queen commanded Harley] d'agir avec ses amis et de mettre en mouvement leur c'est a dire les Torys et les Whiggs mecontens des autres,

*Niedersachsisches Staatsarchiv, Calenberg Briefe Archiv, 24 (England) 92.

qui paroissent avoir formé un Parti considerable dans la Chambre des Communes. Mr Harley Harcour l'Attorney general et quelques autres chefs de ce Parti ayant depuis consideré cette affaire d'un si grand poids representoient a S.M. [la Reyne] qu'ils n'etoient pas assez authorizez pour se faire croire dans une chose de cette importance, mais que S.M. devoit y employer My Lord Thresorier et le Duc de Marlborough qui par leur authorité pouvoient seuls persuader les gens de ses intentions. Mais s'etant addressée a eux, Elle les y trouva peu disposer, ils Luy en parlerent comme d'un conseil pernicieux qui venoit de Mr Harley et ils Luy firent entendre qu'ils ne pouvoient plus la servir avec luy. C'étoit, dit on, dimanche dernier que cela ce passa, jour du conseil...

A Londres le 17/28 fevrier 1708:

La disgrace de Mr Harley donne tant de matiere de parler qu'elle n'a pû s'epuiser tout d'un coup et il n'etoit pas aisé non plus a gens qui voyent les choses de loin d'en dire les circonstances bien juste. Lors que Mrs Harley, Harcourt Attorney general et St Jean Secretaire de guerre firent entendre à la Reyne qu'ils n'étoient pas assez authorizez, pour pouvoir mettre leurs Parti en mouvement en des choses de tant d'importance, si des gens plus accreditez qu'eux et qui avoient la confiance de S.M. ne s'employoient a faire connaitre eux mêmes Ses intentions, Elle prit le parti les écrire au Duc de Marlborough, par une lettre dont fut chargé Mr St Jean, qui paraissoit estre bien dans l'esprit du Duc et ayant par sa charge de grandes relations avec luy. Le Duc recevant cette lettre dit d'abord que tout cela ne pouvoit venir que de Mr Harley, qui mettoit ces choses dans l'esprit de la Reyne. Il prit le parti de l'aller trouver et de luy representer la necessité qu'il y avoit de complaire aux Whiggs dans la conjoncture ou l'on se trouvoit, puis qu'ils ne demandoient sinon qu'on tirast Mr Harley d'employ. La Reyne se tenant dans ses premiers sentimens de ne pas se laisser ainsi faire la loy sur un homme dont Elle se croyoit bien servie, le Due Luy representa que pour luy il scavoit bien vivre avec tout le monde et s'accommoder de Mr Harley comme d'un autre, mais que S.M. ne trouveroit pas si aisé la dessus my Lord Thresorier et que tant de liens l'unissoient avec luy qu'il ne pourroit pas s'en detacher. S.M. envoya vers luy l'Attorney general pour luy faire connoitre les sentimens où Elle étoit et pour tacher de l'y faire entrer. Le Thresorier parut trouver mauvais que Harcourt se fût chargé de ce message, surquoy il luy répondit qu'il avoit alai en cela d'autant plus volontiers qu'il luy avoit souvent tenu des discours et donné des ordres semblables. Le Thresorier luy demanda enfin que puis qu'il étoit un si bon porteur de messages, si'il ne voudroit pas se charger de celuy qu'il luy donneroit, qu'etoit de faire entendre a S.M. que si Elle persistoit dans cette resolution, qu'il La supplioit d'agreer qu'il Luy remist sa charge, de quoy Harcourt s'acquita, mais rien n'ebranla S.M. jusqu'à lundy suivant que la necessité des affaires, plus que son penchant, l'obligea de relacher de ses premiers sentimens.

SELECT BIBLIOGRAPHY

This list is intended principally to give the location or title of manuscript and printed sources mentioned in the Notes by more abbreviated descriptions. Unless otherwise stated, the place of publication is London.

Other sources which are traceable directly from the Notes, including most of the contemporary tracts and modern articles cited, are not listed here.

I. Main Manuscript Collections

Bank of England
Court Books (Directors)
General Court Books

Blenheim Palace
Churchill Papers, now in British Library, Additional MSS.

Bodleian Library
Ballard MSS
English MSS
North MSS
Rawlinson MSS

Brampton Bryan (available at the Herefordshire Record Office)
Harley MSS

British Library
Additional MSS (the Additional MSS. referred to throughout this volume)
Lansdowne MSS
Loan 29 (Main collection of Harley's papers)
Sloane MSS
Stowe MSS

Cambridge University Library
Anonymous diary (printed by W.A. Speck – see II Printed Sources)
Cholmondeley (Houghton) MSS.

Codrington Library, All Souls, Oxford
Luttrell Diary (printed by Henry Horwitz – see II Printed Sources)

Niedersächsisches Staatsarchiv, Hannover
Calenberg Briefe Archiv

Nottingham University Library
Portland (Nottingham) Papers

Public Record Office
State Papers, Domestic
State Papers, Foreign
Treasury Papers
P.R.O. 31 (transcripts)

II. Printed Sources

Addison Letters	*The Letters of Joseph Addison*, ed. Walter Graham, Oxford, 1941.
Ailesbury Memoirs	*Memoirs of Thomas, Earl of Ailesbury*, ed. W.E. Buckley, 2 vols, Roxburghe Club, 1890.
[Allen, John]	'Cooke's Life of Bolingbroke', *Edinburgh Review*, lxii (1835), 1–34.
Anne Letters	*The Letters and Diplomatic Instructions of Queen Anne*, ed. Beatrice C. Brown, 1935.
Baillie Corr.	*The Correspondence of George Baillie of* Jerviswood, 1702–8, ed. Gilbert Elliot, Edinburgh, 1842.
Berkeley Corr.	*The Correspondence of George Berkeley and Sir John Percival*, ed. Benjamin Rand, Cambridge, 1914.
Berwick Memoirs	*Memoirs of the Marshall Duke of Berwick written by himself*, 2 vols, 1779.
Bolingbroke Corr.	*Letters and Correspondence of Lord Bolingbroke*, the four-volume edition, ed. Gilbert Parke, 1798.
Boyer, *Annals*	Abel Boyer, *The History of the Reign of Queen Anne, digested into annals*, 11 vols, 1703–13.
Boyer, *Quadriennium*	Abel Boyer, *Quadriennium Annae postremum: or the Political State of Great Britain during the last four years of the late Queen's reign*. 1718, four vols. each containing two volumes, numbered consecutively [This work is a revised edition of the same author's *Political state of Great Britain* for the years 1710–14].
British Diplomatic Instructions: France	*British Diplomatic Instructions, 1689–1789*, Volume II – *France, 1689–1721*, ed. L.G. Wickham Legg. Camden Society, 1925.
Burnet	Gilbert Burnet, *The History of my Own Time*, [ed. M.J. Routh], 1833.
Burnet *Supplement*	*A Supplement to Burnet's history of his own time*, ed. H.C. Foxcroft, 1902.
CSP Dom. Anne	*Calendar of State Papers, Domestic, Anne*, 1916-
CTB	*Calendar of Treasury Books*, xxiv-xxviii (1710–1714) ed. W.A. Shaw et. al., 1950–5.
CTP	*Calendar of Treasury Papers*, vols by date, 1702–7, 1708–14, ed. J. Redington, 1874 and 1879.

Carstares, *State Papers* — *State Papers and Letters Addressed to William Carstares*...ed. Joseph M'Cormick, 1774.

Chalmers, *Treaties* — *A Collection of Treaties between Great Britain and other powers*, ed. George Chalmers, 2 vols, 1790.

Chandler, *Debates* — *The History and Proceedings of the House of Commons, 1660–1743*, ed. Richard Chandler, 1742–3.

Clarendon Corr. — Diary of Henry, Earl of Clarendon, *The Correspondence of Henry Hyde, Earl of Clarendon*, ed. S.W. Singer, 1828.

Cole, *Memoirs* — Christian Cole, *Historical and Political Memoirs of the affairs of state...1697–1708*, 1735.

Commons Journals (CJ) — *Journals of the House of Commons*

Conduct of the Duchess — *An Account of the Conduct of the Dowager Duchess of Marlborough from her first coming to Court to the year 1710*, by herself, 1742.

Court and Society — Manchester, Duke of, *Court and Society from Elizabeth to Anne*, 1864.

Cowper, *Diary* — *The Private Diary of Lord Chancellor Cowper*, ed. E.C. Hawtrey, Roxburghe Club, 1833.

Lady Cowper, *Diary* — *Diary of Mary, Countess Cowper...1714–1720*, ed. S. Cowper, 1865.

Coxe, *Marlborough* — William Coxe, *Memoirs of John, Duke of Marlborough* 3 vols, 1818–1819.

Cunningham — Alexander Cunningham, *The History of Great Britain from the Revolution in 1688 to the accession of George I*, (translated from the original Latin MS. by William Thomson), 2 vols, 1787.

Dalrymple, Sir J. — *Memoirs of Great Britain and Ireland*, 2 vols, 1771–3.

Davenant, Charles, — *The True Picture of a Modern Whig...* three parts, 1701.

Davenant, Charles — *Sir Thomas Double at Court...* 1710.

Davenant, Charles — *New Dialogues upon the Present Posture of affairs...*, 1710.

Defoe, *Union* — Daniel Defoe, *The History of the Union between England and Scotland*, ed. J.L. de Lolme, 1786.

Defoe, Daniel — *The Secret History of the White Staff* (1714)

Defoe, *Political Paper* — 'An unpublished political paper by Daniel Defoe', ed. G.F. Warner, *EHR*, xxii (1907), 130–43.

Evelyn Diary — Evelyn, John, *The Diary of John Evelyn*, ed. E.S. de Beer, Oxford, 1955.

Feldzüge Eugen — *Feldzüge des Prinzen Eugen von Savoyen*, ed. H.S.E. von Eberswald, Wien, vol. 14 (ii Serie, Band v.), 1889.

Grey, *Debates*, — Anchitell Grey, *The Debates of the House of Commons*, 1763.

Grimblot, Paul — *Letters of William III and Louis XIV... 1697–1700*, 2 vols, 1848.

Guise, Sir John — *Memoirs of the family of Guise of Elmore, Gloucestershire*, 1917.

Hatton Corr. — *Correspondence of the family of Hatton*, ed. E. M. Thompson, Camden Society, 1878.

Hanmer, Corr. — *The Correspondence of Sir Thomas Hanmer bart.*, ed. Sir Henry Bunbury, 1838.

Harcourt Papers — *The Harcourt Papers*, ed. Edward W. Harcourt, Oxford, 1880.

Hardwicke *State Papers* — *Miscellaneous State Papers from the Collection of the Earl of Hardwicke*, ed. Philip Yorke, 2 vols., 1778.

Hearne, *Diary* — *Remarks and Collections of Thomas Hearne*, ed. C.E. Doble and D.W. Rannie, ll vols., Oxford 1885–1921.

Hill Corr. — *The Diplomatic Correspondence of the Right Hon. Richard Hill (ed. Rev. W. Blackley, 1845), 2 vols.*

H.M.C. — *Historical Manuscripts Commission*, Seventh Report (Denbigh MSS), Eighth Report (Marlborough MSS), Twelfth Report (Rutland MSS), Portland MSS, vols i-x, Bath MSS. vols i-iii, Mar. and Kellie MSS., Ancaster MSS., House of Lords MSS., vols v-x, Dartmouth MSS., vol i, Cowper MSS., vol iii, Buccleuch MSS., vols i-ii, Stuart MSS., vol i, Downshire MSS., Finch MSS., Hastings MSS., Kenyon MSS.

Horwitz, Henry — *The Parliamentary Diary of Narcissus Luttrell, 1691–1693*, Oxford, 1972.

Howell, *State Trials* — *A Complete Collection of State Trials*, ed. T.B. Howell, 34 vols, 1809–1928.

Huntingdon Library Bulletin — Correspondence of James Brydges, viz: – Letters and accounts 1705–13, Vol, 2 (1931), 123–47, Letters of Henry St. John to J.B. Vol, 6 (1935) 153–70.
Letters of J.B. to Henry St. John, Vol, 7 (1936), 119–66.
Letters of J.B. and Robert Harley, Vol, 1 (1937), 457–72.

Huntingdon Library Quarterly (the same, continued) — Letters on Godolphin's dismissal, Vol, 3 (1939), 225–42.

Japikse, *Correspondentie* — N. Japikse, *Correspondentie van Willem III en van Bentinck*, 6 vols, 'S-Gravenhage 1927–1937.

Journal to Stella — Jonathan Swift, *Journal to Stella*, ed. Harold Williams, 2 vols, Oxford 1948, and other editions.

Kemble, J.M. (ed). — *State papers and correspondence from the Revolution to the accession of the House of Hanover*, (1857).

Krämer, *Archives*

F.J.L. Krämer, *Archives ou Correspondance Inedite de la Maison d'Orange-Nassau*, 3rd series, Leyden, 1907–9.

Lamberty, *Memoirs*

Guillaume de Lamberty, *Memoirs pour servir à l'histoire du xviii siecle*, Amsterdam, 1735–40.

Legg, L.G. Wickham (ed).

'Extracts from Jacobite correspondence, 1712–1714', *Eng. Hist. Rev*, xxx (1915), 501–18.

Lexington Papers

The Lexington Papers... extracted from the Official and Private Correspondence of Robert Sutton, Lord Lexington, ed. H. Manners Sutton 1851

Locke Letters

Original Letters of Locke, Shaftesbury, A. Sidney..., ed. T. Forster, 1847.

Lockhart Papers

The Lockhart Papers, containing Memoirs and Commentaries upon the affairs of Scotland from 1702 to 1715, by George Lockhart Esq., of Carnwath, 2 vols, 1817.

London Diaries

The London Diaries of William Nicholson, Bishop of Carlisle, 1702–1718, éds. Clyve Jones and Geoffrey Holmes, 1985.

Lords Journals (LJ)

Journals of the House of Lords.

Luttrell

Narcissus Luttrell, *A Brief Historical Relation of State Affairs from September 1678 to April, 1714*, 6 vols, 1857.

Macky, *Memoirs*

Memoirs of the life of Sir John Clerk of Penecuik, baronet... 1676–1755. ed. John M. Gray [to which is apended the 'Memoirs of the secret services of John Macky in the reigns of William, Anne and George I, 1733], Roxburghe Club, 1895.

Macpherson, *Original Papers*

James Macpherson, *Original Papers containing the secret history of Great Britain*, 1776, 2 vols.

Madresfield Court MSS.

Letters of Sarah, Duchess of Marlborough, from the original manuscripts at Madresfield Court, 1875.

Marchmont Papers

A Selection from the Papers of the Earls of Marchmont... 1685 to 1750, ed. G.H. Rose, 3 vols. 1831.

'Mesnager, Nicholas' [attributed to Daniel Defoe]

Minutes of the negotiations of Mons. Mesnager at the Court of England, 1717.

Morrison Collection

Catalogue of the Collection of Autograph Letters and Historical documents formed by Alfred Morrison, privately printed, 1883–1892, 6 vols.

Norris Papers

The Norris Papers, ed. Thomas Heywood, Chetham Society, Manchester, 1846

Oldmixon, John

The History of England during the reigns of William and Mary, Anne and George I, 1735.

Parliamentary History

William Cobbett (and J. Wright), *The Parliamentary History of England*, vi, 1810.

Pauli, *Aktenstücke* — *Aktenstücke zur Thronbesteigung des Welfenhauses in England, in Zeitschrift des Historischen Vereins für Niedersächsen,* 1883.

Private Corr. — *The Private Correspondence of Sarah, Duchess of Marlborough,* 2 vols, 1838.

Revue Nouvelle — P[aul Grimblot], 'Documents inédits sur l'histoire d'Angletere: intrigues jacobites...' *Revue Nouvelle,* iii (Paris, 1845).

Seafield Corr. — *The Seafield correspondence from 1685 to 1708,* (ed. James Grant), Edinburgh, 1912.

Seafield Letters — *Letters relating to Scotland in the reign of Queen Anne by the Earl of Seafield and others* (ed. P. Hume Brown), Edinburgh, 1915.

Shaftesbury Letters — *The Life, Unpublished Letters, and Philosophical Regimen of Anthony, Earl of Shaftesbury,* (ed. Benjamin Rand), 1900.

Sharp, Thomas, — *Life of John Sharp, Archbishop of York,* 2 vols, 1825.

Shrewsbury Corr. — William Coxe, *Private and Original Correspondence of Charles Talbot, Duke of Shrewsbury,* 1821.

Snyder, Henry L. — *The Marlborough-Godolphin Correspondence,* 3 vols, Oxford 1975.

Speck, W.A. — *An Anonymous Parliamentary Diary, 1705–6,* Camden Miscellany, xxiii, Royal Hist. Soc., 1969.

Spence's Anecdotes — *Anecdotes, Observations and Characters of Books and Men collected from the Conversations of Mr. Pope and other Eminent Persons of his Time by J. Spence,* (ed. S.W. Singer) 2nd edition, 1858.

Swift Corr. — *The Correspondence of Jonathan Swift,* (ed. F. Elrington Ball), Vols i-iii, 1910–11.

Swift Corr. (Williams Edition) — H. Williams, *The Correspondence of Jonathan Swift,* Clarendon, 1965.

Swift, Ford Letters — *The Letters of Jonathan Swift to Charles Ford,* (ed. David Nichol Smith), Oxford, 1935.

Swift, Jonathan — *Prose Works...Political Tracts 1711–13.* Ed. H. Davis, Oxford, 1951.

Toland, *Works* — *The Miscellaneous Works of Mr. John Toland,* ed. P. Des Maizaux, 2 vols, 1747.

Torcy, *Account* — 'Torcy's account of Matthew Prior's negotiations at Fontainbleau in July 1711', *EHR,* xxix (1914), 525–32.

Torcy, *Journal inédit* — *Journal inédit de Jean-Baptiste Colbert Marquis de Torcy* (ed. Frederic Masson), 1903.

Torcy, *Memoirs* — *Memoirs of the Marquis of Torcy,* 2 vols, 1757.

Van 'T Hoff — B. Van 'T Hoff, (ed.) *The correspondence of Marlborough and Heinsius,* Ütrecht, 1951.

Vernon Corr.	*Letters Illustrative of the Reign of William III from 1696 to 1708 addressed to the Duke of Shrewsbury by James Vernon, Esq.*, ed. G.P.R. James, 3 vols, 1841.
Welbeck Letters	*A Catalogue of Letters and other Historical documents exhibited in the Library at Welbeck*, ed. S.A. Strong, 1903.
Wentworth Papers	*The Wentworth Papers, 1705–1739*, ed. J.J. Cartwright 1883.
Wodrow, *Analecta*	*Analecta: or Materials for a History of Remarkable Providences*, Maitland Club, Edinburgh, 1842–3, by Robert Wodrow.

III. Secondary Works

Baxter, S.B.	*William III*, 1966.
Baxter, S.B.	*England's Rise to Greatness, 1660–1783*, California U.P., 1985.
Beattie, J.M.	*The English Court in the Reign of George I*, Cambridge, 1967.
Bennett, G.V.	*The Tory Crisis in Church and State, 1688–1730: the Career of Francis Atterbury, Bishop of Rochester*, Oxford, 1975.
Bennett, G.V.	*White Kennett, 1660–1728, Bishop of Peterborough*, 1957.
Biddle, Sheila	*Bolingbroke and Harley*, 1975.
Browning, A.	*Thomas Osborne, Earl of Danby and Duke of Leeds 1632–1712*, 3 vols, Glasgow, 1944–51.
Burton, I.F., Riley, P.W.J. and Rowlands, E.	*Political Parties in the Reigns of William III and Anne: The Evidence of Division Lists*, BIHR, Special Supplement No. 7, 1968.
Churchill, Winston, S.	*Marlborough, his Life and Times*, 4 vols, 1933–38.
Clapham, J.H.	*The Bank of England, a History*, 2 vols, Cambridge, 1944.
Colley, Linda,	*In Defiance of Oligarchy. The Tory Party 1714–60*, Cambridge, 1982.
Cruickshanks, E. (ed.)	*Ideology and Conspiracy: Aspects of Jacobitism 1689–1759*, Edinburgh, 1987.
De Krey, Gary Stuart	*A Fractured Society. The Politics of London in the First Age of Party, 1688–1715*, Oxford, 1985.
Dickinson, H.T.	*Bolingbroke*, 1970.
Dickinson, H.T.	*Liberty and Property, Political Ideology in Eighteenth Century Britain*, 1977.
Dickson, P.G.M.	*The Financial Revolution in England*, 1967

Douglas, David, C. *English Scholars, 1660–1730*, 1951 edn.

Downie, J. *Robert Harley and the Press: Propaganda and Public Opinion in the Age of Swift and Defoe*, Cambridge, 1979.

Feiling, Keith, *A History of the Tory Party, 1640–1714*, Oxford 1924.

Foster, J. *Alumni Oxonienses*, Oxford, 1887–92.

Foxcroft, H.C. *Life and Letters of. . .Halifax*, 1898.

Foxcroft, H.C. See also under II. Printed Sources; Burnet Supplement

Gaedeke, A. *Die Politik Oesterreichs in der Spanischen Erbfolgefrage*, Leipzig, 1877.

Geikie, R. and I.A. Montgomery *The Dutch Barrier, 1705–1719*, Cambridge, 1930.

Gregg, Edward *Queen Anne*, 1980.

Hatton, Ragnhild *George I. Elector and King*, 1978.

Hamilton, Elizabeth *The Backstairs Dragon, a Life of Robert Harley, Earl of Oxford*, 1969.

Henning, B.D. *The House of Commons 1660–1690, (The History of Parliament)* 1983, 3 vols.

Hill, B.W. *The Growth of Parliamentary Parties, 1689–1742*, 1976.

Hoare, H.P.R. *Hoare's Bank, a record, 1673–1932*, 1932.

Holmes, Geoffrey *Augustan England: professions, state and society, 1680–1730* 1982.

Holmes, Geoffrey *British Politics in the Age of Anne*, 1967.

Holmes, Geoffrey *Politics, Religion and Society in England, 1679–1742*, 1986.

Holmes, Geoffrey *The Trial of Dr. Sacheverell*, 1973.

Holmes, Geoffrey (ed). *Britain after the Glorious Revolution*, 1969.

Holmes, Geoffrey, and Speck, W.A. *The Divided Society: Parties and Politics in England, 1694–1716*, 1967.

Hoon, E.E. *The Organisation of the English Customs System, 1696–1786*, New York, 1938.

Horsefield, J.K. *British Monetary Experiments, 1650–1710*, 1960.

Horwitz, Henry *Parliament, Policy and Politics in the Reign of William III*, Manchester, 1977. (cited in the Notes as 'Horwitz').

Horwitz, Henry *Revolution Politicks: the Career of Daniel Finch, Second Earl of Nottingham, 1647–1730*, Cambridge 1968.

Hughes, Edward *Studies in Administration and Finance, 1558–1825*, Manchester, 1934.

Jones, Clyve (ed) — *Party and Party Management in Parliament, 1660–1784*, Leicester, 1984.

Jones, J.R. — *Country and Court 1658–1714*, 1978.

Jones, J.R. — *The First Whigs: the Politics of the Exclusion Crisis 1678–1683*, Oxford, 1961.

Jones, J.R. — *The Revolution of 1688 in England*, 1972.

Jones, J.R. (ed) — *The Restored Monarchy, 1660–1688*, 1979.

Kenyon, John P. — *The Popish Plot*, 1972.

Kenyon, John P. — *Robert Spencer, Earl of Sunderland*, 1958.

Kenyon, John P. — *Revolution Principles: the Problems of Party 1689–1720*, Cambridge, 1977.

Klopp, Onno — *Der Fall des Hauses Stuart, und die Succession des Hauses Hannover*, Vienna 1875–1888, vols 13–14.

Lacey, Douglas R. — *Dissent and Parliamentary Politics in England, 1661–1689* New Brunswick, 1969.

Legg, L.G. Wickham — *Matthew Prior, a Study of his Public Career and Correspondence*, Cambridge, 1921.

Legrelle, Arsene — *La diplomatic francaise et la succession d'Espagne*, iv., Gand, 1892

Lenman, Bruce — *The Jacobite Risings in Britain, 1689–1746*, 1980.

McInnes, Angus, — *Robert Harley, Puritan Politician*, 1970.

McLachlan, J.D. — *Trade and Peace with Old Spain, 1667–1750*, Cambridge 1940.

Miller, John — *James II: a Study in Kingship*, 1978.

Miller, John — *Popery and Politics in England 1660–1688*, Cambridge 1973.

Nicholson, T.C. and Turberville, A.S. — *Charles Talbot, Duke of Shrewsbury*, Cambridge, 1930.

Pares, Richard and Taylor, A.J.P. — *Essays Presented to Sir Lewis Namier*, 1956.

Plumb, J.H. — *The Growth of Political Stability in England 1675–1725*, 1967.

Plumb, J.H. — *Sir Robert Walpole, Vol. 1, The Making of a Statesman*, 1956.

Plumb, J.H. — *Sir Robert Walpole, ii The King's Minister*, 1960.

Ranke, Leopold von — *A History of England, Principally in the Seventeenth Century*, Oxford, 1875, 6 vols.

Riley, P.W.J. — *The English Ministers and Scotland 1707–1727*, 1964.

Roberts, Clayton — *The Growth of Responsible Government in Stuart England*, Cambridge, 1966.

Sachse, W.L. — *Lord Somers, A Political Portrait*, Manchester 1975.

Salomon, Felix — *Geschichte des lezten Ministeriums Annas von England (1710–1714) und der Englischen Thronfolgefrage*, Gotha, 1894.

Schwoerer, L. — *The Declaration of Rights, 1689*, Johns Hopkins U.P. 1981

Sedgwick, Romney — *The House of Commons, 1715–1754, (The History of Parliament)*, 1970, 2 vols.

Somerville, D.H. — *The King of Hearts: Charles Talbot, Duke of Shrewsbury*, 1962.

Somerville, Thomas — *The History of Great Britain during the Reign of Queen Anne*, 1798.

Sperling, John F. — *The South See Company*, Boston 1962.

Speck, W.A. — *Stability and Strife: England 1714–1760*, 1977.

Speck, W.A. — *Tory and Whig: the Struggle in the Constituencies, 1701–1715*, 1970.

Szechi, D. — *Jacobitism and Tory Politics*, Edinburgh, 1984.

Thomson, Mark A. — *The Secretaries of State, 1681–1782*, Clarendon Press, 1932.

Trevelyan, G.M — *England under Queen Anne*, i. *Blenheim* (1948 edn.), ii. *Ramillies and the Union with Scotland* (1932 edn.), iii *The Peace and the Protestant Succession* (1946 edn.)

Turberville, A.S. — *The History of Welbeck Abbey and its Owners*, 2 vols.

Walcott, Robert — *English Politics in the Early Eighteenth Century*, Oxford, 1956.

Ward, W.R. — *The English Land Tax in the Eighteenth Century*, Oxford, 1953.

Weber, Ottocar — *Der Friede von Utrecht*, Gotha, 1891

INDEX